"While we eagerly await the promised kingdo[...] the better that is far short of the best. This bo[...] ment for faithful strivers."
THE LATE RICHARD JOHN NEUHAUS, editor-in-chief, [...]

"Prudence, especially in the context of politics and the struggle for social reform, is a poorly understood, largely neglected and desperately needed virtue. We have long needed an intellectually coherent and compelling treatment of the subject. Happily, Clarke Forsythe has met the need. Drawing on the wisdom of Aristotle, Wilberforce, Lincoln and other theorists and practitioners of political prudence, Forsythe has written a book that will both instruct and inspire all who work to protect the weak and vulnerable and to advance the cause of justice."
ROBERT GEORGE, McCormick Professor of Jurisprudence, and director of the James Madison Program in American Ideals and Institutions, Princeton University

"Early in these absorbing pages, Clarke Forsythe stresses the virtue of perseverance as the essential twin sister to prudence in pursuing a politics of human dignity. In a democracy, a prudent 'strategic' and incremental 'tactical' approach to legislation usually gets better results than an all-or-nothing perfectionism—but only if we also stay honest and zealous in our goal; only if we persevere as William Wilberforce did in his lifelong struggle against slavery. This is a thorough, carefully reasoned and provocative reflection on the realities of the American political scene by a veteran legal scholar. Highly recommended."
CHARLES J. CHAPUT, O.F.M. Cap., Archbishop of Denver

"Clarke Forsythe's *Politics for the Greatest Good* is an invaluable contribution to reflection within the pro-life movement on the best strategy to adopt in vindicating the right to life. He grounds his analysis on important historical materials, both from early American political thought and from the career of William Wilberforce, in making his case for an incremental strategy to reverse *Roe v. Wade*. He also provides effective critical analysis of the misguided argument that political morality requires never voting for laws that expand protection of the unborn, but do not prohibit all abortions (for the time being), due to the lack of the necessary political support for broader protection. As a long-time leader in the pro-life movement, who has done so much to craft and defend legal and legislative strategies to protect the right to life, he is intimately familiar with the often difficult circumstances facing those who would reestablish an American commitment to protecting all innocent human life from conception to natural death. Christians involved in pro-life work should be thankful for, and attentive to, his astute analysis and advice."
CHRISTOPHER WOLFE, codirector, Ralph McInerny Center, and Emeritus Professor, Marquette University

Clarke D. Forsythe

POLITICS FOR THE

GREATEST GOOD

The Case for Prudence in the Public Square

IVP Books
An imprint of InterVarsity Press
Downers Grove, Illinois

InterVarsity Press
P.O. Box 1400, Downers Grove, IL 60515-1426
World Wide Web: www.ivpress.com
E-mail: email@ivpress.com

InterVarsity Press® is the book-publishing division of InterVarsity Christian Fellowship/USA®, a student movement active on campus at hundreds of universities, colleges and schools of nursing in the United States of America, and a member movement of the International Fellowship of Evangelical Students. For information about local and regional activities, write Public Relations Dept., InterVarsity Christian Fellowship/USA, 6400 Schroeder Rd., P.O. Box 7895, Madison, WI 53707-7895, or visit the IVCF website at <www.intervarsity.org>.

Design: Cindy Kiple

Images: William Wilberforce: Portrait of William Wilberforce (1759-1833) Aged 29 (oil on canvas) by John Rising (1753-1817) © Wilberforce House, Hull City Museums and Art Galleries, UK/ The Bridgeman Art Library Nationality

   Abraham Lincoln: The Granger Collection

   pro-life demonstration: AFP/Getty Images

ISBN 978-0-8308-2922-4

Printed in the United States of America ∞

Library of Congress Cataloging-in-Publication Data

Forsythe, Clarke D., 1958-
 Politics for the greatest good: the case for prudence in the public
 square / Clarke D. Forsythe.
   p. cm.
 Includes bibliographical references and index.
 ISBN 978-0-8308-2922-4 (pbk.: alk paper)
 1. Prudence. 2. Wisdom—Religious aspects—Christianity. 3.
Christian ethics. 4. Christianity and politics. I. Title.
BV4647.P8F67 2009
261.7—dc22

                                                 2009000456

P	20	19	18	17	16	15	14	13	12	11	10	9	8	7	6	5	4	3	2	1
Y	26	25	24	23	22	21	20	19	18	17	16	15	14	13	12	11	10	09			

To Karen, Sally, Elena, Caroline, Lara and Maria.

And to all my colleagues

at Americans United for Life (AUL),

past and present, who have labored so long

for the greatest good possible.

CONTENTS

ACKNOWLEDGMENTS

Although their names are not on the cover, I am grateful to many, without whose support, I could not have completed this book.

I want to thank

Richard and Imogene Forsythe, for their enduring love and support.

The past president of Americans United for Life, Peter Samuelson, and the board of directors, for supporting my M.A. degree program and the work on this book.

Peg Kucharz, for her professional support in dozens of ways over the past several years.

Professor John Kilner, for his support, encouragement, intellectual inspiration and academic guidance over several years.

Erika Bachiochi, for her initial editorial critique and help.

Jerry and Joanne Frazel, for the use of their summer home to work and for their support and encouragement.

The librarians and staff of Homewood Public Library, for help with many resources over the past several years.

Paige Cunningham, for her initial encouragement to undertake the M.A. program.

Michael Paulsen and Christopher Wolfe for their comments on earlier drafts. Any remaining mistakes and errors are, of course, mine.

"If mankind were to resolve to agree in no institution of government, until every part of it had been adjusted to the most exact standard of perfection, society would soon become a general scene of anarchy, and the world a desert. Where is the standard of perfection to be found? Who will undertake to unite the discordant opinions of a whole community in the same judgment of it; and to prevail upon one conceited projector to renounce his infallible criterion for the fallible criterion of his more conceited neighbor?"

Alexander Hamilton, *Federalist* 65

"What is prudent and what is good are substantially one and the same; they differ only in their place in the logical succession of realization. For whatever is good must first have been prudent."

Josef Pieper (1904-1997)

PREFACE

The day after the November 2008 election, I spoke to a lunch gathering about dealing with political frustration. Many Americans were frustrated with politics during the long election season of 2007-2008. And the credit and housing crisis only heightened the anxiety.

Numerous issues sparked the frustration—the state of party politics, "partisan wrangling" in Congress, negative campaign ads or the failure of their party or candidate to win. Many believe that corruption in politics is inevitable. Others are frustrated by the incremental nature of any progress in policy and politics in a democratic society. Little good ever seems to be achieved; nothing but half-measures seems to result. Many of these people have voted year after year, and after little change seems to occur they wonder if their vote really matters or whether politics is really part of the answer.

I wrote this book to address that frustration. I also wrote it to address the nagging concern that citizens and public officials sometimes have: *whether it's moral or effective to achieve a partial good in politics and public policy when the ideal is not possible.*

It's often claimed that it's "moral compromise" to aim for anything less than the perfect. I've heard that objection repeatedly during the past twenty-four years that I've been involved in public policy through the courts and legislatures. By showing that it is both moral *and* effective to achieve political and legal reform through the momentum created by incremental changes, I hope to encourage citizens and activists to persevere in politics and public policy.

Our high expectations sometimes tempt us to think that an "all or nothing" approach must govern politics. But in the face of the institutional constraints, competing interests and real obstacles that prevent *any* political reform, I contend that there is no moral compromise when we make the aim of politics not the perfect good but *the greatest good possible.*

By showing that it is both moral *and* effective to achieve political and legal reform through the momentum created by incremental changes, I hope to encourage citizens and activists to persevere in politics and public policy.

The frustration that comes from high expectations that aren't realized might be tempered by looking more deeply into the obstacles that block political and legal change.

First, political change usually comes slowly in a democracy. One of the main reasons is that political power is diffused through the three branches of government—legislative, judicial, executive. And in the United States power is further diffused in our federal system between the national government and the fifty states. This separation of powers was intentional—to prevent the consolidation of power in one person or branch that could result in tyranny. The upside is that tyranny is prevented; the downside is that the three branches of government often move slowly or piecemeal.

Second, in a representative democracy—a republic—politics inherently involves a clash of contending interests. This is the result of free people in a free society deciding how to live together.

Other obstacles include public opinion, legal constraints, procedural hurdles, opposing parties, money, and human vices and weaknesses, among others.

But progress can be made.

To persevere in pursuing political reform, it's important to understand and contend with these obstacles, as citizens and voters, and find some way to *identify effective solutions to the particular obstacles.*

In light of the clash of interests and competing obstacles in politics that block progress and change, it is possible to advance partial changes when complete change is not possible. And such a strategy can be both moral and effective.

It is moral when a legislator aims to achieve a partial good or limit an unjust law or condition but is prevented by countervailing forces beyond his or her control. It's always good to decrease and lessen an evil when we cannot completely end it due to forces beyond our control. That's not cooperation or complicity or compromise.

Building momentum through partial changes can also be effective as part of a strategy to achieve greater change. The effectiveness of such a strategy is seen—to give just two examples—in the forty-five-year campaign of William

Wilberforce against the slave trade and slavery in the British empire, and in the strategy of the Whigs and Republicans against slavery in the United States in the 1840s and 1850s. The example of Wilberforce and others shows that partial advances, even if they are no more than limitations on an existing unjust law or condition, can create momentum for progress.

And it's absolutely necessary to persevere, against all odds. William Wilberforce devoted virtually his entire parliamentary career to the campaign against the slave trade and against slavery in Great Britain, dying three days after Parliament voted to the abolish slavery. William Lloyd Garrison is usually credited with launching the nineteenth-century anti-slavery movement with the publication of his newspaper, *The Liberator*, in 1831 in Boston. Though considered "antipolitics" in the 1830s, Garrison lived to support Abraham Lincoln for a second term in 1864 and see the results of his long labor come to fruition.

It may seem counterintuitive, but one solution to the frustration that results from high expectations in politics is to get *more* involved and better informed. That may mean spending more time keeping up to date on political events and studying government—whether it's the state legislature or the U.S. Congress—or, better yet, actually visiting an elected representative or helping in a political campaign.[1] By spending more time understanding politics and public policy, we can have more confidence that we know how to contend with the obstacles to political reform and have a better understanding of which candidates or party have a better grasp on just and effective solutions.

Our inability to achieve, so far, the ideal need not lead to our giving up. But rather, by taking up such an informed and morally sound strategy, we will become better citizens and voters. But more than that, grasping such a prudentially informed political aim is necessary to enable our community, our state and our nation to achieve the greatest good possible in our time.

INTRODUCTION

Is it Immoral to Be Prudent?

Any exhilaration that Abraham Lincoln felt on being elected president of the United States in the early morning hours of November 7, 1860, was fleeting. The election left Lincoln feeling, in his words, "as I never had before, the responsibility that was upon me."[1] He was quickly confronted with profound issues of political prudence.

Because Lincoln was elected on a Republican platform opposing the extension of slavery, Southern cries for secession came quickly. Talk of "compromise," set against the backdrop of the Missouri Compromise of 1820 and the Compromise of 1850, was on everyone's lips, but was rejected by many Americans—North and South—as opinions hardened.

Congress convened on December 3, twenty-six days after the election. Congressman David Clopton of Alabama counted heads for secession and concluded, "I cannot see how a collision of arms can be avoided."[2] Many Republican leaders "disliked the very idea of concession as implying timidity and apology."[3] After the first Senate caucus, Republican Senator William H. Seward, summed up the situation: "The Republican Party today is as uncompromising as the Secessionists in South Carolina."[4]

On December 18, the first Southern state, South Carolina, seceded, and the Senate formed a committee to address the crisis. The leader of the committee, Democratic Senator John J. Crittenden, proposed six constitutional amendments to resolve the crisis, including one that would extend slavery into the territories.[5]

The committee began work on December 22. Of seven proposals put forward in the committee, only Crittenden's seems to have captured significant public support.[6] But his proposal was quickly rejected by the committee. After six more days of debate, on December 28, "the committee reported to the Senate that it could reach no conclusion."[7]

President-elect Lincoln, with no constitutional authority until his inauguration on March 4, was in no position to negotiate a settlement. When he issued what he intended as a conciliatory statement in a speech by Republican Senator Lyman Trumbull, it was attacked by both sides. Nor were Southerners in a position to overturn the election or extend slavery into the territories through Congress. But Republicans were under pressure to grant concessions.

Lincoln quickly decided that he could make no concession on the issue of *the extension of slavery in the territories*,[8] "believing that the doctrine *of* the exclusion of slavery from the Territories must be defended as their supreme citadel."[9] Lincoln was "determined to stand behind the Republican platform, believing that any attempt to soften his position would dishearten his supporters in the North without producing any beneficial impact on the South."[10] This was a fence against slavery which he would not tear down.

In so doing, Lincoln reaffirmed a national policy against the extension of slavery by Whigs, Free Soilers and Republicans going back at least to the Mexican War and the Wilmot Proviso of 1847, and held with growing tenacity throughout the 1840s and 1850s.[11] And it was a policy strongly articulated by Lincoln in numerous speeches between 1854 and his election in 1860.

Lincoln's letter to Senator Trumbull on December 10—repeated in other letters to Republican members of Congress—summarized his position: "Let there be no compromise on the question of extending slavery. If there be, all our labor is lost, and ere long, must be done again. . . . The tug has to come, and better now than at any time hereafter."[12] Lincoln disseminated his position to Republican Party leaders, and it was published in the *New York Tribune* on December 22.

Was Lincoln's rejection of the Crittenden Compromise—as history has called it—right or wrong? Should Lincoln have accepted some extension of slavery into the territories?

Lincoln's consideration of the Compromise is a classic example of prudential reasoning. Prudence is practical wisdom. Prudence has been considered a cardinal (preeminent) virtue since at least the time of Aristotle.

Prudence is concerned with right action and requires deliberation, judgment, decision and execution. Wisdom understands what is right; prudence involves making the right decision and implementing it well. Prudence takes account of limitations in a world of constraints and strives to achieve the greatest measure of justice—the greatest good possible—under the particular circumstances.

Although politics is perhaps the first arena that comes to mind when we think about prudence, prudence is a virtue first cultivated or neglected in our personal lives. Americans live in a culture of choice. Choice is a major theme of marketing. We shape our identity and our legacy through our choices. We make hundreds of choices a day, from the trivial to the profound, and we love to choose. When I asked my six-year-old daughter to get ready to go grocery shopping with me, she looked me in the eye and asked, "What are my options?"

We spend much more time making choices than we do thinking about making *good* ones. What are our goals and priorities? Are they the right ones? How we will use our time and resources? Who can give us good counsel? What is the right decision in these circumstances? And, having made a decision, how do we implement it effectively?

But considerations of prudence inevitably extend to public policy and politics. Questions about the goals of politics, the purpose of law, the effective use of law, the moral boundaries of law, are as old as the Greek philosopher Aristotle.

These concerns were traditionally debated against the backdrop of the classical virtue of prudence. Greek, Roman, Stoic and Christian philosophers, like Aristotle, Seneca, Cicero, Augustine, Thomas Aquinas and Immanuel Kant, reflected on the nature and application of prudence. Political leaders like Edmund Burke and William Wilberforce, and American founders like Thomas Jefferson, John Jay and John Adams expressly relied on prudential decision making.

A prudential political (and legislative) strategy focuses on worthy goals, identifies effective means to achieve those ends and the wise use of limited resources, recognizes the limitations of the fallen world and its constraints on political action, and seeks to preserve the possibility of future progress. A prudential approach balances zeal with knowledge, especially knowledge of the current obstacles and of effective ways to overcome them.

Prudence used to be part of the common vocabulary of Americans.[13] But despite their long history spanning several civilizations, the cardinal virtues—prudence, courage, temperance, justice—are rarely taught today. For some, what's useful (utility) is more important than the moral reasoning required by prudence. For some, prudence has been reduced to pragmatism or whatever works. For others, prudence is equated with moral compromise.

Yet, whether or not we use the term *prudence*, and understand its long history in philosophical and political theory, we commonly rely on prudential reasoning. The war in Iraq since 2003 is a vivid example of prudential reasoning and debate.[14] Two individuals may have opposite views of the war, but it is quite likely that they think (and maybe argue) in terms of the publicly stated goals for the war, whether the goals are good and achievable, the effective relationship between ends and means, and the likelihood of success. We use prudential reasoning, well or poorly, whether we recognize it or not.

A reflection of prudence is also seen in the terms we use to discuss politics. Throughout our political history, Americans have used shorthand phrases, almost clichés—like "political compromise," "settling for half a loaf," "accepting the lesser of two evils" or "getting what you can"—to refer to incremental gains when seeking political change. Behind these shorthand phrases, which really do little to guide ethical decision making, lies the classical tradition of political prudence.

Whether it is ethical and effective to seek to secure "half a loaf" when the moral ideal in politics is not achievable, is a common question faced by political activists and politically involved citizens, both in policymaking and in elections. It is a dilemma faced by political leaders throughout American history.[15]

Voters may feel this most acutely when they vote for president, sometimes referring to the "lesser of two evils." But that common phrase is really a cliché that obscures the need for prudential reasoning about political choices. Voters sometimes feel torn between an all-or-nothing approach, which resists regulations or partial prohibitions of a social problem as "compromise," and an all-or-something approach, which seeks to secure as much progress as possible when obstacles make complete success legally or politically impossible.

The theme of this book is the recovery of a rich understanding of prudence, as it has been understood by philosophers and statesmen, for its application by policymakers and citizens to contemporary public policy. Although the primary focus is on bioethical issues, the analysis will be useful to citizens interested in any political issue.

Among the range of bioethical issues in public policy, abortion is a particularly sensitive and difficult issue that calls for prudence. The confirmations of Chief Justice John Roberts and Justice Samuel Alito to the Supreme Court in 2005-2006 sparked widespread political speculation about the potential overturning of the Supreme Court's 1973 decision in *Roe v. Wade*. A reversal of *Roe* would not outlaw abortion but would, instead, return the issue of abortion to the people and the electoral and legislative processes. The prudential deliberations over the right public policy would then intensify dramatically.[16]

An understanding and a cultivation of prudential reasoning is needed as these political questions intensify in the coming years. Prudence will not ensure unanimity, but prudence can clarify the debate, focus it on the most important questions and teach us wisdom in political decision making.

In the past few centuries since the rise of representative government, other social reform movements have faced similar tensions. Difficult questions of political prudence can be seen in the British anti-slavery movement of the eighteenth and nineteenth centuries. After many years of effort, division hindered the British anti-slavery movement in 1830 before the slave trade was successfully prohibited in 1833.[17]

Despite the long history of classical prudence—its support in moral philosophy and theology, and its historical effectiveness in the examples of Wilberforce and Lincoln—it continues to be subject to strident criticism. Like the William Lloyd Garrisons of the nineteenth century, a minority today challenges this understanding of political prudence as immoral, at least when moral issues are the focus of politics; they assert, instead, that only an all-or-nothing approach is legitimate. This challenge overlooks the classical understanding of prudence and would sideline our traditional moral understanding of political change in a representative democracy. A right understanding of prudence is necessary to realistically make a moral difference in politics.

One critic of prudence is moral perfectionism. Is legislation morally illegitimate unless it prohibits a social evil completely? Or can legislation properly limit a social evil if a prohibition is not possible? A recent book by British activist Colin Harte, *Changing Unjust Laws Justly*, takes the position that any partial prohibition is "intrinsically unjust," which I will refer to as the "perfectionist" view. *Is it immoral to be prudent?* is the paradox moral perfectionism poses.

The perfectionist challenge to prudential legislation effectively calls into question the morality of democracy itself (and the structural constraints on government). Change usually comes slowly and incrementally in a democracy. This is so for several reasons, but the primary one is that political power is more diffused in a democracy than in a monarchy or authoritarian government. That diffusion of political power is intentional, and the main reason is to preserve liberty by preventing the consolidation of power that might lead to tyranny.

Prudence is not pragmatism; prudence requires moral purpose. Prudence aims to achieve the greatest good possible in the concrete circumstances. Prudence does not require an all-or-nothing approach to public policy. In fact, an all-or-nothing approach, generally speaking, is often neither prudent nor effective. An all-or-nothing approach is not dictated by divine or natural law, moral philosophy, or ethics. Prudence must necessarily guide the consideration of constraints and contingencies in politics, especially when lawmakers begin to grapple with the specifics of legislation and efforts to limit unjust laws and conditions.

The related ethical and legal doctrines of *cooperation* and *complicity* complement a prudential analysis, and support the wisdom of an *all-or-something* approach to public policy. They confirm that legislators and citizens can establish a legislative fence around an unjust law or condition without participating in the problem.

It is not possible to say that any partial prohibition of a social evil is "intrinsically unjust" without considering various factors, including the specific intent of the legislators, the particular language of the law, and—perhaps most importantly—the existing institutional, legal, social and political constraints. While it is not possible to say, in the abstract and without considering the concrete circumstances, that any law permitting a social evil is unjust, such a law may be prudent or imprudent in the particular circumstances.

Chapter one recovers the ethical teaching of Aristotle, Augustine and Thomas Aquinas. Since prudence involves action, it's necessary to examine political leaders who have actually employed prudence in making political decisions. Hence, chapter two looks at prudence in the thought of the American founders. The prudential tradition is richly exhibited in the thought and practice of these founders. The famous *Federalist Papers*, advocating the adoption of the Federal Constitution in New York State, is the supreme example of the founders' prudential reasoning about government. Chapter three looks at prudence in the decision making of William Wilberforce. Chapter four examines prudence in the decision making of Abraham Lincoln. The historical examples of Wilberforce and Lincoln—just two of numerous examples that could be cited—reveal that these leaders relied on prudence and effectively employed an all-or-something approach. Chapter five rebuts the challenge to prudence by moral perfectionism. The last two chapters apply the insight of classical prudence to contemporary policymaking in a democratic republic. Chapter six addresses the question of abortion. Chapter seven addresses the regulation of biotechnology. I conclude by addressing several obstacles to prudence in the contemporary thinking of those like Catholics and evangelicals with strong moral positions on bioethical issues.

Although prudential reasoning is necessary for political leaders, it is also essential for citizens in a republic, a system of representative government where we choose our political leaders. Prudence is a habit that can be learned by experience, a habit that will contribute to the flourishing of our lives as parents, citizens and voters. It is vital for all of us to develop mature prudential reasoning in our assessment of public policy and in our voting for political leaders, if our democratic republic is to reflect the greatest measure of justice possible in a world of constraints.

PRUDENCE AND THE FULFILLED LIFE

"It is not possible to be good in the strict sense without practical wisdom, nor practically wise without moral virtue."

Aristotle

To the extent we desire a life of meaningful accomplishments, significant purpose, loving and enduring relationships, prudence—making right decisions and implementing them well—is a necessary part of such a life.

The Greek philosopher Aristotle (384-322 B.C.) believed that the practical reasoning at the core of prudence was the ability to deliberate about "living well as a whole."[1] And fifteen hundred years later, the philosopher-theologian Thomas Aquinas (A.D. 1225-1274) said that "through prudence we deliberate well about matters pertaining to the whole of human life and the ultimate end of human life."[2] To the extent we desire to fulfill our greatest potential, we will consistently pursue prudence. Prudence is a virtue, a habit to be constantly pursued.

Prudence—sometimes described as practical wisdom or practical reasonableness—is one of the four cardinal virtues, along with justice, courage and temperance.[3] Prudence is more than wisdom. Wisdom is knowing what's right; prudence is making good decisions *and* implementing them effectively. Aquinas called it simply "right reason about what is to be done."[4]

Prudence was highly valued for two millennia across at least four civilizations: Greek, Roman, Jewish and Christian.[5] Plato and Aristotle praised the cardinal virtues, as did Cicero.[6] The book of Proverbs suggests that zeal without knowledge is imprudent, and the apostle Paul virtually quotes Proverbs when he expresses regret that his brethren's "zeal is not based on knowledge"

(Romans 10:2). Paul's epistles to Timothy and Titus (1 Timothy 3 and Titus 1)
suggest that prudence is a requirement of a leader in the church. The book of
Wisdom (the Wisdom of Solomon) highly praises the four cardinal virtues.[7]

But prudence, unfortunately, has fallen out of favor. Prudence has been
gradually misunderstood or denigrated over the past four centuries for several
reasons. Sometimes it is reduced to sheer pragmatism or simply cautious moderation. In modern ethics, prudence is often reduced to utility or self-interest.
The modern view of prudence is derived from a misunderstanding of prudence as pragmatic self-interest rather than from the classical tradition.[8] For
example, a recent book conceives of prudence as cautious moderation or pragmatism, and then dismisses prudence as an enemy of excellence and an obstacle to heroism.[9] And many will recall Dana Carvey's satire of President
George H. W. Bush with the phrase "It wouldn't be prudent."

Prudence is often confused with another cardinal virtue, temperance (as in
the phrase "prudent moderation"). The confusion of prudence with caution
may be deeply ingrained in American culture: when I used the term *prudence*
in an interview with a journalist, she replaced the word with *caution* in her
final story. A recent book on the Supreme Court repeatedly refers to "prudence
and caution" and "restraint and prudence."[10] It's time to restore a right understanding of prudence.

Prudence as a Cardinal Virtue: The Classical Tradition

Although prudence starts as a personal virtue, it has application to all areas of
our lives in which we make decisions—family, organizations, community, politics. Prudential decision making is needed to identify good goals, set priorities
and follow through to make an effective difference. Prudence is essential in all
that we do because *it makes zeal effective.*

Reflection on prudence has a long history. For more than two millennia
reflections on human nature and virtue looked at the four cardinal virtues:
prudence, justice, courage and temperance. They are called the cardinal virtues because *cardinal* is derived from the Greek word for "hinge." The cardinal
virtues are those on which all the other virtues depend or hinge. The understanding of prudence (or practical wisdom) developed over time from Plato to
Aristotle to Thomas Aquinas.

Significant reflections on the meaning and importance of prudence start with Greek philosophy. Plato addresses the cardinal virtues in his dialogues, though not with the attention that Aristotle subsequently gave the virtues in his *Ethics* or with the systematic thoroughness with which Thomas Aquinas eventually gave them in his treatise on prudence in his *Summa Theologica* (also known as *Summa Theologiae*).

Aristotle's legacy. Much of the classical political tradition owes a great debt to Aristotle (384-322 B.C.), one of the most influential philosophers in history. He authored great works such as *The Politics*, *The Nicomachean Ethics* and *The Metaphysics*, and influenced Muslim and Christian philosophers for centuries.[11]

Aristotle was an insightful observer of nature, including human nature. (His emphasis on nature was more profound and much different from the reductionist tendencies of modern sociobiologists.)[12] Today, in what some have called a post-Christian world, an Aristotelian evaluation of human nature may be one of the most effective ways to explain human nature in the public debate over the regulation of biotechnology.[13]

That's because Aristotle's moral philosophy begins with human nature and the natural end of human beings. His view is teleological; that is, he started with the *telos*, the end or goal, of a thing or person, and defined the " 'success,' 'completion,' or 'fulfillment' of that thing or person by its end. That which contributes to the agent's success, completion or fulfillment is the good or morally appropriate."[14] Aristotle considers happiness to be the most important *good* in life, but he concludes that happiness is achieved not by wealth or power or fame, but through virtue. Thus Aristotle's ethics focuses on virtue.

A human virtue is a human excellence. The virtues are prized because they "enable man to attain the furthest potentialities of his nature."[15] Aristotle (following Plato) identifies four cardinal virtues: prudence, justice, courage and temperance.

In his *Ethics*, Aristotle describes prudence or practical wisdom as an intellectual virtue. "Moral virtue concerns excellence in the development of a person's character, while intellectual virtue concerns excellence in the development of one's intellect or understanding."[16] Aristotle distinguishes theoretical wisdom from practical wisdom or prudence (*phronēsis* in Greek).

An important element of Aristotle's ethics is his doctrine of the mean. Aristotle defined virtue as the mean between two extremes or vices.[17] Courage, for example, is the mean between recklessness and timidity. And prudence is necessary to perfect the virtue by finding the mean.

Thus, prudence is not just one of the cardinal virtues; it is preeminent, the key to all the others. "Aristotle . . . links the 'unity of the virtues' directly with prudence."[18] Prudence shapes the other virtues and enables them to be virtues and not vices.

In Josef Pieper's instructive book *The Four Cardinal Virtues*, he emphasizes the point:

> Prudence is the *cause* of the other virtues being virtues at all. . . . Virtue is a "perfected ability" of man as a spiritual person; and justice, fortitude, and temperance, as "abilities" of the whole man, achieve their "perfection" only when they are founded upon prudence, that is to say upon the perfected ability to make right decisions.[19]

Philosophical realism, to a large extent, begins with Aristotle. Aristotle understood our world as a world of limits and constraints.[20] John Hallowell explains the "the principles of classical realism," which go back to Aristotle: First, "there exists a meaningful reality whose existence does not depend on our knowledge of it." Second, "man is endowed with a faculty which enables him, at least dimly, to grasp the meaning of this reality." Third, "through knowledge of what we are, we obtain knowledge of what we ought to do."[21] Hence, knowledge does not involve the making or constructing of anything but rather the discovery of what already exists.

Aristotle concluded that prudence required both practical wisdom and moral virtue, or, to put it another way, that practical wisdom and moral virtue were inextricably intertwined. For example, Doris Kearns Goodwin, in her assessment of Abraham Lincoln's political wisdom, observes that Lincoln combined "tough-minded" political skills with an

> extraordinary array of personal qualities that enabled him to form friendships with men who had previously opposed him; to repair injured feelings that, left untended, might have escalated into permanent hostility; to assume responsibility for the failures of subordinates; to share credit with ease; and to learn from mistakes.[22]

Some Christians became skeptical of the importance of the cardinal virtues because of their classical or pagan roots. One reason for this may be captured by Josef Pieper's observation that "the classic origins of the doctrine of virtue later made Christian critics suspicious of it. They warily regarded it as too philosophical and not Scriptural enough. Thus, they preferred to talk about commandments and duties rather than about virtues."[23]

However, J. Budziszewski explains why this rejection of Aristotle was unwarranted. Aristotle's philosophy focuses on human nature and the *good* of human beings. The good of any thing is its proper work or function. "If X is a thing's function, then the good of the thing lies in the activity of performing X, and its highest good lies in the activity of performing X excellently."[24] We find the highest good of a human soul in its function or proper work—"the activity it performs that nothing else can perform or that nothing else can perform as well."[25]

Budziszewski describes Aristotle's conclusion as to the human soul's proper work: "The good of a human soul lies in the activity of using and following reason, and its highest good lies in the activity of using it and following it excellently." For anything to fulfill its purpose excellently, it must possess a "special quality that enables it to perform its function or proper work excellently."[26] It must possess an excellence or virtue. Hence, by his observation of human nature, Aristotle produced a philosophical system that focused on virtues which enabled humans to achieve their ultimate purpose.

Today, Aristotle's ethics is classified as "virtue ethics," and virtue ethics is sometimes considered to be insufficient to comprehensively explain all of human moral obligation. Virtue has to be tied to some adequate metaphysical reality, and Christians would largely agree that the theological virtues (faith, hope and love) are superior to the cardinal virtues.

But as Budziszewski concludes, "There is no reason for not taking Aristotle as far as he can be taken."[27] Aristotle can help us think more deeply about human nature and virtue, and help us understand Thomas Aquinas's philosophy and development of prudence fifteen hundred years later. Any residual doubts about Aristotle's ethics should not lead people to ignore prudence, however, which continues to be emphasized in the Catholic tradition, in the teachings of Thomas Aquinas (and many others) and in the evangelical tradition, through Scripture.

Augustine's political realism. Augustine (A.D. 354-430), bishop of Hippo in northern Africa, was one of the first church fathers who prominently integrated the classical virtues with Christian faith. Augustine's best known works are *The City of God* and *Confessions*.[28]

Augustine's legacy, however, is not an advanced analysis of prudence as much as a moral and political realism that undergirds a clear-sighted understanding of the limits and constraints of this world. By distinguishing the City of God from the City of Man, Augustine pointed out "the abiding wisdom of not locating the City of God in any political order of this world."[29]

Augustine also expounded on the relationship between Christian faith and politics in his monumental classic, *The City of God*. Augustine strikes a balance in the function of politics and the state. His realism does not descend to the sheer pragmatism of the sixteenth-century philosopher Machiavelli; he retains the goal of achieving good in "the fallen world," a world constrained by human weakness and sin. But his realism and understanding of God also limits what the state can and should achieve in that fallen world.[30]

As Augustine scholar Graham Walker has said:

> Politics functions not in a morally blank world but in a fallen one. . . . Augustine is happy for political rule to take its bearings from moral truth, or even to promote some virtue and some true piety, to the extent feasible. But feasibility is determined by the fallen condition of nature. As a result, both the tasks and the tools of political rule are limited in scope.
>
> Of course politics and law are valuable, but the possibilities of inculcating virtue through law are real but narrow. Political rule does what good it can while the central drama proceeds on other levels. Because he recognizes nature as both created and fallen, Augustine's thinking forbids both moral vacuity and moral transformationalism in politics. . . . It amounts to a principled argument against a politics of principle—not, of course, against a politics that consults principle, but against one that takes the attainment of principle to be its prime task. . . . [T]his is because politics is in essence a provisional palliative for the fallen condition.[31]

In light of Augustine's realistic view of human nature, politics cannot be the means for ultimate human fulfillment. As James Schall has observed, "Political entities . . . were at best, for St. Augustine, remedial institutions designed mostly to prevent the worst, rather than establish the good, let alone the best."[32]

Augustine's realist theology reached all the way to the American colonists. Augustine heavily influenced Calvin, and Calvin informed the Puritans. "It seems likely that by [James] Madison's time, the theology of creation and fall would have been so widely shared among Americans of the ratifying generation as to constitute a kind of common sense hardly in need of statement."[33]

Prudence recognizes that what can be accomplished through politics is limited by the fallen world. Those limits help us to evaluate and understand the obstacles around us and temper our expectations of what can be effectively accomplished—through politics—even with the best of efforts.

THOMAS AQUINAS'S DEVELOPMENT OF PRUDENCE

Aristotle's *Ethics* and his reflections on prudence influenced Thomas Aquinas (A.D. 1225-1274).[34] Aquinas adopted Aristotle's philosophy over Plato's, and developed Aristotle's philosophy more fully, including his explanation of prudence. For Aquinas, prudence is a moral and intellectual virtue concerned with action.[35] An "intellectual virtue . . . resides in the . . . rational part of the soul."[36] Prudence is the intellectual virtue that "perfect[s] the reason and makes it suitably directed towards means ordained to the end."[37]

Aquinas, following Aristotle, distinguished speculative reason (concerned with "necessary things") from practical reason ("concerned with contingent matters, about which human actions are concerned").[38] "Practical wisdom . . . is an intellectual virtue directed towards practical action. . . . [T]he practically wise person has directed his wisdom towards conceptualizing the appropriate courses of action and in habituating the appropriate character. This is done by regularly directing our feelings, desires and emotions along the lines dictated by reason. . . . Practical wisdom, then, brings rationality to bear upon our actions and passions."[39]

Prudence is oriented toward achieving the good. Prudence, according to Aquinas, explores how the good can be "procured and preserved."[40] As James Schall says, "Prudence deals with our will in its search for our authentic good as it is manifested through what we do and through the circumstances of each particular case that comes up before us."[41]

Why is prudence preeminent among the cardinal virtues? For Aristotle, "there are two major categories of virtue—character virtue and intellectual virtue—which correspond to the major division in the soul between its two major parts—the nonrational and the rational. The nonrational part of the soul becomes authentically virtuous when it is guided and cultivated by the rational part."[42] Aquinas puts it this way:

Prudence is a virtue most necessary for human life. For a good life consists in good deeds. Now in order to do good deeds, it matters not only what a man does but also how he does it; that is, that he do it from right choice. . . . Rectitude of choice requires two things; namely, the due end, and something suitably ordered to that due end. . . . Consequently, an intellectual virtue is needed in the reason, to perfect the reason, and make it suitably disposed towards things ordered to the end; and this virtue is prudence. Consequently, prudence is a virtue necessary to lead a good life.[43]

Prudence provides the necessary guidance to the human will to choose the good.[44]

THE PROCESS OF PRUDENTIAL DECISION MAKING: DELIBERATION, JUDGMENT, DECISION

The heart of prudence is making decisions to take the right action and implementing those decisions effectively. Prudential decision making rests on a foundation of philosophical and moral realism, accurate perception, and understanding (cognition) of the real world—the world as it is and not as we would like it to be. This includes, especially, realism about human nature and the human condition.[45]

Reinhold Niebuhr, for example, distinguished the political dispositions he called idealism and realism. " 'Realism' denotes the disposition to take all factors in a social and political situation, which offer resistance to established norms, into account, particularly the factors of self-interest and power." Idealism is "characterized by a disposition to ignore or be indifferent to the forces in human life which offer resistance to universally valid ideals and norms."[46]

Prudential decision making has four primary elements: discerning the good that can be accomplished, deliberation, judgment and decision (or command).[47] A number of different skills are needed in this process, including planning and preparing to take the right action at the right time.

Practically applying prudential reasoning requires an intimate knowledge and understanding of the actual circumstances at the particular time, including real obstacles, and identifying effective solutions to those obstacles. *It requires that we tie good and effective means to good ends.* That requires three primary qualities: seeking good counsel, exercising good judgment and implementing that judgment effectively.

The foundation of prudence is the understanding of basic moral principles applicable to the act under consideration. Thomas Aquinas called this conscience or *synderesis*.[48]

We typically seek to understand the good through reason and faith, with the aid of religious authority, moral philosophy, governing laws and relevant experience, and through reading, reflection and counsel on these sources of authority.

Aristotle said that the person of practical wisdom needs both knowledge of universals (or principles) and knowledge of particulars. "The prudent person differs from others in assessing just which such universal and particular premises are the appropriate ones to consider and act on in any given situation."[49]

Prudence requires a clear understanding of reality and the real nature of problems. In the middle of the American Civil War, for example, Abraham Lincoln expressed the frustration of how "hard it is to have a thing understood as it really is."[50] The uncertainty of military actions is expressed in the familiar phrase "the fog of war." For example, a significant part of the public debate in the United States over the Iraq War is due to different perceptions of the nature of the reality of Islamic terrorism. Is it global or regional? Would it disappear if the United States left the Middle East? Does it require military force to effectively restrain it? Different perceptions of the nature of that reality lead to opposing policies. And those policies will fundamentally shape American security and the future of the United States and the Middle East.

> Dennis Ross, special Middle East Coordinator in the Clinton Administration, noted, "Statecraft is often about working to transform current realities so what is not possible today becomes possible over time. Before you can change an unacceptable reality, you have to understand it in the first place."
>
> ("What Went Wrong," *Wall Street Journal,* June 19, 2007)

In understanding the reality of the problem and obstacles before us, memory, open-mindedness and clear-sighted objectivity are needed.[51]

First, memory involves recalling "the truth of real things" and avoiding false recollection.[52] Memory of what has previously been done and its success or failure is important. It was said of Abraham Lincoln that "to see memory as the essence of life came naturally to" him for he was a man who "seemed to live most intensely through the process of thought, the expression of thought, and the exchange of thought with others."[53]

Second, open-mindedness is required to sift the data and to make the most of counsel.

Third, "clear-sighted objectivity in unexpected situations" is invaluable. This is the virtue, in Josef Pieper's words, by which a person

> when confronted with a sudden event, does not close his eyes by reflex and then blindly . . . take random action. Rather . . . he can swiftly, but with open eyes and clear-sighted vision, decide for the good, avoiding the pitfalls of injustice, cowardice, and intemperance. Without this virtue of 'objectivity in unexpected situations,' perfect prudence is not possible.[54]

A recent and vivid example of the need for such clear-sighted objectivity is that of New York City mayor Rudy Giuliani and other city officials when the World Trade Center was attacked on September 11, 2001. While key members of his administration were killed that day, Giuliani acted in the chaos of that morning, projecting a sense of calm and purpose, and rallying New Yorkers in recovering from that terrifying day.[55]

Fourth, Aristotle refers to prudence as having a capacity for foresight.[56] Pieper describes this as "the capacity to estimate, with a sure instinct for the future, whether a particular action will lead to the realization of the goal. *At this point the element of uncertainty and risk in every moral decision comes to light.*"[57] For example, it was said of Lincoln that "his crowning gift of political diagnosis was due to his sympathy . . . which gave him the power to forecast with uncanny accuracy what his opponents were likely to do."[58]

How well one thinks through the process of deliberation, judgment and decision will likely determine how steadfast one is in the decision made. Lincoln biographer Richard Carwardine observed about Lincoln that "he thought so long and hard before taking a new position that, as Charles Sumner told Harriet Beecher Stowe, 'it is hard to move him . . . once he has taken it.' "[59]

Finally, experience is essential to prudence.[60] While defining the elements of prudence is relatively easy, practically applying prudential reasoning requires knowledge and understanding of the actual circumstances, including opportunities and obstacles, at the particular time.

For example, Aristotle said, "While young men become geometricians and mathematicians and wise in matters like these, it is thought that a young man of practical wisdom cannot be found. The cause is that such wisdom is concerned not only with universals but with particulars, which become familiar from experience, but a young man has no experience, for it is length of time that gives experience."[61]

What does it mean to be imprudent? Is imprudence simply a conclusion that a particular decision was not wise? Or is it simply the failure at any point in the decision-making process during deliberation, decision or execution?[62]

Because there are many facets to prudence, there are many routes to imprudence. Generally, imprudence results from a false course of reasoning or an inaccurate perception of events and circumstances.[63] It is possible to identify specific weaknesses or defects that lead to imprudence: thoughtlessness, impulsiveness, uncontrolled or undirected passion, being dominated by sensual desires, indecisiveness, negligence, or blindness to the concrete realities which surround our actions.

To the extent that "the moral virtues discipline the feelings and desires," imprudence often results from our unchanneled passions, feelings and desires.[64] Imprudence sometimes leads to recklessness out of a misdirected passion, emotion or zeal. Some people are impulsive, passionately angry or tired of waiting, and they move ahead recklessly, without sufficiently weighing the implications. Some are so sure of the righteousness of their position that practical obstacles are dismissed as a nuisance, and those who point out such obstacles are dismissed as compromising traitors.

Sometimes imprudence results from misguided religious zeal that excessively relies on divine intervention or spirituality to the disregard of human reason and responsibility. This type of imprudence has a long history in American politics. In the midst of the anti-slavery politics of the 1840s and 1850s, for example, Abraham Lincoln debated anti-slavery advocates who did not vote for a particular candidate in reliance on the proverb "do not do evil that good may come" (Romans 3:8). However, they could not identify the "evil" that would be done. Likewise, he debated anti-slavery citizens whose motto was "do your duty and leave the consequences to God" without identifying precisely what their duty was or what their responsibility might be for the consequences. They did not closely consider the role of individual responsibility or consider the implications of the different public policies that would result.

Another example of imprudence is "cleverness" without moral purpose, as Aristotle noted.[65] Pieper refers to it as "the insidious and unobjective temperament of the intriguer who has regard only for 'tactics,' who can neither face things squarely nor act straightforwardly."[66]

In contrast, prudence requires moral purpose. Aristotle taught that "practical wisdom . . . requires cleverness but goes beyond it by having a conception of the good which directs the uses to which one's skill at matching means to ends is put."[67]

Prudence does not guarantee success or the elimination of all conflict. That would be contrary to the recognition of a world of constraints. Prudence does not mean that one should pursue such a "moderate" course as to always avoid failure. This would be contrary to the orientation to the good and to prudence's perfection of the other cardinal virtue, courage, in seeking the good.

Prudence and Natural Law

Prudence has an intimate relationship with natural law, but the precise relationship is much debated by lawyers and philosophers, and it may be one of the most complicated issues in this book.[68] I will merely outline the issue here but address it at greater length in chapter five.

Insofar as prudence looks to the good that can be accomplished, prudence considers natural law's definition of the good, as it does other sources of moral guidance. Prudence requires us to consider how moral law, including natural law, defines the good. On an elementary level, the connection is readily apparent: prudence is "right reason about what is to be done"[69] and natural law guides our understanding about what is right.[70]

But does the natural law dictate specific decisions in public policy? Does the natural law dictate specific means to achieve the end of limiting unjust laws and conditions? Or does prudence instead guide our conclusions about the dictates of the natural law?

One difficulty in answering these questions is that the study of natural law is a rich and diverse field. The American founders relied on a long line of authorities—including Aristotle, Thomas Aquinas, William Blackstone—in recognizing natural law as a basis for human law and written constitutions.[71] The Declaration of Independence, citing "the Laws of Nature and of Nature's God," reflects this reliance on natural law.

Within the Christian tradition alone there is substantial diversity in perspectives on natural law, including the Catholic and Thomistic tradition, the Reformed tradition, and other schools of Christian thought.[72] Although the connection between natural law and prudence may not be systematically addressed in all of these traditions, they are well connected in the writings of Aquinas, the Thomistic tradition.

Aquinas defines law as "nothing else than an ordinance of reason for the common good, made by him who has care of the community, and promulgated."[73] Natural law, as a type of law, "is promulgated by the very fact that God instilled it into man's mind so as to be known by him naturally."[74]

Prudence (as right reason) then looks to natural law (as an ordinance of reason), as one source of several in determining the good, in reaching a judgment about "what is to be done."[75] And prudence relies on conscience in doing so.[76] If conscience is correctly formed and employed, prudence will recognize the principal or primary precepts of natural law, which are self-evident.[77] The first principle or precept of the natural law, according to Aquinas, is that "good is to be done and ensued and evil is to be avoided."[78]

What is the relationship of prudence and conscience in discerning and applying the natural law?

Even if one agrees that natural law may dictate the morality of individual acts (e.g., the principle of no intentional killing of innocents), it is a different question whether natural law dictates the details of human law, and a still different question whether natural law dictates the details of *how* legislators in a constitutional republic, governed by majority rule, may go about limiting evil laws or conditions.[79]

Daniel Mark Nelson, for example, argues that "prudence and the virtues have priority over natural law in [Aquinas's] account of moral understanding and decision-making."[80] According to Nelson, "Reason . . . does not operate autonomously in determining the good, but is perfected for that task by the virtue of prudence, which directs the activity of various virtues."[81]

Terry Hall describes the process of reasoning:

> Aquinas emphasizes that in applying the most general principles of the natural law to particular legislative situations we are engaged in *an exercise of practical and not speculative reason*. And . . . this involves not deducing a conclusion from

premises but discerning the application of a rule of action; it is a determination, not a deduction. . . . [W]hereas some further amplification of the general principles of the natural law are brought to light by deduction, most, it seems, will certainly not be. . . .

How is one to determine when these considerations ought to be in play in the deliberations of the natural law legislator? The only answer is that prudence must decide. Aquinas' practical advice to legislators is thus at once both sparse and profound, and can be summed up in the admonition: exercise prudence.[82]

Consider, for example, the role of judicial review in a constitutional system. Does the natural law dictate a system of judicial review? Princeton professor Robert George writes:

The questions of whether to vest courts with the power of constitutional review at all, and, if so, what the scope of that power should be, are in important ways underdetermined by reason. As such, [they] are matters to be resolved prudently by the type of authoritative choice among morally acceptable options—what Aquinas called "determinatio" and distinguished from matters that can be resolved "by a process akin to deduction" from the natural law itself.[83]

The same reasoning about natural law and the power of judicial review in the courts is applicable to the question of legislative means to limit unjust laws and conditions. Thomas Aquinas never applies natural law, as a matter of logical deduction, to address the question of the prudence or justness of legislative attempts to limit unjust laws or conditions. For example, as we will see in chapter five, Aquinas and Catholic Church teaching may affirm that laws which command abortion, authorize abortion or declare abortion to be a "right" are all unjust, but this is a very different circumstance from a legislative attempt to limit an unjust law or condition when a prohibition is not possible. No tradition of natural law, whether anchored in nature or God, overrides prudence to dictate the illegitimacy of legislative fences around a social evil.

RECOGNIZING OPPORTUNITIES, OBSTACLES AND CONTINGENCIES

An essential part of prudence is accurately perceiving the reality of obstacles. The classical tradition of prudence starts from the premise that we live in a world of constraints. Aristotle recognized that humans are limited in power and situated in a context that limits what can be achieved.

One of the main temptations of religiously minded, politically involved citizens is letting their zeal race ahead of realism, obstacles, available resources and other constraints. Prudence requires an accurate view of reality and of human nature, both its potential and limits.[84]

Realism has serious implications for how we order and plan our lives. We are embodied beings in a world of limits and constraints. We do not conduct our lives in disregard of the physical laws of nature, expecting divine intervention when we transgress those laws. We do not plan our lives based on the expectation of miracles, however much we may pray for them. This obviously has significant implications for the relation of faith to planning our lives, including our work in the political world. Some are tempted to believe that good intentions (or religious piety or prayer) will overcome all of the constraints of the fallen world.

In his book *Good to Great,* Jim Collins examines how business leaders must honestly evaluate the obstacles—the "brutal facts"—facing their business. Collins emphasizes the point by looking at the heroic honesty and realism that Admiral James Stockdale exhibited while a leader of prisoners of war during the Vietnam War. To the optimists who were sure that they would all be released by Christmas, Collins imagined that Stockdale's response was blunt: "We're not getting out by Christmas. Deal with it!" Stockdale's experience led him to a lesson of balance: "You must never confuse faith that you will prevail in the end—which you can never afford to lose—with the discipline to confront the most brutal facts of your current reality, whatever they might be."[85] A prudential analysis should yield realistic hopes instead of merely naive optimism.

One of the most consequential questions of political prudence in the twentieth century was the accurate perception of Hitler's designs in Germany in the 1930s. Two consequential people who had quite different perceptions of Hitler's designs were Winston Churchill and Neville Chamberlain. Roy Jenkins, Churchill's biographer, concluded that Churchill's "instinctive sense of the movements of geo-politics far exceeded Chamberlain's clear but narrow-sighted view of the chessboard."[86] Churchill's insight was aided by a trio of advisers who supplied him with accurate research regarding what was happening inside Germany, including the rebuilding of the Luftwaffe, the German air force.[87] Because of Churchill's close analysis of the German reality, "for many years Churchill saw [Hitler] and the rise of his aggressive, armed Germany as a mortal danger. Until the late spring of 1939 Chamberlain and his people did not."[88]

When we deliberate, prudence requires us to see and act on genuine opportunities and to recognize and deal with real obstacles and constraints. Understanding the realities of public opinion and of political institutions like courts and legislatures is necessary for effectively shaping public policy.[89] This requires balance and judgment.

The combination of being oriented toward the good and recognizing that we live in a world of constraints leads to the conclusion that prudence in politics aims not at the perfect good but at the greatest good possible in the real world.

LEARNING FROM EXAMPLES OF PRUDENTIAL DECISION MAKING

Prudence can be gained by reflection, by case studies of decision making— through observation and reading—and through personal experience in decision making. Prudence in specific arenas cannot be perfected without personal experience.

This combination of case studies and personal experience is part of education in both business and military affairs. Politics, business and the military are rich sources for learning prudence because they involve making and implementing decisions. (Although housekeeping and raising children well do not usually capture the attention of historians and novelists, they also require great prudence.[90] Indeed, Aristotle and Aquinas both observed that before people can govern others with prudence, they must be able to govern their household.)

An example of counsel's role in prudence is found in Winston Churchill's prosecution of World War II. A vivid example of the management of Britain's fight in World War II is told by Arthur Bryant through the diaries of Field Marshall Alanbrooke.[91] G. M. Trevelyan observed Churchill's qualities (perhaps with exaggeration) from Bryant's record: "Napoleon fell because he would never take counsel; his marshals were only his servants, whereas Winston treated his generals as his advisers. This habit of taking counsel, combined with his own personal qualities, is what won the war."[92] Among the factors that made up Churchill's style, Bryant writes, "Having chosen the best and stoutest [military] Service advisers he could find, through constantly probing and prodding them, he knew he could rely on their resistance if he went too far and always deferred in the end to their considered and united opinion."[93] Perhaps it is the need for counsel that prompted Aquinas to say that "no man is altogether self-sufficient in matters of prudence."[94]

The example of Churchill points out that prudence also requires becoming personally comfortable with disagreement and controversy, when many people avoid it at all costs and consider it to be inherently bad. Having multiple advisers or constituents inevitably leads to disagreement. To lead an organization, it is necessary to develop sufficient consensus (not necessarily complete agreement) for action among the necessary members. That often involves exposing and probing disagreement, and examining alternative positions and points of view, with clear mindedness as free of emotion as possible, to determine the best course of action.

Military examples of prudential decision making abound because they involve the relation of means to ends. General Dwight D. Eisenhower, for example, exhibited different qualities of prudence in preparing the Allied plan for the D-Day invasion of Western Europe. He had experience in previously commanding three successful invasions. He was a "master" at logistics and administration.[95] He delegated well. Stephen Ambrose emphasized Eisenhower's qualities: "Eisenhower was a team player, a manager of vast enterprises, a general who led by deciding what was the best plan after careful consultation with his staff and field commanders, then getting everyone behind the plan."[96] He worked to develop the best of relationships with his British counterparts, and his success with teamwork was a key reason for his selection.[97] Throughout his command, he felt it necessary, like Field Marshall Alanbrooke, to demonstrate "confidence, enthusiasm and optimism in the command."[98]

Business education and practice emphasize many aspects of prudence because business leaders have to make dozens of daily decisions and effectively execute them.[99] For example, a Chicago businessman, Ken Chastain, deliberated and planned for months about a decision to move his engineering business after being in the same location for three decades. In making that decision, he talked with employees and customers. He considered dozens of factors, including taxes, travel, traffic and the location of his customers. After making the decision to move his business, he spent months implementing that decision. He found it made a "world of difference" in reducing overhead and locating the business closer to projects and clients, which, among other things, saved on energy costs.

POLITICAL PRUDENCE

Ethan M. Fishman notes:

> Essentially, prudent political leaders are able to translate morally preferable ideals into politically feasible policies. They possess the remarkable ability to reconcile morality with practical politics without compromising the integrity of their ideals. . . . Prudence is a process that depends upon the fortuitous confluence of a leader's often fragile inner resources with political, economic, and social conditions that frequently are beyond the leader's control.[100]

The same reasoning that is part of prudence as a moral and intellectual virtue for making and implementing right decisions is necessary for political prudence. Prudence in political affairs has been the subject of reflection since ancient times.[101] Plato, Aristotle and Aquinas addressed the challenge of political prudence in the context of an individual, authoritarian ruler, which was the most common form of government in their time.

Aristotle held up Pericles as a statesman who embodied political prudence because he could "reckon what things are good both for themselves and others."[102] For Aristotle:

> Practical reason and judgment . . . contain two separate elements: knowledge of the relation of means to ends and a commitment to and understanding of moral purpose. One cannot properly exist without the other. Political skill, without moral goodness, is sterile. And good character, without the craft of politics, is ineffective. . . . Only prudence, in Aristotle's sense, captures the elastic balance between means and ends because it actively seeks that balance and other political modes of thought do not.[103]

The chief end of political prudence is the common good.[104]

Part of political prudence involves understanding that politics is limited, that politics is not the most important thing in life, that politics should not take the place of theology, or, to use James Schall's words, "that politics, to be politics, ought not to seek to explain all reality by itself."[105] Ultimate questions are properly left to theology and philosophy, because they are beyond the competence of politics. This has important implications for civility in public policy.

Four questions. Many citizens in a democracy are interested in making a difference, standing up for what's right, defending important principles and achieving good results. Many who are interested in political, legal or social progress are committed to effectively changing unjust laws and conditions without moral compromise. It is an enduring political dilemma in a constitutional democracy where political power is decentralized and diffused.

This is hardly the first generation to face this challenge. In the 1780s, William Wilberforce faced the challenge in attempting to end the slave trade in the British empire. Abraham Lincoln and many other political leaders faced the challenge in attempting to restrict slavery in the United States from the 1830s to the 1850s.

How can we make a difference in politics without compromising important principles? Harry Jaffa, the Aristotelian scholar who wrote the classic examination of the Lincoln-Douglas debates, *Crisis of the House Divided*, summarizes the Aristotelian-Thomistic tradition on political prudence with four questions for political leaders:

- Is the goal worthy?

- Does the political leader exercise wise judgment as to what's possible?

- Does he or she successfully apply means to ends?

- Does he or she preserve the possibility of future improvement when all of the good cannot be immediately achieved?[106]

Good goals. The goal of politics is the common good. Prudence is not mere pragmatism or cautious moderation because it aims to achieve the good; it calls upon us to persevere in seeking the good, even when we are tired, discouraged or weighed down by obstacles.

How can the elected political leader harness the means of power to achieve good goals?[107] This is examined at length in Ethan Fishman's book, *The Prudential Presidency*. Fishman mounts a pointed and thorough response to recent scholars of presidential politics over the past forty years, including James David Barber, Richard Neustadt, James MacGregor Burns and George Edwards III. "The problem lies with what the scholarship of Neustadt, Barber, and Edwards omits. Since they are unable to tell us much about the ethical purposes of political power, their analyses of presidential leadership are flawed and incomplete." Fishman contrasts the prudential politician with the "deal-making pragmatist, the naïve idealist, and the cynical realist."[108] Fishman and Jaffa agree in starting with the question of determining good goals. Prudence supplies that orientation in politics. While good goals are key, however, they are not enough.

What's possible? One of the most difficult challenges is accurately understanding the constraints that limit the political leader in the good that can be achieved. Outsiders are prone to criticize political leaders for what appears in newspaper headlines, but an accurate assessment must be based on an analysis of the four questions that Jaffa poses. Political leaders must understand the constraints and work to successfully overcome them.

The American constitutional democracy imposes unique constraints on what can be accomplished politically. While classical reflections on prudence span civilizations and centuries, Plato, Aristotle and Thomas Aquinas did not deal with the unique aspects of modern democracy, where political power is widely diffused rather than held by one authoritarian ruler.

Modern politics is constrained by laws and procedures. Procedural constraints exist in every court and legislature. The procedural rules are complex, and only those who are legislators, or who assist legislators, or who have taken the time to understand that arena, can fully understand the existing constraints.

There are also constraints on communication in a culture of mass media. In one sense the freedom to communicate seems greater than ever. But the proliferation of the modes of communication means increasing competition for people's attention. And the costs of *effective* communication can be enormous. For example, one reason why political campaigns are increasingly expensive is the cost of paid media—the cost of getting out the candidate's message to the public.

Outsiders sometimes exhibit one of three responses to political constraints: overlook them, fail to dig deep enough to understand them or purposely ignore them. Experienced realists know that if they do not understand the existing constraints, they cannot identity any effective solution, let alone implement one. These constraints limit the good that can be achieved in any year, in any given circumstance. Joseph Fornieri, in his study of Lincoln, points up the problem of "failing to appreciate the extent to which the application of moral principles is constrained by the limits of politics."[109] Political prudence requires realism about human nature, limited resources, cultural obstacles, and the power and constraints of public opinion.

Successfully applying means to ends. How do political leaders apply limited resources to achieve the greatest good possible? Individual legislators work within the context of a group, and the work of that group is typically constrained by a constitution and its structure of government. As we will see in the next chapter, such constraints were intentionally built into the American constitutional structure to restrain and channel political power.

What is the role and responsibility of a legislator in seeking to achieve the most good, surrounded by colleagues with differing values, intentions and goals? And how does she or he justly decide how to accomplish important goals when the legislator is constrained by the group and has purposes different from other majorities or minorities within the group?

Successfully connecting means to ends requires an understanding of the particular circumstances. As a lawyer, I am often called upon for advice about a legislative bill in a particular state. Unless I am to immerse myself in the myriad factors in the particular state, I can only make general recommendations. It is often necessary to ask specific questions about the factors that will shape the success of a particular bill. Knowledge of local proceedings and constraints is essential.

Avoiding a permanent compromise that prevents improvement. One of the most difficult acts of political judgment involves assessing whether the decision made to achieve the greatest good possible under the circumstances involves a decision which will prevent future improvement.

Massachusetts Senator Daniel Webster was criticized for taking such a step when he supported the Compromise of 1850 in his famous speech of March 7. His support surprised many Northerners, and his reputation was significantly and permanently impaired.[110]

William Wilberforce, by contrast, consciously avoided permanent compromise that would prevent future progress. In 1812 he wrote to Zachary Macaulay that they "should be 'guarded against any measures which might ever totally obstruct our future reforms.' "[111] This is perhaps the most difficult of prudential judgments.

Jaffa's four questions merely summarize Aristotelian prudential reasoning

in politics. The intensity and complexity of political devleopments may obscure these factors in day-to-day political judgment. But prudence is precisely
needed to orient political leaders toward the good. We hear leaders explain
that orientation through their rhetoric. That orientation won't determine a
leader's success, however, unless it is combined with proper judgment as to
what's possible and the skill to execute a plan to connect means to ends.

Winston Churchill, who was well acquainted with naval policy, once used
the metaphor of navigation to explain this complex balance in his essay on
"Consistency in Politics":

> A Statesman in contact with the moving current of events and anxious to keep
> the ship on an even keel and steer a steady course may lean all his weight now on
> one side and now on the other. His arguments in each case when contrasted can
> be shown to be not only very different in character, but contradictory in spirit
> and opposite in direction: yet his object will throughout have remained the
> same. His resolves, his wishes, his outlook may have been unchanged; his meth-
> ods may be verbally irreconcilable. We cannot call this inconsistency. The only
> way a man can remain consistent amid changing circumstances is to change
> with them while preserving the same dominating purpose.[112]

Voting. The closest many Americans may come to the public policy process
is through elections, yet elections are key opportunities to exercise our re-
sponsibilities as citizens. We live in a republic, not a direct democracy, and can
enact laws only through political representatives. Elections require us to make
a judgment between competing candidates, and due to the dominant two-
party system in the United States for the past 150 years, the number of candidates is usually limited to two, especially in general elections.

Unfortunately, the phrase "the lesser of two evils" is often voiced when elections roll around. But does it really capture the choice in most elections? Voters casually use that phrase to refer to two choices, neither of which excites
them. But the phrase often masks the failure to identify a true evil in both
candidates or a failure to carefully evaluate different candidates.

Except in local elections, it's virtually impossible to personally know the
candidates. Thus we are left to rely on the counsel of knowledgeable friends,
party affiliation, and our own research and inquiry into the candidate's record
in order to make the most informed judgment we can.

A prudential judgment of candidates should be guided by Harry Jaffa's four questions. Does the candidate have the moral purpose, character and skill to make good political decisions and to implement them well? What has the candidate proposed to do? What is the candidate likely to do based on his or her record in past political positions and policy statements? We cannot hope for the candidate who perfectly represents us. The choice often boils down to the candidate, among those available, who will most closely represent us or a choice between those pursuing injustice and those with whom we might differ regarding truly prudential questions.

Avoiding cooperation in the unjust actions of others. How do political leaders or politically active citizens pursue good goals in politics without being sullied by the social evils that they are trying to limit or eliminate?

There is a long ethical tradition, called the *doctrine of cooperation*, that seems ideally suited to answer this question and to ethically evaluate the actions of legislators and political leaders. A related concept is the notion of *moral complicity*. Both cooperation and complicity look to one's *intent* and to the degree of one's *participation* in unjust actions. The doctrine of cooperation is not a competing way of thinking about these issues but is really subject to prudence. Decisions about appropriate cooperation often require a prudential judgment.

Prudence starts with identifying the good, but quickly moves to identifying the greatest good possible in the concrete situation. Cooperation, in turn, is concerned with separating good from evil when working with others—and politics and public policy inevitably involve working with others. Cooperation involves how individuals or institutions can work with other individuals or institutions to achieve the greatest good possible in concrete situations without involving themselves in the unjust actions of others. Cooperation is precisely about group action and acting justly while avoiding the taint of the unjust action of others. It is precisely about working in politics or legislation "without dirtying your hands."

For example, do taxpayers cooperate in evil when they pay taxes to a government that engages in evil actions? Was the North complicit in slavery in the South before the Civil War?

The doctrine of cooperation goes back at least as far as Aquinas, and its modern formulation was developed by St. Alphonsus Liguori.[113] It is well-developed, it deals with group actions, and it seeks to separate good actions and goals from evil ones. Though it seems ideally suited for analyzing legislative strategies in a modern mass democracy, in the long history of the doctrine of cooperation few seem to have devoted focused attention on thoroughly evaluating how cooperation applies to democratic legislators.[114] But the foundation for reasoning about this problem and the answer to this dilemma has a long history in the doctrine of cooperation.

"Cooperation is any assistance or agreement with another person in an evil act."[115] Can one cooperate with the evildoer without being morally culpable? How can one work with others (who may have different motives and objectives) to achieve good goals?

The traditional doctrine of cooperation has developed certain distinctions that can help legislators (and activists) think through how to work with others to achieve good goals. So, it is a precise tradition in moral reasoning that applies, for example, to establishing legal fences around unjust situations or laws. Instead of using the ambiguous notion of *compromise*, which is often thrown about in political debates, political dialogue would be more productive if attention was given to the distinctions of *cooperation* in evaluating political action.

The doctrine of cooperation has established the primary distinction between *formal* and *material* cooperation.[116] With formal cooperation the cooperator *intends*, *agrees with* or *approves* the wrongdoer's unjust act. One can never formally cooperate in unjust acts. Formal cooperation with evil is evil and is prohibited. With material cooperation there is no intent to *participate* in the wrongdoer's morally evil act.

> That [cooperation] is material which occurs only in the bad action of the other, apart from the cooperator's intention. But the latter [material cooperation] is licit when the action is good or indifferent in itself; and when one has reason for doing it that is both just and proportioned to the gravity of the other's sin and to the closeness of the assistance which is thereby given to the carrying out of that sin.[117]

The doctrine of cooperation also understands that prudential judgments are inherent and unavoidable in determining whether one is cooperating in injustice. The notion that prudence applies only to nonmoral judgments, not moral, is alien to the Thomistic moral tradition, as is the notion that there is no room for prudential judgments in decisions about cooperation because the natural law dictates the answers.

However, it's important to emphasize that there is no cooperation whatsoever, formal or material, if an individual *does not contribute in some way to the wrongful action of the principal agent.* If there's no help, there's no cooperation.

Cooperation and legislative fences. How does the doctrine of cooperation apply to establishing legislative fences around a social evil? The answer requires a careful evaluation of (1) the intent of the legislator, (2) the means employed, and (3) an understanding of the legal and practical constraints on the legislator's action, including the effect of the shifting votes that legislators face working within the structure of majority rule. The two primary questions—"Is the end intended proper?" and "Are the means appropriate?"—must be considered in the context of surrounding constraints.

Social evils, such as unjust laws and conditions, are often supported by cultural, social, legal (including constitutional) and political forces. It is often impossible to overcome those obstacles in their entirety. But it may be possible to limit or constrain the unjust laws and conditions through legislation.

Promoting or voting for legislation intended to limit a social evil is not a question of illicit cooperation, formal or material.[118] For example, in a situa-

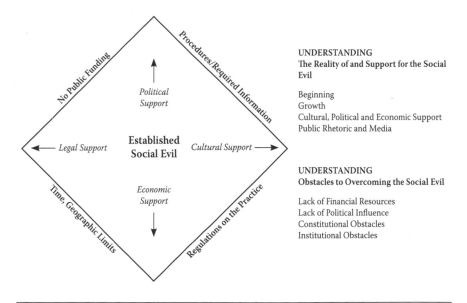

Figure 1.1. Legal fences around social evil when prohibition is not possible

tion where permissive abortion exists and is maintained by either a legislative majority or a judicial decision, the aim of pro-life legislators can be to limit it as much as possible. That degree of permissive abortion that remains will not need or depend on their votes; indeed, it will remain (due to a majority or a judicial decision) despite their votes. Their aim and focus is to limit it as much as possible, as though they are erecting fences or barriers. By "limiting the harm done" or "lessening the negative consequences," legislators do not admit or support the rest of the evil that they do not have the power (legal or political) to touch now.[119]

Legislators do not "cooperate" in all legislative acts simply by virtue of being a member of the legislative body. Germain Grisez provides the following explanation:

> Cases of cooperation among equals usually pose no special problem. Both (or all) share the same purposes and do the same act together. Both (or all) have the same moral responsibility. Morally speaking, it is as if each were acting alone. The classical problem of cooperation arises where people acting together are not really doing the same (moral) act, even though they are cooperating in the same (external) behavior. The relevant question here is: What is one willing?[120]

Grisez's analysis shows why seeking to limit evil laws or their evil effects does not involve cooperation at all, formal or material, precisely because the attempt to establish a legislative fence does not help or assist the efforts of others—perhaps a majority—to retain as much of abortion as possible. There is no cooperation of equals. What is willed is key. The intent is to limit the evil effects.

Compare the issue of legalizing no-fault divorce. A legislator in some countries or states may confront a situation in which divorce is being legalized to a degree that he or she thinks is unjust or may confront an existing legal regime in which divorce is tolerated to an unjust degree. Law professor John J. Coughlin applies the reasoning of Pope John Paul II's 1995 encyclical, *Evangelium vitae* §73, in an illuminating way:

> To the extent that one participates in the legislative, executive, and judicial powers of a system of law, one has an obligation to endeavor to render the law as just. The legislator would seem to have the most serious obligation in rendering just laws. To a more limited extent, those with executive and judicial power also have an obligation to execute and interpret existing law in ways that are consis-

tent with natural justice. With the primary responsibility on the legislator, it is fundamental that one may not vote in favor of a new divorce law that permits divorce for unjust reasons. The legislator, for example, should not vote to introduce unilateral no-fault divorce into a jurisdiction where it does not already exist as a legal option. It is perhaps more realistic, however, to discuss the situation of the legislator who confronts an already existing regime of statutory law that has led to the deterioration of the traditional concept of marriage as an objective social reality with all of the good that it promises. According to *Evangelium Vitae* 73, it seems permissible for the legislator to vote in favor of new legislation that restricts divorce but which legislation does not represent the ideal law through which to regulate divorce. During the process, it seems helpful for the legislator to explain publicly when possible his or her reason for the affirmative vote. [In] other words, it is licit to vote in favor of legislation that restricts a more permissive statute. The new law obtains the most protection for the sanctity of marriage in the here and now. . . . [Pope John Paul II's 1995 publication] *Evangelium Vitae* 73 permits a legislator to vote for a less than ideal but more restrictive provision.[121]

Moral complicity. A concept closely related to cooperation is moral complicity; in fact, they are largely the same thing. Complicity is closely related to the legal concept of accomplice (as in accomplice liability to a crime).

Responsibility as an accomplice requires an intent to aid or assist. To be an accomplice one must aid or abet a crime. The law uses terms like *aid, abet, advise, assist, hire, induce* or *procure* to refer to the actions of an accomplice. One can be an accomplice without providing physical assistance if one counsels or encourages another to commit a crime.[122]

Thus, like cooperation, the doctrine of moral complicity shows that legislators who attempt to establish a legislative fence around a moral evil are not helping or assisting in the legislative majority's (or the court's) retention of abortion. Both their actions and their intent prove exactly the opposite. They don't aid or assist an abortion. Nor do they aid or assist the legalization of abortion, since the legislative majority (or a court) preserves the legalization of abortion. And their intent is not to aid but to limit as much as possible.

Nevertheless, legislative situations are sometimes far from clear, but difficult and complex, due to shifting groups of majorities and minorities, especially if multiple votes are involved and the outcome is uncertain. Prudence is necessary to decide whether one is cooperating or complicit in an evil act.

The misuse of "compromise." This dilemma—attempting to limit unjust laws when it is not possible to prohibit or overturn them outright—is often framed as a question of "moral compromise."[123] It is sometimes claimed that law must embody perfect justice, and that those who seek anything less are not just imprudent or ineffective, but are "compromisers." This is misguided.

In its briefest definition *compromise* means mutual concession. The *Oxford English Dictionary* defines compromise as "a coming to terms, or arrangement of a dispute, by concessions on both sides; partial surrender of one's position, for the sake of coming to terms." That was, for example, Lincoln's understanding of compromise. Describing the Missouri Compromise of 1820, he said, "At length a compromise was made, in which, like all compromises, both sides yielded something."[124] Compromise assumes an even distribution of power between two sides who each "give up" something in order to achieve a settlement.

Because compromise involves *mutual* concession, "compromise" would not be considered accurate when applied to a situation in which a person's will is overpowered by the will of another individual or a group. Thus it is not plausible to refer to a woman raped by a man, or a group of soldiers who retreat in the face of a superior force, or a person who gives up his wallet at the point of a gun, as having compromised. We understand that people in such situations are defeated by a counter- and overwhelming force, and we hold responsible those who defeated the weaker person with overwhelming force.

This is analogous to the situation where legislators seek to establish a legislative fence around a social problem when they cannot eliminate it entirely due to legal or political obstacles beyond their control. The term *compromise* suggests a situation in which legislators sit in a backroom and give up certain principles in order to gain something else. That's hardly the situation when a minority seeks to establish a legislative fence. In such situations the use of the term *compromise* is merely a political epithet and not accurate in evaluating the prudence of the action taken. Being blocked from achieving more—by laws or political obstacles—is not a concession or a compromise.

PRUDENT RHETORIC AND "MESSAGE STRATEGY"

Political prudence also requires prudential rhetoric. The implication of the Declaration of Independence's proposition that government rests on "the consent of the governed" is that "democracy is first of all governed by persuasion and deliberation."[125] Securing the consent of the governed requires persuasion. For example, Lincoln biographer Richard Carwardine points out that for Lincoln "articulating the aims and rationale of war was essential to Union victory."[126]

Rhetoric is the ancient art of persuasion, not deceptive speech as it has been derided in modern times.[127] Persuasion involves inducing people to agree with you on some proposition, fact or truth. Some have called this "a cultural apologetic."[128]

As C. S. Lewis explained, the purpose of rhetoric is to move people to action:

> Both these arts [rhetoric and poetry] . . . definitely aim at doing something to an audience. And both do it by using language to control what already exists in our minds. The differentia of Rhetoric is that it wishes to produce in our minds some practical resolve . . . and it does this by calling the passions to the aid of reason. It is honestly practiced when the orator honestly believes that the thing which he calls the passions to support *is* reason, and usefully practiced when this belief of his is in fact reason. . . . The proper use is lawful and necessary because, as Aristotle points out, intellect of itself "moves nothing": the transition from thinking to doing, in nearly all men at nearly all moments, needs to be assisted by appropriate states of feeling. . . . Very roughly, we might almost say that in Rhetoric imagination is present for the sake of passion (and therefore in the long run for the sake of action) while in poetry passion is present for the sake of imagination, and therefore in the long run for the sake of wisdom or spiritual health.[129]

Three of the most effective means of persuasion are appeals to authority, moral principle and utility (or consequences). Persuasive public rhetoric often involves appeals to some or all of these.

Persuading different audiences. Prudent rhetoric requires communicating differently with different audiences in ways that effectively help them understand and accept important political propositions. And it must be aimed, in a democratic republic, toward producing and sustaining majority support for political and legislative actions.

The American public is made up of increasingly diverse audiences, including a wide range of religious believers, utilitarians, Enlightenment rationalist secularists and postmodern antirationalists.[130] Political leaders need to effectively articulate for them ethical principles that protect human beings and human dignity.

For example, Abraham Lincoln's rhetoric recognized the contrast between a moral ideal and the limits of human nature in the real world. He argued that the authors of the Declaration of Independence "meant to set up a standard maxim for free society, which should be familiar to all, and revered by all; constantly looked to, constantly labored for, and even though never perfectly attained, constantly approximated, and thereby constantly spreading and deepening its influence, and augmenting the happiness and value of life to all people of all colors everywhere."[131]

In 1841, Lincoln encouraged political activists to be winsome. He counseled the local temperance leaders of his day that "if they continued to denounce the dram seller and the drinker in 'thundering tones of anathema and denunciation,' nothing would be accomplished. Far better to employ the approach of 'erring man to an erring brother,' guided by the old adage that a 'drop of honey catches more flies than a gallon of gall.' "[132]

In the public policy process on bioethical issues there are many critical audiences, including the American public (which influences legislators), activists and activist organizations, individual legislators, legislative committees, judges, and the media. All of these play a different role in shaping law and policy.

Case study: Two sides of the coin. Public education cannot be effective without understanding public opinion. For example, mistakes in public education on abortion have been made over the past thirty years by sometimes focusing on the wrong message to the wrong audience. Pro-life education has mostly focused on driving home one and only one theme: abortion kills an unborn child (or takes a human life). This is only one-half of the message that is necessary on this multifaceted issue. The other half is that abortion is bad for women. Americans are impressed by nuance, contingencies and the weighing of competing interests. It has always been the case that there are two sides of the coin on abortion, the impact on women and on the unborn child.[133]

Similarly, most pro-life education has been focused on the choir or the media or abortion advocates, when the most important audience is Middle America—the 60 percent in the middle who are neither consistently pro-life nor consistently pro-abortion.[134]

There is abundant evidence that Middle America sees abortion as something of an evil. A 1991 Gallup Poll on abortion and moral beliefs, the most detailed and in-depth ever undertaken, found that 49 percent considered abortion to be murder, while an additional 28 percent saw abortion as at least "the taking of human life."[135] That is, a total of 77 percent saw abortion as at least the taking of human life, if not murder itself.[136]

But even though many Americans view abortion as an evil, many believe it is a *necessary evil*. "Necessary" for what? In many Americans' minds it is necessary to avert the "back alley." Or more generally, necessary for "women's health."

We do not know precisely why Middle America considers abortion to be a necessary evil. But whether the precise reason is the "back alley" or women's health more generally, pro-life advocates will effectively address it by raising public consciousness that abortion is not good for women. The myth of abortion as a "necessary evil" has enormous implications for future public education.

Confronted with the persistence of these moral qualms by a substantial majority of Americans, abortion advocates make use of "choice" rhetoric to sideline Americans' qualms. Wielding the resonant language of "choice," proponents of legalized abortion have convinced Americans that, no matter how they feel about abortion, legal prohibitions would only make the problem worse. The tactic is to convince Americans that the only real option is to persuade women to choose something other than abortion because legal prohibitions are not a reasonable or effective option.

This tactic is exemplified by the most enduring and effective symbol that abortion proponents have used over thirty years—the coat hanger. Surrounding the coat hanger are a number of myths about the impact of abortion law in the pre-*Roe v. Wade* era and about the safety of abortion since legalization. More than ideological, it is practical.

The myth of abortion as a "necessary evil" explains why some polls can show that a majority of Americans think that abortion is "murder" or "taking a human life," and yet think it should remain legal. While they are against abortion, they don't think that criminalizing it is a realistic solution. Alternatives, prevention, adoption, yes. Criminalization, no. This tension is heightened by the additional myth that pre-*Roe* state abortion prohibitions targeted women, when, in fact, the consistent target of the law was *practitioners*. This explains why most Americans support practically any regulations short of criminalization. If abortion prohibitions are not a reasonable option, the most opponents can do is to persuade women to choose an alternative ("choice").

The myth of abortion as a "necessary evil" also explains why 50 percent of Americans may believe that abortion is "murder" without translating this into fervent social or political mobilization. While Middle Americans may view abortion as an evil, they view it as intractable. Likewise, they view fervent campaigns to prohibit abortion as unrealistic if not counterproductive, while they are drawn to realistic alternatives and regulations. They agree that there are too many abortions and would like to see them reduced. Abortion is not a galvanizing electoral issue for Middle America because Middle America doesn't see that much can be done about the issue legally or politically.

Consequently, effectively engaging Middle America in the abortion debate requires addressing both sides of the coin—addressing the impact on women as well as the impact on the child. Helping the public understand the impact on both and the alternatives available may contribute to a heightening of public understanding that we so sorely need on this issue.

What about other bioethical issues? What will it take to get the right message to the right audience in the coming debates on genetic engineering and manipulation? It will not be possible, or perhaps even beneficial, to oppose genetic engineering based on vague notions of "playing God" or of "changing human nature." If the genetic engineering of the future, for example, is truly voluntary and informed, it will be very difficult to enact any legal constraints on it. Instead, it will be necessary to define and identify real harms to human beings that require social protection through public policy. As Leon Kass has pointed out, many have a natural "repugnance" to the notion of human cloning.[137] But can they articulate convincing ethical or practical arguments against it?

Effectiveness will require understanding the likely conflicting opinions of the American public. Opinion polls won't tell us what is right, but they can tell us what our challenges are and where we can most effectively focus our energies. Arguments from principle do not have to be abandoned entirely—they are necessary but not sufficient—but they must be tied to pragmatic arguments more persuasively.[138]

These arguments will not be simple to construct. For example, human embryos, conceived in vitro, will be a convenient and primary target for much genetic engineering. In so-called therapeutic cloning, an embryo would be engineered for stem cells or other tissue to meet the needs of a human being. Can we articulate ways in which such "use" of human beings for others' sake represents harm that public policy ought to prevent? Can we indeed make the case that genetic manipulation of born, even consenting, human beings actually works to their harm?

The lessons of the abortion debate lead to a broader conclusion—in our utilitarian culture, we must supplement principled arguments in utilitarian ways, pragmatic ways. Appealing exclusively to religion, or even moral principle, is often ineffective. Americans are concerned about the practical effect of public policy and weigh the pros and cons.

As George Weigel has put it, we need to address the public with "a language that communicates public concerns in a public way . . . a language that does not require that the participants in the public debate share all the theological convictions" of people of faith.[139]

For better or worse public opinion necessarily plays a heavy role in a democracy. As Lincoln put it, "In a government like ours, public sentiment is everything, determining what laws and decisions can and cannot be enforced."[140] Rather than disdain secular culture, activists should strive to sincerely and effectively engage it. We must take our ambivalent culture as it is and not as we would like it to be. It is the essence of prudential leadership to know your audience.

THE DEMISE OF PRUDENCE

Unfortunately, prudence has fallen into disuse. Why have we forgotten prudential reasoning? There are several possible cultural reasons. Carnes Lord attributes the demise of prudence to the rise of modern, pragmatic political science that focuses on technique and empirical results.[141]

A partial explanation for the decline of prudence lies in modern ethics. Douglas Den Uyl writes:

> It is the self-regarding character of prudence that constitutes its essence; but with the abandonment of teleology, "self-regarding" came to be understood in terms of the satisfaction of one's own desires or interests, while "other-regarding" came to form the core of ethical theory. As a result, prudence lost its significance as a virtue.[142]

In other words, Den Uyl attributes the demise of prudence to Thomas Hobbes and Immanuel Kant.[143] Robert Kraynak would also attribute its demise to what he calls "the politics of moral imperatives" of Kant.[144]

James Davison Hunter and others would likely attribute it, in large part, to the decline in moral education in American education.[145] Hunter in his important book *The Death of Character* traces the evolution in education and the training of children in virtue in the nineteenth century. The evidence is that prudence in American textbooks came to be confused with another cardinal virtue, "moderation."[146]

None of these is a compelling reason for disregarding the virtue of prudence in our lives (and those of our families) and in our public discourse. We need to evaluate political and legislative strategies, in terms of prudential reasoning. Recovering prudence and developing prudential reasoning is essential for effective political action and policymaking to achieve the greatest good possible in this world.

2

POLITICAL PRUDENCE IN THE THOUGHT OF THE AMERICAN FOUNDING

If mankind were to resolve to agree in no institution of government, until every part of it had been adjusted to the most exact standard of perfection, society would soon become a general scene of anarchy, and the world a desert. Where is the standard of perfection to be found? Who will undertake to unite the discordant opinions of a whole community in the same judgment of it; and to prevail upon one conceited projector to renounce his infallible criterion for the fallible criterion of his more conceited neighbor?

Alexander Hamilton, *Federalist* 65

Virtue and prudence were strong themes of the American colonists of the eighteenth century. Prudence is a virtue reflected in the political writings of many of the leaders of the founding generation. This emphasis was derived from both the classical education of the founders and the biblical heritage of the Protestantism that was pervasive throughout the colonies. The founders learned from classical sources and from the Bible. They sought wisdom from historical experience and, in regard to politics, from the experience of historic republics.

Their integration of classical and Christian philosophy in founding the American republic was a key to the success of the founding and the establishment of republican government.[1] Indeed, the Declaration of Independence was the direct result of prudence: Jefferson held that prudence dictated that the justification for American independence in the Declaration be published for the world.[2] The colonists' pursuit of prudence influenced individual behavior and the formation of governmental structures, as exemplified in the teaching of the *Federalist Papers*. Conscious of human limits and constraints, the founders aimed for the *best* regime, not the perfect.[3]

ON "TWO WINGS": FAITH AND REASON

In his book on the founders' intellectual heritage, *On Two Wings: Humble Faith and Common Sense at the American Founding*, Michael Novak documents the reliance of the founding generation on faith and reason. The founders were influenced by the Jewish metaphysics of the Old Testament as well as the commonsense practical reasoning of the Enlightenment.

The founding generation was deeply rooted in the classical tradition.

> Among the more widely read Romans were Cicero, Livy, and Tacitus; among the Greeks, Demosthenes, Aristotle, and Polybius. Doubtless the most widely read ancient work, however, was Plutarch's Lives. Writers of political tracts for the newspapers conventionally signed their articles with pseudonyms, often taken from Plutarch, and they could assume that their readers would understand something of their message from their choice of pen name.4

This is necessary to understand the significance of "Publius" as the "author" that Hamilton, Madison and Jay gave to *The Federalist* tracts that they wrote in 1787-1788. Publius was the Roman "who following Lucius Brutus's overthrow of the last king of Rome," established "the republican foundation of the government."[5] *The Federalist* cites the history of Greece and Rome in *Federalist* 8–9.

They studied classical sources for the lessons of human experience. The life and violent death of ancient republics reinforced the view of human nature that they derived from the Jewish and Christian Scriptures. Through the Scriptures the American colonists were thoroughly educated in virtue generally and prudence specifically. Although there were possible conflicts between the sources of and understanding of prudence in the classical tradition and in Scripture, the founding generation could also look to combine them consistently. Virtue was a strong theme derived from both "wings."

Classical learning. In colonial education the Jewish-Christian Scriptures were supplemented by classical learning. Latin and Greek were considered the "learned tongues."[6]

Moral philosophy was commonly taught in American schools in the seventeenth and eighteenth centuries. This included the cardinal virtues. Norman Fiering documents the training in moral philosophy that was reflected in commencement theses at Harvard in the 1640s and 1650s.[7] Some of these addressed practical wisdom or *prudentia.*

Students studied both Aristotle and Aquinas.[8] Other widely used texts on moral philosophy included Eustache de Saint-Paul's *Ethica* (which largely followed Thomas Aquinas) and David Fordyce's *Elements of Moral Philosophy.*[9] In the 1760s, John Jay's education at King's College in New York City (the forerunner to Columbia University) included Latin, for which the tutor used "a reader on moral philosophy, with sections on virtues such as prudence and fortitude."[10]

Prudence in the scriptural heritage of the founding generation. "And we prayed to our God and set a guard as a protection against them day and night" (Nehemiah 4:9 ESV).

A key part of the founders' intellectual heritage was the Scriptures, specifically the Jewish Scriptures and the Christian New Testament. The Scriptures hold a rich reservoir of teaching on wisdom and prudence, both individual historical experiences and doctrinal teaching.

In contrast to Aquinas, Scripture does not include a systematic analysis of prudence. But there is both doctrinal teaching and examples that exemplify each part of Aquinas's explanation of prudence. More practical than systematic, the book of Proverbs addresses virtually all aspects of prudence that Aquinas does. It emphasizes practical aspects over ethical theory.[11]

The Old and New Testaments emphasize virtue generally and each of the classical virtues specifically: prudence, justice, courage and temperance. Proverbs repeatedly enjoins individuals to be prudent. Justice is an attribute of God (Psalms 9:16). Political leaders are enjoined to rule justly (Psalms 58; Proverbs 29:4); individuals have an obligation to act justly (Psalms 106:3). This is a theme of the Minor Prophets. The children of Israel (Deuteronomy 31:6) and their leaders (Joshua 1:6)—and believers under the new covenant—are enjoined to be courageous (1 Corinthians 16:13). Leaders in the first-century church were required to be temperate (1 Timothy 3:2, 11; Titus 2:2). The examples are innumerable.

The Hebrew words for wisdom and prudence are different, and wisdom and prudence are sometimes compared (Proverbs 8:12) but often distinguished (Proverbs 8:12; 14:8).[12] Prudence is often associated with action: "Every prudent man acts out of knowledge, / but a fool exposes his folly" (Proverbs 13:16; see also Proverbs 22:3; 27:12). "A fool shows his annoyance at once, / but a prudent man overlooks an insult" (Proverbs 12:16). "A prudent man keeps his knowledge to himself, / but the heart of fools blurts out folly" (Proverbs 12:23).

Prudence involves deliberation and planning (Proverbs 14:8). "A simple man believes anything, / but a prudent man gives thought to his steps" (Proverbs 14:15). Wisdom and prudence involve counsel (Proverbs 8:14). More than once, prudence is contrasted with the "simple": "The simple inherit folly, / but the prudent are crowned with knowledge" (Proverbs 14:18; see also Proverbs 1:4; 8:5); "Flog a mocker, and the simple will learn prudence" (Proverbs 19:25). The simple lack judgment (Proverbs 9:4, 16). The wise accept correction: "A fool spurns his father's discipline, / but whoever heeds correction shows prudence" (Proverbs 15:5; see also Proverbs 9:8-9).

Though Proverbs 3:5 is sometimes taken out of context to suggest that one can never rely on his or her "own understanding," Proverbs repeatedly enjoins one to seek "understanding" (Proverbs 3:13; 4:1, 5, 7) and to seek the counsel of others.[13] Thus Proverbs 3:5 is better understood to warn against relying *exclusively* on one's *own* understanding to the exclusion of God or the counsel of others.

Proverbs is a key Old Testament book for the study of wisdom. Much of the book of Proverbs is about wisdom and prudence (Proverbs 8:5, 12; 12:16). Indeed, it is the stated purpose of the book: "the Proverbs of Solomon / . . . for giving prudence to the simple" (Proverbs 1:4).

Proverbs teaches wisdom and the benefits of wisdom. Proverbs 8 is particularly important. Wisdom is a public reality, accessible to all human beings (Proverbs 8:4). Prudence is not private knowledge but calls out to all, even unbelievers. Wisdom "dwell[s] together with prudence" (Proverbs 8:12).

One of the primary passages on prudence is Proverbs 19:2: "It is not good to have zeal without knowledge, / nor to be hasty and miss the way." Some have translated this: "zeal without knowledge is not good" or "zeal without knowledge is folly." The apostle Paul virtually quotes Proverbs 19:2 in his letter to the Romans, where he says, regarding his Jewish brothers, that "I can testify about them that they are zealous for God, but their zeal is not based on knowledge" (Romans 10:2).

Proverbs endorses the importance of knowledge, discernment of principles of morality and justice, sound judgment and discernment, counsel, correction, planning, judgment, wisdom in speech, and integrity.[14] But there are four recurrent characteristics associated with prudence: discernment (Proverbs 10:13; 17:24; 18:15; 19:25), understanding (Proverbs 10:23; 11:12; 16:16), giving thought to one's ways (Proverbs 14:8, 15) and discipline (Proverbs 1:2, 3, 7; 9:13; 10:17; 12:1).

In addition to principles, the Bible taught the American colonists through stories of prudence and imprudence. One example is Abigail's negotiation with David when her husband Nabal deals foolishly with David (1 Samuel 25). The problem is reported to her; she conceives a plan; and she executes it quickly and successfully, with words of diplomacy and wisdom. Abigail's quick decision, which was well-implemented, saved her husband's life and saved David from rash vengeance. In Chronicles, a nurse's prudent decision rescued the young prince Joash, secreted him away and saved his life (2 Chronicles 22:10-12). Years later, he became king.

Moral and political realism in the Jewish Scriptures. "As far as possible, we have bought back our Jewish brothers who were sold to the Gentiles" (Nehemiah 5:8).

The Old Testament also conveyed a strong picture of moral and political realism. The recognition of human evil was present from the Fall, seen most vividly in the story of Cain and Abel.

Kings, unrestrained by law or a balance of powers, could be corrupt and murderous. Even the best of kings, like Josiah, faced foreign invasion, defeat and death. Good kings, like Solomon, did not necessarily train wise sons to succeed them.

Under both the old and new covenants the most virtuous and religiously devoted faced hardship, obstacles, assassination threats, slavery or death. The American colonists read that King Hezekiah had to face the threat and challenge of Sennacherib despite the king's reforms and religious faithfulness

(2 Chronicles 30). They also learned that bad kings served a long time without divine intervention replacing them. As Abraham Lincoln observed, "God has his own purposes."

The realism of biblical morality includes the recognition of constraints, the fallen world and human evil. Proverbs recognizes the context of moral acts and the dependence of moral responsibility on one's freedom to act.

> Do not withhold good from those who deserve it,
> *when it is in your power to act.*
> Do not say to your neighbor,
> "Come back later; I'll give it tomorrow"—
> *when you now have it with you.* (Proverbs 3:27-28, emphasis added)

Examples of prudence are found in the books of Nehemiah and Esther. With the counsel of Mordecai, Esther exercises prudence in executing a number of plans. She exposes the treachery of Hamon and saves the Jewish people. Then, Esther and Mordecai execute a second plan to save the Jewish people from a massacre. Esther and Mordecai show prudence: Mordecai in how he activates Esther's support, and Esther in her request to the king.

Nehemiah gives a unique perspective on prudence and moral and political realism. Because of their failure the exiles in Jerusalem serve a foreign king (Nehemiah 9:37). Nehemiah is appointed governor by a foreign king and returns to Jerusalem to rebuild the wall of Jerusalem, despite many difficulties and obstacles. Nehemiah combines moral realism with a confidence in divine inspiration (Nehemiah 9:20, 30). Nehemiah shows prudence in combining prayer with practical wisdom: "We prayed to our God and posted a guard" (Nehemiah 4:9).

Like Nehemiah, Daniel is a book in which prudence (wisdom in action, strictly speaking) is emphasized. Daniel and his colleagues are men of "wisdom and understanding" (Daniel 1:17, 20). Daniel "set [his] mind to gain understanding and to humble [him]self before . . . God" (Daniel 10:12). Daniel has a habit of praying on his knees three times a day, "giving thanks to his God" (Daniel 6:10). God is emphasized as the source of this wisdom (Daniel 2:21). Wisdom is emphasized at the end of Daniel: "Those who are wise will shine like the brightness of the heavens, and those who lead many to righteousness, like the stars for ever and ever" (Daniel 12:3). In the end, "None of the wicked will understand, but those who are wise will understand" (Daniel 12:10).

Moral and political realism in the New Testament. "Wisdom is proved right by her actions" (Matthew 11:19).

In the Gospels, Jesus emphasizes the importance of results in the testing of wisdom. He recognizes the Pharisees' charges against John the Baptist and himself:

> For John came neither eating nor drinking and they say, "He has a demon." The Son of Man came eating and drinking, and they say, "Here is a glutton and a drunkard, a friend of tax collectors and 'sinners.'" But wisdom is proved right by her actions. (Matthew 11:18-19)

This example has interesting implications for the charge of *scandal*. Both John and Jesus were attacked, and their reputations were inevitably sullied by innuendo. But rather than express concern about the possibility that good people will misunderstand or be led astray, Jesus puts the emphasis on the end result, seemingly disregarding the possible confusion resulting from the slander.

Paul emphasizes the need for elders to be able to administer their households wisely. Aristotle first, and then Aquinas in his commentary on Aristotle's *Ethics*, made a similar judgment; Aquinas noted that Aristotle "says that the particular good of each individual person cannot be attained without domestic prudence, i.e., without the proper administration of the household."[15]

Paul recognizes the contextual limits on moral responsibility, declaring: "If it is possible, so far as it depends on you, live at peace with everyone" (Romans 12:18).

Virtue and wisdom are repeatedly praised by the New Testament authors.[16] It is not wisdom per se but worldly wisdom that is criticized (2 Corinthians 1:12). The New Testament concludes by emphasizing that discernment about the end times requires wisdom.[17]

The American colonists and the founding generation found a rich teaching of prudence in the principles and stories of Scripture. Scriptural learning, combined with their classical learning, shaped their cultural and political institutions.

What the Founding Generation Learned About
Civil Government from the Bible

The American colonists searched the Bible for its teaching about the structure and content of civil government.[18] Many different answers have been offered throughout history. In the sixteenth century, proponents argued that the divine right of kings was dictated by Scripture.[19] In the twentieth century some Christians argue that liberal democracy is the only form of government consistent with Christianity.[20] And Christian Reconstructionists argue that government and society must follow virtually the entire corpus of Old Testament law.[21]

Does Scripture dictate theocracy, monarchy, aristocracy, democracy or some other form of government? The colonists and founders generally concluded that Scripture did not dictate any particular form of government, though it did outline a minimal moral content for just government.[22]

Their reasoning might have been along the following lines. Numerous Scriptures speak to the providence of God and his sovereignty over the political affairs of nations; some relate to God's specific intervention in the political affairs of nations in history.[23] God delivered judgment on rulers that violated his law.[24] However, this general providence does not necessarily mean that God selects individual rulers by name, or their particular form of government. It is possible to see, as recorded in hindsight in Scripture, when such selection served God's plans in history. It is much less possible to see this under the new covenant, which is transpolitical.[25] Even if God has enabled or (merely) used rulers to fulfill his plans, however, it does not necessarily mean that he selected them personally, merely that he used whoever happened to rule the particular nation. Nor does it indicate his blessing of that leader or government, since God used even despotic regimes for the fulfillment of his plans.[26]

A key passage of Scripture often cited is Romans 13:1: "Everyone must submit [Greek, *hypotassō*] himself to the governing *[hyperechō]* authorities *[exousia]*, for there is no authority *[exousia]* except that which God has established. The authorities *[exousia]* that exist have been established *[tassō]* by God."

Does the second part of Romans 13:1 indicate that (1) God has chosen *individual rulers*, or that (2) God has chosen various *forms* and *spheres* or *jurisdictions* of governmental authority? A number of scholars endorse the first proposition.[27] But there are significant reasons to indicate that the latter is a more accurate reading of Romans 13.

First, the Greek word for authority in verse 1 is *exousia*, which is used elsewhere in the New Testament as a general term for different types of authority other than governmental authority (in the first instance *exousia* is modified by *hyperechō*). Matthew 7:29 and Mark 1:22 use the term to refer to the authority Jesus taught with. It is also used in Matthew 21:23 and Mark 11:28 when the Pharisees question the authority by which Jesus does miracles. Paul uses the word in 2 Corinthians 10:8 to refer to apostolic authority.

Second, the second clause of verse 1 begins with "for," indicating that it provides a reason for the first clause. And the reason is a more general principle ("no authority *[exousia]* except that which God has established"), and the more general principle refers to virtually all other forms of human authority. In other words, verse 1 implies "obey the government because God has ordained government as he has other authorities" (like parents and the church).

Third, the word "authority" *(exousia)* in the second part of verse 13:1 and 13:2 is general rather than specific or individual, like "ruler" (*archōn* in Matthew 9:18 and Luke 18:18) or "governor" (*hēgemōn* in Acts 24:1).[28] There are several other passages in the New Testament where *exousia* is used with more specific words like *ruler* and also used in reference to apostolic authorities and spiritual or angelic beings.[29]

Finally, while Scripture says that God chose particular leaders to guide the nation of Israel to fulfill his purposes (his plans under the old covenant), the proposition that Romans 13:1 means that God selects individual rulers threatens to bring Romans 13 into serious and unnecessary contradiction with the example of the apostles in Acts 4–5 to obey God rather than men. Disobeying Moses, as God's personal appointee, was tantamount to disobeying God. *If all rulers are God's personal appointees, there can be no distinction "between obeying God and obeying men."*

Moral standards for a just government. In contrast to the form or structure of government, the American colonists discerned that the moral order of the Old Testament contained fundamental standards of justice for governors.[30] The Mosaic law set basic standards for governors, both moral standards and standards for the administration of justice.[31] Isaiah, Amos and

Micah all spoke to this. Isaiah addressed his condemnation to both the leaders and the people.[32]

These injunctions go to the heart of any system of justice. They address basic standards of guilt and innocence, and detecting truth and falsehood. This consistent theme, addressing those fundamentals, runs through the prophets. This supports the proposition that these admonitions of moral guidelines for government apply to any civil government, not just Israel's.[33]

The conclusion that Scripture does not dictate any one particular form of civil government is supported by a comparison of the old and new covenants, the teachings of Christ, his recognition of the king's sphere and his emphasis on the kingdom of God, and the injunction of the apostles to obey even pagan governments unless God's command is directly contradicted by human command. *Since the design of government is not dictated by divine law, it is a matter of prudence, seeking to achieve the greatest good possible under the circumstances.*

In addition to the good, prudence looks to experience. The American experience in the 1600s and 1700s is one of experimentation within a biblical worldview. The Puritans of the 1600s experimented unsuccessfully with a "Bible state," founded on Old Testament law. The New Haven Colony of the 1640s made the law of God the law of the colony (though it is important to note that this was "by full and general consent" of the colony). The New England Puritans "constantly drew parallels between themselves and the people of Israel and Judah" and "conceived that by going out into the Wilderness, they were reliving the story of Exodus."[34]

Why did this fail? There is no indication from Scripture that theocratic government was ever intended under the new covenant. To that must be added changes in culture, geography and ethnicity that compelled growth and experimentation. The Puritans that landed in America were not the Israelites of 1200 B.C., despite the fact that they had the Old Testament. The religious wars of seventeenth-century Europe reminded the American colonists of human sinfulness and the need to constrain governmental power.

All these experiences shaped the growth of American constitutionalism in the 1770s and 1780s. The importance of reason, wisdom and experience in establishing just governmental forms is often ignored. The American founders of the 1770s were highly conscious of the biblical inheritance and sought the wisdom derived from experience.[35] They were concerned with ordered liberty and preventing the misuse of governmental power. There were concerned about the religious strife in Europe. There was also the demographic and religious diversity of America.[36]

The American founders looked to the experience of republics in history, primarily Greece and Rome, and what they could learn about the negative outcomes of those republics. They did not find enduring republics in Greek history, and observed the failure of Athenian democracy. They looked to Plutarch for his history of Solon's attempt to establish just laws and constitutions and "mixed government." They examined the classical political forms of government by one, government by a few, government by many, and the notion of "mixed government" combining the best of these forms. They looked for "practical models of sound government" that could be applied to "American circumstances."[37]

The colonists found that although Scripture does not dictate any specific form or structure for civil government under the new covenant, there are moral constraints that define a minimally just government. Perhaps one phrase captures the minimal content of just government: constitutionally limited government under God.[38]

Within that minimally just framework, governmental judgments are subject to constitutional constraints and prudential judgments. In Robert Kraynak's analysis, the "four leading Christian theologians of the premodern era— St. Augustine, St. Thomas Aquinas, Martin Luther and John Calvin . . . shared a common approach to politics based on the Two Cities."[39] Their differences "are attributable to judgments of prudence, meaning practical disagreements about how far the state should go in trying to realize the hierarchy of ends proper to the temporal realm."[40] It is consistent with Scripture and American constitutionalism to pursue the essential role of government to punish the unjust. What goals civil government should pursue beyond that is a matter of prudence, constrained by positive law and the practical limits of "the consent of the governed."

The two wings—classical learning and the biblical heritage, faith and reason—undergirded the colonists' prudential approach to organizing political structures, first with state constitutions, then in the framing of the federal constitution. Realistic about human nature and the tendency of political power to be consolidated in a tyranny, the colonists adopted practices such as the separation of (political) powers, checks and balances, and ultimately federalism.

THE MORALITY OF DEMOCRACY

The American republic is founded on the belief in the principle that the consent of the governed is the foundation of the moral legitimacy of democracy, and that no government is legitimate that does not rest on the consent of the governed. That is the core of the Declaration of Independence.

Yet some religious believers may have an uneasy suspicion that democracy is immoral because it allows unjust results in public policy. How can democracy be defended as moral if it allows immoral results? The American colonists struggled with these questions too.

The short answer is that history shows that all forms of government lead to unjust results to some degree, because all government, to one degree or another, is a reflection of flawed human nature. As James Madison famously wrote in *Federalist* 51:

> But what is government itself but the greatest of all reflections on human nature? If men were angels, no government would be necessary. If angels were to govern men, neither external nor internal controls on government would be necessary. In framing a government which is to be administered by men over men, the great difficulty lies in this: you must first enable the government to control the governed; and in the next place oblige it to control itself. A dependence on the people is, no doubt, the primary control on the government; but experience has taught mankind the necessity of auxiliary precautions.

In other words, the problem is not that democracy leads to unjust results (laws and conditions) but that all government leads to unjust results to one degree or another. Long experience demonstrates that government is made up of limited and fallible individuals, and the centralization of power in one or a few does not lead to perfectly just laws and conditions. The Old Testament, with which the American colonists and founders were intimately familiar, showed the experience of fallible human rulers.

Second, government resting on the "consent of the governed" is not entirely an American invention. Aquinas, for example, rejected the divine right of kings and held that the ruler must govern for the common good and not his own self-interest. Government resting on the consent of the governed was conceived as a form that, among other benefits, might minimize injustice, in part by requiring government to look to the interests of the governed and (with the prudential arrangements identified by the founding generation) by distributing power to preserve liberty and prevent tyranny.

In the middle of the twentieth century, John Hallowell confronted an intellectual climate that challenged the morality of democracy by claiming that the moral principles underlying democracy were irrational, were "superstition or prejudice," that none could be "scientifically" supported.[41] Hallowell, relying on Aristotelian realism, argued that democracy had roots in objective reality.

> No one denies that there is often a wide discrepancy between professions of faith and actual practice, between principles and actions. The question is how we should interpret such discrepancies. The immature reaction is to say that if I cannot attain perfection, I will not even try; if practice can never be squared with principles, then principles are nonexistent. The mature man, on the other hand, learns to live with imperfection—in himself, in others and in society—without making a standard of imperfection.[42]

The issues that Hallowell explored in the mid-twentieth century are the same ones that Hamilton, Madison and Jay addressed in *The Federalist*, and they are the same ones we debate today: What political institutions and arrangements can best prevent tyranny and ensure just government and political liberty? What is the role of political parties, and should they represent principles or interests? How can citizens effectively work through parties to see that just government is the party's policy? What political arrangements can best ensure a public policy that protects family life and religious liberty?

The need to defend the morality of democracy is no less today. The morality of democracy is challenged on many different fronts. Public policy in a democracy yields imperfect, sometimes clearly unjust, results. Those imperfections are mediated by the forms of representative government. They should render more realistic our expectations of what government can or should achieve in this life.

REPUBLICAN GOVERNMENT AND VIRTUE

Faith and reason, as the two wings of the intellectual heritage, influenced the founding generation in their eventual devotion to republican government—

representative democracy, government by the consent of the people. The founding generation believed virtue was critical to a republic because government rested on the people. The founders respected the virtue of prudence in individual behavior and in politics.

Forrest McDonald records that "a few of the Framers questioned the desirability of adhering to a republican form of government, thinking that form to be less compatible with liberty than limited monarchy was, *but none believed that any other form would be acceptable to the American electorate.*"[43]

The founders' understanding of republican principles were derived from Montesquieu, David Hume, Algernon Sidney, John Milton and James Harrington.[44] Independence in July 1776 forced more and more of the public to study political theorists and republican principles, leading to the adoption of the Constitution eleven years later, in 1787.[45]

But with that devotion to republican government came a consistent theme in the writings of the founders and American political leaders for the half century between 1760-1810—the necessity of virtue in any people who hoped to create and sustain a free republic.[46]

Virtually every familiar American leader in the founding era wrote on the importance of virtue in a republic, including George Washington, Thomas Jefferson, John Adams, Samuel Adams,[47] John Jay,[48] James Madison, Alexander Hamilton, Benjamin Rush and James Wilson.[49]

For example, John Adams, who drafted the Massachusetts state constitution of 1780, the oldest operating, written constitution, declared in the opening paragraph that the dissemination of virtue among the people was necessary to preserve their rights.[50]

James Madison, at the Virginia constitutional ratification convention of June 1788, declared: "If there be . . . [no virtue among us], we are in a wretched situation. No theoretical checks, no form of government, can render us secure. To suppose that any form of government will secure liberty or happiness without any virtue in the people, is a chimerical idea."[51]

Benjamin Rush said, "The only foundation for a useful education in a republic is to be laid in religion. Without it there can be no virtue, and without virtue there can be no liberty, and liberty is the object and life of all republican governments."[52] Rush, in his own educational plan for Pennsylvania in 1786, wrote, "religion is the foundation of virtue, virtue is the foundation of liberty;

liberty is the object of all republican governments; therefore, a republican education should promote religion as well as virtue and liberty."[53] And Samuel Cooper declared in 1780, "As piety and virtue support the honour and happiness of every community, they are particularly required in a free government. Virtue is the spirit of a republic; for where all power is derived from the people, all depends on their good disposition."[54]

The early state constitutions, including Massachusetts and Pennsylvania, explicitly emphasized the need for virtue. They went so far as to provide public support to ensure public virtue.[55] The earliest state constitutions emphasized virtue in political life.[56] The Northwest Ordinance of 1787 affirmed that "religion, morality, and knowledge, being necessary to good government and the happiness of mankind, schools and the means of education shall forever be encouraged."[57]

Even Jefferson emphasized the importance of virtue in public education that "the supports for freedom must come from the virtue of the people."[58] In later years Jefferson recalled Washington's character, emphasizing his prudence.[59] This was affirmed by others. Delegates to the Constitutional Convention of 1787 were concerned about the relationship between power and virtue in political leaders. One delegate, Pierce Butler, observed, "I do [not] believe they [the executive powers] would have been so great had not many members cast their eyes toward George Washington as president; and shaped their ideas of the powers to be given the president, by their opinion of his virtue."[60]

NATURAL LAW

The American founders were committed to natural law and natural rights. Scholars point out that many founders, including James Otis, Samuel Adams, Thomas Jefferson, Alexander Hamilton and John Adams appealed to natural rights.[61] The Declaration of Independence appealed to "the Laws of Nature and of Nature's God." Their understanding was not derived from a single source.[62] The founders retailed their natural law and ethics. As Michael Novak observed, "The founders were not primarily metaphysicians; they were nation-builders."[63]

It was a mixed understanding of natural law, derived from a number of sources, including Hooker (who was heavily influenced by Thomas Aquinas), John Locke, Blackstone and others.[64] But "the founders use Locke's terms [for the laws of nature and the natural rights of humans] in more traditional ways, consistent with Hooker and Sidney, even Cicero, Seneca, and Aristotle."[65]

Forest McDonald has written,

> The Patriots had turned to Locke rather than to the other great natural-law theories—Hugo Grotius, Samuel von Pufendorf, Thomas Rutherford, Burlamaqui, Vattel—for the reason that none of the others was so well adapted to their purposes. Vattel, the most respected of the lot, went so far as to say that rights were "nothing else but the power of doing what is morally possible," that is to say, what is proper and consistent with duty; and none of the theorists except Locke furnished a clear-cut rationale for independence.[66]

McDonald's point emphasizes the pragmatism of the founders in looking to natural law—which version suited their purposes?

Some founders believed that natural right was reflected in human nature. The Declaration, of course, states that men are "endowed by their Creator with certain inalienable rights." John Adams found natural law "in the frame of human nature, in the constitution of the intellectual and moral world."[67] Jefferson wrote, "The God who gave us life gave us liberty at the same time."[68]

In expounding his understanding of natural law in his 1790 lectures on law, James Wilson, a delegate to the Convention of 1787 and among the first group of Supreme Court justices, emphasized the relationship between reason and revelation:

> How shall we, in particular cases, discover the will of God? We discover it by our conscience, our reason, and by the Holy Scriptures. The law of nature and the law of revelation are both divine; they flow, though in different channels, from the same adorable source. It is, indeed, preposterous to separate them from each other. The object of both is—to discover the will of God—and both are necessary for the accomplishment of that end.[69]

Among all the founders, Wilson was perhaps the foremost scholar on natural law.[70] He clearly believed that "human laws created in opposition to these [natural] rights must be considered void."[71]

The founders were prudential in the classic sense of prudence as practical reason. In his *Defense of the Constitution of Governments of the United States*, written in the 1780s before the Federal Convention, John Adams critically contrasted Locke's brilliant philosophical abstractions with Locke's "absurdity" in drafting a constitution for Carolina in 1663 that consolidated the legislative and executive power in eight proprietors; Adams derided the consolidation as a "new oligarchical sovereignty."[72]

There is nothing in the record of the colonists or the founding generation, however, to think that the founders would have thrown out prudence in considering the application of natural law, or that they would have considered natural law to dictate the specifics of legislation, especially legislative attempts to limit unjust laws and conditions. That was not their understanding of natural law. This is confirmed in the drafting and enactment of the federal constitution, which points out the relationship between prudence and natural law in the thought of the founders. *The Federalist* is the culmination of that thought.

THE FEDERALIST

> The choice must always be made, if not of the lesser evil, at least of the GREATER, not the PERFECT good; and that in every political institution, a power to advance the public happiness involves a discretion which may be misapplied and abused. (*Federalist* 41)

The American founding generation's understanding of virtue and political prudence is reflected in *The Federalist* (often called *The Federalist Papers*). Clinton Rossiter, professor of politics at Cornell in the 1950s, argued that *The Federalist* was "the most important work in political science that has ever been written, or is likely ever to be written, in the United States."[73] More than two centuries later, *The Federalist* remains a national treasure for teaching political prudence.

The Federalist was written by three men of experience: Alexander Hamilton (1755-1804), James Madison (1751-1836) and John Jay (1745-1829), but was published under the pseudonym of Publius. It is a series of eighty-five essays, written mostly by Alexander Hamilton and James Madison, and published in New York newspapers to argue for the ratification of the U.S. Constitution. It had an agenda in the sense that its purpose was to persuade New York delegates to vote for the proposed federal constitution, but it argued for the proposed constitution on prudential grounds.[74]

The authors were realistic about human nature, including the tension between passion and reason (*Federalist* 10, 50, 55, 76). As Hamilton wrote in *Federalist* 6: "Is it not time to awake from the deceitful dream of a golden age and to adopt as a practical maxim for the direction of our political conduct that we, as well as the other inhabitants of the globe, are yet remote from the happy empire of perfect wisdom and perfect virtue?"

Graham Walker summarized the doctrine of human nature reflected in *The Federalist* (esp. 6, 10, 76):

> Men are inclined to vice but capable of virtue, and those with political power are not exempt from this condition. People who think this way are obviously not moral cynics or even moral relativists. They simply believe that human sinful inclinations make it necessary to place limiting safeguards around human political powers—including around the power to promote virtue.[75]

Consequently, Publius emphasized that wisdom and virtue among the people was essential to the perpetuation of liberty and republican government.

The Federalist explicitly relies on natural and divine law for the most general goals of civil government. Madison in *Federalist* 43 cited "the transcendent law of nature and of nature's God, which declares that the safety and happiness of society are the objects at which all political institutions aim and to which all such institutions must be sacrificed." But Publius never cites natural law as dictating the specifics of civil government—a written constitution, federalism, separation of powers, and checks and balances. To support the specifics, Publius relies on prudence.

The Federalist starts with a prudential question, "whether societies of men are really capable or not of establishing good government from reflection and choice, or whether they are forever destined to depend for their political constitutions on accident and force" (*Federalist* 1). The authors argued for the "common good" (*Federalist* 57), popular or republican government (*Federalist* 39), and liberty. They argued against the dangers and weaknesses of confederacy and disunity generally (*Federalist* 6-8), and the defects of the Articles of Confederation in particular, and they argued for the ratification of the federal constitution and for American union, which will contribute to the security, prosperity and liberty of the American people.

They argued for the merits of the proposed Constitution, that it was "true" to republican principles and much like their own state constitutions. In particular, they argued for the separation of governmental powers (*Federalist* 47), a strong executive (*Federalist* 70), majority rule, government resting on "the consent of the people," (*Federalist* 22) and for "divided, balanced, and limited government."[76]

Because of its realism about human nature, *The Federalist* seeks to explain the prudential arrangements struck in the proposed federal constitution. As Madison wrote in *Federalist* 51:

> Ambition must be made to counteract ambition. . . . It may be a reflection on human nature that such devices should be necessary to control the abuses of government. . . . These inventions of prudence cannot be less requisite in the distribution of the supreme powers of the State.

A second implication of political prudence was establishing a system of government that preserved liberty and prevented tyranny by controlling and balancing power. To do this, the founders carefully designed political structures and arrangements. These included limited government, republicanism, a mixed constitution (with elements of monarchy, aristocracy and democracy), separation of governmental powers (legislative, executive, judicial), checks and balances on governmental powers, and—with the constitution of 1787—federalism.

For example, some claim that the framers created a "godless constitution," but that is a false understanding of their prudential structure. The Establishment Clause of the First Amendment left the issue of religion to the states. As Jean Yarbrough puts it:

> while the Framers made no more than passing references to character at the Federal Convention, and failed to provide for it in the Constitution or to discuss it in *The Federalist*, they passed over the subject not because they were indifferent to these concerns or because they took its continuance for granted but because these matters were the preserve of the states, and the states were unlikely to ratify any charter that asked them to surrender these powers to the central government. Moreover, to recommend that the newly created federal government become actively involved in education, religion, and civil participation flew in the face of even the most radical nationalists' understanding of the scope of federal powers. Consequently, if we are to understand the significance of character in the American constitutional system, we must direct our

attention toward the state constitutions. In contrast to the federal Constitution, the Revolutionary state constitutions actively sought to promote the moral and civic virtues that would restrain the excesses of the commercial principle. And although the leading statesmen-educators divided on the question of which system would best form republican character—religion and a stern moral education or a more secular and enlightened emphasis on history and literature coupled with the right economic and social environment—there is no doubt that they considered some combination of these institutions to be vital to the preservation of free government.[77]

Another of the most controversial prudential decisions was the framers' handling of slavery at the Convention of 1787. One of the framers, James Wilson, for example, believed that slavery was "repugnant to the principles of natural law."[78] Yet he was a principal author of the federal constitution, which did not prohibit slavery. When challenged on this at the Pennsylvania ratifying convention of 1788, he pointed to the powers granted to Congress to limit or prohibit slavery (after 1808) and stated that the restrictions on slavery in the Constitution were "all that could be obtained. I am sorry it was no more; but from this I think there is reason to hope that yet a few years, and it will be prohibited altogether."[79] Wilson's statement was tragically excessively optimistic, but it reflected the judgment that the union of the states could not be accomplished in conjunction with prohibiting slavery; and, of course, had the federal constitution been rejected in 1787, slavery would have, in any case, been secured for the foreseeable future in the Southern states. Ultimately, it was eighty years of union that rallied Northern opinion to fight the war that ended slavery in 1865.

CONCLUSION

The two wings of the American founding reinforced the significant role that prudence played in the social and political thought of the American founders. They believed virtue was a necessary part of the foundation of republican government. Imbued with moral realism they constructed governmental structures to preserve liberty and prevent tyranny. Their moral realism led to their political realism, and their political realism concluded that the Good could be only imperfectly achieved in this fallen world. The American founders did not contribute a unique ethical understanding of prudence to the world, but their exercise of political prudence—in creating independent colonies, new state constitutional governments and a federal constitution—was unprecedented and far-reaching, and it is has had profound implications for the American legal and political system, and for world history.

WILBERFORCE'S PERSEVERANCE

"Persistence is the most important quality in politics. It was possessed in heroic quantity by Wilberforce."

Hugh Thomas, *The Slave Trade*

In the year that the U.S. Constitution was cast, William Wilberforce began his prudential campaign to abolish the slave trade in the British empire. One of the great social reform movements of the eighteenth and nineteenth centuries was the British anti-slavery movement. If England, the world's leading slave-trading nation, had not ended the slave trade, it would have inevitably expanded. The British historian George Macaulay Trevelyan (1876-1962) considered the British abolition of the slave trade "one of the turning events in the history of the world."[1]

One of the key leaders in that movement was William Wilberforce (1759-1833), a member of Parliament for nearly forty-five years from 1780-1825. In 1780, Wilberforce entered Parliament at the remarkably young age of twenty-one and eventually developed a reputation as an independent reformer. Wilberforce became the parliamentary leader of the movement in 1787, only a few years after it began with a small group of Quaker Dissenters. Wilberforce and his compatriots struggled for twenty years, from 1787 to 1807, to abolish the slave trade, and then for another twenty-five years to emancipate the slaves, until Parliament prohibited slavery in July 1833, three days before Wilberforce's death. The movement slowly reversed Britain's involvement in the slave trade, influencing several other nations, including the United States, to end the trade between 1807 and 1820.

From his position in Parliament, Wilberforce influenced the king and the most important political leaders of his day, worked with growing networks throughout different spheres of British life, took strategic steps to change British public opinion and law, and persevered over a half century despite chronic health problems. His life's work changed the course of slavery throughout the Western world.[2]

In 1787, the movement made a deliberate decision to aim first to abolish the slave trade and, after that victory was secured, to then emancipate the slaves. In both phases they sought to enact regulations or partial prohibitions on the slave trade or slavery when they could not obtain complete prohibition. The movement's campaign against the slave trade and slavery is a rich and rewarding case study of prudential action over several decades. The 2007 film *Amazing Grace* hopefully spurred many to look deeper into Wilberforce's strategy.

The Reality of the Slave Trade

In 1786-1787, Wilberforce undertook a crash course to understand the context and reality of slavery and "the Trade" (as it was called). He singled it out as "the greatest of all human evils."[3] Wilberforce described his new newly found mission in life in his diary on Sunday, October 28, 1787, when he was a twenty-eight-year-old member of Parliament (MP): "God Almighty has set before me two great objects, the suppression of the Slave Trade and the Reformation of Manners." These twin goals became the focus of the rest of his parliamentary career.

The slave trade had been going on for at least 275 years, since 1502, and British involvement had been going on for a century, since 1672, when "the Royal African Company became the first chartered British enterprise involved in the Trade."[4] England became the leader of the slave trade after 1713, when the Treaty of Utrecht "gave Britain the right to import slaves into Spanish American colonies."[5] The trade was "an unregulated, and essentially unchallenged, enterprise for most of the" 1700s.[6] The right to own slaves in England itself seemed established since the early 1700s.

But a few years before the Quaker abolition committee was founded in 1783, an attempt was made through legal test cases to establish the illegality of slavery in England, in which Wilberforce's eventual compatriot, Granville Sharpe, played a key role.[7] Only in the 1770s was the legality of slaves in England itself effectively ended.

One of Wilberforce's biographers, Robin Furneaux, describes the transport of slaves from Africa across the Atlantic Ocean—the Middle Passage, as it was called:

> The slaves were kept chained in these crowded holds. . . . When weather permitted they were taken up on deck and made to jump around under the threat of the lash. But when the weather was bad the buckets in the hold overflowed or upset and the slaves lay in their own filth for weeks on end in an atmosphere which gutted the seamen's candles and could be smelt across a mile of ocean. In these foul conditions they were ravaged by epidemics; but some captains would risk losing many of their slaves in exchange for the high profits that could be expected from "tight packing." In these ships the slaves were crammed in "spoon-fashion" always lying on their right sides because this was thought to be better for their hearts. Slaves suffered more from seasickness than Europeans and sometimes died of this complaint. Others were driven mad by the conditions and by terror of the unknown future. Mad or dead they were thrown overboard to feed the sharks that followed the slave ships all the way across the Atlantic. Those who survived would have to endure a journey that averaged about one hundred days. At the beginning of the voyage the crew would take their pick of the slave women. The slaver who wrote, "Once off the coast the ship became half bedlam and half brothel," has left us the pithiest summary of conditions in the Middle Passage.[8]

One of Wilberforce's compatriots, Thomas Clarkson, drew a detailed diagram of the slave ship *Brookes,* which crammed 609 slaves into its hold where they were "kept chained in a space smaller than a coffin."[9]

In response to the first move in Parliament to investigate the slave trade in December 1787, the traders raised four primary rebuttals. Some denied outright any harsh treatment of slaves; at least one was so bold as to "express his wish that English laborers might be but half as happy."[10] They contended that slavery really freed slaves from a life of uncertainty, violence and famine in Africa. They argued the futility of regulation—that if Britain didn't conduct the slave trade, France, Spain and Holland would simply step in ("Every Negro lost to a British ship by regulation would be a Negro won by a French ship").[11] This was a powerful argument by commercial interests for most of the twenty years between 1787-1807 and motivated Wilberforce to work for an international agreement.

And they pushed the fear of uprising, insurrections and massacres.[12] After the French revolution began, they associated the abolitionists with revolutionaries who wanted to foment rebellion and overturn established government, and they blamed every slave revolt on the agitation of the abolitionists. In 1791-1792, a slave revolt in San Domingo so prejudiced the climate that Prime Minister William Pitt apparently urged postponement of a motion to abolish the trade.[13]

But the most powerful rebuttal—perhaps the biggest obstacle—that undermined the abolition campaign for twenty years was the belief that the slave trade was a "necessary evil" for the British economy. Furneaux writes that despite "the incredulous horror of the House of Commons when the full iniquity of the Trade was revealed to it,"[14] Parliament refused to abolish "what it regarded as a profitable and necessary branch of commerce. . . . In an age in which suffering abounded the Slave Trade was accepted as a painful necessity, as one of the many unpleasant facts of life."[15]

It was this entrenched, profitable, expanding trade, supported by the most powerful political and economic forces in England, that Wilberforce took on in 1787. John Wesley captured Wilberforce's position in one of the last letters Wesley wrote, describing Wilberforce as an "Athanasius contra mundem" (Athanasius against the world).[16]

WILBERFORCE'S GIFTS

Wilberforce's prudential use of his personal gifts, as he matured, played a significant role in his eventual success. The son of a successful merchant, Wilberforce was raised in middle-class comfort. But his father died in 1767, when Wilberforce was just eight. From his college days at Cambridge, Wilberforce had great social gifts—witty and the center of attention, despite being little more than five feet tall.

Wilberforce decided to enter politics and used his twenty-first birthday party on August 24, 1780, as a launching pad for his campaign to represent Hull, his hometown. His election on September 11, 1780, was attributed to his "connections, charm and purse."[17]

Wilberforce was a charismatic and eloquent figure. "His voice, as fine in song as in rhetoric, was a social grace much in demand."[18] In a parliamentary age of great orators—including Edmund Burke, Charles Fox, George Canning, Richard Sheridan and William Pitt the Younger—Wilberforce was one of the best.[19] It was said by one parliamentary reporter that his speaking "was so distinct and melodious that the most hostile ear hangs on it delighted."[20] Canning commented on how skilled Wilberforce was in debate: "If there is any one who understands thoroughly the tactics of debate, and knows exactly what will carry the House along with him, it certainly is [Wilberforce]."[21]

One example is his first speech against the slave trade, on May 12, 1789, in which he laid out the facts about the trade over three hours:

> The nature and all the circumstances of this trade are now laid open to us; we can no longer plead ignorance—we cannot evade it—it is now an object placed before us—we cannot pass it; we may spurn it, we may kick it out of the way, but we cannot turn aside so as to avoid seeing it. . . . [I]t is brought now so directly before our eyes, that this House must decide, and must justify to all the world, and to their own consciences, the rectitude of the grounds and principles of their decision.[22]

Wilberforce was winsome: "The charm and charity of his severest strictures astonished an age used to furious religious arguments. . . . [H]e was that rare being, a man of strong convictions who could embrace those who differed."[23] Wilberforce shared with Abraham Lincoln a willingness to accept common blame without finger-pointing or invective. In his inaugural speech against the trade on May 12, 1789, Wilberforce said:

> I mean not to accuse anyone but to take the shame upon myself, in common indeed with the whole Parliament of Great Britain, for having suffered this horrid trade to be carried on under their authority. We are all guilty—we ought all to plead guilty, and not to exculpate ourselves by throwing the blame on others.[24]

He described how he sought cordial relations even with political enemies. Of a slaveholding gentleman, Wilberforce commented: "There is in grammar what they call a disjunctive conjunction. . . . So there is in society; it is thus with that gentleman and me—he is so great a slave holder. . . . But we do very well when we meet; we pass by topics upon which we should not agree, and exchange the small shot of conversation."[25] As one biographer said, he "attacked evils vigorously but worked with a spirit of respect and tolerance for people of very different allegiances."[26]

One mark of Wilberforce's political ability is that after a few years representing Hull (his boyhood home) he moved and won election in the most coveted seat in Parliament, Yorkshire, "with some 20,000 voters, the most populous as well as the largest constituency in the country," which was "a sounding board for national public opinion, for its electorate was diverse."[27] Wilberforce decided to do this on his own, remarking that "to anyone else it would have appeared a mad scheme. . . . It was very contrary to the aristocratic notions of the great families of the County to place the son of a Hull merchant in so high a situation."[28] He attended a political meeting at York on March 25, 1784, ostensibly to speak briefly, but with his own plan of becoming a candidate for the seat. Despite speaking at the end of a long, outdoor meeting in which "the crowd was lashed by wind, rain and hail," Wilberforce "made one of the best and most important speeches of his life. . . . He spoke for an hour and held his audience enthralled from beginning to end." It was this speech that prompted the famous quip from John Boswell, the biographer of Samuel Johnson, who was in the crowd: "I saw what seemed a mere shrimp mount upon the table; but as I listened, he grew, and grew, until the shrimp became a whale."[29] Not yet twenty-five years old, he was elected on April 7.

Wilberforce was afflicted with chronic ill health throughout his life, debilitating him for extensive periods, and he lived decades longer than colleagues thought he would. He suffered from "weakness of the lung, bowel . . . and eye."[30] At times, his exertions were such that his doctors predicted his imminent death. In February 1788, shortly after he began his focus against the slave trade, he was "felled by a nearly fatal gastric illness,"[31] which sidelined him for nearly the entire year. His eyes bothered him as early as 1786 and grew worse as he aged, to the point where he lost sight in one eye.[32] Obeying the standard medical advice of his day, Wilberforce became a regular user of opium, which was prescribed not as a cure but to relieve symptoms, the "only medication then known for his digestive condition."[33] This remedy apparently saved his life but regular use led to weak eyesight, which grew progressively worse.

He also suffered from a curvature of the spine, such that as he advanced in middle age his head "dropped forward until it almost touched his chest" unless he consciously raised it. In his last years in Parliament, he suffered from gout. In 1818, at the age of fifty-eight to fifty-nine, he was described as "shattered in constitution and feeble in body,"[34] but still exhibited a great and cheerful spirit.[35] He possessed self-awareness, knew his limitations and pursued "seasons of study, rest and renewal."[36]

ZEAL MADE EFFECTIVE BY PRUDENCE

Prior to his conversion to evangelical Christianity in 1784-1786, Wilberforce was an unlikely candidate to become the parliamentary leader against the slave trade. In his first four years in Parliament, Wilberforce energetically engaged in the luxuries and party life of London, which he later recalled as "dissolute" and "frivolous." Although he changed the way he spent his time after his conversion, he retained his charm, gaiety and wit. Hearing of his conversion, his family (prejudiced against "enthusiasts," as evangelicals were then called) was wary of an impending visit. But, after the trip, one relative remarked, "if that is madness, I hope he bites us all."[37]

Just after his twenty-fifth birthday and the summer after winning the Yorkshire seat, he toured France with a former tutor, Isaac Milner, a fellow of the Royal Society (of Science), a Cambridge mathematician, and later president of Queen's College. Milner agreed to join the months-long journey that stretched from October 1784 to February 1785, followed by a second trip with Milner that lasted from June to October 1785.[38] The conversations with Milner sparked a religious conversion. "By October 1785, the 'great change,' as he afterward termed it, had driven Wilberforce to rise early each morning to pray."[39] In effect, Wilberforce had become an evangelical Anglican.

Due to his conversations with Milner, he was in substantial turmoil between October and December 1785 as to what to do with his career. Wilberforce impulsively considered resigning from Parliament, seeing the dissolute and frivolous life surrounding Parliament as an obstacle to his newfound faith. He sought out John Newton for advice on December 7, 1785, after seeking a secret meeting.[40] A former slave trader, Newton was then pastor of a church in London. But over some months of careful reflection and counsel (with Pitt, John Wesley, Newton and others), Wilberforce came to see his parliamentary career as a calling, which induced a "higher sense of the duties of my station, and a firmer resolution to discharge them with fidelity and zeal."[41]

He pursued abolition at significant personal and financial cost. Many think he could have succeeded as prime minister when Pitt died in January 1806 had Wilberforce not championed the abolition of the slave trade. He spent a fortune, literally, combating the trade and on many other charitable endeavors. And his physical safety was frequently threatened.

Though it's uncertain whether Wilberforce ever studied Aristotle's *Ethics* or Thomas Aquinas's *Treatise on Prudence*, prudence was part of Wilberforce's common vocabulary and of his political deliberations.[42] In describing his religious conversion, Wilberforce wrote a friend:

> It is scarce too strong to say, that I seem to myself to have awakened about nine or ten years ago from a dream, to have recovered, as it were, the use of my reason after a delirium. In fact till then I wanted [i.e., was in want of] first principles; those principles at least which alone deserve the character of wisdom, or bear the impress of truth.[43]

In an early speech of February 22, 1782 (against the British government's prosecution of the American war), Wilberforce argued that "the ministers' conduct had resembled the career of furious madmen rather than the prudent exertions of statesmen."[44]

Wilberforce had a strong apprehension of moral purpose. Emancipation was consistently his goal. Pollock writes that "he aimed at an entire end to Slavery itself."[45] While Wilberforce did not deny that emancipation was a desire, he did not make it a parliamentary objective in the early years when enormous obstacles prevented it. In an April 2, 1792, speech on the subject, Wilberforce sidelined the subject of emancipation in these words: "I am not afraid of being told I design to emancipate the slaves; I will not indeed deny that I wish to impart to them the blessing of freedom. . . . But the freedom I mean is that of which, alas! [they] are not capable. . . . The soil must be prepared for its reception."[46]

But even when emancipation was not his immediate parliamentary objective, he deftly emphasized the principle of the matter, as in his February 18, 1796, parliamentary speech, responding to MP Robert Banks Jenkinson's proposal that consideration of abolition be postponed until "the return of peace":

> There is something not a little provoking in the dry calm way in which gentlemen are apt to speak of the sufferings of others. The question suspended! Is the

desolation of wretched Africa suspended? Are all the complicated miseries of this atrocious trade—is the work of death suspended? No, sir, I will not delay this motion, and I call upon the House not to insult the forbearance of Heaven by delaying this tardy act of justice.[47]

Similarly, he responded to the claim that the slaves were "well-fed":

What! Are these the only claims of a rational being? Are the feelings of the heart nothing? . . . So far from thanking the honorable gentleman for the feeding, clothing and lodging of which he boasts, I protest against the way in which he has mentioned them as degrading men to the level of brutes, and insulting all the higher qualities of our common nature.[48]

Wilberforce consciously avoided permanent compromise that would prevent future progress. In 1812, he wrote to Zachary Macaulay that they "should be 'guarded against any measures which might ever totally obstruct our future reforms.'"[49]

In Wilberforce's time, the notion of "political expediency" was a prudential consideration. Wilberforce wrote: "In the case of every question of political expediency, there appears to me room for the consideration of times and seasons—at one period, under one set of circumstances it may be proper to push, at another and in other circumstances to withhold our efforts."[50]

One of the lures of imprudence is to fail to see the great (though uncertain) good that might be obtained because of the real and daunting costs of achieving it. The great good of ending the slave trade was uncertain, and it was made more uncertain by the vigorous and insistent claims that it could not happen or would lead to even greater evils. The traders were effective in sowing doubt in the minds of members of Parliament and the public.

There was a general belief—which Wilberforce apparently shared—that immediate emancipation "would be productive of universal anarchy and distress."[51] The claims by traders that insurrections would result concerned him, and he was also concerned that insurrections would lead to "further repression."[52]

Prudence aided Wilberforce in articulating the practicable good that could be achieved and in persevering in its pursuit despite great obstacles and uncertainty.

WILBERFORCE'S NETWORK

Sociologist James Davison Hunter argues that the driving force of cultural change in history is not the solitary genius but the network.[53] Wilberforce frequently sought the counsel of many, surrounded himself with experts and relied on his associates in the movement.

Wilberforce was a promising MP to advance the movement's goals in Parliament. The abolition movement began with the Quakers. "There was little or no coordinated abolitionist effort, no 'movement' as such, until the 1780s."[54] John Wesley's 1774 pamphlet against the slave trade, *Thoughts on Slavery*, was "one of the very first," according to one Wilberforce biographer, John Pollock. The Quakers had opposed the slave trade throughout the eighteenth century and, apparently, first presented a petition against the trade to Parliament in 1783. (Another Wilberforce biographer Furneaux suggests that this was instigated by the atrocity aboard the slave ship *Zong* in March 1783.)[55] But the Quakers, as dissenters from the established church, were on the outside of British society and their influence was limited.[56] Wilberforce gave them crucial influence in Parliament.

As Pollock observed, "Wilberforce proved that a man can change his times, but that he cannot do it alone."[57] He became intentional about building a network, or what he called "bringing together all men who are like-minded, and who may probably at some time or other combine and concert for the public good."[58]

He was always willing to work with coalitions on particular issues without regard to personalities and disagreements on other issues. One biographer reports that " 'measures, not men' became one of his favorite sayings."[59]

Perhaps Wilberforce's most significant relationship was with William Pitt the Younger (1759-1806), just three months older than Wilberforce, son of the famous prime minister who died in 1778, and destined to be the dominant political leader of his generation.[60] His father having been prime minister, Pitt had a fast education in politics and was gifted with an excellent mind and a sparkling wit. Shortly after Wilberforce, Pitt entered the House after the Christmas 1780 recess. Within twenty months, Pitt was Chancellor of the Exchequer (the rough equivalent of the U.S. Treasury Secretary) and became prime minister in December 1783.

Furneaux observes:

> Pitt's character was complementary to Wilberforce's and it is not strange that
> they became such close friends. Wilberforce had the vivacity, charm, and gre-
> gariousness that Pitt lacked, but he tended, at the beginning of his career, to see
> politics as a game, as a contest of eloquence and wits in which victory was its
> own reward. Pitt introduced Wilberforce to the serious side of politics; until his
> conversion all of Wilberforce's political ideas were taken from Pitt and even af-
> ter it they seldom found themselves in disagreement.[61]

Wilberforce was destined to be disappointed with Pitt's seeming lack of
complete commitment to abolition. An analyst of Wilberforce's anti-slavery
strategy, Jay Sappington, says,

> it is a debated point whether his [Pitt's] inconstancy was due to a lack of full
> sympathy with or commitment to the cause, or was a matter of political expedi-
> ency on the part of one who, as a PM with the Government and the King to
> manage, had more at stake then did Wilberforce. There is no doubt that he re-
> frained from using his full influence on the issue.[62]

Wilberforce had known John Newton (1727-1807) since he had listened to
Newton's sermons as a child. A former slave trader, John Newton—the author
of many hymns, including "Amazing Grace"—became rector of Olney and
then of St. Mary Woolnoth Church in London, and eventually testified against
the slave trade before Parliament. During the turmoil of reconsidering his career, Wilberforce wrote to Newton, seeking his counsel, in December 1785.[63]
Later, at a moment of great despair for Wilberforce in 1796, Newton encouraged Wilberforce to persevere.

Admiral Sir Charles Middleton, an MP who entered Parliament shortly before Wilberforce, and "mastermind" of the 1805 British naval victory at Trafalgar, was also a committed abolitionist. Sometime after Wilberforce visited the
Middletons in the fall of 1786, Middleton (along with others) recruited Wilberforce to be the parliamentary leader.[64]

MP Henry Thornton was a wealthy banker who resided with Wilberforce in
the Clapham community, which Thornton did much to start. At least five
members of the Clapham community were members of Parliament. Thomas
Clarkson was a researcher and skilled propagandist who published a two-
volume history of the movement in 1808.[65] Wilberforce worked effectively

with Hannah More, a writer and poet, on philanthropic endeavors.

Wilberforce met James Stephen, a leading maritime lawyer, in January 1789; Stephen became his brother-in-law.[66] Seventeen years later, it was Stephen who eventually created the parliamentary strategy that resulted in the successful vote abolishing the trade. In 1821, Wilberforce passed the torch as parliamentary leader to MP Thomas Fowell Buxton, "a young Quaker MP whose efforts to secure prison reform Wilberforce greatly admired."[67]

These networks reached into different segments of British society. They served to counsel Wilberforce and advance his numerous endeavors. Historian Roger Anstey observed: "As in every stage of the abolitionist campaign, Wilberforce used the friends both from his old and his new life. . . . Certainly his popularity paid unforced dividends for one secret of such triumphs as the abolition movement gained was Wilberforce's popularity and connections."[68]

One key network in the fight against the slave trade was the London Abolition Committee. Legal, educational and political efforts against the slave trade were sporadic and lacked significant momentum until April-May 1787, when the Committee was formed and recruited Wilberforce.

Sometime in 1787, the Committee made the prudential judgment to focus first on the slave trade. Jay Sappington outlines the decision of the committee to focus on the trade, drawing from Thomas Clarkson's *History*. The committee concluded that "prudence dictated a two-phrase strategy, and the trade was seen as the root of slavery, not vice versa."[69]

Roger Anstey's *The Atlantic Slave Trade and British Abolition 1760-1810*, is an enthralling analysis, full of subtle insights into the strategy of the British abolition movement and sensitive to the "balancing of tactical considerations" that was "a keynote of abolitionist conduct in 1801-1802."[70] Anstey quotes Clarkson's *History* on what apparently was the essential reasoning—*matching means to ends*:

> According to Clarkson, "it appeared soon to be the sense of [the London Abolition Committee], that to aim at the removal of both would be to aim at too much, and that by doing this we might lose all." Theoretically, so reasoning in the Committee continued, it did not matter which evil should be selected for attack, for each would be vitally weakened by the successful onslaught on the other.[71]

Furneaux gives a lengthy recitation of additional reasons for that prudential decision:

> The first thing that the Abolitionists had to decide was what, precisely, they
> wished to abolish. There were faced with two distinct evils, the Slave Trade and
> the institution of slavery. With the exception of Granville Sharpe, who did not
> recognise the impossible, they agreed that their chances of success would be
> greater if they concentrated on one of these evils. They also agreed that it "did
> not matter where they began, or which of them they took as far as the end to be
> produced was the thing desired." If slavery were abolished, the Trade would
> clearly die at the same time. The Foreign Slave Trade would then stand out as a
> moral anachronism and economic folly. If the Trade were abolished, planters
> would be forced to treat their slaves well in order to preserve their numbers.
> Greater leniency must grow into greater privileges and rights and, at length,
> into freedom. The last argument seems weak even assuming that the planters,
> when faced with Abolition, would react logically; they had seldom done so in
> the past, nor were they to do so in the event. No such doubts seem to have
> struck the Abolitionists in 1787, and even if they had, they would still have been
> justified in concentrating their attack on the Trade. An attack on slavery would
> have been an open assault on "property," a word which in the eighteenth cen-
> tury had deep emotional overtones. The Abolitionists would have been charged
> with letting loose an irresponsible race; they would have had slave revolts flung
> in their teeth and been challenged to prove that the slaves were ready for free-
> dom, a statement with which few of them then agreed. There would have been
> grave constitutional questions of the powers of Parliament over the internal
> affairs of semi-independent colonies. Secession would have been threatened. . . .
> On the other hand, Parliament had an indisputable right to regulate or abolish
> any branch of commerce, and to prohibit the Trade would interfere with no
> one's property or security.[72]

Although Wilberforce agreed with the Committee's strategy, his consistent
goal was always emancipation.[73] As he explained thirty years later in a letter to
Joseph Gurney:

> It is most true, that it has ever been and still is, both the real and the declared
> object of all the friends of the African race, to see the W.I. [West Indian] slaves
> GRADUALLY *transmuted* into a free Peasantry; but this, the ULTIMATE ob-
> ject, was to be produced progressively by the operation of multiplied, chiefly
> moral causes; and to appear at last to have been the almost insensible result of

the various improvement: not to have been an object all along in view, and gradually but slowly advanced upon (like an obelisk at the end of an avenue) but like the progress of vegetation which appears to have gradually changed barrenness and desolation into virtue and beauty.[74]

Pollock concludes that "Wilberforce knew that to secure sudden emancipation from Parliament was politically impossible."[75] For example, during the final debate on the abolition bill on March 16, 1807, MP Windham (apparently disingenuously hoping that Parliament would ban neither the slave trade nor slavery) argued that "if Parliament abolished the Slave Trade they should abolish Slavery too, and not outlaw the one without the other." Wilberforce replied that "he indeed looked forward to a change in the status of the negroes but 'it was not in our power to heal up both the wounds immediately.' "[76]

CONFRONTING OBSTACLES

From the outset Wilberforce and his allies were opposed by the most powerful forces in England: the Royal family, most of the Cabinet, vested economic interests and naval heroes like Lord Nelson who referred to "the damnable doctrine of Wilberforce and his hypocritical allies."[77]

In addition to this general opposition, four major obstacles prevented success between 1787-1807: making the case to the public and mobilizing public opinion through petitions, the belief that the Trade was necessary to the British economy, the failure of England to control the seas, and the perceived authority of the colonial assemblies.

In 1804, Wilberforce wrote, "Remember, our grand practical difficulty in Abolition is that the Colonial legislatures will not concur and that without their concurrence we can do nothing."[78] Pollock explains that "Wilberforce believed with almost everyone, . . . that Emancipation could come only with the consent of the colonial assemblies, who were adamant."[79]

In addition, *unanticipated obstacles*—principally the war with France until the victory at Trafalgar in 1805—disrupted momentum and stalled progress. Ironically, the war with France, which inhibited success for over a decade between 1792 and 1805, resulted in British victory and command of the seas, which, in turn, resulted in progress in the abolition of the slave trade.

At the outset of the campaign Wilberforce and his allies lacked prudence in two crucial misunderstandings of the reality of the slave trade. First, they assumed that moral arguments would be enough and failed to perceive the strength of the notion that the trade was a "necessary evil." They "at first believed abolition would be fairly simple matter, taking only a couple of years to accomplish. All that was required, they thought, was to confront Parliament with the horrors of the Trade."[80] They failed to recognize that self-interest is always intertwined with political issues. Second, they failed to see that their progress would be influenced by "unrelated" issues of national interest. Anstey agrees that the abolitionists in the early stages did not "properly appreciate" the "political and constitutional obstacles in the way of a speedy abolition."[81]

The prevalent belief was that "abolition would instantly annihilate a trade, which annually employed upwards of 5,500 sailors, upwards of 160 ships, and whose exports amount to 800,000 sterling; and would undoubtedly bring the West India trade to decay, whose exports and imports amount to upwards of 6,000,000 sterling, and which give employment to upwards of 160,000 tons of additional shipping, and sailors in proportion." The trade "upon which two thirds of the commerce of this country depended" was thought to be essential to the British economy.[82]

They did not anticipate the strength of the notion of the trade as a necessary evil.[83] This assumption even infected the abolitionists. As Pollock describes it, "even among supporters . . . few believed . . . that Abolition would be sound policy, whether economic or political." They frankly "regarded it as a quixotic act of national self-sacrifice demanded by humanity and justice."[84]

It was precisely this reliance on "humanity" that was rejected by the commercial interests, as reflected in the Earl of Abington's speech against abolition in 1793. Reginald Coupland, another of Wilberforce's biographers, reports that Abington "swept aside the noxious bundle of petitions. What was the ground of them? Humanity! 'But humanity is no ground for petitioning. Humanity is a private feeling and not a public principle to act upon. It is a case of conscience, not of constitutional right.' "[85]

Eventually, however, the Committee concluded that the moral case had been effectively made and turned to confront the notion that the slave trade was a necessary evil, what Wilberforce and Clarkson called "the impolicy of the Trade."[86] Anstey reports that "the Abolition Committee soon concluded that the general, moral case against the slave trade had been made and that the way to induce a positive readiness to end the trade was to demonstrate that it was impolitic as well as unjust and inhumane." The Committee reported by early 1788 that "they have more particularly directed their attention to the plea of political necessity which is frequently urged to justify . . . this traffick."[87]

Clarkson published a book, based on considerable research and data, that specifically attacked the "impolicy" of the Trade.[88] Anstey observes, "Here was the first assertion of a conscious balance in advocacy which was henceforth to be frequent in the whole abolition campaign."[89] Wilberforce and his allies consciously balanced arguments of "justice" and "humanity" and "policy" in parliamentary debates over the next twenty years.

The slow pace and procedures of Parliament—the key legislative forum in Britain—were certainly part of the reason for the length of the campaign. After Wilberforce's May 1789 speech, for example, the House voted in June to hear more evidence in the "next session," which meant the following year. Typically, the House would conduct substantive business February to May and then adjourn until the next January. For these and others reasons, Wilberforce became an advocate for parliamentary reform.

With a problem as complex and longstanding as the international slave trade, it is doubtful whether Wilberforce and the movement could accurately understand all of the obstacles, much less their solutions, before the problem was thoroughly engaged. It took considerable time, effort and resources to understand the obstacles, to implement strategies and to learn from their failures and adjust their strategies in light of increased knowledge and changing circumstances and obstacles. But, as they gained experience, their understanding of each of these obstacles increased. Experience was vital to their prudence.

FENCES AROUND THE TRADE

For the forty-five years between 1787 and 1833, Wilberforce and his allies consistently favored partial prohibitions when they could not achieve general and immediate abolition or emancipation.[90] They sought regulations or partial prohibitions of the trade and of slavery. Sappington summarized several regulatory fences that Wilberforce and other MPs sought to put around the slave trade when they could not abolish it outright:

"Slave Carrying Bills: These bills, such as the Dolben Slave Limitation Act, reduced the number of slaves that could be carried per ship."

"Slave Trade Limitation Bills: If enacted, these bills would have prohibited slave exports from specific parts of Africa."

This would, in effect, limit the trade geographically. This had a strategic tie to colonial conquests made during the war with France. Abolitionists were able to argue that "prohibiting the importation of slaves into the captured islands" prevented the possibility that with the potential return of these islands to France, Britain would not have foolishly invested in its enemy's economy.[91]

"Foreign Slave Trade Bills: These statutes prohibited the importation of slaves to foreign countries and their colonies, as well as to captured colonies. Both shipments originating in Africa and those originating in other colonies, which could then be re-supplied from Africa, were banned."[92]

In light of the war with France in 1793, "all present attempts to carry a general vote of Abolition [were] suspended," and abolition of the slave trade was deemed politically and legally impossible. In the alternative, Wilberforce "pro-

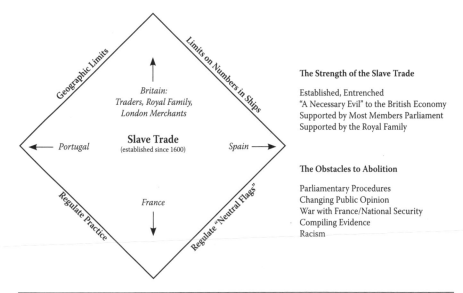

Figure 3.1. Legal fences around slave trade when prohibition was not possible (1787–1807)

posed some restrictive regulations which might mitigate the present evils of the trade, and prepare for its entire suppression."[93] On May 14, 1793, Wilberforce introduced a more limited bill, the Foreign Slave Bill. This "would limit and regulate the importations into our own colonies"[94] and thereby forbid the selling of slaves to foreign colonies. It passed the House but was rejected by the Lords. In February 1794, Wilberforce again introduced the Foreign Slave Bill. It passed the House but not the Lords.

Sappington summed up the point of these regulations. There were two broad categories:

> Measures which actually and immediately ended some part of the trade (such as the Foreign Slave Trade Bills), and regulations which in some way ameliorated the ongoing horrors of the trade (such as the Slave Carrying Bills). Bills in the latter category were beneficial in two senses. First, they were good in and of themselves, by virtue of the reduction in suffering and loss of life they affected, even if they could not reduce the traffic. Second, both types of laws were seen as stepping stones to further regulation and/or incremental abolition because the public debates that surrounded these bills increased the visibility of the Trade and its horrors.[95]

Although Wilberforce sponsored a motion for general and immediate abolition annually for several years, abolition came not immediately and totally but, by intent and in effect, incrementally. The slave trade was incrementally reduced by regulations and partial prohibitions, and those incremental reductions were tied, in public debate, to issues of national interest rather than strong arguments of morality—"justice" and "humanity"—which were reserved until the final stroke. The incremental reductions served to eliminate the fears raised by the claims of the slave traders. Though Wilberforce and his allies had the strongest moral motivations, they exhibited strategic, tactical and rhetorical flexibility in their actions and arguments in large part because they stayed focused on the end result and did not confuse the goal with their motivations.

By 1806 these bills had substantially reduced the trade. And the argument against abolition was weakened and "could not be threatened with ineffectiveness by foreign rivals since they lacked either the inclination or the ability to take up Britain's share of the trade."[96]

The notion that mere regulations might imply approbation of the slave trade was openly debated in Parliament. Sir William Dolben prefaced his slave-carrying bill on May 9, 1788, with the statement that "he did not mean, by any regulations he might introduce for this purpose, to countenance or sanction the Slave-trade, which, however modified, would be always wicked and unjustifiable."[97] Another historian of the abolition of the trade states that "Pitt himself demanded the one-year limitation to counteract the argument that regulation implied approbation of the slave trade."[98] In 1802 Canning, in proposing an exclusion of slavery from Trinidad (captured during the war with France), appealed to committed abolitionists "not to oppose a partial measure from the belief that this would be to condone the essential evil."[99]

Wilberforce and his allies were forced to make prudential judgments about the impact of regulations or partial prohibitions, and Wilberforce, for the most part, accepted regulations and partial prohibitions when general and immediate abolition was not possible. In *The Atlantic Slave Trade and British Abolition*, Roger Anstey documents how frequently the abolitionists resorted to "partial measures" when general and immediate abolition was not possible and how they were effective in promoting the ultimate goal.

PERSISTENCE IN THE CAMPAIGN AGAINST THE TRADE

Much can be learned from the strategic and tactical adjustments that the anti-slavery movement made between 1787 and 1807.[100] While Wilberforce made it an annual strategy to move for general and immediate abolition of the trade, other strategies and bills were offered by other MPs. In June 1788, MP Sir William Dolben introduced the first regulation that the movement attempted, a slave limitation (or carrying) bill. The Dolben bill was an important vehicle for the abolitionists to gather and present evidence to Parliament on the reality of the trade and the Middle Passage.[101]

For the two years between May 1787 and May 1789, the movement was occupied with gathering data and "preparing the case against the Slave Trade."[102] In January 1790, Wilberforce proposed a select committee in the House to investigate the trade, and this dragged on for nearly two years. The debate did not actively renew until April 1791. Wilberforce made a speech of four hours on April 18, 1791, leading to one of the major votes testing their strength on the abolition of the trade. They lost 88 to 163, and the fight in Parliament was again postponed until the following year.

A critical change in the external environment and in tactics came in 1792. In March to April 1792, Wilberforce again moved for abolition of the slave trade, with a speech on April 2, 1792. But then Home Secretary and MP Henry Dundas intervened and offered an amendment for "gradual" abolition, a move which gave MPs a safe "out" to avoid the difficult question. Though Wilberforce opposed it, it passed the House 230 to 85. The Commons approved the amended bill and identified January 1, 1796, as the "target date for complete abolition," but the amended bill was defeated in the House of Lords. The House backtracked a year later and refused to confirm the date for "gradual abolition."[103] After a fight now going on five years, Wilberforce became more resigned to a longer fight instead of quick success.[104]

Dundas's move was a significant detour that seemed to haunt Wilberforce for years. Years later Wilberforce wished he "had called the bluff in 1792 when, in effect, he had been offered gradual Emancipation if he would abandon the fight for immediate Abolition."[105] In contrast to Wilberforce's support of Dolben's regulations, Jay Sappington notes that Wilberforce "opposed Dundas' gradualist proposals in 1792 when the House seemed likely to pass his own immediatist one."[106]

The French Revolution disrupted the campaign for more than a decade. Although revolution broke out in France in 1789, Anstey observed that "the French Revolution . . . had no significant effect on the abolition cause until the autumn of 1791," by late 1792 the French Revolution damaged the abolition movement when abolition began to be associated with radicalism.[107] The French Revolution ripened into war in February 1793. Pitt put national security issues first, and the House rejected Wilberforce's motion to merely introduce his abolition bill in 1793.

Two years passed, and at the end of 1795, when Wilberforce returned to Parliament victorious after his Yorkshire speech in support of the government's policies, he immediately employed his greater popularity by moving for a general and immediate abolition of the slave trade.[108] His motion would have effectively implemented Dundas's schedule for "gradual" abolition by 1796, but Hugh Thomas notes that the "the public mood was in favor of indefinite delay. The consequences of the revolutions in France and Saint-Domingue, the war, and the social problems at home caused the opposition to abolition to become far stronger."[109]

In 1796 the abolitionists were as close as they ever came to a successful vote in the House before 1807. Popular sentiment swung back toward Wilberforce and his motion for immediate abolition of the slave trade was defeated by just four votes, 70 to 74, on March 15, 1796. (The loss by four votes was attributed to the absence of friendly votes attending a new opera, allegedly sponsored by the slave traders.) In the summer of 1796, Dolben attempted a stricter version of his Slave Limitation (Carrying) Bill, which lost,[110] and Wilberforce unsuccessfully tried to convince Pitt and Dundas to include abolition in treaty negotiations with France. The defeat in 1796 was "the most devastating defeat of the entire 20 year fight to abolish the slave trade."[111]

Why did it take eleven more years to abolish the slave trade after coming so close in March, 1796? The answer is largely the war and national security. Anstey comments that "both from the viewpoint of the abolitionists themselves, and in the context of the whole history of abolition, the years 1796-1804 may appear barren and sterile. . . . Yet the events of the eight years after 1796 both reveal the reasons why the abolition still was not achieved and contain the seeds of developments in abolitionist thinking and tactics which were shortly to be important ingredients of success."[112]

In 1799, Wilberforce's motion to abolish the trade was defeated 74 to 82. The movement also tried a number of regulatory bills in 1799. MP William Smith "revived the Slave Carrying Bill" (restricting the number of slaves that could be carried per ton of British shipping), which passed the Commons but was defeated in the Lords. MP Henry Thornton's bill to forbid slave exports also lost. Pitt also supported a "Slave Trade Limitation" bill, intended to restrict the areas of the West African coast open to the trade, but while it passed the House of Commons it got nowhere in the Lords."[113] According to Hugh Thomas, the slave carrying regulations reduced the profitability of the trade.[114]

Between 1797 and 1799, Wilberforce established an annual practice of moving for general and immediate abolition, but the Commons rejected these motions by slim margins (74 to 82 in May 1797; 83 to 87 in April 1798, but 54 to 84 in March 1799).[115] However, "the political obstacles to a general abolition continued to be insuperable."[116] For the four years between 1800 and 1803, Anstey reports that Wilberforce suspended this practice "for tactical reasons." Wilberforce "refrained from his annual motion in 1800 and 1801, and could only introduce it too late for effective action in 1802, whilst in 1803 the imminent threat of invasion led him to stay his hand."[117]

Anstey summarized Wilberforce's strategic considerations: "Complete British abolition remained the goal but Wilberforce withheld a motion on this in years when to introduce such a motion might prejudice a wider purpose, such as a general convention, or when some partial measure had a better chance of success."[118]

A significant external political change during these years that eventually contributed to abolition was the Act of Union with Ireland in 1801, which resulted in bringing into Parliament new Irish MPs who supported abolition. Wilberforce saw the need to educate these hundred new Irish MPs on the abolition question and rightly perceived that many would favor abolition, as they were to show in the 1804 parliamentary vote.

War with France resumed in 1803, and there was great fear of an invasion by Napoleon. The "question of abolition was put aside for the more immediate concern of national security."[119]

Toward the end of the 1804 session a motion by Wilberforce to abolish the slave trade, supported by Pitt and MP Charles Fox (leader of the political opposition to Pitt), won with a significant majority. The first clear vote for immediate abolition in the House, it gave the impression that abolition was in sight. Abolition prevailed in the Commons 99 to 33 on third reading, but lost in the Lords. Belmonte writes that "popular support for abortion had been steadily growing, in great part due to the sustained campaign to convince the public of the slave trade's immorality. Many in Parliament felt the shift in momentum, or were themselves convinced, and began to support Wilberforce."[120]

Sappington gives some insight into the spectrum of views in Parliament: "there was a minority at either end of the spectrum of positions on abolition. . . . Victory for the reformers lay with the remaining votes in the middle. . . . [M]any of their gains and losses in the legislative battle resulted from the interplay of several factors. Over the decades, shifts occurred in the circumstances related to each of the three issues of national interest: Britain's economic security, its internal political and social stability, and its external stability and ascendance as an empire in relation to the other western powers."[121]

Frank Klingberg observed that "it was a convergence of national interest issues with the abolitionists' goals—and the reformers' brilliance at capitalizing on this convergence—which finally yielded success. Early in the game, however, the reformers did not fully perceive the necessity of exploiting these non-moral issues."[122] It was this convergence on which James Stephens acted, as we will see, with his successful strategy in 1806.

THE FINAL PUSH: 1805-1807

By 1805 Wilberforce and his allies had learned to effectively tie the goal of abolition to national security issues. Although the Commons voted down abolition 77 to 70 early in 1805, strategic progress was gained through a change in external conditions.[123] In August to September 1805, Pitt "finally delivered on a promise he had made to Wilberforce in March to have the Government stop the Guiana and Surinam Trade . . . by an Order in Council." This maneuver effectively bypassed Parliament.[124]

Nelson's famous victory at Trafalgar came in November 1805. "The completeness of the victory, by giving Britain total command of the seas, was to have a very definite effect on Abolition prospects."[125] Sometimes fortuitous, external events arise that can be acted on to advance the cause. Prudence counsels being sensitive to these opportunities, and planning for them, if possible.

Pitt's unexpected death at forty-seven in January 1806 actually removed an obstacle by changing the government and the cabinet. Pitt was succeeded by William Grenville as prime minister, and Charles Fox became foreign secretary.[126] Both were strong abolitionists who had consistently supported abolition in the 1790s, though they had conflicted with Wilberforce, personally and politically, at various times over the past two decades. These two worked more closely with the abolition movement, and Wilberforce's political independence made it easier for him to work with this new coalition. "Wilberforce and Fox now consulted with one another about matters of legislative strategy, and Fox secured a promise from the Prince of Wales that he would not adversely stir up the opposition of the royal family to abolition."[127] Thus in February 1806 "the coalition ministry which came to power was dominated by men who favoured abolition," and the cabinet itself became more favorable.[128]

The attorney general introduced a Foreign Slave Trade Bill to "strengthen, by statute, the royal proclamation of 15 August 1805 which prohibited, with exceptions, the supply of slaves to conquered territories."[129] It was proposed as a matter of national interest, and arguments about "justice" and "humanity" for the slaves were intentionally downplayed.[130] Wilberforce supported this and deferred, waiting to introduce his own general abolition bill.[131] Hugh Thomas records the strategy:

> This was a stepping stone to full abolition, but it was introduced quietly, so that Sir Robert Peel, the cotton manufacturer and slaveowning member for Tamworth, had to admit, in a speech on the third reading, that he had not been present during the earlier discussions because he had not realized the bill's importance. The Commons voted 35 to 13 in favor [on May 1]. In May 1806, this bill passed even the Lords (by 43 to 18). By then, a new economic argument had been added to the purely humanitarian one: the West Indies were in debt, there was a large sugar surplus and the "saturated" old colonies did not want new slaves.[132]

STEPHEN'S SUCCESSFUL TACTIC

By 1806 the war measures taken against the slave trade were beginning to take effect. "The measures against the trade to conquered islands operated ever more widely as conquest followed conquest and could scarcely have been repealed during wartime, whilst the years from 1806 onwards saw the successively more rigorous application of the measures which [James] Stephen had proposed."[133]

The connection between the trade and foreign policy laid the foundation for a creative strategy largely conceived by Wilberforce's brother-in-law, James Stephen, an admiralty lawyer, who had published two books that argued that the misuse of neutral flags in colonial trade worked to Britain's economic and strategic detriment.[134] Stephen made a strong argument in general, laying a solid foundation for its application to the slave trade, but left the application to the slave trade largely to the imagination.

> Grenville introduced a measure in the House of Lords to codify Pitt's Order in Council regarding the Guiana Trade, and to expand the restriction to all foreign countries as well as to captured and ceded colonies (i.e., a substitute for the Foreign Slave Bill, which had never passed both houses). The immorality of slavery was purposely side-stepped during the debate which followed. Instead, Stephen's economic analysis was used to argue that the bill was essential to national security. The strategy worked, and the bill was carried in both houses.[135]

Anstey summarizes the incremental impact of Stephen's strategy:

> Stephen's masterly tactic of concentrating first on the abolition of those branches of the trade which could be represented as harming the national interest in time

of war, and the way in which this measure was played down, meant that the political nation was confronted all of a sudden with the fact that it had abolished what was believed to be nearly two-thirds of the British slave trade almost without realising it. . . . The decision to go first for the ending of the British slave trade to foreigners, by an appeal to sound policy, and then to introduce the wavering ranks of independent men gently to a total abolition, based additionally on justice and humanity, by means of a declaration of intent, was of immense importance.[136]

In other words, Stephen's strategy "showed that abolition would actually help the war effort."[137] Stephen's prudence was a result of his experience in working with Wilberforce and the movement over the past seventeen years since 1789 and of capitalizing on the national security issues which shaped the context of 1804 to 1807.

In early 1807 they changed tactics. Instead of Wilberforce moving in the House, Grenville introduced the bill in the Lords first in January 1807. "After a bitter and emotional month-long fight, at 4 am on the morning of February 5, 1807, the bill passed, 100-36" in the Lords.[138] According to Stephen's strategy, this was followed by a resolution in the Commons, which prevailed 114 to 15, declaring the slave trade "contrary to principles of justice, humanity, and sound policy and pledging abolition with all practical expediency." On February 22, 1807, the night of second reading, the bill passed 283 to 17 in the House. The royal assent was declared on Wednesday, March 25, 1807.

ENFORCEMENT PROBLEMS AFTER 1807

Pollock notes that with the royal assent in March, 1807, "The Bill for the Abolition of the Slave Trade became law. The problems of enforcing it began."[139] The trade was legally prohibited but not eliminated.

After a twenty-year fight, success in the vote to abolish the slave trade led to a lull, as Parliament focused its attention on other issues. There was a certain pause to rest from exertions of the past twenty years.

The anti-slavery movement shifted its attention to effective enforcement of abolition. Wilberforce did not speak again on the subject in Parliament for four years, until 1811. But Frank Klingberg concluded that "the results of the efforts made in the years 1807-1815 were quite as important as those of the years 1787-1807."[140]

Jay Sappington summarizes four goals of the bills that were introduced over the next twenty-five years, leading to emancipation in 1833: (1) improved enforcement of abolition as "an illicit Trade continued to flourish despite the new law," (2) adoption of abolition by other nations through abolition clauses in international treaties, (3) gradual emancipation, (4) immediate emancipation (steps toward gradual emancipation having failed led to calls for immediate emancipation).[141] The first bill, by MP Brougham, was passed to thwart illegal trade and increased the penalty from a misdemeanor to a felony. Wilberforce supported this.

During these years an international strategy was renewed and the movement emphasized enforcement efforts in Parliament. On January 1, 1808, the American slave trade was officially abolished. Other countries agreed in following years.

A major tactic to monitor enforcement was a registry bill. A campaign for registry bills began in 1811. The drive for comprehensive and effective registration took eight years.

Prime Minister Spencer Perceval approved an Order in Council in January 1812 that required Trinidad to create a slave registry system to help detect illegal importation, the first effort to get registry to prevent illicit importation.[142] Having established this foothold, the movement then sought to expand registry to encompass other colonies, but that required parliamentary approval.

In 1815, "Wilberforce proposed expansion of the registry system to all colonies."[143] In the summer of 1816 the Slave Registry bill, which Wilberforce referred to as "my chief Parliamentary object," was debated.[144] The slavers took advantage of a slave revolt in Barbados, attributing its cause "to the Registry Bill having raised hopes of immediate Emancipation," which "led to violent attacks on Wilberforce."[145]

The registry effort was intertwined with the international strategy. "The campaign for Registration was . . . complicated by the current negotiations with Portugal and Spain for Abolition of their Slave Trades."[146] The international strategy slowly bore fruit, through several steps over a decade.

The Napoleonic wars riveted British public attention in 1814-1815. In 1814 Wilberforce decided "to concentrate on international abolition and to put aside their agitation to stop up the holes in the British Abolition laws."[147] When

Napoleon abdicated in April 1814, "Wilberforce perceived this as a splendid opportunity to negotiate European abolition by holding captured French colonies as ransom to the agreement being forged at the first Peace of Paris. . . . The British public—stimulated by the discrete but effective agitation of Wilberforce and his associates—was incensed" and opposed the Treaty's weak abolition stance.[148]

Between 1814 and 1815, Wilberforce worked for a requirement in the treaty with France that the trade be abolished. In January 1815, those hopes were temporarily dashed, despite hundreds of petitions and a million signatures. Upon launching his campaign that culminated in Waterloo in 1815, Napoleon issued a decree abolishing the French slave trade. With Napoleon's defeat at Waterloo, in July 1815, "Louis XVIII [was] reinstalled as King of France," and he kept his promise to abolish the Trade."[149] After renegotiating the treaty, Foreign Secretary Castlereagh wrote to Wilberforce on July 31, 1815, "I have the gratification of acquainting you that the long desired object is accomplished . . . the unqualified and total Abolition of the Slave Trade throughout the dominions of France."[150]

Spain fell next. In September 1817, the British foreign secretary, Castlereagh, successfully negotiated a treaty with Spain on the slave trade.

Finally, in 1820, a Uniform Registry Bill was enacted. Sappington referred to it as a "key step, not only in the enforcement of abolition, but in the progress towards emancipation. The resulting data gave abolitionists hard proof of abolition's failure to halt the traffic."[151]

THE CAMPAIGN FOR EMANCIPATION

Although Wilberforce's ultimate goal was emancipation, it was not an immediate practical objective in Parliament until after abolition of the slave trade was secured. By 1818 Wilberforce had concluded that the abolition of the trade had not produced the hoped-for amelioration in the lives of the slaves and turned more resolutely toward a focus on emancipation, but political, social and economic unrest made emancipation politically untenable before 1823. A renewed concerted push for emancipation was instigated in 1823. "Early in 1823 Wilberforce, Stephen, Macaulay, Buxton, Clarkson and others determined to delay no longer."[152] According to Pollock, "Clarkson the skilled and tireless propagandist fanned public opinion until it surged in sympathy towards the slaves. On 31 January a great meeting founded the Antislavery Society with the Duke of Gloucester as the president whose emotional speeches were cheered to the echo."[153]

At sixty-three, Wilberforce passed the mantle of leadership in Parliament to MP Thomas Fowell Buxton to lead the campaign for emancipation. But before doing so Wilberforce added to the push with a new tract, the fifty-six-page "Appeal to the Religion, Justice and Humanity of the Inhabitants of the British Empire in Behalf of the Negro Slaves in the West Indies."

Then a slave uprising in the Caribbean island of Demerara, which resulted in many deaths, put the abolitionists on the defensive. This allegedly occurred due to the government's abrupt order that whips be disused in crown colonies, an order which Wilberforce criticized as insufficiently prepared and explained. The counterattack against Wilberforce and his compatriots after Demerara "forced the abolitionists to conduct a painstaking investigation of the colonial slave system, which eventually resulted in much more widespread knowledge of the abuses connected with slavery."[154]

Foreign Secretary George Canning then undercut them. In October 1823 Canning used the "insurrection of blacks at Demerara" to justify certain "reforms" for the treatment of slaves in the West Indies. Debate ensued over Canning's proposed reforms, which "formed the basis of the Government's policy almost up to the time of the emancipation act in 1833."[155] Wilberforce opposed delegating reforms or measures to alleviate slavery to the colonial assemblies or legislatures, which he consistently distrusted. In June 1824 Wilberforce made his last appeal to the House of Commons. He virtually collapsed in June, and his wife pressed him to "resign his seat before the next Session." After 1825 Wilberforce remained a leader in the movement but withdrew from Parliament.

The new parliamentary leader, Buxton, presented evidence to Parliament of an illicit slave trade between 1823 and 1830. Terrible conditions were brought to Parliament's attention in 1825. The miscarriage of justice and tragic death of Methodist missionary John Smith turned public opinion in 1825. Smith became "the Anti-Slavery martyr."

A major anti-slavery meeting convened in May 1830, chaired by Wilberforce. Younger activists called for immediate emancipation and formed a new "Agency Anti-Slavery Committee."[156] One measure of the movement's political progress was shown in the general election of 1830 when Yorkshire, with four representatives, elected four abolitionists.[157]

Parliament was diverted in 1832 from the slavery issue by the issue of parliamentary reform. In June, 1832 Parliament enacted the Great Reform Bill of 1832, granting the vote to middle-class men. But this aided the push for emancipation.

Buxton moved for immediate emancipation in 1831 and in 1832. He moved in May for a select committee to create a plan for emancipation. Although the motion lost 163 to 90, according to Sappington "this only proved the strength of the abolitionists."[158]

In 1832 the Cabinet began to draft a comprehensive plan for emancipation. The government brought in a plan "whose main elements were: (1) that all slaves be freed, (2) that all freed slaves be apprenticed to their current owners for a time period to be determined by Parliament, (3) that all slave children age six or under be declared free, and (4) that slave owners be loaned LB15 million pounds to ease the transition from a slave economy to the apprenticeship system."[159]

These proposals were "debated extensively in and out of Parliament over the next several months."[160] Victory came on July 26, 1833, when the Parliament bill mandating abolition passed on second reading in the House of Commons. Wilberforce died three days later, July 29, 1833. One year later—July 31, 1834—800,000 slaves were freed.

The Reformation of Manners

An account of Wilberforce's campaign against the slave trade would be incomplete without mentioning the second major life "objective" that he outlined in his diary in October, 1787, "the reformation of manners." Although some of his modern biographers spend little time explaining his strategy, Wilberforce believed that the objectives were intertwined and that virtue among the people, especially the upper classes in eighteenth-century Britain, was necessarily related to the cultural renewal that would end the slave trade. Belmonte presents perhaps the best account of this "second object," which was to "make goodness fashionable among the leadership class."[161]

As early as August 1785, Wilberforce expressed his concern in a letter to his friend, Lord Muncaster:

It is not the confusion of parties, and their quarreling and battling in the House of Commons, which makes me despair of the Republic, . . . but it is the universal corruption and profligacy of the times, which taking its rise among the rich and luxurious has now extended its baneful influence and spread its destructive poison through the whole body of the people.

Wilberforce "began to actively research historical models for moral and cultural renewal" and found that the proclamation issued by William and Mary was more effective than others. In part at Wilberforce's behest, George III reissued a proclamation against vice on June 1, 1787.

Among his network for this object was the bishop of London, Beilby Porteus. Porteus expressed his own prudential reasoning on the object: "The design appeared to me to be in the highest degree laudable, and the object of the greatest importance and necessity; but I foresaw great difficulties in the execution of it unless conducted with great judgment and discretion, especially in the first outset."[162]

As part of this campaign Wilberforce in April 1797 published *A Practical View of the Prevailing Religious System of Professed Christians in the Higher and Middle Classes in the Country Contrasted with Real Christianity*. This book (usually referred to as *A Practical View*) served as an impetus for evangelism for two generations.

At forty-eight years old, during "the five years of the Portland and Perceval ministries, 1807-1812," Wilberforce saw "the peak of his influence on the men who governed Britain as he struggled to raise the standards of public life."[163]

CONCLUSION

After nearly fifty years of struggle, against innumerable setbacks and countless periods of despair and depression, Wilberforce and his allies succeeded in partially preventing a great evil. Effective enforcement efforts actually took another three or four decades. American slavery was not abolished until 1865.

Assessing Wilberforce's prudence over his forty-five-year parliamentary career depends on our understanding of his opportunities, obstacles and actions. Wilberforce understood this and summarized well the challenge of assessing the prudence of historical action:

How can we judge fairly of the characters and merits of men, of the wisdom or
folly of actions, unless we have . . . an accurate knowledge of all particulars, so
that we may live as it were in the times, and among the persons, of whom we
read; see with their eyes, and reason and decide on their premises?[164]

Despite his eventual success, Wilberforce had some personality traits that
may have actually distracted him from engaging his twin objects with more
vigor. First and foremost he had a tendency to be unfocused by lending his efforts to dozens of charities. A partial list of Wilberforce's charities include the
Sierra Leone Company (to establish a colony of freed slaves), the Society for
the Education of Africans, the Society for Bettering the Condition and Increasing the Comforts of the Poor (the Bettering Society), the Society for the
Relief of Debtors, the Relief fund for starving north Germans, Rumford Eating
Houses, the Friends of Foreigners in Distress, the British and Foreign Bible
Society, the French Bible Society, the Society for the Relief of the Manufactur-
ing Poor, the Society for destitute Lascar seaman, the Kensington, Chelsea and
Fulham Bible Society, the African Institution, and the Royal Society for the
prevention of cruelty to animals.[165]

As Pollock summarizes it, "his own charities were legion and it has been
reckoned that he was president, vice-president, or committee man of no less
than sixty-nine societies."[166] Was Wilberforce's involvement in so many truly
essential to their success or the development of British humanitarianism during the half century after his death, or could he have made more progress toward the twin "objects" if he had been more focused?

Part of the problem was his nature. Furneaux states frankly that Wilberforce was "never quite successful in disciplining his butterfly mind."[167] But
Wilberforce did possess the self-awareness to recognize this as a weakness
and sought to be more disciplined and focused. Whether or not Wilberforce
consistently and successfully resisted these tendencies, he possessed the self-
awareness to address them from time to time, and his self-awareness was essential to his prudence.

In addition—and perhaps related to the first—Wilberforce had a tendency
to speak to both sides of any question and to reflect "indecisiveness."[168] Some
said he was "without any fixed opinions, except on the Slave Trade and the
essential doctrines of Christianity."[169] Others countered that "men might
doubt about his vote on minor matters, but where the interests of morality,

or humanity, or religion were involved, there Wilberforce's perception of what was right appeared intuitive, and his vote was certain."[170] But this contrast raises a question, Was there a reasoned priority to his thinking? On the most important moral questions of his time, prudence led him to be steadfast, whereas he exhibited more flexibility on more pragmatic questions of lesser importance.

One chronicler, Douglas Holladay, has aptly summarized several principles that defined Wilberforce's character and strategy: First, "Wilberforce was committed to the strategic importance of a band of like-minded friends devoted to working together in chosen ventures." Second, "Wilberforce believed deeply in the power of ideas and moral beliefs to change culture through a campaign of sustained public persuasion." Third, "Wilberforce was willing to pay a steep cost for his courageous public stands and was remarkably persistent in pursuing his life task." Fourth, "Wilberforce's labors and faith were grounded in a genuine humanity rather than a blind fanaticism." Finally, "Wilberforce forged strategic partnerships for the common good irrespective of differences over methods, ideology, or religious beliefs."

Throughout, as Holladay puts it, "compromise on principle was unthinkable, but compromise on tactics was never a problem."[171] One weakness of movement activists is a tendency to confuse every compromise of tactics with a compromise of principle. By equating a compromise of tactics (tactical flexibility) as a compromise of principle, activists can undermine their own strategy and strip themselves of energy. This requires a clear understanding of the reality of the problem and a clear perception of the greatest good possible and the right goals that will achieve that.

Sappington summarizes Wilberforce's legislative strategy:

> His ultimate goal was the non-legislated end of slavery. To help bring that about, he sought the end of the slave Trade. Until that could be accomplished, he pursued incremental legislation and partial abolition, he sought to mitigate its evils by incrementalist measures, taking as much ground as he deemed politically possible at each stage of the fight. . . .
>
> For Wilberforce, then, gradualism was a way to coax some gains from a situation where political reality (e.g., lack of votes, in the case of abolition; potential anarchy, in the case of immediate emancipation) made total gains impossible or inadvisable.[172]

Assessment of Wilberforce's prudential judgment must go back to the twin "objects" he set for himself in October 1787. In concert with various networks, he substantially achieved those goals and laid a foundation for social progress through public policy and numerous charitable institutions, which continued for decades after his death.

LINCOLN'S JUDGMENT

"They [the authors of the Declaration of Independence] meant to set up a standard maxim for free society, which should be familiar to all, and revered by all; constantly looked to, constantly labored for, and even though never perfectly attained, constantly approximated, and thereby constantly spreading and deepening its influence, and augmenting the happiness and value of life to all people of all colors everywhere."

Abraham Lincoln

Abraham Lincoln and William Wilberforce are an instructive contrast in examining political prudence because they dealt effectively with different political realities in different countries in different eras. Decisions of political prudence are situated within the context of concrete circumstances, with opposing political and cultural forces and constraints on resources and decision making. Those realities must be understood within their unique context. Many of these factors and forces are beyond a leader's complete control but can be shaped by prudent decisions and implementation.[1]

Wilberforce was a British legislator, not a chief executive, and although he was involved with hundreds of issues as a legislator, he persevered for forty-five years on two related issues: abolishing the slave trade and emancipating the slaves.

Lincoln was conscious of Wilberforce's example and perseverance.[2] Lincoln served in the Illinois state legislature and for one term in the U.S. House of Representatives in the 1830s and 1840s. Between 1850 and 1860, he was a prominent lawyer and rising leader in Illinois and in Republican politics, who twice ran unsuccessfully for the U.S. Senate. He became a national political leader only after his debates with Senator Stephen Douglas during the course of the Illinois Senate campaign of 1858. He became the Republican nominee for president in 1860 by successfully making himself the acceptable second choice of the Republican convention delegates. As president, Lincoln made hundreds of decisions as an executive, though two issues, the war and slavery, dominated his presidency across five Aprils. The purpose of this chapter is to focus on nine of Lincoln's presidential decisions. While they do not all deal with slavery, each is examined through the lens of prudence.

If Wilberforce's defining characteristic was perseverance, Lincoln's was his judgment—about the greatest good possible in the particular circumstances, about political actions, about leadership and public opinion, about human relationships, about the Constitution, about effectively suppressing the rebellion (as Lincoln characterized the war).

As Harry Jaffa summarized Lincoln's prudential judgment: Lincoln "understood the task of leadership . . . to know what is good or right, to know how much of that good is attainable, and to act to secure that much good but not to abandon the attainable good by grasping for more."[3] Understanding Lincoln's prudence requires a balanced inquiry into his judgment of proper ends and appropriate means in the context of the particular opportunities and obstacles he faced.

LINCOLN'S CHARACTER AND PHILOSOPHY

Assessing Lincoln's prudence starts with evaluating his political principles. These were fundamentally shaped by his view of the natural rights doctrine of the Declaration of Independence and the U.S. Constitution, which established the political structure within which Lincoln acted. The Declaration and the Constitution directly shaped Lincoln's political philosophy and his sense of his duty as president.[4] Joseph Fornieri explains,

> The Declaration proclaimed the moral end to which the Union was dedicated. Lincoln read the Constitution in view of the Declaration. . . . Lincoln consistently emphasized the continuity between the Declaration and the Constitution

as two complementary and founding documents of American republicanism. The Constitution provided the specific institutions and framework whereby the aims of the Declaration could be realized prudently.[5]

Lincoln biographer Richard Carwardine and many others have noted Lincoln's personal gifts: "his mental toughness, including tenacity in thought and a firm resolve once his purpose was fixed."[6] He

was blessed with an unusual confidence in his own judgment. . . . But this conviction of his own worth—which made him unusually resistant to feelings of political jealousy and toughened him against the chronic abrasion of wartime criticism—stopped short of becoming an overdeveloped self-regard.[7]

He also had a "conscious striving for self-restraint, . . . anger and personal hostility should not be allowed to compromise political and military objectives."[8] Lincoln possessed "an unsurpassed understanding of human nature" and a "formidable memory."[9] Lincoln's secretary of the Navy, Gideon Welles, commented on his "wonderful self-reliance." After a critical review of Lincoln's administration, Daniel Farber concluded that "Lincoln had an ability to work his way unflinchingly to the heart of an issue and act accordingly, without self-righteousness or arrogance."[10]

Lincoln was known for his shrewd assessment of human nature generally and of the personalities of individuals in particular. In his book *We Are Lincoln Men*, Lincoln biographer David Donald recounts how Lincoln developed an effective relationship with William H. Seward. Seward had been governor of New York and was Lincoln's key rival for the Republican presidential nomination of 1860. When Lincoln was elected, he asked Seward to be secretary of state. Professor Donald writes, "During his first few days in Washington, Lincoln had arrived at a shrewd understanding of the personality of his secretary of state. The President was neither a psychoanalyst nor a biographer, but he recognized intuitively that Seward would defer to an authority figure."[11]

While many have noted Lincoln's "powerful ambition,"[12] the key question is *whether it was truly tied to worthy goals.*[13] Lincoln methodically climbed the right steps to the Republican presidential nomination of 1860. He nearly tied Douglas in the 1858 Illinois Senate race, made famous by the Lincoln-Douglas debates, and established himself as a national political leader without holding political office after 1850. His Cooper Union address of February 27, 1860, in New York City made a significant impact in building his reputation as a national Republican leader. He effectively used his network of Illinois political operatives to capture the 1860 Republican presidential nomination.

Lincoln developed a morality in politics that emphasized incremental gains. In a speech on internal improvements during his single term in Congress in 1848, Lincoln stated:

> The true rule, in determining to embrace, or reject any thing, is not whether it have *any* evil in it; but whether it have more of evil, than of good. There are few things *wholly* evil, or *wholly* good. Almost every thing, especially of governmental policy, is an inseparable compound of the two; so that our best judgment of the preponderance between them is continually demanded.[14]

Lincoln was not here talking about the morality of individual actions but of the complex impact of public policies.

Lincoln's prudence looked to the practical impact of public policies rather than to the personal vices of candidates. The moral position of "doing one's duty and leaving the consequences to God" in elections has a long history in American politics. Lincoln biographer William Lee Miller refers to this as "individualistic perfectionism."

Lincoln evaluated this notion of political morality in an October 1845 response he wrote to Williamson Durley in the aftermath of the 1844 presidential election.[15] One of the most important issues in the 1844 election was the annexation of Texas, which abolitionists opposed, believing it would result in at least one or more new slave states. Polk (who supported annexation) beat Clay (who opposed annexation) by just 38,792 votes, while the Liberty Party candidate James Birney (who opposed slavery) garnered 62,263 votes. Lincoln supported and campaigned for Clay.

In his letter to Durley, Lincoln rebutted the reasoning of one Liberty man who had rejected voting for Clay on the basis that "we are not to do evil that good may come." The "evil" was allegedly voting for Clay, because Clay was a slaveholder, despite the fact that Clay opposed annexation and Polk supported it. Thus, the position of the Liberty man was that voting for Clay was an evil (because he was a slaveholder) that couldn't be justified by the good (the nonannexation of Texas) that might follow.

Lincoln accepted the moral proposition but denied that it applied to the selection of Clay. In his response to Durley, Lincoln alluded to Christ's Sermon on the Mount where Christ urges his followers to be wary of false prophets, testing their claims by their "fruit."

> This general, proposition is doubtless correct; but did it apply? If by your votes you could have prevented the *extention* [*sic*] . . . of slavery, would it not have been *good* and not *evil* so to have used your votes, even though it involved casting of them for a slaveholder? By the *fruit* the tree is to be known. An *evil* tree can not bring forth *good* fruit. If the fruit of electing Mr. Clay would have been to prevent the extension of slavery, could the act of electing him have been *evil?*[16]

What Clay would do, as an elected official supporting a policy, was more important than the personal characteristic that he was a slaveholder.

Another significant example of Lincoln's political morality is the contrast between Charles Sumner's speech at the June 1848 convention of the "Conscience Whigs" in Worcester, Massachusetts, and Lincoln's speech months later in that same town during the 1848 presidential campaign. Sumner was a "Conscience Whig" who opposed slavery. He opposed both the Whig candidate Taylor and the Democratic candidate Cass, and supported the Free Soil candidate Martin Van Buren. After the convention Lincoln traveled to Worcester to support Taylor and argue against desertion to Van Buren. Lincoln asserted:

> In declaring that they [the Free Soilers] would "do their duty and leave the consequences to God" [they] merely gave an excuse for taking a course that they were not able to maintain by a full and fair argument.
>
> To make this declaration did not show what their duty was. If it did we should have no use for judgment; we might as well be made without intelligence, and when divine or human law does not clearly point out what is our duty, we have no means of finding out what it is [except] by using our most intelligent judgment of the consequences. . . .
>
> If there were a divine law, or human law, for voting for Martin Van Buren, or if a fair examination of the consequences and first reasoning would show that voting for him would bring about the ends they pretended to wish he [Lincoln] would give up the argument. . . .
>
> But since there is no fixed [moral] law on the subject, and since the whole probable result of their action would be an assistance in electing General Cass, he must say they were behind the Whigs in the advocacy of the freedom of the soil.[17]

Prudence was part of Lincoln's public vocabulary, and he was familiar with the principle of moral complicity in evil. For example, by the spring of 1864 he came to believe that "God now wills the removal of a great wrong, and wills also that . . . the North as well as . . . the South, shall pay fairly for our complicity in that wrong."[18] This theme was repeated in his second inaugural address.

Lincoln historian Richard Current captured Lincoln's prudential sense of the relationship between means and ends:

> He has been characterized as a flexible man rather than one of fixed determina-
> tion. In fact, however, he was flexible and pragmatic only in his choice of means
> and in his sense of timing. Though no doctrinaire, Lincoln was a man of deep
> conviction and settled purpose. Only by compromising with the necessities of
> the time could he hope to gain and hold political power. And only by holding
> political power could he hope to give reality, even in part, to his concept of the
> Union and its potentialities.[19]

ESTABLISHING FENCES AROUND SLAVERY

Lincoln's public opposition to slavery extended as far back as 1837, when as an Illinois state representative he presented to the Illinois House of Representatives a public "protest" with Dan Stone, his fellow representative from Sangamon County. Their nuanced position stated that they "believe[d] that the institution of slavery [was] founded on both injustice and bad policy," that Congress had no constitutional authority to interfere with slavery in the existing slave states but could abolish slavery in the District of Columbia, and that "the promulgation of abolitionist doctrines tends rather to increase than to abate its evils."[20]

During the 1850s Lincoln articulated a position against slavery that was "moderate" in the context of the times—opposing slavery but not supporting immediate abolition (which was not possible in the Southern states, in any case, for political and constitutional reasons). He opposed the extension of slavery and articulated a widespread hope (and belief) that if slavery was confined to the Southern states it would be left on the road to extinction. In Lincoln's view this was the expectation of the framers of the Constitution.

Lincoln worked within the limits of majoritarian politics to build the Republican Party, which he saw as an essential bulwark against the extension of slavery. The most effective way of doing that, while the Whig Party was disintegrating in the early 1850s, was to articulate the broadest policy against the extension of slavery around which disparate ethnic and political groups (whatever their motives) could unite.

During the 1850s Lincoln became a rising leader against the extension of slavery into the territories. In 1854 the Kansas-Nebraska Act—which repealed the Missouri Compromise and opened the Kansas-Nebraska territory to slavery—dramatically changed sectional politics and brought Lincoln—who had been working as a private lawyer in Springfield since 1850—back into active political life. He strongly opposed that Act, which ignited a firestorm in the North, significantly weakened the Democratic Party in the North and fostered the rise of the Republican Party.

Lincoln biographer Richard Carwardine has summarized the complexity of Lincoln's "principled but prudent set of views"[21] of slavery, which combined "moral repugnance at the institution, sympathy for the slave, respect for the protection the federal Constitution afforded slavery, commitment to preserving social order, belief in the essential goodwill of the Southern slaveholder, and the need for common, gradual action by North and South on a problem for which they shared responsibility."[22]

The development of slavery politics included the development of the anti-slavery movement. "Toward the end of the [1830s], the movement split, with one part getting involved in politics and the other maintaining 'purity.'"[23] Lincoln developed a politics within that context that was clear-eyed and realistic about obstacles and limitations, and attempted to achieve the greatest good possible.

Like the slave trade in England in the 1780s, slavery in the United States was regarded by many as a necessary evil. As historian Henry Mayer described the contemporary scene, by the 1820s "for most Americans . . . a fatalism had set in that regarded slavery as an immutable feature of the landscape, an unlooked-for evil that had been fastened upon them by generations long past and whose resolution had to be left to enlightened generations not yet born."[24]

Until the 1840s, anti-slavery strength in Congress was too weak to establish any legal fences around slavery.[25] During his single term in Congress (1847-1849), Lincoln supported the Wilmot Proviso, which would have prohibited slavery in any territory acquired during the war with Mexico, though the Proviso never became law.[26] In January 1849, during his last few months in Congress, Lincoln drafted a bill to abolish slavery in the District of Columbia (subject to congressional control) and provide compensated emancipation, but it was apparently never introduced.[27] (Lincoln signed such a bill as president in April 1862.)

Lincoln was not an anti-slavery leader, however, until 1854. Leaving Congress after one two-year term in 1849, Lincoln concentrated on his legal practice for five years until Senator Stephen Douglas championed the Kansas-Nebraska Act in 1854. The Act served as "a wake-up call" to Lincoln.[28] The Act "would pull his antislavery convictions to the center of his politics, and 'arouse' the universalism and egalitarianism, and the moral concept of the nation, that they rested upon."[29]

Lincoln's philosophy was well defined after 1854, through two campaigns for the Senate and numerous public speeches. Lincoln's Peoria, Illinois, speech in October 1854 marked his renewed entry into politics. He denounced the Kansas-Nebraska Act as "removing the restrictive fence,"[30] and made a strong argument against the repeal of the Missouri Compromise and for keeping slavery out of the western territories. He compared the prohibition on the slave trade to a prohibition on extending slavery into the territories.[31] He admitted that while he had no solution to slavery in the Southern states, he strongly opposed its extension.

The momentum in the 1850s, especially after the Supreme Court's March 1857 *Dred Scott* decision struck down congressional limits on slavery in the western territories, was moving in favor of the extension of slavery, the "nationalization of slavery," and threatened the Republican belief that slavery was confined to the Southern states and on "the road to extinction." Lincoln's speeches increasingly addressed the importance of limiting slavery, opposing its spread and nationalization.

After the Supreme Court's *Dred Scott* decision, Lincoln denounced the decision in a speech at Springfield on June 26, 1857. Lincoln became the Illinois Republican nominee for the U.S. Senate in 1858. And in his debates with Senator Stephen Douglas, Lincoln espoused the wrong of slavery and the importance of limiting it when it was impossible to prohibit it. As Lincoln stated the policy and the rationale for legislative limits:

The Republican Party . . . look[s] upon [slavery] as being a moral, social and political wrong; and while they contemplate it as such, they nevertheless have due regard for its actual existence among us, and the difficulties of getting rid of it in any satisfactory way. . . . Yet having a due regard for these, they desire a policy in regard to it that looks to its not creating any more danger. They insist that it should as far as may be, *be treated* as a wrong, and one of the methods of treating it as a wrong is to *make provision that it shall grow no larger.*[32]

During the Lincoln-Douglas Senate debates of 1858, Lincoln struck what he thought was a prudent balance, given public opinion and contemporary racial prejudices. He denied that he supported "political and social equality" for slaves while arguing that "there is no reason in the world why the negro is not entitled to all the natural rights enumerated in the Declaration of Independence, the right to life, liberty, and the pursuit of happiness. I hold that he is as much entitled to these as the white man."[33] He opposed Senator Stephen Douglas's "popular sovereignty," which (in Lincoln's view) would have allowed slavery to be introduced into the western territories and would lead to the nationalization of slavery. In taking this position Lincoln implicitly acknowledged a natural law limitation to majority rule.

And the following year in Ohio, he repeated the position he had articulated in the 1858 Senate race against Douglas, referring to

the Republican principle, the profound central truth that slavery is wrong, and ought to be dealt with as a wrong, though we are always to remember the fact of its actual existence amongst us and faithfully observe all the constitutional guarantees—the unalterable principle never for a moment to be lost sight of that it is a wrong and ought to be dealt with as such.[34]

Republicans believe that slavery is wrong, and they insist, and will continue to insist upon a national policy which recognizes it, and deals with it, as a wrong. There can be no letting down about this.[35]

Finally, in his Cooper Union address (New York) of February 1860, Lincoln argued for the constitutional authority of Congress to control slavery in the territories. There he stated that the Republican policy was to consider slavery "as an evil not to be extended, but to be tolerated and protected only because of and so far as its actual presence among us make that toleration and protection a necessity. Let all the guaranties those fathers [the Constitution's framers] gave it, be, not grudgingly, but fully and fairly maintained."[36]

But Lincoln's positions were nuanced and not without moral concern. Indeed, his biggest "compromise" with slavery might appear to be his reluctant support for the Fugitive Slave Law during the 1850s.[37] But Lincoln likely saw it as an unavoidable rhetorical concession—he never actually voted for the federal Fugitive Slave Law—given the fugitive slave clause in the text of the Constitution.

Lincoln frankly admitted the difficulty of identifying any successful solution to slavery in the original slave states, given its pervasive reality and (what he believed to be) the protection the Constitution's text afforded slavery in those states. By 1860 he had articulated a three-part program against slavery, believing that Congress had no constitutional authority to end slavery in the slave states. This involved gradual emancipation, compensated emancipation and approval by the majority of the voters of a state. He had expressed this three-part plan at least as early as his 1858 debate with Senator Stephen Douglas in Freeport, Illinois. He also consistently supported colonization until late in his presidency. Though Lincoln tried to obtain border-state support for such a policy in the early years of the war, it was seriously hampered by border-state opposition and by the slow progress of the war. This policy was eventually superseded by the Emancipation Proclamation.

Lincoln and Garrison. Lincoln's views on slavery and its resolution are usefully contrasted with the views of Boston abolitionist leader William Lloyd Garrison. Historians often mark the beginning of the nineteenth-century anti-slavery movement with the publication of Garrison's newspaper, *The Liberator*, in Boston on January 1, 1831.

Though Garrison "regularly derided the Republicans for diluting their platform in the quest for fusion,"[38] Garrison knew little about Lincoln before the Lincoln-Douglas debates of 1858. In March 1858 Lincoln's law partner, William Herndon, visited Garrison in Boston. According to Garrison biographer Henry Mayer, Herndon sought a meeting with Garrison under the auspices of the Illinois Republicans. This was before the Illinois Senate campaign that sparked the Lincoln-Douglas debates—so Lincoln was not a national figure in the Republican Party—and it was twenty-three months before Lincoln's Cooper Union address in New York that was the centerpiece of Lincoln's "eastern campaign" for the Republican nomination.

Mayer's analysis is that the slavery issue in American politics had entered a new stage by 1858, which caused Garrison to consider politics in a new light. "For Garrison, however, there was no question that abolitionism had arrived at the threshold of a fresh relationship to politics. . . . One by one the institutions that had collaborated to keep slavery out of politics had collapsed."[39] "Garrison preferred to continue his high-minded appeal for a moral reformation that might yet break the impasse, and to accomplish this he had to engage in some kind of productive tension between Republican politicians and the abolitionist conscience."[40]

The Civil War and its impact on slavery eventually brought Lincoln and Garrison together. Though Garrisonian activism may have conflicted with Lincoln's incremental approach within the Republican Party in the 1850s, by the time of Lincoln's 1864 reelection campaign, in Carwardine's words, "Garrison's wing of abolitionism and its newspaper presses" supported "the National Union coalition. They joined mainstream evangelicals to form a broad front of political activists."[41]

THE CONTEXT AND CONSTRAINTS OF LINCOLN'S ELECTION

Lincoln was elected after forty years of anti-slavery agitation (starting from the Missouri Compromise of 1820) that shaped law, public opinion and politics in ways that established hard and substantial limits on what Lincoln could achieve as president in the limited time of four or eight years. These included the annexation of Texas and the Wilmot Proviso, the hardening of opinion in both the North and South by 1850, the Compromise of 1850 and the Fugitive Slave Law, the Kansas-Nebraska Act of 1854 which overturned the Missouri Compromise, the Supreme Court's *Dred Scott* decision in 1857, the Lecompton controversy in Kansas, John Brown's attack at Harpers Ferry in October of 1859, and the sectional divide that resulted in the political divide between the Democratic and Republican parties.[42] Lincoln was an acute observer and realist about these constraints and discussed them repeatedly in his public addresses.

Lincoln's essential plan for his presidency was rooted in basic Republican Party principles and the Republican platform of 1860. But secession and the war raised new and unprecedented challenges; it was the gravest crisis the country had seen in its eighty-year existence.

Lincoln's decisions as president must be understood against the backdrop of slavery politics in the 1850s, the development of his own views as a political leader expressed in dozens of political speeches, and the Republican Party's principles and platform of 1860.

Essential to an understanding of Lincoln's decisions as president is a close reading of his own statements, especially his first inaugural address and his numerous presidential documents. Many of these were widely published and substantially affected public opinion and the public's view of Lincoln, and they defined his leadership.

LINCOLN'S PRESIDENTIAL DECISIONS

Lincoln faced the greatest crisis any U.S. president had faced at his inauguration. Seven Southern states had seceded; at least four—Georgia, Mississippi, South Carolina and Texas—published declarations of secession that described slavery as the essential, if not sole, reason for their secession.[43] He was surrounded by disloyal personnel in every department. Lincoln had to give immediate attention to staffing a new administration, which would effectively carry out the policies of the first Republican president, before he and his tiny staff were quickly consumed by other pressing emergencies. President Buchanan left him a federal government that was deeply in debt, and Lincoln was pressed to finance the forces to "enforce the law" and suppress the rebellion.[44] The War Department consisted of fewer than two hundred staff. There was a minimal army that lacked basic and sufficient supplies.

One of his first and most important decisions was the selection of his cabinet of ten, a series of shrewd decisions most thoroughly explored by Doris Kearns Goodwin in her book *Team of Rivals*. Lincoln included in his cabinet the three men who had been his main adversaries for the Republican nomination, Seward, Chase and Bates. As the first Republican president, Lincoln sought strong men who represented the different constituencies of the Republican Party. These also provided the essential counselors that Lincoln relied on for the next four years.

The essence of prudence is making good decisions and implementing them well. As an executive Lincoln made dozens of decisions daily. The ones highlighted here are considered among the most serious and controversial, and my focus is on the reasons for those decisions based on available historical data and Lincoln's own explanations in his public documents and speeches. The sustained and reflective study of political decision making provides important lessons for prudential reasoning.

1. Using force to restore the Union (December 1860 to July 1861). Although the first significant clash of Union and Southern forces did not occur until July 1861, the decision to use force (if necessary to restore the Union) was virtually made by the time of Lincoln's first inaugural address, the statement of his administration's policy.[45]

What good, what moral purpose, might justify using force to fight the secessionists or put down "the rebellion," as Lincoln referred to it? (Lincoln intentionally referred to it as the "rebellion" to emphasize his view of its illegal character under the Constitution.)

Two purposes are often cited: restoring the Union and ending slavery. But there are at least two additional reasons: enforcing the laws and the Constitution, which flowed from the presidential oath, and preserving self-government. The most familiar expression of the latter is in Lincoln's Gettysburg Address of November 1863, but Lincoln cited it as early as May 1861 in a statement to his secretary John Hay:

> I consider the central idea pervading this struggle is the necessity that is upon us, of proving that popular government is not an absurdity. We must settle this question now, whether in a free government the minority have the right to break up the government whenever they choose. If we fail it will go far to prove the incapability of the people to govern themselves.[46]

Lincoln elaborated on this theme in his first message to Congress on July 4, 1861: "This issue embraces more than the fate of these United States. It presents to the whole family of man, the question, whether a constitutional republic, or a democracy—a government of the people, by the same people—can, or cannot, maintain its territorial integrity, against its own domestic foe."[47]

Critics of Lincoln often overlook the power of the Union in American politics and in the rise of the Republican Party in the 1850s. While Lincoln consistently supported the Union in the 1840s and 1850s,[48] critics overemphasize Lincoln's personal opposition to secession, without considering the broad political support for the Union which Lincoln gave voice to.

The preamble to the Articles of Confederation of 1778 twice referred to the Articles as "articles of Confederation and perpetual Union."[49] And the preamble to the U.S. Constitution of 1789 declares, as the first purpose, that the Constitution is "ordained" "in Order to form a more perfect Union."[50]

Lincoln biographer Richard Carwardine summarizes the powerful icon of the Union in public opinion by 1860:

> The Union was not just politically significant; it had meaning for the romantic and spiritual sensibilities of Americans. Protestants prized it as the vehicle for God's unique role for America within human history. The "acute millennial consciousness" of North American Protestants, carried to the New World by the original Puritan settlers and successively passed down to each new generation, gave the new nation a powerful sense of being God's instrument in the coming of his Kingdom. . . . And whereas in the antebellum generation the call to defend the Union had been the cry of Northern conservatives eager to find common ground with Southern churches, it now became, in the historian James Moorhead's words, a cry "infused with a new moral significance. . . . The holy Union that Northerners defended was no longer the compromise-tainted object of earlier years; it was democratic civilization in collision with an alien way of life."[51]

Just weeks before Lincoln's inauguration, Senator Seward gave a speech in the Senate on January 12 with the central theme of preserving the Union ("to set forth the advantages, the necessities of the Union to the people . . . and the vast calamities to them and to the world which its destruction would involve"), which reportedly reduced Senator Crittenden (D-Ky.) to tears.[52]

The Union was not just a Republican idea. After Lincoln's call for the militia on April 15, Democratic senator Stephen Douglas rallied to his support and called for Northern Democrats "to sustain the President in the exercise of his constitutional functions to preserve the Union."[53] Douglas's public support was effective in "mobilizing Democratic support."[54]

Lincoln's position was that he was enforcing the laws against unlawful secessionists as required by the presidential oath of office set forth in the text of the Constitution. In addition, he believed that his constitutional role as commander in chief compelled him to act.

Though abolitionists were upset with Lincoln's refusal in 1861 to publicly express slavery as one purpose of the war, Lincoln felt constrained for at least three reasons. The same Constitution, which he believed the rebellion (secession) violated, also protected slavery; an all-out war against slavery would contradict his belief that the Constitution protected slavery in the slave states and the position he had taken in his inaugural address. Second, he could not act aggressively against slavery without losing the border states, like Kentucky, which were essential to Union victory. And if the Union lost, slavery would be secure in the slave states. Finally, neither his cabinet nor Northern public opinion (the cabinet reflecting Northern opinion) supported slavery as the main purpose—or perhaps a purpose at all in 1861— and Lincoln needed a united cabinet and North to put down the rebellion. Critics of Lincoln ignore the fact that the debate over slavery as a purpose of the war was raging in Congress and in public opinion throughout 1861. For example, on July 22, the day before the Union defeat at Bull Run, Congress passed a resolution by Senator Crittenden 117 to 2, which stated that "this war is not waged upon our part in any spirit of oppression, nor for any . . . purpose of overthrowing or interfering with the rights or established institutions of those States."[55]

Generally, Lincoln considered the slavery issue so sensitive that he reserved to himself the policy decisions about slavery during his administration.[56] And his policy on slavery evolved slowly, affected by the border states, Northern public opinion, the realities of growing numbers of slaves coming into Union control and progress in the war.

Lincoln's letter to Horace Greeley of August 22, 1862, is often quoted, but usually quoted incompletely. The passage concerning Lincoln's desire to restore the Union with or without slavery is usually quoted, but his distinction in the last sentence between "official duty" and "personal wish" is often ignored.[57] That distinction is critical to the entire letter and reflects Lincoln's position on slavery throughout his candidacy for president and his presidency. What he could and would do as president was limited by his understanding of the Constitution.

2. Resupplying Fort Sumter (April 1861). However silent and ineffective Lincoln appeared during the secession crisis (when he had no constitutional authority), he made a number of bold decisions in the eight weeks after his inauguration. (In 1861, Inauguration Day was March 4, an unfortunate delay, and only moved up to January 20 at the time of Franklin Roosevelt.) His executive actions were set against a history of weak predecessors as president, conflicting legal opinions about the extent of executive authority, and new constitutional and political challenges that had no precedent.[58]

By the time of Lincoln's inauguration and address of March 4, 1861, seven states had seceded from the Union—South Carolina, Mississippi, Louisiana, Florida, Alabama, Georgia, Texas. South Carolina had occupied Fort Moultrie on December 27, 1860, after Major Robert Anderson had abandoned it. And Congress adjourned in the midst of the crisis, according to the calendar of the day.

Lincoln's "First Inaugural Address" was truly the first public declaration of his proposed policy for his administration, and the first one to hold any weight due to his new constitutional authority.[59] (In his second inaugural address, Lincoln stated that his first inaugural address, which he considered his most important public statement of the proposed aims of his administration, was "devoted altogether to saving the Union without war.")

Lincoln sought to balance conciliation with a clear statement of his constitutional duty. He tried to be conciliatory in his address—some Republicans thought too conciliatory—and, in consultation with William Seward and others, changed earlier drafts to delete words and phrases that might be considered provocative by the South.[60]

Lincoln repeatedly emphasized the presidential oath. The fact that the presidential oath is part of the text of the Constitution, and the importance that Lincoln placed on the presidential oath, is often overlooked. The presidential oath in article two of the Constitution states: "I do solemnly swear that I will faithfully execute the office of President of the United States, and will, to the best of my ability, preserve, protect, and defend the Constitution of the United States."

Lincoln declared to the South: "You have no oath registered in Heaven to destroy the government, while I shall have the most solemn one to 'preserve, protect, and defend it.' " As Professor Michael Paulsen emphasizes, "Lincoln fought the Civil War out of a sense of constitutional duty, flowing from his oath of office to 'preserve, protect, and defend' the constitution and his sworn duty to take care that the laws be faithfully executed."[61]

Preparing to "faithfully execute" the laws required preparations to protect Fort Sumter. There was "no symbol of Federal authority . . . more important than Fort Sumter."[62] Fort Sumter was one of the earliest and most important applications of Lincoln's oath to "faithfully execute" the laws.

In the following months Lincoln cited and relied on his oath in explaining his decisions. He referred to his oath in a meeting with a Baltimore committee in April 1861 when he attempted to quell rioting in Baltimore and bring Union troops into Washington to guard the capital.[63]

In his first inaugural address, Lincoln argued for the "perpetual" union of the states based on "universal law," contract law, the history of the nation and the Constitution, and he referred to secession as anarchy:

> No State, upon its own mere motion, can lawfully get out of the Union,—that *resolves* and *ordinances* to that effect are legally void; and that acts of violence, within any State or States, against the authority of the United States, are insurrectionary or revolutionary, according to circumstances.
>
> I therefore consider that, in view of the Constitution and the laws, the Union is unbroken; and, to the extent of my ability, I shall take care, as the Constitution itself expressly enjoins upon me, that the laws of the Union be faithfully executed in all the States. Doing this I deem to be only a simple duty on my part; and I shall perform it, so far as practicable, unless my rightful masters, the American people, shall withhold the requisite means, or, in some authoritative manner, direct the contrary.[64]

Lincoln's view that no state had a unilateral constitutional right to secede was supported by the Articles of Confederation, which referred at least six times to a "perpetual Union" and which suggested in Article 13 that no state could secede without the unanimous consent of the other states. Lincoln's rejection of secession was also supported by James Madison's view during the 1830 South Carolina nullification crisis.[65] And Lincoln relied on President Jackson's exercise of presidential authority.[66]

Lincoln's position was directly contrary to the position of outgoing President James Buchanan that, even if secession was unconstitutional, the federal government could not "make war" against a state and thus was powerless to prevent secession.[67] Lincoln's response was that "this was not 'making war against another sovereign, for secession was not legally possible and the Confederacy did not exist as a legal entity. Rather, this was suppressing an unlawful rebellion and executing the laws of the United States in all of the states to the full extent possible."[68]

Because of the presidential oath, Lincoln declared at the outset of his inaugural address that he would enforce all the provisions of the Constitution. He would not interfere with slavery in any state. Believing he had no other choice under the Constitution, he promised to enforce the controversial federal Fugitive Slave Law of 1850 and the fugitive slave provision in the Constitution.

He also referred to the policies expressed in his own previous speeches, and in the Republican platform of 1860, for evidence that his administration would not threaten slavery in the Southern states. ("I have no purpose, directly or indirectly, to interfere with the institution of slavery in the States where it exists. I believe I have no lawful right to do so, and I have no inclination to do so.")

The inaugural address established his administration's policy, and when Seward challenged him in subsequent weeks that the administration "had no policy," Lincoln pointed back to his address.

Lincoln continued the argument from his first inaugural address, in his July 4, 1861, special message to Congress, where he gave an extended explanation of the factors that he evaluated in making the decision to resupply Fort Sumter.

The collision at Fort Sumter was shaped by secessionist moves before Lincoln's inauguration. Southern demands for a federal slave code preceded Lincoln's election; such demands split the Democratic Party in mid-1860, which led to the Republican victory in November. Secessionists were opposed to the election of any Republican, secessionist talk preceded the election, and some states might have seceded if *any Republican* had been elected.

The collision at Fort Sumter was also shaped by Lincoln's (and his cabinet's) understanding of reality.[69] The day after his inauguration, Lincoln received a "bleak report" from Major Anderson, with the recommendation of General Scott that Sumter should be surrendered.[70] He felt bound by his inaugural address to balance conciliation with securing federal properties. As part of his deliberations Lincoln posed additional questions to General Scott to assess the situation more precisely and carefully.

Lincoln's deliberation extended over three weeks. He attempted to balance a blizzard of pressing decisions. His cabinet was divided about Sumter until deliberation and accumulating information formed a consensus. He consulted with his cabinet over a period of eleven days and then posed the following question to them, asking for a written response: "Assuming it is possible to now provision Fort-Sumpter [sic], under all the circumstances, is it wise to attempt it?" The majority of the cabinet was initially against resupplying Sumter but changed by March 27 as new information was gathered.

As David Donald and others have pointed out, Lincoln had several options: he could resupply (with provisions), reinforce (with arms) or vacate. After several discussions with his cabinet Lincoln, on April 4, approved the expedition to resupply Fort Sumter with provisions. On April 6 Lincoln sent a message (intended to be made public) to Governor Pickens of South Carolina as a statement of Lincoln's nonconfrontational intent. Fort Sumter was attacked on April 12 and Major Anderson surrendered the fort on April 14. Whether or not Lincoln tried to "maneuver" the South into the first aggression, the attack on Fort Sumter clearly and dramatically galvanized public opinion in the North, which propelled Lincoln and his administration forward.

3. Lincoln's call for militia and convening Congress (April 15, 1861). While Lincoln was deciding whether to resupply Fort Sumter, he was also evaluating other actions to suppress the rebellion.

The day after Sumter fell, April 15, Lincoln issued a proclamation, pursuant to Article 2 of the Constitution, calling out the militia and calling for 75,000 troops, on the basis that "the laws of the United States have been for some time past, and now are opposed, and the execution thereof obstructed, in the States of South Carolina, Georgia, Alabama, Florida, Mississippi, Louisiana, and Texas, by combinations too powerful to be suppressed by the ordinary course of judicial proceedings, or by the powers vested in the Marshals by law."[71] In consultation with his cabinet Lincoln also called Congress into special session on July 4 and indicated that the actions he had taken would be submitted to Congress when it convened. He explained his action in terms of the duty of the presidential oath, to duly execute the laws.[72]

As feared, Lincoln's April 15 proclamation calling up the militia led to other states seceding, including Virginia on April 17. While perhaps the most legally defensible action (supported by federal law going back to the early days of the nation), it had the political effect of alienating several other states. Lincoln was left with concern about the border states of Maryland, Missouri and Kentucky, believing that Kentucky was the key.

Even Chief Justice Taney (who opposed Lincoln) had previously (in 1849 in a case called *Luther v. Borden)* "endorsed the inherent right of every government to 'use its military power to put down an armed insurrection, too strong to be controlled by civil authority,'" which power "'is essential to the existence of every government' and 'essential to the preservation of order and free institutions.' "[73]

On April 19, two days after Jefferson Davis had invited privateers to attack American shipping, Lincoln proclaimed a blockade of Southern ports. Although it is questionable whether Lincoln had any alternative in suppressing the rebellion, this blockade caused subsequent legal and diplomatic problems, and his cabinet was split on the propriety of blockading rather than closing the ports.

Judicial opinions and constitutional scholars have supported the constitutionality of Lincoln's action. Constitutional scholar James Simon concluded that Lincoln's "proclamation" to call up the militia was "well within his executive authority, having been first exercised by President Washington in 1795."[74] Justice Nelson, dissenting in *The Prize Cases* in 1863,[75] demonstrated Lincoln's authority to call out the militia to put down the rebellion.[76]

4. Suspending the writ of habeas corpus (April 1861). Perhaps the most controversial of Lincoln's actions before Congress convened in July 1861 was his limited suspension of habeas corpus. The charge that Lincoln and his administration "violated civil liberties" during the Civil War primarily involves three policies: the suspension of the writ of habeas corpus, the suppression of newspapers and the opening of the mail, and military arrests and trials of civilians. And the most serious charge is whether Lincoln and his administration leveled these policies against the Democratic opposition. These charges raise the prudential question of whether Lincoln used proper means in restoring the Union, fulfilling his constitutional oath and presidential role, and eventually ending slavery.

Habeas corpus is a longstanding legal procedure to test the legality of someone's arrest and detention—whether the arrest is justified in law. The writ of habeas corpus was a significant common-law protection against arbitrary police or executive power, going back centuries in English legal history. Upon a petition for the writ, a judge can issue a writ of habeas corpus (Latin for "have the body") to be delivered to the constable (who has "the body" of the individual imprisoned), requiring the constable to give legal reasons justifying his arrest and detention of the individual.[77] The suspension of habeas corpus means that individuals can be arrested and imprisoned without such judicial process. Lincoln suspended habeas corpus at least eight times during the war.

Based on information that mobs intended to destroy train tracks between Philadelphia and Annapolis to prevent Northern troops from reaching Washington, Lincoln suspended habeas corpus for the first time on April 27 "along the military line" between Washington and Philadelphia.

Lincoln's decision was shaped by his constitutional and legal evaluation, his focus on the goal of preserving the Union and suppressing the rebellion, his recognition of the geographic and political vulnerability of the national capital, Washington, D.C., and the geographic, strategic and political significance of the border states. How much of the South could secede, and how much could the nation lose and still hope to suppress the rebellion?

Critics of Lincoln's suspension often overlook the complex balancing of factors that Lincoln conducted in April 1861. Among the most pressing: there were only two thousand troops defending Washington. An invasion or an attack was expected imminently, and the threat that Lincoln and others in his administration might be captured was widely feared, not just in Washington but across the country. For weeks Lincoln had no idea when troops might arrive to protect the city. It was not until noon on April 25 that the Seventh Regiment finally arrived in Washington.

At the same time that Fort Sumter was falling, Maryland was becoming a significant geographic center by virtue of Washington's geographic vulnerability. Maryland effectively controlled access to Washington. Northern troops were attacked in Baltimore on April 19. Local forces burned Baltimore's bridges and cut telegraph lines to the North in April, effectively cutting off communications with the North while Lincoln was seeking militia to defend Washington. Confederate troops were positioned across the Potomac, apparently ready to lay siege to or invade Washington. In the aftermath of April 15, leading Southern officers in the army and navy resigned. The uncertainty stretched on for a week.

Rioting in Baltimore continued. Though concerned that the Maryland legislature would vote for secession, Lincoln refused on April 25 to authorize General Scott to disband the legislature or arrest legislators, with a thoughtful analysis.[78] (When he allowed the arrest of Maryland legislators in September 1861, he published a statement in a local paper defending the action.)

Critics of Lincoln's suspension of habeas corpus also tend to exaggerate the extent of his suspension of habeas corpus before Congress convened on July 4, 1861. His suspension was limited to the military line between Washington and Philadelphia, because that was the route along which the reinforcements were coming. (Lincoln did not suspend the writ nationwide until September 1862, after Congress passed the Militia Act of 1862 in July.)

What was problematic about Lincoln's suspension of the writ is that the Constitution arguably intends that Congress shall have the exclusive power of suspension. Lincoln asked Attorney General Edward Bates for a legal opinion on the potential suspension of habeas corpus and on the potential declaration of martial law as early as April 20.[79] The U.S. Constitution provides: "The privilege of the Writ of Habeas Corpus shall not be suspended unless when, in Cases of Rebellion or Invasion, the public Safety may require it." But this provision is included in Article 1 (involving legislative powers), not in Article 2 (involving presidential powers), leading Chief Justice Roger Taney to subsequently conclude that Congress had exclusive authority to suspend habeas corpus.

Lincoln's suspension of the writ on April 27 was quickly challenged in the famous case of John Merryman, who was arrested and detained on May 25.[80] Chief Justice Taney, the author of the Supreme Court's *Dred Scott* decision of 1857, acting in his single capacity as a circuit judge, concluded that Lincoln's action was unconstitutional. Lincoln ignored the judgment and continued the suspension.

After April 1861 Lincoln suspended the writ (or authorized Secretary Seward or military commanders to suspend the writ) of habeas corpus on eight occasions. In subsequent suspension orders, Lincoln issued a standard to guide the military commanders: "Unless the necessity for these arbitrary arrests is manifest, and urgent, I prefer they should cease."[81]

Lincoln responded to critics, including Chief Justice Taney, and defended his suspension of the writ in his July 1861 message to Congress in special session. (According to congressional practice in the 1850s and 1860s, Congress was not in session in March 1861, when Lincoln was inaugurated.) What was Lincoln to do as commander in chief until Congress could be convened? He justified his suspension of habeas corpus as a matter of necessity related to his oath to "preserve, protect, and defend the Constitution."

To state the question more directly, are all the laws, *but one*, to go unexecuted, and the government itself go to pieces, lest that one be violated? Even in such a case, would not the official [presidential] oath be broken, if the government should be overthrown, when it was believed that disregarding the single law, would tend to preserve it? But it was not believed that this question was presented. It was not believed that any law was violated. . . . Now it is insisted that Congress, and not the Executive, is vested with this power. But the Constitution itself, is silent as to which, or who, is to exercise the power; and the provision [the clause in Article 2 of the Constitution] was plainly made for a dangerous emergency, it cannot be believed that the framers of the instrument intended, that in every case, the danger should run its course, until Congress could be called together; the very assembling of which might be prevented, as was intended in this case, by the rebellion.[82]

Attorney General Bates issued a legal opinion on July 5, 1861, defending Lincoln's action as constitutional and "prudent,"[83] supporting Lincoln's "lawful discretionary power to arrest and hold in custody, persons known to have criminal intercourse with the insurgents."[84]

Through his proclamation of September 24, 1862, Lincoln suspended habeas corpus nationwide "in certain kinds of cases" to enforce Congress's conscription law, the Militia Act of July 17, 1862.[85] He defended his actions through a number of different public outlets, including his famous April 1864 letter to Albert Hodges:

I did understand . . . that my oath to preserve the constitution to the best of my ability, imposed upon me the duty of preserving, by every indispensable means, that government—that nation—of which that constitution was the organic law. Was it possible to lose the nation, and yet preserve the constitution? . . . I felt that measures, otherwise unconstitutional, might become lawful, by becoming indispensable to the preservation of the constitution, through the preservation of the nation. Right or wrong, I assumed this ground, and now avow it.[86]

Concerning Lincoln's early suspension of the writ in Maryland, Daniel Farber concludes: "Although the constitutional issue can hardly be considered free from doubt, on balance Lincoln's use of habeas in areas of insurrection or actual war should be considered constitutionally appropriate."[87] Carwardine puts the issue directly: "Military coercion of the Confederacy involved political coercion on the Union home front. Few aspects of Abraham Lincoln's presidency have attracted more discussion than his use of emergency executive powers."[88] The three most important considerations that shaped Lincoln's actions were his understanding of the Constitution, the Republican commitment to restoring the Union and effectively dealing with the complex obstacles that impeded that.

5. Lincoln's "suspension of civil liberties" (1861-1865). Beyond the specifics of the suspension of the writ of habeas corpus is the broader charge that Lincoln "violated civil liberties," including suppressions of free speech and free press, and military arrests of civilians outside the war zone. Lincoln was very conscious of the tension between suppressing the rebellion and its impact on civil liberties. He frankly posed the dilemma in his July 1861 message to Congress, "Must a government, of necessity, be too *strong* for the liberties of its own people, or too *weak* to maintain its own existence?"[89]

One of Lincoln's essential arguments was that these emergency measures were necessary to preserve the Union itself. Years afterward, Secretary of the Navy Gideon Welles recalled:

> Few, comparatively, know or can appreciate the actual condition of things and state of feeling of the members of the Administration in those days. Nearly sixty years of peace had unfitted us for any war, but the most terrible of wars, a civil one, was upon us, and it had to be met. Congress had adjourned without making any provision for the storm, though aware that it was at hand and soon to burst upon the country. A new Administration, scarcely acquainted with each other, and differing essentially in the past, was compelled to act, promptly and decisively.[90]

Such a doctrine of necessity is a dangerous and controversial notion, and one of the ultimate prudential questions about Lincoln's administration is whether he was justified in employing such means to suppress the rebellion to preserve the Union.[91]

The telegraph office in Washington was first shut down by Secretary of State William Seward on April 19, the same day that the Lincoln administration began to blockade Southern ports. In May, Lincoln closed the mails to "disloyal" publications.[92] The administration shut down "allegedly disloyal newspapers."[93] It also engaged in government oversight of private correspondence. According to Carwardine, Lincoln "was probably behind the War Department's executive order of July 22 [1861] empowering commanders to seize and use civilian southerners' property for military purposes."[94] His special message to Congress when Congress convened on July 4 gave an elaborate defense of his actions "to prevent . . . such attempt to destroy the Federal Union."[95]

The extent and propriety of the Administration's suppression of "disloyal" newspapers is a serious question. University of Chicago law professor Geoffrey Stone, author of *Perilous Times: Free Speech in Wartime from the Sedition Act of 1798 to the War on Terrorism*, reviewed the book *Lincoln's Wrath*, a critical account of the Lincoln administration's attempt to shut down various "disloyal" newspapers.[96] Stone concluded that the book "offers no evidence to support" its thesis that "Lincoln was a skilled manipulator of the press whose Machiavellian machinations secretly encouraged and even directed the dismantling of the opposition press." Instead, Stone concluded that the authors resort "to innuendo, loaded rhetorical questions, dubious inferences, and spurious conspiracy theories in lieu of proof."[97]

Lincoln was also charged with suppressing what was merely "disloyal speech." Two of the most famous "civil liberties" cases during the Civil War involved the arrest of Ohio Democratic Congressman Clement Vallandigham by General Ambrose Burnside after a speech in Mt. Vernon, Ohio, on May 1, 1863,[98] and the arrest of Indiana Democrat Lambdin P. Milligan in 1864.[99] These examples "raise[d] suspicions that Republicans attempted to combat the opposing political party by means other than the ballot," and Democrats "maintained that such cases were the tip of an iceberg of Republican interference at the polls that froze the political opposition."[100]

Constitutional law professor Michael Paulsen points out that Lincoln thoughtfully explored the First Amendment questions surrounding the arrest of Vallandigham.[101] Lincoln had to balance the policies in the immediate present with the threats imminent and the future uncertain. Lincoln believed "as commander in chief that he must deal decisively with threats to the nation's security posed by men like Vallandigham."[102]

In response to the Vallandigham arrest, Lincoln broadly defended those actions in a June 1863 public letter to Erastus Corning and other New York and Ohio Democrats.[103] Lincoln defended military arrests of civilians "outside of the lines of necessary military occupation" as "constitutional *wherever* the public safety does require them; as well in places to which they may prevent the Rebellion extending as in those where it may be already prevailing;

as well where they may restrain mischievous interference with the raising and supplying of armies to suppress the Rebellion, as where the rebellion may actually be."[104] As Mark Neely points out, one of the remarkable things about the letter is that Lincoln's defense did not rely on Congress's habeas corpus act of March 1863, believing that his authority as president and commander in chief was sufficient.[105]

Among the most controversial actions was Secretary of War Stanton's order of August 8, 1862, which ushered in a "brief period of sweeping and uncoordinated arrests" between August 8 and September 8, 1862, with the purpose of preventing "draft resistance."[106] These were "authorized by the president and designed to enforce America's first national military draft, the Militia Act of July 17."[107] Historian Mark Neely concluded that Stanton's August 8 orders "had momentous effect on civil liberties in the United States" and allowed "a horde of petty functionaries to decide without any legal guidelines one of the highest matters of state: precisely who in this civil war was loyal or disloyal."[108] Neely concluded that "the authorities were in many ways sincerely attempting to end resistance to enlistment and the draft" and that there were 354 well-documented cases of arrests (and perhaps another 100 to 200 other cases) during that month period.[109]

In October 1863, Lincoln wrote to the military commander of Missouri, General John M. Schofield, who was "accused of abusing his authority by arresting leading radicals and suppressing radical papers under the guise of military necessity."[110] Lincoln directed Schofield to "only arrest individuals, and suppress assemblies, or newspapers, when they may be working *palpable* injury to the Military in your charge; and, in no other case will you interfere with the expression of opinion in any form, or allow it to be interfered with violently by others."[111]

Mark Neely's unique 1991 book, *The Fate of Liberty*, was the first to examine hundreds of Civil War arrest and military-trial records. Neely concluded that, for Lincoln, "Suspending the writ of habeas corpus was not originally a political measure, and it would never become primarily political."[112] Although significant power for military arrests was delegated to Secretary Seward, "In truth, Seward and the State Department ordered few arrests." Instead, the "responsibility for initiating arrest lay with some authority outside the department in at least 43 percent of the cases."[113] The "statistical record proves that Seward by no means crushed dissent," for he "presided over the arrest of only 864 civilians."[114] Modern estimates put the total number of civilian arrests in the North by Union forces at 13,000 to 14,000.[115] In any case, "Republicans would later enjoy substantial bipartisan agreement on the necessity of the early arrests in Maryland," which was widely believed to have successfully kept the state in the Union. The crucial border state of Missouri was the focus of arrests of a "disproportionately large numbers of civilians," the origin of trials by military commission and the most difficult prudential questions.[116] Missouri was, in Neely's conclusion, the "low tide for liberty."[117] But Neely concluded:

> The only large group of arrests that appeared in any way to resemble what most Democrats complained about at the time, the sort that really disturbed historians and civil libertarians, were those that followed the August 8, 1862, orders. And those were sincerely meant to enforce conscription rather than stifle dissent—which explains their relaxation in one month's time after most draft quotas had been filled.[118]

Professor James Simon concluded:

> The Lincoln administration censored the mails and military commanders sporadically shut down newspapers that opposed the war. But Lincoln never proposed, nor did the Republican-controlled Congress pass, a mid-nineteenth century version of the Alien and Sedition Acts. The opposition press remained robust during the war and continued savagely to attack administration policies.[119]

The exercise of such emergency powers raised charges that Lincoln was a tyrant. But there were at least *five obvious checks* on Lincoln's exercise of these emergency powers: the constitutional provision for impeachment; the other branches of government, specifically Congress and its appropriation powers; the congressional elections of 1862 and 1864; his own reelection of 1864 (which Lincoln in fact came close to losing until September 1864); and a critical Democratic press in the North. These checks were recognized by the framers and by Lincoln, who publicly acknowledged to a group of Ohio Democrats: "If he uses the power [of suspending the writ] justly, the same people will probably justify him; if he abuses it, he is in their hands, to be dealt with by all the modes they have reserved to themselves in the constitution."[120]

6. Lincoln's amendment of Fremont's proclamation (September 1861).
While some critics condemn Lincoln for taking private property during the
course of the war, others criticize Lincoln for not acting against slavery more
directly and quickly.

In late August 1861, General John C. Fremont—commander of the entire
Western Department—declared martial law throughout the state of Missouri
and directed Union troops to affirmatively confiscate the slaves of all persons
"who shall be directly proven to have taken an active part with their enemies
in the field." Congress had passed the First Confiscation Act earlier that
month, but Fremont's proclamation went beyond that law.[121] Lincoln rescinded
Fremont's proclamation because it went further than Congress's Confiscation
Act and for the purpose of quelling dissension in the border states.

Fremont made his proclamation public, and Lincoln learned about it, along
with the public, in the press. Abolitionists obviously praised it, but Lincoln's
supporters in the border states warned that it would endanger the loyalty of
the border states. Lincoln heard from an old friend in Kentucky that "it will
crush out every vestage [sic] of a union party in the state."[122]

Lincoln attempted to quietly urge Fremont to "conform" the order on his
own to the Act of Congress, but Fremont refused.[123] Lincoln then publicly ordered him to conform it to the terms of Congress's First Confiscation Act.[124]
This provoked the consternation of abolitionists like Ohio senator Benjamin
Wade and Frederick Douglass.

As Lincoln wrote in a private letter to Orville Browning, his action to curtail
Fremont's proclamation was ultimately shaped by principle—his conviction
that presidential power and military law did not extend so far as to free the
slaves permanently by fiat—and by policy—his need to keep both the border
states and abolitionists within his working coalition, his impression of public
opinion, and his decision to reserve to himself decisions about slavery.[125]

7. The timing of the Emancipation Proclamation (October 1862). One of
the most difficult, controversial and momentous decisions of Lincoln's presidency was the Emancipation Proclamation of January 1, 1863.[126] His decision to
issue it and announce that to his cabinet in July 1862 was preceded by substantial deliberation and efforts to encourage the border and other states, like Dela-
ware, to accept compensated emancipation, and by his conclusion that the Confederacy's use of slavery to support its war power needed to be undermined.

Lincoln's opposition to slavery, tempered by his sense of constitutional and political constraints, was well-established. As long ago as 1854, in opposing the Kansas-Nebraska Act, Lincoln opposed slavery as a matter of principle:

> This *declared* indifference, but as I must think, covert *real* zeal for the spread of slavery, I can not but hate. I hate it because of the monstrous injustice of slavery itself. I hate it because it deprives our republican example of its just influence in the world—enables the enemies of free institutions, with plausibility, to taunt us as hypocrites—causes the real friends of freedom to doubt our sincerity, and especially because it forces so many really good men amongst ourselves into an open war with the very fundamental principles of civil liberty—criticizing the Declaration of Independence, and insisting that there is no right principle of action but *self-interest*.[127]

Such principles were repeated in his June 26, 1857, speech against the Supreme Court's March 1857 *Dred Scott* decision and in his June 16, 1858, "house divided" speech in which he accepted the Illinois Republican Senate nomination against Douglas.[128] Subsequently, in his Chicago speech, responding to Douglas's criticism of the "house divided" speech, Lincoln called slavery "a vast moral evil." At the same time, Lincoln had long expressed a widely held recognition of the Constitution's protection of slavery in the Southern states.[129] He frequently stated that he expected the ultimate extinction of slavery and that the framers had anticipated the ultimate extinction.[130]

The Emancipation Proclamation was preceded by repeated attempts by Lincoln to offer compensated emancipation to the border states in March, May and July 1862. Lincoln wrote to Albert Hodges in April 1864 that he resisted emancipation by military officers when it was not "an indispensable necessity" to the suppression of the rebellion and that when he made those "earnest, and successive appeals to the border states to favor compensated emancipation, I believed the indispensable necessity for military emancipation, and arming the blacks would come, unless averted by that measure."[131]

As Lincoln wrote to Hodges:

> I am naturally antislavery. If slavery is not wrong, nothing is wrong. I can not remember when I did not so think, and feel. And yet I have never understood that the Presidency conferred upon me an unrestricted right to act officially upon this judgment and feeling. It was in the oath I took that I would, to the best of my ability, preserve, protect, and defend the Constitution of the United States.

. . . I did understand however, that my oath to preserve the constitution to the best of my ability, imposed upon me the duty of preserving, by every indispensable means, that government—that nation—of which that constitution was the organic law.[132]

While Lincoln believed that he had no authority under the Constitution to directly prohibit slavery in the slave states, he came to believe that he could attack slavery to prosecute the war within his constitutional authority as commander in chief.[133] This explains the limitation of the Emancipation Proclamation to the states in rebellion. Lincoln's views on the expansiveness of the war powers was not unprecedented. John Quincy Adams articulated such a broad understanding of the president's war powers over slavery in a famous statement in Congress in 1842.[134] After the Union victory at Antietam, Lincoln "judged that inaction [against slavery] was an even greater danger."[135]

Lincoln's Emancipation Proclamation was taken by many as his statement of abolition as a second goal of the war, but it reflected the sentiment of a growing number of Northerners that the abolition of slavery must play a role as a purpose of the war. These combined goals were part of the platform of a broad-based National Union Party for the 1864 election campaign.

He saw the "time coming" for a constitutional amendment on slavery in late 1863 but deemed, at that time, that the country was not yet ready.[136] But in 1865 Lincoln "worked effectively behind the scenes to persuade wavering congressional Democrats to support it."[137] And his reconstruction plans required that states accept the amendment to reenter the Union.

8. Declaration of martial law "behind the lines" (1861-1865). Lincoln's judgment is also questioned for his imposition of martial law "behind the lines," or outside the theater of war, or allowing that to occur by his military commanders. Martial law substitutes military rule and legal process for civilian legal process. Legal scholar Daniel Farber, in his book *Lincoln's Constitution*, sustains the case for the legality of the use of martial law *in the theater of war* itself.[138]

The more difficult question, however, is the imposition of martial law *outside* the theater of war. After a critical review of Lincoln's protection of civil liberties during the war, Farber concluded:

The verdict on the Lincoln administration's civil liberties record is mixed. Many of the acts denounced as dictatorial—the suspension of habeas at the beginning of the war, emancipation, military trials of civilians in contested or occupied territory—seem in retrospect to have reasonably good constitutional justifications under the war power. Other leaders, faced with half the country in open rebellion, would have gone much farther than Lincoln did. But there were clear excesses like the treatment of Milligan, Vallandigham, and the *New York World*. Such actions were generally not taken at Lincoln's initiative, but as president, he retained ultimate accountability.[139]

Farber also concluded that military trials

in occupied Southern territory or contested areas of border states probably involved a justifiable application of martial law. Arrests in the North were more problematic. Roughly 5 percent of military trials—about two hundred—took place in uncontested territory, outside of the South or the border states. . . . But some others . . . merely involved disloyal speech.[140]

Farber concluded that "interference with free speech during the Civil War was sporadic"[141] and points out that "Lincoln's insistence to the Missouri general [Schofield] on the need for 'palpable injury' as a basis for suppressing speech" adheres closely to stricter judicial standards for protecting free speech not developed until a half century later.[142] Farber also concluded that "Lincoln played only a secondary role in the most famous instance of interference with free speech, the Vallandigham case."[143]

Lincoln subsequently defended his administration's policy on military arrests in the same public June 1863 letters to New York and Ohio Democrats on the basis of public necessity:

Inasmuch . . . as the Constitution itself makes no such distinction, I am unable to believe that there is any such constitutional distinction [between inside or outside the theater of war]. I concede that the class of arrests complained of can be constitutional only when, in cases of rebellion or invasion, the public safety may require them; and I insist that in such cases they are constitutional *wherever* the public safety does require them; as well in places to which they may prevent the Rebellion extending as in those where it may be already prevailing; as well where they may restrain mischievous interference with the raising and supplying of armies to suppress the Rebellion, as where the Rebellion may actually be.[144]

Vallandigham's arrest "was not for criticizing the administration or General Burnside, which Lincoln conceded would be wrong," but, in Lincoln's words, "because he was laboring, with some effort, to prevent the raising of troops; to encourage desertions from the army; and to leave the Rebellion without an adequate military force to suppress it."[145] Farber concluded that Lincoln's views "are consistent with our current views of legitimate executive power."[146] And Lincoln's defense in the letter was persuasive with the public.[147]

After Appomattox, in 1866, the Supreme Court ruled in the *Milligan* case[148] and rejected the use of trials by military commission outside the lines of necessary military occupation. The Supreme Court did not directly challenge the suspension of the writ of habeas corpus or the military arrest of civilians.[149]

There is no basis for any conclusion that Lincoln ever "acted in knowing violation of constitutional standards."[150] As of 1860, there was little developed law on the extent of executive authority or the interpretation of the First Amendment, and the standards Lincoln applied thoroughly examined the heart of the issue and anticipated legal standards that wouldn't be developed by the courts for decades.[151]

Throughout, Lincoln was clearly guided by his understanding of presidential authority under the Constitution to defend the Constitution, preserve the Union and faithfully execute the laws. Within his constitutional role, Lincoln sought to successfully connect the means at his disposal to the end of suppressing the rebellion and preserving the Union.

9. Lincoln's veto of the Wade-Davis Reconstruction Bill (July 2, 1864). The war to preserve the Union introduced new political and constitutional problems and implications that were unprecedented. These were multiplied many times over by the ending of slavery through the war and the proposed Thirteenth Amendment, approved by Congress but not ratified by the states until after Lincoln's assassination.

The issues that eventually were called "Reconstruction" emerged as early as 1862, as soon as Union forces began to take control of certain seceded territories. However, as hopes for Union victory rose in the middle of 1863, the question of Reconstruction of the Union was more intentionally raised in newspapers, public discussion and congressional debate.

The issue of reconstruction divided the Republican Party. Some in Congress wanted the most lenient requirements for Reconstruction while others wanted the most severe requirements. In calling Reconstruction "the greatest question ever presented to practical statesmanship," Lincoln called it, in effect, the most difficult prudential question he faced.[152]

Lincoln's developing policy was outlined in four public documents: his December 8, 1863, annual message to Congress, including his Amnesty Proclamation; his December 1864 annual message to Congress; his second inaugural address on March 4, 1865; and his last public address on April 11, 1865.[153]

In his 1863 annual message to Congress, Lincoln set forth strong positions that any returning rebel swear allegiance to the Union and accept emancipation. He declared, "I shall not attempt to retract or modify the emancipation proclamation; nor shall I return to slavery any person who is free by the terms of that proclamation, or by any of the acts of Congress."[154]

On the other hand, Lincoln resisted the extent to which radical Republicans sought to "punish" the South, and he resisted being pinned down on other specifics, like black suffrage, the "most fundamental and controversial of all Reconstruction issues."[155] Bills to enfranchise freedmen were introduced in Congress but rejected in the spring of 1864. These bills tested Northern opinion on black suffrage.

Another aspect was reintegrating Southern states back into the Union. Lincoln set forth his "ten percent plan": "when the number of loyal men taking the oath reached ten percent of the votes cast in the 1860 election, they could 're-establish a State government' recognized by the United States."[156]

As long as the war continued, Lincoln needed to maintain both radical and conservative Republicans in a united front against the rebellion. This was Lincoln's political challenge from the beginning of the war to its end, and is reflected in his dogged effort to keep conservatives and radicals united in his cabinet and in his effort to bridge divisions in Missouri politics in the fall of 1863.

Carwardine records that Lincoln "did develop a broad approach to reconstruction, shaped by his own temperamental preference and constitutional conviction, and by military and political need. The law and the Constitution would be his guide to action, not vindictiveness or hatred."[157]

However broad Lincoln's assertion of federal power to meet these problems, it was not as broad as the radical Republicans would have employed. Carwardine observes that

Lincoln's gradualism served a progressive purpose. His approach to social improvement was that of a political realist who knew that for every radical action there was the real threat of a conservative counterreaction and that thoroughgoing changes could prove self-defeating. Lincoln formulated both his emancipation and his reconstruction policies convinced not only that they were true to the Founders' values, but that they offered the best means of making progress and maintaining the momentum of change.[158]

For example, Lincoln "remained firmly attached to the new government in Louisiana as a sure guarantor of 'perpetual freedom' and as the most available means of bringing the state 'into proper practical relations with the Union.'"[159]

The policy debate over reconstruction in the Republican Party came to a head with the Wade-Davis Bill, which passed Congress on July 2, 1864. The bill was more stringent than Lincoln's December 1863 proclamation in two crucial respects: the bill required 50 percent rather than Lincoln's 10 percent, and required "a provision guaranteeing freedom be incorporated in the restored states' new constitutions."[160] In effect, the bill postponed reconstruction when Lincoln wanted to use such policies as a "carrot" to encourage loyal citizens in the South to rejoin the Union.

Michigan senator Zachariah Chandler confronted Lincoln as he was signing bills in the Senate, emphasizing that "the important point is that one prohibiting slavery in the reconstructed states." Lincoln reportedly responded, "That is the point on which I doubt the authority of Congress to act." Chandler protested, "It is no more than you have done yourself." Lincoln replied, "I conceive that I may in an emergency do things on military grounds which cannot be done constitutionally by Congress."[161] Lincoln refused to sign the Wade-Davis Bill and thus pocket-vetoed it. Progress on reconstruction was effectively postponed until after the fall 1864 elections.

The radical Republicans criticized Lincoln specifically for his alleged "misreading of events."[162] To their mind Lincoln was, by purpose or effect, "trading black freedom for magnanimity toward rebels."[163] In response to what Lincoln perceived as the "exclusive" and "inflexible" plan for reconstruction proposed by the radicals, Lincoln believed that Louisiana had to be examined individually. Lincoln's last public speech on April 11, 1865, after the surrender at Appomattox, directly addressed the impending reconstruction and his characterization of the Louisiana government: "Grant that [the freedman] desires the elective franchise, will he not attain it sooner by saving the already advanced steps toward it, than by running backward over them? Concede that the new government of Louisiana is only to what it should be as the egg is to the fowl, we shall sooner have the fowl by hatching the egg than by smashing it?"[164]

Carwardine concludes that "Lincoln kept his humility and his temperamental distrust of the absolutism, the pretensions of superior sanctity, and pharisaism of those religionists who pressed him toward more radical action against the South."[165] What actually transpired in the Reconstruction period we now know was strongly shaped by Booth's bullet, not simply in killing Lincoln but in strengthening a spirit of vengeance toward the South. Lincoln's assassination was a disaster for the freedman and the South.

Conclusion

To a great extent Lincoln's prudence as president comes down to his judgment of the good, more specifically whether there was a right to unilateral secession by any state or minority of states. Lincoln's explanation for his judgment and his stated goals and intentions in suppressing the rebellion are a matter of public record in his numerous speeches and official documents.

Lincoln's prudence (right reason about what is to be done) cannot be rightly assessed against a standard of perfection. Prudence assesses how much good is possible by fallible people in this world of constraints and limits. Nor can it be assessed against judicial decisions of a future age. Rather, it must be assessed against how well Lincoln understood the good, made decisions in light of the good and implemented them effectively in the face of countervailing obstacles.

Lincoln's greatest shortcomings are seen in his management of his generals and the war. He had the steepest learning curve here. Perhaps the most important controversies were the general issue of the progress of the military campaign and Lincoln's supervision of the imposition of martial law by officers in the field. But Lincoln's challenge in 1861 and 1862 was not only to manage his generals as commander in chief but to change the contemporary military mindset to recognize that the goal was *not* capturing the opposition's political capital (Richmond) but destroying their army. Even as late as the battle of Gettysburg, July 2-4, 1863, General Meade communicated that he had driven "the invader from our soil." Whereupon Lincoln responded to his staff, "Will our

generals never get that idea out of their heads? The whole country is our soil."[166]
This was something that he, his cabinet, the generals and the North gradually
learned, but the implications were ever-growing bloodshed and destruction.

Nevertheless, Richard Carwardine—whose biography of Lincoln focuses
more than any other on political prudence—concludes that "as a commander-
in-chief with little military experience, but one who gave hours to hard strategic thought, Lincoln has subsequently won high marks from historians.
Operating from first principles . . . he came to see much earlier than his commanders the best means of exploiting the Union's advantage in numbers,"
and the "hard war" policy at the end was based on the fact that "to destroy
armies you had to deny them food, ammunition, and other supplies."[167] Add-
ing the secondary goal of the war, emancipation, to the initial goal of restoring the Union, "made conciliation and compromise with the armed South an
impossibility."[168] Carwardine strikes an appropriate balance in his assessment of Lincoln:

> Through this formidable, if unspectacular, combination of personal qualities,
> political authority, and diagnostic ability, Lincoln sustained what proved to be a
> stunningly effective overall strategy. Historians have rightly made much of his
> caution, especially in the earlier phases of the war, as he knit border conserva-
> tives, residual Whigs, and War Democrats into the Union coalition. Rather less
> has been made of Lincoln's understanding of the need to inspire and energize
> the North, and to inoculate it against the most virulent strains of war-weariness
> and defeatism, by articulating an ideal of the nation that spoke to a higher pa-
> triotism and an expanded vision of the Union. He did this on his own terms and
> not the radicals'. . . . His commonly noted fatalism induced not political passiv-
> ity but an understanding that the individual politician would fail if he tried to
> swim against or resist the larger tide. "Lincoln's whole life was a calculation of
> the law of forces, and ultimate results." . . . This did not encourage inertia in a
> man for whom "work, work, work" was "the main thing." Rather it meant identi-
> fying and promoting the means by which the larger forces at play could be ad-
> vanced. Convinced that the Union both should and could be saved, and sure
> that slavery's days were numbered, Lincoln seized his historical moment as the
> instrument of a providential purpose.[169]

5

THE CHALLENGE OF MORAL PERFECTIONISM

Broadly speaking, William Wilberforce and the Whigs in the 1780s and Abraham Lincoln and the Republicans in the 1850s employed similar strategies: erecting legal fences against a social evil when they could not prohibit it. In seeking to overturn or limit unjust laws and conditions, what moral obligations do political leaders, like Wilberforce and Lincoln, have in deciding which goals to seek and which means to pursue? Must they exclusively pursue the perfectly just in law? Were Wilberforce and Lincoln morally obliged to support only legislation that would completely prohibit slavery? Could they, as a means to the ultimate goal of abolition, propose legislation that would limit the evil (by regulating it) without prohibiting it outright? Despite the success of Wilberforce and of anti-slavery opponents in fencing in slavery, the legitimacy of such an approach is widely questioned.

Many Americans might see Wilberforce's dilemma as a question of "saving as many lives as possible" and accept the commonsense morality of such a goal. But a number of voices have challenged that commonsense morality when it comes to abortion legislation, the main subject of this chapter. Some rhetorically claim that regulations or partial prohibitions "abandon" the victims. Others claim that they constitute moral compromise or contradict principled rhetoric or are counterproductive.[1]

The most elaborate criticism of this "commonsense morality" is by British activist Colin Harte in his book *Changing Unjust Laws Justly*.[2] Harte's is a very personal and heartfelt attempt to articulate a moral public-policy strategy, and his case against unjust laws is a serious and important one ("Woe to those who make unjust laws" [Isaiah 10:1]). Harte reflects the frustration that many feel at the slow pace of legal reform and at the imperfections and inequalities that often result from the democratic process.

Harte's focus is on abortion. He opposes "restrictive abortion legislation"—his term for "proposals that would in themselves restrict abortion to particular (categories of) unborn children—the proposals referring to such things as the gestational age of the unborn child, his or her state of health or disability, the circumstances of the conception, etc."[3] In Harte's view, voting for a law that leaves some abortions in place is "an intrinsically immoral action."[4]

Unfortunately, Harte fails by virtually ignoring both prudence and the doctrine of cooperation in his analysis. Instead, Harte's argument is based on an extrapolation of Thomas Aquinas's "Treatise on Law" and of certain papal encyclicals and Catholic Church documents. Consequently, this chapter involves a close examination of Aquinas's writings and Church documents because these are the authorities on which Harte relies.

There are six primary elements to Harte's argument. (1) He contends that the principle of "solidarity," as expressed in the writings of the late Pope John Paul II, requires the complete legal protection of every single human being in any abortion law. (2) According to Harte the natural law condemns "intrinsically unjust" laws, as that concept is used in §22 of the 1974 "Declaration on Procured Abortion" from the Catholic Church's Congregation for the Doctrine of the Faith[5] and in Pope John Paul II's 1995 encyclical *Evangelium vitae*.[6] "The concept of intrinsic unjustness in law is *implied* in the Church's traditional teaching and . . . is articulated in recent magisterial teachings," according to Harte.[7] As Harte readily admits, "The concept of intrinsic unjustness of restrictive abortion legislation is central to my argument that it is unethical to vote for it."[8] (3) He argues that any law which "permits" or "tolerates" abortion is "intrinsically unjust."[9] Harte asserts that "no bill that permits or tolerates abortions"—as he broadly defines those terms—"can be judged to be either wise or humane or just or civilized."[10] (4) "The identification of a law as intrinsically unjust is sufficient to judge that the act of voting for it is intrinsically unjust and never an ethically good choice."[11] No legislator can vote for an intrinsically unjust law. (5) The "object" of the legislator's vote is the key for Harte, but that object is not determined by the legislator's intent but by the bill that is finally enacted by the entire legislature. (6) The "common good" requires a devotion in any bill to every single human life.

Harte sets his understanding of natural law against the classical prudential tradition. Harte poses the paradox that it is immoral to be prudent; classical prudential reasoning is overriden by the dictates of the natural law. Harte paradoxically exalts the right to life to such a preeminent position that it cannot be actively protected in human law unless it is perfectly protected. But few if any human goods can be perfectly protected in this world of constraints.

Even conceding the proposition that the natural law may dictate absolute (exceptionless) moral norms for personal behavior (e.g., no intentional killing of innocent human beings), it is a big step removed from that to argue that the natural law dictates *the details of human laws*, and it is another step removed from that to argue that the natural law dictates the details of *legislative attempts to limit existing unjust laws and conditions*. Legislators don't kill or commit abortion when they pass laws or amendments to limit unjust laws, and legislators don't necessarily endorse a right to abortion when they attempt to legally prohibit as many abortions as possible.

The linchpin of Harte's book is not the concept of "intrinsically unjust" but his extrapolation that *any law that "permits" abortion (as he defines it) is "intrinsically unjust."* Harte's definition of *permit* is not limited to its meaning of "authorize" in Aquinas or John Paul II, but broadly includes *any bill that leaves any abortion unprohibited*.[12]

Harte's argument rests on a unique and narrow interpretation of Aquinas (natural law) and of the writings of various popes, principally John Paul II. Harte's novel extrapolation of the writings of Aquinas and John Paul II are frankly at odds with the conclusions of the statements of national bishops' conferences and individual cardinals and bishops over the past thirty years in Ireland, England, Australia and the United States. These statements have been remarkably consistent in teaching that the specific elements of legislative policy are left to the guidance of prudence and not dictated by natural law, and that legislative attempts to limit unjust laws and conditions are morally sound (licit).[13] This should be enough to cast substantial doubt on Harte's novel extrapolation of Thomistic and Catholic Church teaching.

UNDERSTANDING OBSTACLES:
THE SUPREME COURT'S IMPOSED LIMITS AND EXCEPTIONS

Aquinas taught that true prudence requires cognition—that is, understanding reality. An accurate analysis of the legislative and political arena must start with an understanding of the constraints of the real world, why they exist, and what can realistically be done to defeat or overcome them.[14] Prudence requires recognizing the moral and practical complexity in difficult policy issues, even while emphasizing moral ideals and working for solutions.

Abortion is unique among bioethical issues in American society because it is not subject to popular control through representative government. Instead, the Supreme Court intervened in 1973, erased the abortion laws of the fifty states, even the least restrictive prohibitions, and substituted its own national law of abortion on demand in the *Roe v. Wade* decision.[15]

Virtually all other bioethical issues are a matter for legislative debate and decision, without federal court interference. In contrast to *Roe*, the Supreme Court in 1990 left the issue of nutrition and hydration for chronically or terminally ill patients to the states,[16] and in 1997 the Court left the issue of assisted suicide to the states.[17] These issues are decided by the people at the state (not federal) level.

Although it was immediately apparent from the *Roe* decision that states could not prohibit abortion in the first trimester (that no state prohibitions could be enforced), the full sweep of the Court's decision became apparent only over time, as states tried different responses and the Court decided additional cases.

The vague contours of the Court's decision in *Roe* suggested that the "right" could expand, and the limits that states could impose were entirely uncertain. Indeed, for thirty-plus years after the *Roe* decision, the Court has decided twenty-seven to twenty-eight cases which continue to define what the states can do. That "elaboration" of the original decision in *Roe* will continue for the foreseeable future.

In effect, the Court in *Roe* established a national abortion law covering all the states, allowing, but not requiring, regulations around the margins. Unless regulated by federal or state legislation, that national law is an all-encompassing policy of abortion on demand virtually. An unfettered abortion license exists—in all fifty states, at any time of pregnancy, for any reason, for girls of any age who might become pregnant. The Court invalidated prohibitions before viability and required that prohibitions after viability might be possible but only if there was an exception to preserve the "health" of the mother, and then defined "health" as any "emotional" reason related to "well-being."[18] Thus the Court required all kinds of exceptions to prohibitions and regulations before any new state or federal abortion regulation could go into effect, and has done so for more than thirty years.

There were more implications. The Supreme Court's decision in *Roe* swept abortion prohibitions off the legislative and political table by empowering federal courts to slap injunctions on any law prohibiting abortion, to prevent the law from going into effect. On top of all this a federal statute (the Civil Rights Attorneys Fees Act of 1976) requires that a state pay (from tax dollars) the attorneys' fees of the abortion clinics (tens or hundreds of thousands of dollars) when they "prevail" in invalidating a state abortion statute. For example, when the Supreme Court struck down Nebraska's partial-birth abortion prohibition in 2000, it also struck down partial-birth abortion bans in twenty-nine other states. Those thirty states were forced to pay the fees of the abortion attorneys—reportedly totaling $6,000,000.

> The Supreme Court adopted a boundless definition of "health" for purposes of abortion law: "all factors—physical, emotional, psychological, familial, and the woman's age—relevant to the well-being of the patient."

It was immediately apparent with the *Roe* decision that the states could no longer prohibit abortion. Virtually all public officials followed the Court's decision. Abortion clinics quickly opened up in major cities. One state, Rhode Island, tried to immediately reenact an abortion prohibition, and that was quickly invalidated by the federal courts. Three states (or territories) tried again in 1991-1992, and these too were quickly invalidated.

Eventually, abortion prohibitions were swept off the legislative and political agenda. Elected legislators in a democracy have limited time and resources, and their reelection is based on making a difference on public issues that are relevant to their constituents. Knowing the power of federal courts and the certain outcome of bills that prohibit abortion, legislators will not consider abortion prohibitions. Until *Roe* is overturned, such bills have no chance of going into effect and being enforced. If introduced by a single legislator, they will not be considered by a committee and will never come to a vote. Without votes on such bills they will not be part of a legislator's record, nor the subject of any election. Understanding the nature, dimensions and future prospects of this reality is critical.

As long as *Roe* is the law, it is clear—for members of Congress and state legislators at the outset of any legislative session—that no law *prohibiting* any abortion will ever go into effect. The federal courts would block such a law. And the Supreme Court dictates the details of each abortion law and which boundaries (and exceptions) must be included.

The Court's 2007 decision in *Gonzales v. Carhart*[19] effectively restores the *Planned Parenthood v. Casey* decision of 1992.[20] That means more deference to state legislatures in passing regulations. But the *Gonzales* decision gives no green light to broad prohibitions of abortion before fetal viability.

All abortion legislation since 1973, state or federal, has been drafted and enacted against the background of this national law of abortion on demand imposed by the Supreme Court's edict.

POLITICAL AND LEGISLATIVE PRUDENCE: BUILDING FENCES TO CONTAIN SOCIAL EVILS

The purpose for and context of fences. Given the broad, vague and potentially expanding nature of the Supreme Court's abortion license, attempts were immediately made to build fences around the *Roe* decision. How could the abortion license be limited practically, politically, legally?

Faced with that political and legal cataclysm of *Roe*, what should abortion opponents have done? What could they have done? Because there is no monolithic movement, a lot of leaders and organizations tried a lot of tactics. But—at least in the legal and policy arena—three general tactics were tried: state repudiation of the decision (attempting to prohibit abortion despite the *Roe* decision), attempts in Congress to pass a constitutional amendment to overturn the *Roe* decision and attempts to establish state legislative fences around the abortion license. Part of prudential memory requires knowing and understanding what's been tried before, and why.

Fences have different potential functions. They can establish a moral line, clarify a legal boundary (like a property line), keep something good in, keep bad things out, prevent the expansion of an evil, or combine some or all of these objectives.

Fences are also erected within a context. They take account of the terrain and of what's inside and outside the fence. Fences do not *necessarily* establish a right or a principle or legitimize what's inside or outside the fence. Where a fence is placed is sometimes determined by countervailing authority or power. For example, fences established at a property line may recognize the power (or legal rights) of the adjoining property owner and seek to keep his activity limited to his property. The purpose of legislation largely depends on the intent of the author or sponsor, and that is primarily determined by looking at the text and context.

Regulations (like fences) do not necessarily imply or confer legitimacy; they can be entirely practical and functional. Regulation *may* confer legitimacy when the regulation of the activity results in traded benefits to the regulators from the regulated activity (as, for example, in taxing prostitution). The essential elements of prudence—understanding first principles, cognition, deliberation, judgment, decision—are necessary to establish the most effective fences. And how to prudentially establish legal fences calls Harry Jaffa's four questions to mind—good goals, what's possible, connecting means to ends, preserving the possibility of future improvement.

Federal and state laws have attempted to put fences around the abortion license. The object of many legislators was to limit abortions and the abortion "right" when it could not be prohibited. Those fences themselves have been subject to Supreme Court review and have sparked at least twenty-eight cases since *Roe*.[21] The most vital fence was preventing public funding—making clear that neither the federal nor state governments were required to fund abortion from tax dollars. This was the immediate subject of litigation across the country, and the Supreme Court did not clearly confirm the ability of public officials to cut off state or federal funding for seven years, until the Supreme Court's *Harris v. McRae* decision in 1980.

Prudence and incrementalism. Until now I've not mentioned the term *incrementalism*. That's because it has serious limitations as a term of description and explanation. An increment is simply a step; hence incrementalism begs numerous questions: Where is the step going? What is the goal?

Nevertheless, the term *incrementalism* is pervasive—in law, politics and economics. An op-ed on the July 2006 Israeli-Hezbollah war, for example, referred to the military strategy of Israeli prime minister Ehud Olmert as "the incrementalist approach."[22] A reporter for the *New York Times* referred to the Senate's passage of the Child Custody Protection Act in July 2006 as a strategy "to seek incremental changes in federal laws."[23] The metaphor of the flywheel for persevering in producing positive change in an organization—emphasized in Jim Collins's 2001 book, *Good to Great*, expresses the reality of incremental change in business.

While it's not possible to eliminate the use of the term *incrementalism*, caution is warranted in evaluating what is meant by the term in any particular context.[24] Although incrementalism may not be clearly descriptive, it reflects the way the world works in many ways, and it is widely used in law, politics and economics.[25] We might think of prudence as strategic and incrementalism as tactical.

Why is the American policy process recognized to be "incremental by nature"? There are two main reasons. Most important, it is a byproduct of the design of the framers of the state and federal constitutions. The state constitutions, which preceded the federal constitution, separated governmental powers to prevent the undue concentration of power and tyranny. But decentralization also means that government moves more slowly. In addition to separation of powers, there are also checks and balances among the three branches of government. On top of that, the federal constitution established a federal system. The framers designed American government to be "incremental." Second, in the context of any particular policy campaign, with the constraints of time and resources, the amount of change is limited by democratic division and opposition.

> **Prudence supplies the element of moral purpose that "incrementalism" by itself lacks.**

Fences as containment. Most important, fences may embody the moral purpose of *containment*.[26] Harte objects to legislation that, by virtue of majority control over a minority, creates categories that leave some unborn children unprotected by the law. But virtually all line drawing establishes categories, and thus the objection to categories is an objection to all line drawing, and this is ultimately an objection to establishing any fences around the evil. Legislative fences around an evil can only be established by drawing lines, but how the lines are drawn is typically imposed by opposing forces (judicial or political) and rarely by free will.

The important questions are how the fences are established, by whom and

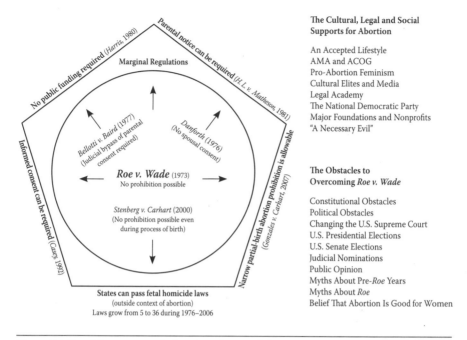

The Cultural, Legal and Social
Supports for Abortion

An Accepted Lifestyle
AMA and ACOG
Pro-Abortion Feminism
Cultural Elites and Media
Legal Academy
The National Democratic Party
Major Foundations and Nonprofits
"A Necessary Evil"

The Obstacles to
Overcoming *Roe v. Wade*

Constitutional Obstacles
Political Obstacles
Changing the U.S. Supreme Court
U.S. Presidential Elections
U.S. Senate Elections
Judicial Nominations
Public Opinion
Myths About Pre-*Roe* Years
Myths About *Roe*
Belief That Abortion Is Good for Women

Figure 5.1. Legal fences around abortion when prohibition is not possible

for what reason. If a legislator votes for a law that regulates abortion, that regulation may restrict the sweep of the abortion license. Various fences around abortion, for example, have been attempted—preventing public funding, parental notice, parental consent, informed consent, clinic regulations, second-physician requirements, postviability regulations and the like.

In all these cases the intent of the thoughtful pro-life legislator, when he or she cannot stop the abortions inside the fence, should be to establish as strong a fence as possible. In effect, the thoughtful legislator is voting for a prohibition—to prohibit abortions outside the fence. The establishment of the fence does not "legitimize" the abortions inside the fence; the Supreme Court did that as a matter of practical politics.

This concept of fences as limits is laid out very well by two members of the U.S. President's Council on Bioethics in a March 2004 report relating to embryo research. They lay out the goal (and principle) of complete protection, cite the (political) obstacles that prevent achieving that goal, and then explain what they are doing and why:

We ourselves are among the members of the Council who favor protecting human life from the very beginning by banning the use of living human embryos
at any stage of development as disposable research material. Until this becomes
politically feasible, we support efforts to accord as much protection as possible
by limiting the number of days beyond which the law tolerates deliberate embryo killing. It is important to understand that the Council's recommendation
here is *not* to authorize embryo-destructive research up to a certain limit. It is
only to prohibit such research beyond a certain limit. Because in the absence of
legislation this research remains unrestricted, a prohibition of embryo-destructive
research beyond a certain limit does not amount to authorizing research up to
that limit.[27]

Some may quibble with the specifics of this statement, but it sets a high standard of public explanation for public officials.

Generally, the specifics of legal fences are not dictated by the natural law for
two primary reasons: the fences are a matter of practical, not speculative, reason, and the location of the fences is not a matter of free choice but is constrained by countervailing forces in the particular circumstances—either judicial imposition or majority rule.

For example, it is arguable that a fence placed at fetal viability is imprudent
because it serves to reinforce the legal (court-imposed) position and the public
view that viability has some intrinsic significance in fetal development. If viability receives any kind of formal or informal support, it might be more difficult to remove it from the law when the Supreme Court's decision in *Roe* is
overturned. A broader application of the same proposition might be that aspects of *Roe* should not be reinforced by legislation now if those aspects might
be more difficult to erase when *Roe* itself is overruled. While the specifics of
those fences are not dictated by the natural law, one fence or another might be
imprudent in the particular circumstances.

Understanding legislative fences. Colin Harte writes from a British rather
than an American perspective, and there is no similar constitutional constraint like *Roe* hovering over British law. (In any case, Harte dismisses the
significance of judicial constraints like *Roe* as irrelevant.) Instead, Harte uses
a 1987 bill by British MP David Alton as his foil to criticize "restrictive laws."
To limit the existing British law broadly legalizing abortion, Alton introduced
a bill with a time limit, prohibiting abortions after a certain time. Then, when

he realized that he could not secure majority support for a prohibition that broad, Alton added a fence (exclusion) that sought to limit abortions based on disability—less restrictive than his original bill but more restrictive than existing law.[28]

In denouncing the 1987 Alton Bill for being "intrinsically unjust," Harte fails to acknowledge that British law allowed abortion for *any fetal imperfection* before the original Alton Bill would have *narrowed* the open-ended policy by prohibiting abortions for *some* disabilities when it could not prohibit *all* abortions for disability. The open-ended abortion policy is still the law today because the original Alton Bill failed.

Harte generally asserts that a law "tolerating" abortion is "intrinsically unjust." But in the case of a fence around abortion, what or who does the "tolerating" and by what means? The Supreme Court required that abortion be "tolerated" in all fifty states by its edict in *Roe*.

For some reason Harte concludes that a bill that "simply repeals an intrinsically unjust Act . . . is not itself intrinsically unjust."[29] He does not say why an amendment that reduced the legality of abortions from twenty-four to sixteen weeks could not be considered to be a repeal of the permission of abortion between twenty-four and sixteen weeks.

For example, assume an amendment intended to put a fence around the abortion license by reducing the time in which abortions could be performed: "In section A of the Abortion Act, the word '24' (weeks) shall be substituted by '16' (weeks)." Harte contends that the justness of the amendment "is determined . . . by considering it with respect to the law it is amending."[30] And he says "the meaning" of the reduction bill "is that it shall not be unlawful for an abortion to be performed if requested by any pregnant woman before the end of the sixteenth week of pregnancy. Insofar as this constitutes the legal toleration of abortion until the end of the sixteenth week of pregnancy, the amendment bill must be judged intrinsically unjust."[31] Who is doing the "tolerating"? Certainly, it is the majority of legislators who support legal abortion up to sixteen weeks.

Harte's criticism of the original Alton bill as "excluding disabled unborn child from legislative proposals" is thus misleading.[32] Given existing British law, the original Alton Bill was realistically an *inclusion*, not an exclusion, because it would have brought more children under the protection of the law than currently existed. Harte implies that existing protection would be undermined by the exclusion when the opposite was true: current policy allowing abortion for *any* imperfection would have been *narrowed* by the Alton's Bill's definition of disability.

Who is responsible for exceptions and exclusions? Critics of fences that restrict but don't completely prohibit an evil often take a snapshot approach. The critics focus exclusively on what's left inside the fence without looking at the whole context, including the original law, how and why the fence got erected, and why the fence was placed where it was.

In the United States, limits or exceptions have been imposed by court edicts or, under the principle of majority rule, by legislative majorities. Either courts require broad exceptions in abortion law or legislative majorities impose them. In a context where the Supreme Court's decision, does not exist, majority rule would establish the fence within which abortions are "tolerated."

Harte disregards the counsel of prudence in several ways. Harte criticizes "exceptions" with particular derision, but he doesn't contend with the reality of the legislative and political process. He doesn't focus on why limits or exceptions in laws occur. It's because courts or legislative majorities *impose* them.

Harte's sweeping proposition that "restrictive legislation will always distort the genuine pro-life view" refuses to consider the context of legislative amendments and voting. He doesn't consider the obvious constraints and the minority's inability to prohibit all abortions. This results in judicial or legislative constraints being dismissed out of his ethical equation.[33]

His insular focus is entirely on the failings of pro-life advocates and largely ignores political, legal and institutional obstacles and how they intervene to obstruct legal or legislative outcomes.[34] He actually blames the legislators in the pro-life minority.[35] Harte broadly criticizes legislatures as a whole for failing to do the right thing without realistically coming to grips with constraints that legislative minorities face in trying to achieve majority support for any legislative proposal.[36] Harte does not evaluate obstacles in his ethical equation; he considers these irrelevant "factors."[37]

Prudence, in contrast, necessarily evaluates both opportunities and obstacles, because it must consider not merely the good in the abstract—prudence is right reason about *what is to be done*—but how much of the good can be accomplished in this world of constraints.

The realities of legislative majorities and minorities. Besides the courts, majority rule is a considerable constraint on political reform and improvements in public policy. Sometimes—as Lincoln acknowledged—it leads to injustice.

Legislative debates and votes may reveal majority and minority blocs that shift depending on the specific proposition, and the outcome may be far from certain or even predictable. This is true not just about abortion but about many legislative issues.

Assume *Roe v. Wade* is overturned and the abortion issue is returned to the state legislatures. Presuming there are 100 legislators, we can expect on the basis of previous votes that certain voting blocs may have formed along the following lines: thirty are pro-abortion, thirty-five are not consistent (will support some restrictions but not others), five are new and unknown, and thirty are predictably pro-life. *This general lineup roughly reflects public opinion in the United States.*[38]

A number of abortion bills would likely be proposed and debated. To make things simple, contrast three bills and how voting blocs might shift.

One bill might seek to retain legalized abortion throughout pregnancy (as currently under *Roe*).[39] Assuming 100 legislators, thirty support; thirty oppose, along with many of the middle forty.

A second bill might, in stark contrast, seek to prohibit abortion entirely. Given previous votes, only thirty votes will support this; seventy oppose a complete prohibition.

The vote of the thirty consistently pro-life is *not needed* to maintain abortion throughout pregnancy; the thirty pro-abortion and some of the middle forty will control. The vote of the thirty consistently pro-life cannot have any effect in preserving or supporting abortion. They are not responsible for what the majority votes for.

In contrast to the "all-or-nothing bills," a third "compromise" bill could also be expected, that might, just for example, authorize abortion up to sixteen weeks, a reduction from the time allowed by the current law. This limitation is supported by the thirty who are predictably pro-life, along with fifteen of the forty in the middle. It is opposed by thirty who are pro-abortion and ten of the forty in the middle. If the thirty consistently pro-life who lost on the first bill abstain, there are seventy legislators left to vote on the second bill. The thirty pro-abortion will support this, along with many of the forty in the middle.

How should the pro-life legislators vote on the sixteen-week bill? The votes of the thirty consistently pro-life are irrelevant to keep abortion legal up to sixteen weeks. Their abstention would do little or nothing to stop the compromise bill from passing; in fact, it would serve mostly to strengthen the majority.

It's neither the intent nor the effect of the thirty anti-abortion legislators to vote *for* abortion up to sixteen weeks. This is made clear by looking at the shifting makeup of majorities that will vote to reduce the time to sixteen weeks compared with the majority that will vote to keep abortion legal up to sixteen weeks. Second, the current law (allowing abortion throughout pregnancy) will continue unless pro-life legislators vote for the reduction. Third, the makeup of the legislature is such that a majority can not be secured that will prohibit abortion entirely. Instead, their objective is to vote for the reduction to sixteen weeks, which could be seen as a prohibition of abortion after sixteen weeks.

Minority blocs are not responsible for what the majority do, but the minority bloc may be able to attract "middle of the road" legislators to prevent (in their view) the worst possible outcome. It may look from the outside as though some compromise has been struck, when the reality is that shifting votes in the middle finally joined with the minority bloc to form a majority on some proposition.

Harte errs by arguing that the justness of a vote for the amendment depends on the law that remains at the end of the day (that allows abortion up to sixteen weeks), despite the fact that the anti-abortion legislators did not vote to allow abortion up to sixteen weeks and did not have the votes (power) to reduce abortion below sixteen weeks.[40]

The law that remains is not the responsibility of the minority of anti-abortion legislators that couldn't change it; it is the responsibility of the majority that voted to preserve abortion. Harte never explains how a legislative minority is responsible for the laws that result from the votes of the opposing majority. This is contrary to democratic theory and government as it has been practiced over the past four hundred years. Not surprisingly, Harte cites no legal or philosophic support for such a proposition. The justness of the fence is not determined by what remains inside that cannot be further limited. Understanding these obstacles and the intent of legislative fences is essential to accurately assessing the intent and ethics of "imperfect legislation."

LAWS THAT AUTHORIZE OR PERMIT A SOCIAL EVIL

Thomas Aquinas observed, "Human law is said to permit certain things, not as approving of them, but as being unable to direct them. And many things are directed by the Divine law, which human law is unable to direct, because more things are subject to a higher than to a lower cause. Hence the very fact that human law does not meddle with matters it cannot direct, comes under the ordination of the eternal law. It would be different, were human law to sanction what the eternal law condemns."[41] Note the distinction between *permit* and *approve.*

Harte defines various legislative categories—bills that obligate, permit, tolerate and prohibit abortion. His central proposition is that laws that obligate, permit or tolerate abortion are all intrinsically unjust.[42] Harte argues that laws that permit abortion are "intrinsically unjust laws" as the latter term is used in §22 of the 1974 *Declaration on Procured Abortion* from the Catholic Church's Congregation for the Doctrine of the Faith and repeated in *Evangelium vitae* §73.

Harte's argument boils down to an interpretation of *permit* and *intrinsically unjust* as those terms are used in Catholic Church documents. Although the Church teaches that laws that "legitimize" or "authorize" abortion are unjust, there is no authoritative Church teaching that laws (or bills) that prohibit some but not all abortions fall within the definition of laws that "permit" abortion or that are "intrinsically unjust." Harte's argument is not based on any explicit passage in Aquinas or in Catholic teaching addressing legislation that partially prohibits a social evil, but instead on his own strained extrapolations of certain general passages.

Harte's attempt to equate *permit* and *authorize* is confusing and contradictory. Harte sometimes uses the term *permit* as meaning "obligate." For example: "A law tolerating some moral evil does not violate God's law, but a law permitting or obligating that evil does do so; it contradicts God's law and, in failing to give what is due to God, can be judged to be intrinsically unjust."[43]

Harte uses the term *permit* so broadly that it loses precise meaning. He writes that the Supreme Court "permitted" abortion by "ruling that women have a 'right' to abortion," and a "more restrictive law" that replaces a "more permissive law" also "permits" abortion if it leaves an abortion unprohibited, and a law that "specifically authorizes abortion" also "permits" abortion.[44] "A 'permissive' abortion law (or, equivalently, a law 'permitting' abortion) refers to the character of the law rather than to the scale of abortion which the law allows."[45] Harte distinguishes a law which "permits" abortion and one which "tolerates" abortion, but then says that "in terms of their practical effect, laws 'tolerating' and 'permitting' abortion may be indistinguishable."[46] Elsewhere, he says that "the four functions of law—obligating, permitting, tolerating, and prohibiting—are mutually exclusive."[47]

This confused discussion of *permit* and *tolerate* is all the more remarkable because Harte puts little significance on Aquinas's emphasis on what *permit* means in *Summa Theologica*. Aquinas says: "Human law is said to permit certain things, not as approving them, but as being unable to direct them" (I-II. Q93. A3).

Following this confusion, Harte claims that "human law cannot permit abortion," and he imports this conclusion into the general rule against "intrinsically unjust" laws.[48]

The important question is whether there are any papal or other Catholic Church teaching that would indicate that a law that "permits" abortion would be among those called "intrinsically unjust" (and, if so, how does the Church define *permit?*). In fact, Catholic Church teaching uses the narrower terms *authorize* or *legitimize* rather than the broader term *permit*.[49]

Instead of limiting the meaning of *permit* to "authorize" (as *Evangelium vitae* uses the term), Harte expands *permit* to mean any bill that, due to countervailing majority will, leaves some abortions unprohibited. Thus he sweeps into the meaning of *permit* laws that Aquinas never meant to include and bills that are specifically allowed by Pope John Paul II in *Evangelium vitae* §73. Harte can never show that a law which attempts to limit an evil is a law that "authorizes" abortion contrary to Aquinas or Catholic Church teaching. In Catholic Church documents, "permit" *never means a law that attempts to limit a social evil but cannot prohibit it entirely due to countervailing political or legal forces.*

Aquinas and natural law. "The law which is framed for the government of states, allows and leaves unpunished many things that are punished by Divine providence. Nor, if this law does not attempt to do everything, is this a reason why it should be blamed for what it does."[50]

There are numerous reasons to think that Aquinas did not believe that natural law dictated the details of attempts to legislatively limit unjust laws and conditions. Such attempts, in Aquinas's reasoning, are instead guided by prudence.

First, legislative details are a matter of practical, not speculative, reason. Thomistic scholar Paul Sigmund, for example, recognizes that "the process of derivation is not a strictly logical or deductive one but involves the use of *synderesis* [conscience] or direct moral intuition to arrive at basic principles and the exercise of practical reason to apply those principles to varying and contingent circumstances."[51]

Second, Aquinas in "On Kingship" counseled in favor of tolerating an unjust form of government in order to avoid a worse form.[52] If he counseled tolerating an unjust form of government, his prudential realism would likewise tolerate a legislative fence that restricted an evil that could not be completely abolished.

Third, Aquinas expressly distinguishes between laws that "permit" and those which "approve" an action: "Human law is said to permit certain things, not as approving them, but as being unable to direct them."[53]

Fourth, there is Aquinas's prudential realization about the limits of the practical enforcement of law in his "Treatise on Law":

> Now human law is framed for a number of human beings, the majority of whom are not perfect in virtue. Wherefore human laws do not forbid all vices, from which the virtuous abstain, but only the more grievous vices, *from which it is possible for the majority to abstain;* and chiefly those which are to the hurt of others, without the prohibition of which human society could not be maintained: thus human law prohibits murder, theft, and suchlike.[54]

While this passage can certainly be unjustly expanded or taken out of context, its most narrow meaning would encompass attempts to limit unjust laws or conditions that the *legislative majority will not completely prohibit.*[55]

Jacques Maritain, a leading Thomistic philosopher of the twentieth century, points to this passage in *Man and the State*, in his recognition that

> legislation could and should permit or give allowance to certain ways of conduct which depart in some measure from Natural Law, if the prohibition by civil law of these ways of conduct were to impair the common good . . . or because it would result in a worse conduct, disturbing or disintegrating the so-

cial body, for a great many people whose moral strength is not on a level with the enforcement of this prohibition.[56]

For example, the failure of the original Alton Bill in Great Britain in 1987, which attempted to tighten the existing abortion license and reduce the permissible conditions for abortions for fetal anomalies, left in place a law permitting abortion for any fetal imperfection that might have been limited by Alton's.

Aquinas's political writings exhibit a strong sense of realism and an aim for the best possible, not the perfect. Aquinas's political writings do not cite the "Treatise on Law" as the exclusive standard by which political action must be judged. For example, in "On Princely Government" *(De Regimine Principum)*, Aquinas writes: "If the tyranny be not excessive it is certainly wiser to tolerate it in limited measure, as least for a time, rather than to run the risk of even greater perils by opposing it." The duty of kings is not to achieve perfect justice for every single citizen but to "strive with all care to avoid tyranny" (chap. 10) and to "foster the common good with all care."[57]

Finally, there are additional passages from Thomas which suggest that the details of human law are not dictated by the natural law: "Nor, if this law does not attempt to do everything, is this a reason why it should be blamed for what it does. Wherefore, too, human law does not prohibit everything that is forbidden by the natural law."[58] Aquinas simply never suggests that the natural law dictates the specifics of attempts to place legal fences around an unjust law or condition.

A careful reading of Catholic Church teaching. Only two Catholic Church documents bear on the issue of "imperfect legislation" as the Congregation for the Doctrine of the Faith uses the term: the 1974 *Declaration*, and John Paul II's 1995 encyclical *Evangelium vitae*.[59] Neither teaches that legislative fences that attempt to limit a social evil (but due to majority rule or other legal or political impediments cannot completely prohibit the evil) are "intrinsically unjust."

The CDF's 1974 *Declaration on Procured Abortion* §22 provides in pertinent part:

> It must in any case be clearly understood that whatever may be laid down by civil law in this matter, man can never obey a law which is *in itself immoral*, and such is the case of a law which would *admit in principle the liceity of abortion*.

Nor can he take part in a propaganda campaign in favor of such a law, or vote for it. Moreover, he may not collaborate in its application. (emphasis added)

The phrase *in itself immoral* is the basis for the phrase *intrinsically unjust.*[60] Note that §22 does not use the broad term *permit*, but refers more narrowly to a law that "would admit in principle the liceity of abortion."

Only one section in *Evangelium vitae* directly addresses "imperfect legislation" or partial prohibitions, §73. Section 73 was not drafted in a vacuum. It was drafted against the background of one thousand years of classical political prudence in the Church's teaching.[61]

Harte rejects the widespread understanding that §73 of *Evangelium vitae* allows legislators to vote for what Harte defines as "restrictive abortion legislation."[62] Paragraph 3 of §73 provides:

A particular problem of conscience can arise in cases where a legislative vote would be decisive for *the passage of a more restrictive law, aimed at limiting the number of authorized abortions, in place of a more permissive law already passed or ready to be voted on.* Such cases are not infrequent. It is a fact that while in some parts of the world there continue to be campaigns to introduce laws favouring abortion, often supported by powerful international organizations, in other nations—particularly those which have already experienced the bitter fruits of such permissive legislation—there are growing signs of a rethinking in this matter. *In a case like the one just mentioned,* when it is not possible to overturn or completely abrogate a pro-abortion law, an elected official, whose absolute personal opposition to procured abortion was well known, could licitly support proposals aimed at *limiting the harm* done by such a law and at lessening its negative consequences at the level of general opinion and public morality. This does not in fact represent an illicit cooperation with an unjust law, but rather a legitimate and proper attempt to limit its evil aspects. (emphasis added)

The initial highlighted portion is the key passage, which describes the type of law that legislators can legitimately vote for. Note that John Paul II does not use the terms *permit* or *tolerate* in 73.3, though he does contrast "a more restrictive law" with "a more permissive law."

There are four key parts in §73.

1. It identifies the intent of the bill as limitation: *"aimed at limiting the number of authorized abortions"* (my emphasis). So, the bill is not a simple regu-

lation but touches on those abortions that are "authorized."

2. By referring to "limiting the number of authorized abortions," the bill must partially prohibit what is authorized.

3. Note that the passage also recognizes a difference in degree—"more restrictive" versus "more permissive"—rather than black or white, all or nothing. And the more restrictive bill must be aimed at replacing a more permissive law. The term *aimed* is repeated. This is very different from the type of law (condemned in the 1974 *Declaration*) that authorizes a right to abortion or "admits in principle the liceity of abortion."

4. Section 73.3 necessarily means that the "more restrictive" law that results will leave some number of "authorized abortions" unprohibited. If the "more restrictive law" that results leaves some abortions in existence, it does not necessarily admit the rightness of abortion in principle. This implication is completely at odds with Harte's position that "a law permitting or tolerating even one abortion violates the natural right to life and is outside the competence of legislators."[63]

Finally, note that John Paul refers to a "problem of conscience." If §73 is only referring to a complete prohibition (as Harte implies) and not a partial prohibition (as a straightforward reading indicates), why does any "problem of conscience" exist for the legislator? Harte's narrow explanation of §73 doesn't take account of John Paul's mention of conscience. No "particular problem of conscience" could arise if the bill involved a complete prohibition. The problem of conscience only arises if the legislator considers "the passage of a more restrictive law, aimed at limiting the number of authorized abortions"—in other words, *a partial prohibition.* Why does the pope mention a problem of conscience if the only type of bill he is referring to is one that completely prohibits? He must have in mind a law that incompletely or partially prohibits, as the text confirms.

Instead of this kind of careful analysis of the specific language of 73.3, Harte quotes different (more general) passages of *Evangelium vitae*, like §§71, 72 or 101, to attempt to limit what the pope plainly wrote in 73. For example, Harte reads his own category of "restrictive abortion legislation" into §71 to limit the meaning of 73.3.

The real purpose of civil law is to guarantee an ordered social coexistence in true justice, so that all may "lead a quiet and peaceable life, godly and respectful in every way" (1 Tim. 2:2). Precisely for this reason, civil law must ensure that all members of society enjoy respect for certain fundamental rights which innately belong to the person, rights which every positive law must recognize and guarantee. First and fundamental among these is the inviolable right to life of every innocent human being. While public authority can sometimes choose not to put a stop to something which—were it prohibited—would cause more serious harm, it can never presume to *legitimize as a right of individuals* . . . an offence against other persons caused by the disregard of so fundamental a right as the right to life. (*Evangelium vitae* 71, emphasis added)

The highlighted language merely repeats the thrust of the CDF's 1974 *Declaration*, the key language being "legitimize as a right."

Section 71 is not referring to attempts to erect a fence around a social evil (by prohibiting a certain number, type or class of abortions) or to the more narrow provision that John Paul addresses in §73, which refers to *"the passage of a more restrictive law aimed at limiting the number of authorized abortions in place of a more permissive law already passed or ready to be voted on"* (emphasis added). This is the key description of the type of bill that legislators can legitimately vote for. Harte errs by reading into §71 his category: "a law permitting or tolerating even one abortion violates the natural right to life and is outside the competence of legislators."

Harte simply rejects, as illegitimate, what the pope quite clearly does in 73.3, comparing a "more restrictive law" with a "more permissive law," and contends that the only question is whether the "more restrictive law" is "in accordance with the moral law, with right reason." Harte simply rejects, per se, the legitimacy of the comparison that the pope makes. Instead, Harte takes very general statements by John Paul and asserts that they preclude partial prohibitions of any kind ("Nor can there be true peace unless life is defended and promoted" [*Evangelium vitae* §101]). John Paul never applies this very general proposition—coming in the conclusion, after the specific conditions of §73—to conclude that every bill must completely protect every human life. Harte simply asserts that the general principle of "solidarity" precludes laws that do not completely prohibit abortion.[64]

"Intrinsically Unjust" Laws

Is there any authoritative Catholic teaching that more restrictive abortion laws, which attempt to replace a more permissive law, are considered as "permitting" abortion or considered "intrinsically unjust"? The answer is no. And here's where Harte's argument falls apart and reveals itself to be an argument about what Harte *wishes* Catholic Church teaching to be.

Harte engages in an extended analysis of Aquinas to attempt to show that "restrictive abortion legislation" is unjust, but he does no more than establish that laws which "authorize" abortion in principle are unjust, something clearly taught by the 1974 *Declaration* and by *Evangelium vitae*.

But Harte argues that there is a distinction between two types of unjustness in Q95 of Aquinas's "Treatise on Law." Harte associates the term *ius civile* with nonmoral political issues on which "compromise" is legitimate, and he associates the term *ius gentium* with moral issues, including abortion.[65] Harte argues that the *ius gentium* (including laws against murder) are specifically dictated or established by the natural law (and not subject to prudential judgment), while the *ius civile* would not be so dictated by reason (and subject to prudential judgment).[66]

This is a doubtful reading of Aquinas and certainly one that the Church has neither adopted nor applied specifically to "imperfect legislation." The context of Aquinas's statement in Q95.A2 regards the specific injunction against personally killing someone (the injunction against killing is derived from the natural law). It does not address the legislator's attempt to establish a just law or attempt to narrow an unjust law. And this certainly has never been applied by the Catholic Church to find that laws which attempt to limit a social evil are intrinsically unjust if they do not completely prohibit the evil. Aquinas acknowledges the judgment of prudence in practically applying the natural law.[67]

What Are Legislators Trying to Do?

Conscientious legislators have a difficult job, especially on the issue of abortion. On one hand, even the most marginal regulation is rhetorically condemned by abortion advocates as just another attempt to "ban all abortions" and "send women to jail." On the other hand, others criticize legislators as horribly unjust for attempting anything other than a complete prohibition on abortion and second-guess their every motive.

How should legislative intent be understood? A third Church document that Harte uses is Pope John Paul II's 1993 encyclical, *Veritatis splendor (The Splendor of Truth)*. John Paul nowhere addresses the subject of "imperfect legislation" in *Veritatis splendor*. Instead, Harte relies on one part of §78, in which John Paul critiques three ethical systems, including proportionalism and consequentialism, which disproportionately emphasize the results (compared to the intent and object of an act) in determining the morality of an act (§§71-75). John Paul emphasizes the importance of the object of the moral act. Harte uses this to analyze a legislator's *real* intent.[68]

Based on his novel interpretation of §78 (which doesn't even address imperfect legislation), Harte claims that legislators who are voting to limit abortion by prohibiting some abortions (and thereby erecting a fence around the abortion license) cannot be judged by their specific intent. This, in his view, is "an unsound theory of legislative voting." Instead, they must be judged by the justness of the norm being enacted—the law that stands at the end of the day.[69] In other words, despite their expressed will and intent that they are voting for the prohibitive part of the law (the fence), Harte contends that they are also responsible for whatever remains inside the fence.

This is contrary to fundamental understandings of human agency, democratic government and majority rule. A legislator's vote for a prohibition that limits the scope of the pro-abortion law would seem—to most people—to be an objection to (not acceptance of) the pro-abortion law, especially when any part of the pro-abortion law is retained by an overwhelming majority that is beyond the legislator's control. Not surprisingly, Harte's novel extrapolation of §78 is refuted by the renowned ethicist William E. May.[70]

The importance of the context of moral actions. Ethical realism requires that we take into consideration, and not ignore, countervailing constraints on human action. For example, if you saw a snapshot of a man firing a gun, you could not determine whether it was a just or unjust act unless you saw what he was firing at (his object) and why. The morality of human acts are inevitably viewed in context. What is the current law? Who caused it? And why? A consistent failing of perfectionists is a failure to understand or consider context, especially current obstacles.[71]

For example, the *Catechism of the Catholic Church* provides:

The morality of human acts depends on: the object chosen, the end in view or the intention, the circumstances of the action. The object, the intention, and the circumstances make up the "sources," or constitutive elements, of the morality of human acts.[72]

A morally good act requires the goodness of the object, of the end, and of the circumstances together.[73]

It is therefore an error to judge the morality of human acts by considering only the intention that inspires them or the circumstances (environment, social pressure, duress or emergency, etc.) which supply their context. There are acts which, in and of themselves, independently of circumstances and intentions, are always gravely illicit by reason of their object; such as blasphemy and perjury, murder and adultery. One may not do evil so that good may result from it.[74]

Harte diminishes, if not rejects, the moral relevance of context and thus the moral relevance of countervailing political power and other obstacles. Harte's position is that "any legislative proposal—even if regarded as 'restrictive' in comparison to an existing law or a law that may otherwise be enacted—that tolerates, permits, or obligates even one direct abortion . . . is always arbitrary and unjust."[75] Harte writes:

The touchstone to which legislators must appeal when judging the justness of a law is the natural law that prohibits all abortions; a law cannot be judged just by considering the context, i.e., whether the previous law permitted or tolerated more abortions, or whether a different law permitting or tolerating more abortions might be enacted if the one subject to a vote is not passed.[76]

This assertion could not be more clearly in conflict with the comparison John Paul makes in *Evangelium vitae* §73 between a "more restrictive" and a "more permissive" law.

Preventing Scandal

One concern of moral theology is public officials and scandal. Scandal is leading someone into sin through one's own actions.[77] Scandal might occur when public officials act corruptly or when they act justly but their actions are misunderstood.

The concept of scandal should not be extrapolated, however, to require public officials to ensure that no misunderstanding results. That is humanly impossible—for church leaders or public officials—in a world of constraints.

The principle must accord reasonable responsibility to citizens for undertaking due diligence to inquire into the facts about the actions of public officials. Scandal is not simply misunderstanding or confusion; the act *must lead someone into sin.*

It is often claimed that legislation partially prohibiting abortion will lead to scandal on the theory that partial prohibitions necessarily imply that "some abortion is okay." For the reasons already laid out, that is a superficial misunderstanding of the legislative process. Is the public more likely to know the "real" intentions of legislators if they adopt an all-or-nothing approach than if they try to erect a fence against as many abortions as possible? This is a prudential question. It will depend on the circumstances and on the skill of legislators in articulating their position and the conscientiousness of citizens in finding out the facts. For example, there was no doubt that the late Congressman Henry Hyde was against abortion, even though he had to accept exceptions for rape and incest in federal funding due to political majorities in the 1990s. His views were clear to all. But, as Aquinas pointed out, "The certitude of prudence cannot be so great as to remove all anxiety."[78]

The broad notion of scandal has implications for legislators on the range of bioethical issues. How do they prudently *limit* an ongoing industry or area of research that is involved in unethical practices that violate human life or dignity?

The openness of the democratic process, combined with media coverage by a free press, minimizes the possibility that the vote of the minority will be misunderstood or that scandal could legitimately be charged. First, the pro-abortion advocates will likely charge (broadcast by the media) that "the real goal" of the anti-abortion legislators is to "ban all abortions." Second, the legislature records all the votes, as a matter of public record (sometimes published in the newspaper). Third, the minority have the capacity to explain, *before* the vote, their principled goals and how or why they were prevented from achieving those principles by the countervailing majority. Fourth, the minority legislators have the capacity through various channels to explain to the public, *after* the vote, what their intent was, why the majority and minority voted as they did, and what they achieved or failed to achieve. Responsible citizens in a democracy with a free press can inquire and find out.

Citizens should responsibly inquire by asking the following questions:

What was the goal of the various bills before the legislature? What was politically possible given the current makeup of the legislature? Were the amendments (limits) proposed by the minority reasonably expected to be effective in achieving their goals? Did the limits (fences) proposed in the bills (or amendments) preclude future improvements (future attempts to prohibit abortion or reduce abortions further)? What other alternatives were considered and could they have succeeded? If the limits proposed in the bills are successful, what next steps do they lead to or prevent? Such responsible inquiry by citizens, instead of undue reliance on certain media reports, could effectively eliminate the risk of scandal.

IS IMPERFECT ABORTION LEGISLATION COUNTERPRODUCTIVE?

Harte applies two general concepts, solidarity and the common good—which have never been applied in papal documents in the context of "imperfect legislation"—to argue that legislation that leaves any abortion unprohibited is "intrinsically unjust."[79]

Since neither Aquinas nor John Paul II applies these general concepts to "imperfect legislation," it would be useful to reflect on whether these general injunctions are more effectively realized through an all-or-nothing approach like Harte's or by seeking the greatest good possible in the particular circumstance.

The assertion that the common good requires the perfect legal protection of every human being is arguably contrary to Aquinas's understanding of the common good. Aquinas says that "the good of the community is greater and more divine than the good of the individual."[80]

In fact, *seeking the good has to take into consideration what is effective in securing any good.*[81] As James Madison reflected in *Federalist* 41, "the choice must always be made, if not of the lesser evil, at least of the greater, not the perfect, good." It is therefore relevant to examine what "imperfect legislation" has accomplished in the United States since *Roe.*

The Supreme Court in *Roe v. Wade* struck down the abortion laws of all fifty states and the District of Columbia, and replaced those laws with a uniform law of virtual abortion on demand, and put the onus on the states, if they chose, to limit abortion on demand with new legislation. If the states did nothing, an unregulated, virtually unlimited abortion right for any woman of any age would be the law in that state. Some states have done virtually nothing, and that unlimited right remains the law thirty-plus years after *Roe*.

Roe caused a great deal of legal uncertainty because the guidelines in it were vague and uncertain, and it was unclear how the courts would receive new state legislation. The only way to find out in the American legal system was by passing new legislation based on the best judgment as to what the courts would allow. (The courts don't issue advisory opinions.)

Any new regulations passed after *Roe* were legislated against the backdrop of what *Roe* said, and with the knowledge that the federal courts would strictly scrutinize what the states did. In a sense, any new state laws were attempts to amend and limit the impact of *Roe* in each state. Every new state law was (and is) subject to at least the possibility of federal court scrutiny (and possibly state court scrutiny), injunction, invalidation and the imposition of fines against the state for passing the invalidated laws.[82]

What were the possible moral responses to *Roe*? Prudence asks us to consider a series of questions: what is the real situation, what is the goal (the good one is trying to achieve), what is reasonably achievable, what is the likelihood of success, how can the obstacles to success be overcome, and does the short-term objective prevent improvement when changed circumstances might allow improvement?

There were several options—legal, political, cultural, educational—for state officials, state legislators and Americans who opposed *Roe* and abortion, and virtually all have been attempted.

1. Under the U.S. Constitution, there are only two ways of overturning a Supreme Court decision: by the Court overturning itself or through a constitutional amendment, which must be approved by both houses of Congress by a two-thirds vote and approved by three-fourths of the states. Both were attempted in the immediate aftermath of *Roe:* Rhode Island tried to pass new legislation to ask the Court to overturn its decision. And a constitutional amendment was attempted in Congress, but it failed repeatedly over the next ten years, and the effort finally came to an end in June 1983, when the Senate voted against the Hatch-Eagleton Amendment 49-50.

2. Congress could attempt to pass federal legislation. This was attempted but was also subject to federal court scrutiny and possible invalidation.

3. States could attempt to enact regulations on abortion.

4. Pro-life Americans could ignore the federal and state legislation process and utilize other means to educate and "change hearts and minds."

Because *Roe* and the abortion policy it established had legal, political and social implications, a legal, political, social and cultural strategy was needed to respond to all aspects of *Roe*. Education alone might be geared to changing hearts and minds, an important objective, but would be too limited in its ability to reduce or stop abortion.

Perfectionist alternatives to state regulations. It's important to examine the implications of two alternative responses that some perfectionists have pursued: the direct challenge along the lines of Rhode Island and "opting out" of state legislation altogether.

Rhode Island tried a direct challenge in 1973-1974; it was rejected by the federal courts, and the Supreme Court refused to hear the case. That set a precedent, and any future attempt to do a similar direct challenge would be treated the same way; a prohibition bill would undoubtedly be struck down, would not even provoke review by the Supreme Court and would result in fines against the state (paid by taxes). That doomed the prospects of such direct challenges; future ones would be treated similarly, and fines (attorneys' fees) would be assessed against the states in favor of the attorneys for the abortion clinics. That meant that legislators would not support prohibitions that had no chance of success. The direct challenge, as a legal or political option, quickly crashed into a brick wall.

One alternative is to opt out of state legislation, to do nothing in the legislature. Opting out of state legislation has significant legal and political implications. The legal implications would include no future abortion cases in the courts, because legislation instigates and defines the litigation (court cases). An opt-out strategy would also effectively shut down political action on abortion, because political action depends on legislative agendas and votes. Citizens vote for candidates because they promise to pursue a certain agenda and support certain policies. Because of *Roe*, abortion prohibitions were swept off the legislative agenda. Since legislatures couldn't pass such prohibitions, candidates couldn't run on an agenda to pass such legislation, and therefore it couldn't be an election issue. Elections are fought over what can be done, what is possible, what legislators voted for and against.

In contrast, consider the impact of an opt-out legislative strategy over thirty years—an all-or-nothing strategy. Without abortion-restrictive bills, no issue of abortion arises in the legislature. With no bill there's no debate and no vote. With no vote there's no abortion record for legislators. With no abortion record there's no election issue; candidates have no record because they had no votes. As time passes, new legislators are elected, but they never have a record on the abortion issue. Abortion as a legislative issue becomes a thing of the past, like voting for "internal improvements" of the nineteenth century to fund postroads and turnpikes. Abortion continues as a cultural issue and it affects individual lives, but it plays no part in legislatures or elections. This is largely what has happened in Great Britain in the aftermath of the Alton Bill.

WHAT "IMPERFECT LEGISLATION" HAS ACHIEVED
OVER THE PAST THIRTY-PLUS YEARS

What *is* possible are certain fences around *Roe*—including parental notice, parental consent, clinic regulations, informed consent legislation, a prohibition on certain types of procedures. What is possible makes up the next election campaign.

Because what is possible is enacted against the backdrop of *Roe*, it is understood by virtually all legislators and lobbyists that these regulations are intended to limit the abortion right because prohibitions are not possible. A regulation is introduced in a legislature because a prohibition is not possible; a partial prohibition may be introduced because a total prohibition is not possible. This might be called an *all-or-something strategy.*

While the first aim of the regulations (the fence) may be to limit *Roe* (the abortion right), there are additional legal and political benefits from attempting to partially prohibit or regulate the social evil.

A second benefit is that regulations make it possible to demonstrate what *Roe* means, the breadth of the abortion right. When the courts, especially the Supreme Court, strike down regulations, it shows the breadth of the abortion right (of *Roe*). What does *Roe* mean? It means what the Supreme Court allows or invalidates. It was apparent in January 1973 that abortion prohibitions in the first trimester were not possible. But the abortion right expanded when the Court bulldozed many of the fences that the states tried to erect. *Roe* came to mean abortion on demand as those cases were decided in the 1970s and 1980s. And with the Supreme Court's *Stenberg* decision in 2000, *Roe* came to mean even partial-birth abortion.

Third, legislative battles, and the court cases that result, are also effective means of national education. If citizens want to educate the public about what *Roe* means, a decision by the Supreme Court (provoking media coverage) educates the public. Likewise, a congressional bill, by attracting national media, goes much further than a state bill in fostering national education. A bill prohibiting partial-birth abortion provokes national education as to what abortion is and what *Roe* means (what the Supreme Court allows). When the Nebraska prohibition on partial-birth abortion (and similar laws in twenty-nine other states) was struck down by the Supreme Court in 2000, one result was public education that *Roe* allows partial-birth abortion, by virtue of Supreme Court order.

Fourth, abortion is still the subject of presidential elections, Supreme Court nominations, and state and federal elections *precisely because* it has been made a legislative (and thus a political) issue. If the legislative and political arenas had been abandoned because total prohibitions were considered "the only moral option," abortion opponents would be relegated to picketing on sidewalk corners. Abortion opposition would be marginalized, and by being marginalized abortion would be much more accepted as a casual and common "right." This merely means that picketing and protest is a limited domain, and that an effective strategy against *Roe* has required engaging the issue across the board, in all available legal, legislative, political, cultural and educational arenas.

Fifth, in a democratic society, it's important to have the sanction of law (approved by public opinion and the system of representative government) behind any moral proposition. It's one thing to *protest* that the unborn child is a human being; it's fundamentally different to be able to *show* that the unborn child is legally protected as a human being in the fetal homicide laws of thirty-six states.[83]

This incidentally may well be one of the reasons why the pro-life movement in Great Britain lacks vitality and why pro-life organizations in other countries envy the intensity of the pro-life movement in the United States. Parliament hasn't really considered an anti-abortion bill in years, maybe decades. In contrast, abortion is a legislative and political issue in the United States because state and federal legislation make it a legislative and political issue. And it is made a legislative and election issue because active citizens demand that it be an issue.

Many legislators would much prefer an all-or-nothing strategy because, since abortion prohibitions are swept off the agenda by the Supreme Court, an all-or-nothing strategy effectively means a "nothing" strategy (in the political and legislative arena), and some legislators would much prefer not to face and debate the abortion issue.

A strategy of rejecting "imperfect legislation" and working only for a perfect prohibition would have quickly meant the end of the abortion debate in legislation and politics. Legislators are elected to get things done, and they are elected because of their position on a range of political, social and economic issues, not just one. Nearly everyone wants their elected representatives to have a stated position on a range of issues. Political campaigns require the identification of differences between candidates and education about those differences. (This is also the essential reason why political campaigns cost so much; educating the public and getting name recognition requires media broadcast time.) A legislator who concentrated on only one issue could never become a candidate. Likewise, if obstacles beyond their control frustrate their ability to achieve success on one issue, legislators are quickly drawn to another issue for which they can make progress toward success.

One example of the impact of an opt-out strategy is seen in the growth of in vitro fertilization (IVF) over the past quarter century, to the point where prohibition in 2009 is unimaginable in any of the fifty states. The example of IVF sheds light on future technologies that might be limited but not prohibited before they become burgeoning industries.

This backdrop has to be understood in order to assess the charge that "imperfect legislation" is a compromise or counterproductive. Some charge that "pro-life rhetoric is drowned out by the legislator's action in voting" for an imperfect bill. The irony is that without the bill, there is no rhetoric at all. The bill—the attempted prohibition or regulation—provides the opportunity for any rhetoric, the opportunity to make abortion an issue in the legislature and in politics—the opportunity for debate. A legislator who introduces a total prohibition will spark no debate and will never get a committee hearing or a legislative vote.[84]

A similar charge is that legislators and activists who support imperfect legislation are compromisers. A compromise is a voluntary giving up of something by parties with equivalent power in order to reach an agreement. Is that what legislators are doing in the face of the Supreme Court's (and the federal courts') power? In light of the impact of *Roe*, a decision to attempt to erect fences around abortion through partial prohibitions or regulations is anything but a compromise.

Sixth, regulatory fences have significantly reduced the number of abortions. Since the states started to put fences around the abortion right, many states have prohibited most public funding, or passed parental notice or consent legislation, fetal homicide legislation, and abortion clinic regulations. And these have significantly reduced abortions since the high point of 1.6 million annually in the 1990s. Research published by The Heritage Foundation provides specific empirical evidence that the drop of 17 to 19 percent in abortions during the 1990s was largely attributable to state legislation establishing fences around *Roe*.[85]

Seventh, the extent and range of regulatory fences that have been enacted demonstrate compelling public opposition to abortion on demand and, by implication, to the Supreme Court's decision. This is an important statement to the nation and the Supreme Court.

Finally, a broader legal foundation for protecting human life has been put in place than existed when *Roe* was decided in 1973, more studies have been published highlighting the negative impact of abortion on women, and public skepticism about the value of abortion has grown.

Despite being constantly and pervasively limited by intense judicial roadblocks, "imperfect legislation" has obtained significant achievements over the past thirty-plus years. Within the very real and harsh (and unconstitutional) constraints imposed by the Supreme Court, pro-life laws have protected important principles (to the extent possible), reduced abortions, kept the issue alive in the states, kept pro-life Americans energized and mobilized in the political and legislative arenas, recorded real votes of legislators on real bills, and demonstrated that the Court has made a mess of the issue (to say the least).

All of this effort, however, is not enough. What more needs to be done?

Roe has to be overturned in one way or another. And, given the position of

Justices Scalia and Thomas, not one justice supports a personhood ruling, while at least two (and maybe more) support overturning *Roe* and returning the issue to the states. Opposition to abortion needs to continue in all sectors of society and through the legal and political system. There is a continuing need to build the legislative foundation in the states, highlight the negative impact of abortion on women in public education, work with researchers to highlight the growing data on the impact, and continue to aggressively litigate abortion cases in the courts, especially (with the new majority) at the Supreme Court. In addition, it is important to highlight, through scholarship, public education and litigation, the mess the Court has made of the abortion issue. New state legislation needs to be solidly backed up by medical data and then needs to highlight the negative effect of abortion on women. Public policy and direct services to women considering abortion are crucial elements in a comprehensive cultural, educational, political and legal strategy.

CONCLUSION

Colin Harte's *Changing Unjust Laws Justly* is a heartfelt attempt to describe a perfectly just public policy, but theory and good intentions are insufficient to be prudent or effective in overcoming unjust laws or conditions. Harte's broad objection to the morality of "imperfect legislation" starts from a very specific (and historically based) point of departure: an emotional objection to any exception that would exclude unborn children with disabilities. Unfortunately, Harte's emotional response to the injustice of such discrimination wrongly leads him to the imprudent rejection of the morality of legal fences as a whole.

In addition to misunderstanding Thomas Aquinas on natural law, Harte makes the mistake, to use Marc Guerra's words, of presuming "that St. Thomas's teaching on natural law constitutes the sum total of his reflections on social and political matters."[86] As Guerra emphasizes:

> St. Thomas did not harbor any utopian expectations about political life. . . .
> St. Thomas realized that no political regime satisfies the strict requirements of justice and that participation in political life always entails the recognition of some form of moral imperfection. Contrary to popular misconception, St. Thomas did not confuse a real concern for the legitimate moral demands of politics with a zealous political moralism.[87]

Harte's incomplete reading of Aquinas, limited to a defective reading of the "Treatise on Law," leaves Aquinas to read like the "categorical imperative" of Immanuel Kant. Harte's "politics of moral imperatives" ignores prudence.[88] In 350 pages, Harte gives virtually no recognition of the classical tradition of political prudence.[89]

The relationship between natural law and prudence—and the debate between the perfectionists and incrementalists—highlights the basic difference between ends and means. Natural law primarily deals with the ends; prudence primarily deals with the means. Natural law may define the ideal as complete legal protection for human life, but what action should be taken to achieve the greatest good possible in this world of constraints? Prudence addresses this.

Harte's argument against abortion legislation that seeks to establish fences around abortion fails to demonstrate that it is "intrinsically unjust" by reference to Aquinas's natural law teaching or to Catholic Church doctrine. He fails to demonstrate that legislators undermine solidarity when, in the minority, they are prevented by countervailing powers from completely prohibiting abortion.

A major point of Harte's is that, when all lives could not be saved, the most vulnerable are not the ones protected first or given priority in legislation like the Alton Bill. This is a clear example of Harte's failure to understand or engage real obstacles. This does not sufficiently take account of the countervailing obstacle of public opinion or legislative majorities who do not support the most vulnerable. Whether "the most vulnerable" can be given priority in protection depends on the same obstacles—including courts, legislative majorities or public opinion—that obstruct the saving of *any* or *all* lives.

While Harte raises some valid concerns about the risks of supporting certain restrictive legislation, these are properly seen as prudential concerns that must be taken into consideration rather than factors that make certain bills "intrinsically unjust." Harte may provide arguments why an abortion prohibition with a time limit (e.g., tied to viability) may be imprudent, but he does not and cannot prove that the natural law dictates the details of legislative attempts to limit unjust laws.

In a democracy with a mass media, it is sometimes difficult for the principles or motives of public officials to be clearly understood. That is a prudential concern but not one that renders a bill "intrinsically unjust."

Harte points out the seriousness of prudential concerns in attempting to limit unjust laws or conditions. However, Harte's ethical analysis suffers from two familiar defects: First, Harte commits the fallacy of refusing to take adequate account of the constraints on public officials' ability to achieve the perfect. Second, he fails to recognize that no formal or material cooperation is involved when public officials try to limit an evil, because their intent is to limit the evil in the face of overwhelming constraints and not to support it. Harte's analysis exemplifies the stubborn tendency, common among the most zealous social activists, to be preoccupied with the problem of moral compromise and fail to seriously consider the real obstacles imposed by opponents in a world of constraints. Consequently, his analysis serves to render any policy efforts futile and to sideline any effective effort in public policy to limit unjust laws or conditions.

It is not enough to simply rhetorically defend a principle; the challenge in a world of constraints is effectively achieving the greatest good possible. The record of legislative attempts to fence in the abortion license over the past thirty-plus years calls us to carefully evaluate the complex obstacles that stand in the way of achieving the good. Understanding those constraints is necessary to chart the path forward in achieving the greatest good possible in this generation.

OVERTURNING *ROE V. WADE* SUCCESSFULLY

The confirmation of Judge John Roberts as Chief Justice of the United States has ushered in a new era in the Supreme Court—the Roberts Court.[1] The addition of Chief Justice Roberts and Justice Samuel Alito in 2005-2006 has spurred renewed debate over the validity of the Supreme Court's 1973 decision in *Roe v. Wade*[2] and whether it could and should be overturned.

These changes in the Supreme Court have heightened media scrutiny of the possibility that the Court might overturn *Roe*. The cover of the June 2006 issue of the *Atlantic Monthly* was devoted to "Life After Roe." This renewed interest had repercussions in the media, state legislatures and congressional hearings, leading up to the 2008 elections.

The Supreme Court's April 2007 decision in *Gonzales v. Carhart*[3] was ambiguous but may prove to be a turning point, a very significant one. Time will tell. The Court upheld the federal partial-birth abortion law (as Congress called it), which was a very narrowly drafted law. The decision will have limited short-term repercussions; abortions will continue relatively unimpeded at the rate of more than one million per year. Five justices, a majority on the Court, still support *Roe*. But the decision has led to heightened speculation that the Court might further limit *Roe*. This chapter outlines a prudential strategy to overturn *Roe* in the wake of *Gonzales*.

Why Roe Should Be Overturned

Why has overturning *Roe v. Wade* been a goal of successive presidential administrations, numerous political leaders at the state and federal level, and millions of Americans represented by dozens of political organizations since the case was decided in January 1973?

First and foremost, many will say that *Roe* has resulted in the deaths of more than forty million unborn children. This recognition is supported by several factors, including the policy of the states in protecting developing human life before *Roe*. There was a long tradition of protecting the unborn child as a human being under the law to the greatest extent possible given contemporary medical technology and the understanding of prenatal life.[4]

Second is the remarkable legal consensus across forty states before *Roe* that the life of a human being begins at conception.[5] The medical development of in vitro fertilization (IVF) in the 1970s only confirmed this biological reality, and it has been recently argued as a philosophical matter by Robert George and Christopher Tollefsen based on the latest science.[6]

Third is the remarkable growth since 1973 of state fetal homicide laws, like "the Lacey Peterson law" in California, that treat the killing of the unborn child (outside the context of abortion) as the killing of a human being (a homicide). Since *Roe*, approximately thirty-six states have passed legislation to treat the killing of the unborn child (outside the context of abortion) as a homicide, and twenty-four of these thirty-six states treat the killing as a homicide *from conception*.

The Supreme Court's 1973 decision in *Roe v. Wade* was an unnecessary, unconstitutional and tragic decision.[7] It abruptly silenced a vigorous national debate that was ongoing among the American people, across the states. It overturned the abortion laws of all fifty states, most of which were actively enforced and many of which had been recently debated, enacted or reaffirmed by the people of the state. It legalized abortion from conception to birth for virtually any reason. A culture of life in America cannot be realized unless *Roe* and its nationwide imposition of abortion on demand is overturned.

With *Roe*, the Supreme Court incurred a self-inflicted wound. It did not understand the history of abortion: while the Court spent half of its opinion trying to base its decision in history, virtually all of its historical propositions have been thoroughly discredited over the past three decades.[8] It did not understand the legal context of its ruling: the states have regularly passed laws since *Roe* that have increased legal protection for the unborn *outside* the context of abortion (fetal homicide laws). And it did not foresee the negative public reaction to its decision that has been sustained over three decades.

Roe was without constitutional authority, without foundation in its text or tradition, and without support in the history of our country. It was an unconstitutional usurpation of the people's authority. From colonial times through 1973, the American people decided the abortion issue for themselves through representative government. The issue of abortion should be decided by the American people, as are most other public issues under our republican system of government, even the most controversial, unless the people specifically withdraw them from the political process (and the control of political majorities) and enshrine them in the Constitution.

The Court has also endangered women's health in at least three ways through its twenty-eight abortion decisions over the past thirty-plus years. First, the Supreme Court has *never required* that women be informed about the medically documented risks of abortion, despite increasing data on numerous medical risks. The Court has merely allowed the states to enact some limited information requirements, subject to lengthy court challenges by abortion clinics. Second, the Supreme Court has never required that abortion clinics be safe or be run by reputable operators. From 1973 to 2000 the federal courts, relying on the Court's decision in *Roe*, uniformly obstructed state clinic regulations. A few states have enacted comprehensive clinic regulations, also subject to lengthy court challenges. Abortion complications are little known because abortion clinics don't track women's complications. Women go to emergency rooms, not back to the abortion clinic, if they have complications, and emergency rooms don't track the abortions. In addition, the state and federal system of health data collection and analysis is haphazard.[9]

Third, the Court has empowered abortion providers who profit from the procedure to unilaterally decide abortion standards. For example, the record evidence in the three federal court cases challenging the Federal Partial Birth Abortion Ban Act of 2003 is that abortion providers (and their trade organizations like the American College of Obstetricians and Gynecologists [ACOG]) have abandoned several decades of evidence-based medicine in favor of risky, unproven innovations (like the dilation and extraction (D&X) procedure, or what Congress called "partial-birth abortion") that suit the convenience of abortionists. The safety and efficacy of the D&X procedure is not demonstrated by empirical evidence, and well-established procedures exist that are effective to treat any maternal or fetal condition.

Roe has corrupted the federal judicial nomination process, in which interest groups pressure U.S. senators to spend an undue amount of time surveying a judicial nominee's views on one issue: abortion. This has undermined the rule of law and the administration of justice in the United States.[10]

Roe has also resulted in considerable confusion among federal judges and state and federal legislators. Federal judges have complained about the ambiguities and contradictions in the Court's abortion decisions. And those ambiguities and contradictions have made it increasingly difficult for state or federal policymakers to predict what the courts will do with abortion legislation.

The public is little aware of the ways in which the Court has obstructed the public will. Take, for example, the New Hampshire parental notice case, *Ayotte v. Planned Parenthood*,[11] which the Court decided unanimously in January 2006. The Court has repeatedly issued pronouncements that the people in the states have compelling interests in regulating abortion and then issued rules that continually stymie any regulations. Necessary health regulations are rendered unenforceable. In *Ayotte*, the Court unanimously declared to the nation—as it has done repeatedly—that the people at the state level have an undoubted right to ensure parental notice before an abortion, and then sent the case back to the lower courts. The press reports the statute as having been upheld. Yet, nearly two years later, the New Hampshire statute—virtually identical to ones enforced in a dozen other states—continued to be mired in litigation with no end in sight. The Supreme Court is not subject to truth-in-advertising and seems completely oblivious to these contradictions in its decisions.

Roe has undermined the protection of human life in other areas of law and diminished human dignity. It has long been anticipated that *Roe* could be applied to numerous other moral and bioethical issues, and take them away from the American people and out of the representative process. The prospects of that may have faded with the additions of Chief Justice Roberts and Justice Alito to the Court in 2005 and 2006, but as of 2008 there are still five justices—Stevens, Kennedy, Souter, Ginsburg and Breyer—who might support an extension of *Roe*. As long as *Roe* stands, it could be expanded to take other issues away that the people now rightfully decide through the representative process—cloning, embryonic stem-cell research, reproductive technology, genetic engineering, nanotechnology or a host of future bioethical issues that we can only now imagine.[12]

In short, the Supreme Court has made a mess of the issue through its twenty-eight contradictory decisions over thirty-plus years. *Roe v. Wade* should be overturned at the earliest possible moment.

But saying so is easier than doing it.

What does "overruling" Roe mean? Throughout 2005-2006, as the Roberts and Alito nominations moved forward, interest groups pointed to public opinion polls showing that the American people supported *Roe* and opposed "overturning *Roe.*" The meaning of those polls largely depends on what the public understands *Roe* to mean and what "overruling" *Roe* means. Some Americans likely believe that overruling *Roe* means that the Supreme Court would make abortion illegal. This is seriously wrong.

Because there is no support on the Court, by any justice past or present, for a" personhood ruling," overruling *Roe* means, as a practical matter, overturning the holding in *Roe* that created a constitutional right to abortion. Overturning that holding would result in returning the issue to the legislative process, mostly likely the states, which had authority to address general criminal matters, like abortion, before *Roe*.

> As a practical matter, due to legislative changes in the states since 1973, if the Court overturned *Roe* today, abortion would be legal in at least forty-three states tomorrow.

It would also mean that those state abortion laws that exist, as of the time of the Court's decision overruling *Roe*, could conceivably come back into force, subject to state constitutional or judicial limitations. Individual state law would be the default position when *Roe* is overturned.

What is the status of state law currently? As a practical matter, due to legislative changes in the states since 1973, if the Court overturned *Roe* today, abortion would be legal in at least forty-three states tomorrow. This is due to three factors: some states repealed their abortion prohibitions before *Roe*; some states have repealed their abortion prohibitions since *Roe*; and in fourteen to fifteen states, activist courts have adopted their own version of *Roe* under the state constitution that would prevent state prohibitions. Until the state legislatures act, and subject to state judicial interference, abortion would be legal in at least forty-three states, and the abortion prohibitions in the remaining seven states might be subject to an immediate suit if *Roe* is overturned. That is the practical, legal meaning of overruling *Roe*. Hence, there will be little immediate legal or social change if *Roe* is overturned.

Why Roe *has not been overturned*. *Roe* has survived for more than thirty years for two basic reasons: (1) Due to the fundamental nature of the American political and constitutional system, it is very difficult to overturn *any* Supreme Court decision. (2) *That* particular Supreme Court decision is staunchly supported by powerful elites: a certain brand of feminism in American society; many elite medical and legal institutions, including the vast majority of law professors; and the leadership of one of the two major political parties in the United States.[13]

In order to successfully oppose and overturn it, the reality of *Roe* needs to be understood in all its dimensions, especially those that contribute to its survival in the law. One of the merits of a law-school education is that it teaches students that they can't argue their position well unless they understand the other side's position better than the other side does. This is part of what Aquinas meant by *docilitas*, or open-mindedness, the ability to clearly see all sides of a question or problem. Advocates for the overturning of *Roe* are ill-equipped if they do not adopt the virtue of open-mindedness in understanding *Roe*, its power and its significance. This needs to be combined with an understanding of the enormous political, cultural and legal hurdles that stand in the way and make the overturning of *Roe* far from inevitable.[14]

Roe v. Wade is a unique decision in American law and culture. Its power in the mind of many Americans as an icon of women's empowerment needs to be fully understood. Professional organizations for women lawyers, for example, commonly promote abortion rights at their meetings, indoctrinating women lawyers on the "need" to preserve abortion rights. *Roe*'s significance and power is reflected in the opinion of the plurality of justices in the Court's 1992 decision in *Planned Parenthood v. Casey* that reaffirmed *Roe*.

> For two decades of economic and social developments, people have organized intimate relationships and made choices that define their views of themselves and their places in society, in reliance on the availability of abortion in the event that contraception should fail. The ability of women to participate equally in the economic and social life of the Nation has been facilitated by their ability to control their reproductive lives. . . . The Constitution serves human values, and while the effect of reliance on *Roe* cannot be exactly measured, neither can the

certain cost of overruling *Roe* for people who have ordered their thinking and living around that case be dismissed.[15]

For many, *Roe* reflects a way of life. It has stood for more than three decades and will not be easily overturned.

In addition, the heightened zeal for overturning *Roe* needs to be tempered by knowledge that it has been attempted, without success, through many cases over thirty-plus years. What can be learned from those prior efforts? What will make any new effort successful when past ones have failed? Because of the nature of the Supreme Court and the legal system, successfully overturning *Roe* will require the confluence of complex social, legal, institutional, political and educational factors. What are those factors? How can they be organized? What will it take to successfully bring them together?

WHAT IS THE RIGHT GOAL?

Prudence requires clearly focusing on which good goals can be realistically achieved in the foreseeable future, in light of the history of the abortion issue in American law and culture over the past four decades, and given contemporary opportunities, resources and constraints.

At one point in American history, perhaps shortly after the ratification of the Fourteenth Amendment in 1868, it might have been possible to persuasively articulate a "right to life" jurisprudence predicated on the Fourteen Amendment's clause declaring that "no state shall deprive any person of life." That jurisprudence could have looked to the protection of human life under the common law.[16] But *Roe* shattered that possibility for constitutional jurisprudence in 1973.

However, protection of developing human beings can and has grown in other areas of law—especially state and federal legislation—since 1973. Judges have been the intellectual class most hostile to protecting developing human life over the past four decades. Legislatures, much more than judges, have been the source of the growth of legal protection for developing human life over the past quarter century. And that will continue to be the case for the foreseeable future.

Roe upset centuries of cultural, political and social traditions, and the understanding that abortion was an issue for the American people to decide through their representatives at the state level. Congress legislated on the issue in very narrow contexts relating to federal territories and jurisdictions. And until the 1960s virtually all states—through state law—prohibited abortion except to save the life of the mother. The federal courts were not involved in the issue, and the assumption was that the U.S. Constitution didn't have anything to say about the issue. It was for the people in the states to decide.

Between 1967 and 1970 approximately fourteen states repealed their abortion prohibitions or introduced broad exceptions into their state laws, though none was as broad as the *Roe* decision would be. Other states—both in their legislatures and through electoral votes—reaffirmed their abortion prohibitions. At the time of *Roe*, thirty states still retained their laws prohibiting abortion except to save the life of the mother. There were no attempts before *Roe* to pass a constitutional amendment to prohibit abortion nationwide. The first attempt to pass such an amendment was a reaction to *Roe's* ruling that the unborn child was *not* a "person" under the Fourteenth Amendment.

The improbability of an amendment. If the goals of a culture of life include effectively reducing or eliminating elective abortion or protecting the unborn child under the law or designating abortion as homicide (the killing of a human being), or a combination of these, then it is a prudential question whether that goal is more effectively achieved in public policy through a constitutional amendment, federal legislation, state legislation or a combination of these.

In the American constitutional system, there are, as a practical matter, two and only two ways to overturn a Supreme Court decision interpreting the federal constitution: a constitutional amendment or a decision by the Court overturning its prior decision. Since the Bill of Rights (the first ten amendments) was ratified by the people in 1791, only seventeen amendments have been approved by the American people. And a lot of popular ones (like the one against flag burning) have failed to make it. Because a federal constitutional amendment is about the most difficult political goal in the American constitutional system, and because the additions of Chief Justice Roberts and Justice Alito to the Court in 2005-2006 have raised hopes that the Court is changing, a federal constitutional amendment on abortion has almost no chance of success in the foreseeable future.[17]

That leaves only one practical option: a decision by the Court overturning its decision in *Roe*. Because the Court in *Roe* decided two main points of constitutional law (two holdings), the Court could, theoretically, revisit either or both of those. The first was that the Liberty Clause of the Fourteenth Amendment contained a national right to abortion. The second was that the unborn child was not a "person" protected by the Fourteenth Amendment to the federal constitution.

The improbability of a "personhood" decision by the Supreme Court. Some Americans would like the Court to declare that the unborn child is a person under the Fourteenth Amendment (a "personhood" decision). Although there is a strong historical argument that the unborn were recognized to be human beings and thus "persons" at the time of the Fourteenth Amendment,[18] the current Court, as a practical matter, will never make such a decision in our lifetime.

There are two compelling reasons for this. First, the most anti-*Roe* justices, Scalia and Thomas, have rejected a personhood argument.[19] The Constitution, they believe, leaves the issue to the states. Because even Justices Scalia and Thomas have rejected it, it is inconceivable that either Chief Justice Roberts or Justice Alito will accept it. As a matter of constitutional law, it may be a plausible theory but it will never be adopted by the Court in the foreseeable future.

Second, and perhaps more important, there are strong *institutional* reasons that the Court will never adopt personhood in our lifetime. Justices Scalia and Thomas (and many others) believe that the Court has been institutionally damaged by taking the abortion issue away from the states and dictating abortion policy throughout the country. A personhood ruling would effectively make abortion illegal everywhere, or (perhaps more legally precise) prevent states from legalizing abortion as a right. Every indication from their past opinions is that *Justices Scalia and Thomas won't vote to take the country from a Supreme Court–dictated policy of abortion on demand to a Supreme Court–dictated policy of no abortions* anywhere. Even if they personally believed that the Fourteenth Amendment protected the unborn child as a person—and they don't—they likely believe that that would possibly damage the Court even more than *Roe* itself.

So, for constitutional and institutional reasons, Justices Scalia and Thomas will leave it to the states. And that's the most that pro-life Americans can hope from the Supreme Court in their lifetime. Given the fact that the judicial class has been one of the most hostile segments of American society to the humanity of the unborn over the past four decades in American law, there's no good reason to put such unwarranted hope in a "personhood" ruling from the judiciary.

Excessive focus on a personhood ruling from the Supreme Court, moreover, tends to disregard what can and has been done to protect the unborn child as a human being through state law. Thirty-six states now have fetal homicide laws. Approximately thirty-eight states have wrongful death (civil) causes of action for the death of an unborn child.

A constitutional amendment may not be needed or prudent. But if it were, the only way to secure a "personhood" amendment (if that's at all possible at any time in the future) is by first overturning *Roe* and returning the issue to the states. Only by first overturning the federal right to abortion, and opening up the state legislative and political process to abortion prohibitions, would the prospects for a constitutional amendment be possible. A personhood amendment is inconceivable while virtual abortion-on-demand *(Roe v. Wade)* is still the law of the land, inconceivable starting from a cultural status quo of abortion on demand. After thirty-plus years of judicially imposed abortion on demand, it will first be necessary to open the way to abortion prohibitions in the law and to promote the public education that might lead to a more comprehensive solution at the national level. The current climate of abortion on demand is hardly the right climate to prudently push a federal human life amendment. Even those who support a national solution through an amendment must recognize that it will not be accomplished without enormous public support.

Because a constitutional amendment is politically impossible at this point, and there is no support by any justice on the Court for a personhood ruling, prudence dictates a focus for the foreseeable future on an overruling of *Roe* that returns the abortion issue to the states. There's a fundamental difference between a "states' rights" policy that cares little about the substance of the matter at hand and an understanding that state criminal laws against abortion were (and may well be) the most effective law-enforcement means to protect unborn children and women from abortion. Many may think that that is not enough, but the obstacles to an amendment and to a personhood ruling, by any objective measure, are overwhelming in 2009.

LESSONS WE CAN LEARN FROM PAST ATTEMPTS TO OVERTURN *ROE*

Aquinas emphasized that prudence requires a good memory. That may seem a strange requirement, until a concrete problem is thoughtfully addressed, and then memory quickly becomes a necessary ingredient. That is vividly seen with the Supreme Court and abortion. A failure of memory led to *Roe*, and a failure of memory may derail efforts to overturn it.

Part of what led to the Supreme Court's tragic decision in 1973 in *Roe v. Wade* was the failure to remember the history of the law's protection of women and unborn children from abortion, and the legitimate moral, practical and medical reasons why those laws were adopted in every state by the American people and supported by virtually all of the leading nineteenth-century feminists in the 1870s and 1880s.

Twenty-seven years later, another failure of memory led the Supreme Court to invalidate the partial-birth abortion prohibitions of thirty states in *Stenberg v. Carhart* in the presidential election year of 2000. The Court failed to remember what it had learned in *Roe*—that the historic legal distinction between abortion and infanticide was birth.

No successful effort can be made to overturn *Roe* in the future without recalling and understanding how the Court and the individual justices have treated abortion since *Roe*. And however much new justices may have a different view of the decision, they do not start on a blank slate and cannot divorce themselves entirely from the past. *Roe*, and the twenty-eight to twenty-nine abortion cases that the Court has decided since *Roe*, will have implications for any future attempt to overturn Roe.

With Chief Justice William Rehnquist's death in October 2004, the last of the nine justices who decided *Roe* in 1973 left the Court. The Supreme Court is an unusual institution. There is a strong sense of history. The justices regularly write of what "we" have done in reference to past opinions, whether or not the justice was on the Court, even if the case is two hundred years old. No lawyer can adequately argue a case before the Supreme Court without a memory of its history and precedents.

I recall being at oral argument in 1988 in *Webster v. Reproductive Health Services* when Justice Scalia questioned Frank Susman, attorney for the abortion clinic, about one of the legal briefs submitted in the case, which contained a great deal of research showing that no right to abortion existed in Anglo-

American legal history. Although Susman derisively dismissed the brief, the brief was thorough and compelling, and from that day forward the majority of the Court has never referred to the existence of a historical right to abortion. Instead, the justices in the *Casey* decision in 1992 abruptly *shifted the rationale* for the abortion right *from history to sociology*, saying that abortion was needed as a backup to failed contraception. This "reliance interests" rationale remains the one unifying rationale among the justices for continuing their national power over abortion.

After the *Webster* case was decided in 1989, pro-life zeal reached a crescendo in the years leading up to 1992. Two states, Utah and Louisiana, and the territory of Guam enacted legislation by the spring of 1992 that prohibited some abortions. I traveled to Utah to work on the language of a bill, and I represented Guam, traveling to Honolulu in early 1992 with my colleague Paul Linton as he argued the defense of the Guam statute before the federal appeals court.

Many thought it was inevitable that the Court would overturn *Roe*, that the momentum was inexorable, that the justices would positively respond to the expression of the people's will in Utah, Louisiana and Guam, that the justices would respond to growing medical and scientific data regarding fetal development. But on June 29, 1992, the Court announced its decision in *Planned Parenthood v. Casey*, and a majority of justices rejected all the arguments for returning the abortion issue to the people.

There seem to be at least three reasons why the Supreme Court reaffirmed *Roe* in 1992 in *Casey*. First, a majority of justices adopted the key sociological premise that abortion was needed as a fail-safe backup to artificial contraception. Second, abortion advocates effectively lobbied Justice O'Connor as the key vote. Third, *Roe* was supported by virtually all of the elite medical and legal institutions in American society, including the American Medical Association and the American Bar Association.[20]

What the Court has done before needs to be remembered in detail. Continuity and stability in constitutional law are relatively important values, and the justices will look for compelling reasons to overturn past decisions, especially *Roe*, the most controversial decision of the past half-century. The zeal of "inevitability" needs to be tempered by knowledge of the reality of frail human beings who live under social and political pressure. As the old proverb says, zeal without knowledge is folly, and that knowledge necessarily includes a good memory and understanding of what has happened and—perhaps more importantly—why.

The overturning of *Roe* isn't inevitable. Even with the change in two justices in 2005-2006 and the *Gonzales* decision in 2007, the odds are against it. Numerous political and legal contingencies could intervene in coming years to interfere with a five- or six-justice majority coming together to overrule *Roe*. The membership of the Supreme Court, the president, the U.S. Senate and public opinion—as it is shaped by the media and elite institutions—will play a key role in the coming years in determining whether *Roe* is reaffirmed or overturned. There is no silver bullet; a broadly based legal, political and cultural strategy will be needed.

OVERCOMING CURRENT OBSTACLES: INSTITUTIONAL, LEGAL, POLITICAL

It's necessary to closely examine—and not blithely ignore—current obstacles before it's possible to identify effective solutions.

The U.S. Supreme Court in 2009 is still dominated by a majority of at least five pro-*Roe* justices—Justices Kennedy, Breyer, Ginsburg, Stevens and Souter. We know that only two—Justices Scalia and Thomas—have publicly stated that *Roe* should be overturned (though even Scalia and Thomas are of the view that the abortion issue is properly a state matter since the Constitution is silent on the issue). We do not know how Chief Justice Roberts or Justice Alito will come out on the ultimate question of the future of *Roe*. Despite the additions of Chief Justice Roberts and Justice Alito, there is still no majority on the Court in 2009 to overturn *Roe*.

The Supreme Court is a highly specialized fraternity. The most reliable way to predict what justices will do in the future is to understand their earlier opinions. These convey what the justices previously know about the issue and what they have done about it. Because there are nine justices, it takes five justices to make a decision and issue a judgment of the Court in a typical case.

But *Roe* is not the typical case. Because the overturning of *Roe* will have unique political reverberations, *five votes will likely not be enough to overturn* Roe. Some justices may hesitate to be the "fifth vote" to overturn *Roe*, as Justice Kennedy reportedly did when he switched his vote to reaffirm *Roe* in 1992 in *Casey*. And given the distinct possibility of a subsequent rereversal of a slim, five-to-four decision (if merely one justice in that majority is replaced), other justices may be concerned about institutional stability. *For these reasons, it will likely take a minimum of six justices to overturn* Roe.

Moreover, no one can force the Court to hear any particular case. The Court controls its own docket, its own work load. The Court accepts cases to hear by the "rule of four"—it takes four justices to hear a case. It is conceivable that the Court could repeatedly refuse abortion cases or any particular type of abortion case. For eight years between *Casey* and *Stenberg*, many abortion cases were appealed to the Supreme Court, and the Court rejected virtually all; those abortion cases it did decide were resolved without a full hearing.

For the foreseeable future it will be harder (socially and politically) for justices to overturn *Roe* than to stand by it. Justices can rationalize why they should not overturn *Roe* in a dozen ways. And many have done just that for thirty-six years; their reasons are stated in numerous opinions that they have authored.

The Court's continuing refusal to overturn *Roe* will be loudly supported by the media, elite legal organizations, elite medical institutions, law schools and faculty, some professional women's organizations, and the leadership of the Democratic Party.

Public opinion will largely tolerate the status quo—as the lack of public reaction to *Casey* and *Stenberg* demonstrates—for at least three reasons: the impact of *Roe* in itself is not largely known, the negative impact on women is not widely disseminated, and the public has a difficult time understanding what "overturning *Roe*" means, even though polls consistently show the public supports broader restrictions on abortion.

For thirty-six years, the Court has, unfortunately, looked at abortion through a paradigm that sets individual autonomy against state action. One practical implication of that paradigm is that the Court has reviewed cases involving state officials defending state abortion legislation and has rejected cases involving private action brought by private or special-interest attorneys. It is more than likely that that paradigm will continue.

Given these obstacles and uncertainties, pro-life political and legislative efforts should focus on legislation with the following short-term goals: *legislation that can put fences around* Roe *and the abortion license, reduce abortions, protect unborn children, protect women from the risks of abortion, encourage alternatives, and educate the public about the negative impact of abortion.*

The right timing. It's not possible to force the Court to reexamine *Roe* in any particular case; this has been repeatedly tried and failed. A state *prohibition* on abortion for the foreseeable future (given the five-to-four composition of the Supreme Court after *Gonzales*) will have a virtually certain outcome: it will never go into effect; it will be struck down by the lower federal district courts, which will be affirmed on appeal; the Supreme Court will deny review; and the state will have to pay hundreds of thousands of dollars in attorney fees to the abortion clinics' attorneys. The likelihood of this outcome is so certain that the risk is unwarranted.

In contrast, there are several types of regulations that can be enforced and make a positive difference now—like parental notice, informed consent and clinic regulations—and states should focus on those types of laws until the current legal and political obstacles change.

In addition, fetal-homicide (unborn victims of violence) laws, like the so-called Lacey Peterson law in California, can protect the unborn child from conception and be enacted and enforced; they are enforced in thirty-six states today. Given current obstacles, state or federal abortion prohibitions in the foreseeable future will be futile and almost certainly counterproductive. Legislation that has no chance of being upheld and no chance of going into effect should be discouraged.

In the meantime, it is important to use current abortion cases to "educate for the future." That includes bringing the reality of abortion and its effect on women to the attention of the justices through current cases.

The right statute. What would be the "ideal" abortion law to present to the U.S. Supreme Court? Even if the ideal law could be identified and drafted, the contingencies of the legislative and judicial process would likely prevent it from becoming the focus of a Supreme Court case. But such a thought experiment should be considered by prudent legislators in the wake of *Gonzales*.

Focusing on the ideal often ignores the countervailing obstacles in the real arenas that we work in. Instead, a realistic and discerning evaluation of those obstacles should lead us to consider the *best* statute under the circumstances.

Generally, the best statute should be good policy, based on sound medical science, that will result in effective protection for women and children. Bills should not try to *force* the Court to decide the most difficult legal or constitutional issues. Statutes that back the Court into a corner will mostly likely be denied review and never be the subject of an effective test case. Essentially, legislators should ask three questions: What will effectively limit the number of abortions? What will raise public understanding about abortion and its negative consequences? What will help limit *Roe* and the abortion license?

The media invariably describes Supreme Court decisions (wrongly) as though the Court "approved" or "disapproved" some law as good or bad policy. The reality is that the Court can decide that Congress or the states have the authority to enact some law, even if the justices don't personally agree with the law. In other words, the media will likely portray the Court in any abortion case as having "approved" the statute rather than merely affirming that the statute was a constitutional option for the states.

For these reasons and others, *the Court should be given the chance to broadly decide that the abortion issue should be decided by the people without having to "approve" the strongest possible abortion prohibition.* If the Court broadly decides that the people in the states should decide the issue, the states can enact broader or narrower regulations or prohibitions, all within their constitutional authority.

Contrary to conventional wisdom, an abortion *prohibition* is *not* necessary to get the Court to reconsider *Roe*. The Court actually reconsidered *Roe* in *Webster* and *Casey*, and neither statute contained an abortion prohibition. Justice Kennedy, in his majority opinion in *Gonzales,* stated that "*Casey* involved a challenge to *Roe v. Wade*," even though the statute in *Casey* did not directly conflict with *Roe*. This understanding confirms that a prohibition is not necessary to set up a test case.

A state legislative proposal must be effectively enforceable and serve its intended function; it can't simply be a marketing tool. And it must be supported by expert medical testimony. As indicated by *Casey, Stenberg* and *Gonzales,* many, if not all, of the justices will be specifically concerned about the impact of the legislation on women's health—not the unlimited emotional "health" definition in *Doe v. Bolton* (emotional well-being), but significant, identifiable medical risks.

The right arguments. Legislation must be drafted with an eye on the public, the courts and the media.

Any future legislation intended to test the limits of *Roe* on abortion must be pursued with the understanding that the following questions are always swirling around the abortion issue in the courts: the effect of abortion on women; the implications of overruling *Roe* on law, society and women's lives; how states might handle exceptions in cases involving the life of the mother, rape and incest; the practical (legal and social) implications of overturning *Roe;* the scope of state legal authority if *Roe* is overturned; and why the people in the states should decide the abortion issue.

The Court will want a clear understanding of what will and won't happen "the day after *Roe*," as the *Atlantic Monthly* framed the cover of its June 2006 issue. These considerations relate to the legal doctrine called *stare decisis*— sticking with what has been decided (precedent). *Stare decisis* is typically thought to be the strongest institutional impediment to overturning *Roe*. Much has been made in the abortion debate about the Supreme Court and the importance of sticking to its precedents.[21]

But the *legal* doctrine of *stare decisis* is most likely a cloak for the political implications. In fact, in *Planned Parenthood v. Casey*, these were intertwined. Because *stare decisis* is treated by some justices as a matter of mere policy, not constitutional principle, the legal doctrine of *stare decisis* is less important than the political aspects, as the *Casey* decision showed. Some justices will undoubtedly be sensitive to public opinion, some more overtly than others. That too was apparent in *Casey*.

Hence, in coming years public opinion needs to be educated about the failures of *Roe*, especially abortion's negative impact on women. And state and federal policy should be shaped in the near term to support these arguments in the courts in the future. As James Hunter's book *Before the Shooting Begins* makes clear, in his analysis of the 1991 Gallup Poll titled "Abortion and Moral Beliefs," public education must address what overturning *Roe* means— including the immediate social, legislative and political implications of overturning *Roe*.

"PLAN B": HOW *ROE V. WADE* MIGHT BE HOLLOWED OUT

Roe v. Wade is an unconstitutional and unjust decision, and the Court *should* overturn *Roe* at the earliest possible opportunity. It has no basis in constitutional law, text or tradition as Joseph Dellapenna's book *Dispelling the Myths of Abortion History* (2006) thoroughly shows. It has encouraged women to rely on abortion as birth control without adequate information about medical risks. The sweeping scope of the Supreme Court's abortion license is not supported by public opinion.

There are, nevertheless, strong medical, institutional and political forces that are working night and day to keep *Roe* the law of the land. And an overruling strategy has been tried before, most prominently in *Webster v. Reproductive Health Services* (1989) and *Planned Parenthood v. Casey* (1992), but also in several other cases that have not been widely publicized.

The institutional and political obstacles are so strong that "Plan B" needs to be thought through. There may be three or more possible alternatives to the Court handling *Roe*. It's important to examine the possible alternatives in order to effectively argue against any partial overturning of *Roe* in the future.

- *Reaffirm* Roe. The Court could, of course, continue to do what it did in *Casey* and reaffirm its decision in *Roe*. Since President Bush finished his second term without another vacancy, leaving five pro-*Roe* justices on the Court, and President Obama has made clear that he will appoint justices who support the most unlimited abortion rights, the Court could stay split five to four (at least) in favor of *Roe* for the foreseeable future.

- *Harsher rejection of state limits on abortion.* If President Obama replaces one of the justices in the Gonzales majority—Chief Justice Roberts, Justices Kennedy, Scalia, Thomas or Alito—the Court could revert to the harsh rejection of state limits reflected in the *Stenberg* decision of 2000 that struck down the partial-birth abortion prohibitions of 30 states.

- *Outright overturning.* While this is the most hoped for by activists, it will be the most difficult to achieve and the most highly criticized.

- *Greater deference to the states and regulations, without overturning* Roe. This could happen in a couple of ways—by changing the "standard of review," the standard that the Court applies to review state legislation. For example, several justices after the Court's 1992 *Casey* decision applied the "undue burden" standard of review and asked whether a state abortion law imposed an "undue burden" on a woman's right to abortion. The Court could redefine the "undue burden" standard to allow greater regulation. It has apparently begun to do this in *Gonzales*, by restoring the deferential standard of review of the 1992 *Casey* decision, in place of the harsher standard from the 2000 *Stenberg* decision.

The political and institutional obstacles to an outright overturning of Roe. As the Court's 2007 decision in *Gonzales* indicates, the likelihood is that the Court will not overturn *Roe* in the foreseeable future. In the judgment of most lawyers and legal scholars, the current Supreme Court will not overturn *Roe v. Wade* in "one fell swoop." Instead, even if the right majority on the Court solidifies, it is more likely that the Court would "hollow out" *Roe v. Wade*, with an overruling postponed to some uncertain point in the future. Experience suggests this; the Court has often changed course gradually to ease social, cultural and political change.

Various institutional and prudential reasons make this more likely than an outright overruling in the short term. For example, Chief Justice Roberts gave a commencement speech at Georgetown University that indicated his policy of trying to decide cases on as narrow grounds as possible. In addition—as explained by federal circuit judge Edith Jones—current standards applied by the Court won't allow lower courts to examine evidence (e.g., of fetal humanity and the negative impact of abortion on women) that would justify overturning *Roe*. The Court would have to change its procedures to allow lower courts to hear such evidence. Accepting that reasoning, in what way and on what time frame might the Court be induced to hollow out *Roe?*

***What hollowing out* Roe *might mean*.** Hollowing out *Roe* suggests removing the core rules (doctrines) of *Roe* that prevent state regulations or prohibitions on abortion, through a series of cases, without a formal, outright overruling of *Roe*. One way would be for the Court to *expressly* change its standard of review by which it examines state abortion regulations and prohibitions. It could reject the "undue burden" standard, for example, and adopt a "rational basis" standard, which would require a state to identify a rational basis for an abortion law. Some think the Court did this in *Webster v. Reproductive Health Services*[23] in 1989. But if so, a majority of the Court clearly replaced that with a less deferential, intermediate standard ("undue burden") in the *Casey* decision in 1992 and then returned to a harsh standard toward legislation (strict scrutiny) in 2000 in *Stenberg*. Given the political reaction to *Webster*, an express and dramatic change in the standard of review might be considered by some justices as too much, too soon.

Perhaps a better (or more likely) way would be for the Court to give an ever-increasing deferential reading to the current "undue burden" standard of review that a majority of the Court adopted in *Casey*. By its inherent elasticity and subjectivity, the undue burden standard is susceptible to evolution, and it could evolve in a new way that would be deferential toward state regulation or prohibition.[24] According to *Casey*, an *"undue burden is . . . shorthand for the conclusion that a state regulation has the purpose or effect of placing a substantial obstacle in the path of a woman seeking an abortion of a nonviable fetus."*[25] In other words, if Justice Stevens, Breyer or Ginsburg define what's "undue," most abortion regulations (and probably any abortion prohibitions) will fall. If Justice Scalia or Thomas define what's "undue," most abortion regulations (and some abortion prohibitions, starting with partial-birth abortion) will pass muster.

***The implications of* Gonzales.** The foregoing analysis is strongly reinforced by the Court's 2007 opinion in the partial-birth abortion decision *Gonzales v. Carhart*. The Court's decision in *Gonzales* has uncertain implications for the future. A narrow majority of five justices upheld the federal partial-birth abortion law. But that federal law is very narrow in its scope, as required by the Supreme Court's 2000 decision in *Stenberg*. On the other hand, of the five in the majority, only two justices, Thomas and Scalia, openly expressed support for overturning *Roe* entirely.

There are passages in the *Gonzales* decision, however, that suggest that this new five-justice majority could uphold virtually any regulations that make medical sense and some limited prohibitions. Justice Kennedy's definition of "undue burden," supported by the four who joined his opinion, will be deferential to state regulations. The decision suggests that states can enact stronger regulations on abortion, and the decision specifically reaffirms the importance of fully informed consent for women.

But this optimistic reading of the *Gonzales* decision (deferential to the states) will depend on a number of contingencies: whether the five justices in the narrow majority remain on the Court, President Obama's Court appointments and the timing of more vacancies. *Gonzales* suggests that stronger fences around the abortion license—if well drafted and strongly supported by medical science—will be permitted as long as the current majority remains. But prudence also requires thoroughly understanding the obstacles that remain with *Gonzales*.

***Some means to hollow out* Roe.** At the outset, it is important to carefully evaluate whether (1) regulations that protect the unborn child or (2) regulations that highlight and protect the health of women are more likely to contribute to the hollowing out of *Roe.* Which type of regulations might be more persuasive to the new majority of Roberts, Kennedy, Scalia, Thomas and Alito?

Regulations that protect women will likely be more important for several reasons. First, concern for women's "health" was the dominant rationale for reaffirming *Roe* in *Casey.* Based on his majority opinion in *Gonzales,* Justice Kennedy apparently still believes that *Casey* is a workable decision. Any future Court will have to deal with the rationale of *Casey.*

In 2007 *Gonzales* again focused the Court on women's health. *Gonzales* appears to properly shift the focus from the unlimited emotional health definition of *Doe v. Bolton* to a more meaningful focus on "significant medical risks." This reinforces the importance of research and data regarding the impact of abortion on women's medical health.

If the undue burden standard becomes more lenient, states will be freer to devise stricter and more detailed regulations to create future test cases. Those new regulations should emphasize the negative impact of abortion on women to (1) bring that medical evidence before the Court and (2) challenge the "reliance interests" rationale of *Casey.*

Second, the facts of fetal life (and the graphic impact of abortion on the unborn child) have been vividly presented to the Court in *Stenberg* and *Gonzales.* This is made clear by Justice Kennedy's acknowledgment in *Gonzales:*

> The State has an interest in ensuring so grave a choice is well informed. It is self-evident that a mother who comes to regret her choice to abort must struggle with grief more anguished and sorrow more profound when she learns, only after the event, what she once did not know: that she allowed a doctor to pierce the skull and vacuum the fast-developing brain of her unborn child, a child assuming the human form.[26]

There is no doubt that the justices know exactly what happens in an abortion. That is not an omission or oversight that keeps them from overturning *Roe.*

Third, the data on the five best medically documented risks from abortion for women highlighted in medical studies over the past ten to fifteen years have not been presented to the Court, or they have not been presented in the case record but only through amicus (friend of the court) briefs. These are the heightened risk of placenta previa, the heightened risk of pre-term birth (PTB), the heightened incidence of drug and alcohol abuse, the heightened incidence of mental trauma and psychiatric admissions, and the loss of the protective effect of a first full-term pregnancy against breast cancer. As the authors of a study in the January 2003 issue of the *Obstetrical and Gynecological Survey* concluded:

> Women contemplating their first induced abortion early in their reproductive life should be informed of two major long-term health consequences. First, their risk of subsequent pre-term birth, particularly of a very low-birth weight infant, will be elevated above their baseline risk in the current pregnancy. Second, they will lose the protective effect of a full-term delivery on their lifetime risk of breast carcinoma. This loss of protection will be in proportion to the length of time that elapses before they experience their first delivery. Increased rates of placenta previa and the disputed independent risk of induced abortion on breast cancer risk warrant mention as well.[27]

The record in *Gonzales v. Carhart* may be the first in which the short-term and long-term medical risks are actually mentioned to any degree. Justice Kennedy acknowledged some of the evidence in passing, but did not emphasize it.

Fourth, when the Court overturns *Roe*, the concern for women's health will be a dominant public concern, and any concern that the justices have about the effect on women's health (by overturning *Roe*) will have to be countered by evidence of the harm of abortion to women. The relative weighing of such public health concerns are for the people to decide, through representative government, as they do other public health issues.

To address these problems from another angle, *what will be the vital issue(s) of persuasion that might induce a future Supreme Court to hollow out or overrule* Roe?

- That abortion kills the unborn child? This seems to be perfectly clear and acknowledged by all justices, as the opinions in *Stenberg* and *Gonzales* make clear.

- That abortion is bad for women? Throughout twenty-eight Supreme Court decisions, there is almost no acknowledgment about the risks *from* abortion for women. Virtually all discussion in Supreme Court opinions focuses on the risks *to the woman if she does not get the abortion.*

• That the Court's vague and contradictory decisions over more than thirty years have confused federal judges and state legislators?

• That the Court's national abortion rule of abortion on demand actually conflicts with public opinion?

• That the facts underlying the decision in *Roe* have changed? Which facts will be relevant here?

• That the Court's decisions have roiled the federal judicial nomination process?

• That there will be no immediate legal change if the Court overturns *Roe?*

• Even if one disparages the notion of "reliance interests" in *Casey*, it can scarcely be denied that there has been reliance with a social impact. Why should such reliance be discounted?

Which one of these (or others) will be more persuasive to the justices?

New Medical Regulations

Some or all of the following regulations might serve to limit *Roe:*

• *Raise the requirements for informed consent.* Make informed consent (women's right to know legislation) more specific by requiring detailed information on the best medically documented risks from abortion. The Court's 2007 decision in *Gonzales* seems to support this.

• *Raise the requirements for clinic regulations.* Abortion clinic regulations might be redrafted along the lines of the Joint Commission on the Accreditation of Heathcare Organizations (JCAHO) guidelines for surgicenters.

• *Ultrasound requirement.* At least sixteen states have enacted or are considering such legislation.

• *Fetal pain legislation.* Such legislation has been introduced in Congress and the states.

• *Prohibition on sex-selective abortion. Gonzales* suggests that a narrow prohibition like this, that does not create a "substantial obstacle" before "the fetus attains viability," might be upheld.

- *Introducing a "balance of harms" analysis into the* Roe/Doe *"health" exception.* Virtually all mention of medical risk in Supreme Court opinions involving abortion refers to "risks" that might flow from the woman *not* getting the abortion. There has been too little recognition of the medical harm to women from abortion. This might be so for at least three reasons: (1) the data haven't been adequately developed until the late 1990s, (2) the pro-abortion justices have no reason to mention this, and (3) the two publicly declared, anti-*Roe* justices, Scalia and Thomas, don't think that such medical and sociological data is particularly relevant to the constitutional issue of whether the Court should be in the abortion business or don't think that the data has been well presented in the record in prior cases.[28]

To introduce a new paradigm, state legislation could introduce some requirement of balancing medical (physical and psychological) risks from the abortion against risks of not getting the abortion. This could be done in more than one way: through (1) the informed consent process (perhaps more likely), (2) through an overt requirement that permission for the abortion depend on a balance of the harms as indicated by evidence-based medicine, or (3) some other mechanism. Justice Kennedy's majority opinion in *Gonzales*, which explicitly acknowledges a "balance of risks," seems to support such evidence in future cases.

Any of these regulations will have to be backed by solid medicine and science. Legislators need to ask themselves, *What is the goal of this legislation, and what is the medical rationale and empirical evidence for such a regulation?*

Until the day the Court completely washes its hands of reviewing state abortion legislation, medical evidence will be a critical support for an abortion regulation or prohibition. This is simply because women's health will always be at the center of the public and legal debate over abortion. For the same reason, it will be necessary to raise public awareness of the negative impact of abortion on women and to build a public consensus for legislation in the states. The Court needs to see the popular will in favor of regulations and prohibitions.

The obstacles to hollowing out Roe. In 2005 renowned federal appeals court judge Edith Jones challenged the Supreme Court's abortion policy-making head-on. In a case brought by the plaintiff in the original *Roe* case, Norma McCorvey, to overturn *Roe*, Judge Jones suggested that federal courts will never be able to consider evidence regarding fetal life or the negative impact of abortion on women unless the Supreme Court changes the standard of review or invites such evidence.[29] Judge Jones wrote:

> The problem inherent in the [Supreme] Court's decision to constitutionalize abortion policy is that, unless it creates another exception to the mootness doctrine, the Court will never be able to examine its factual assumptions on a record made in court. Legislatures will not pass laws that challenge the trimester ruling adopted in *Roe* (and retooled as the "undue burden" test in *Casey* . . .). No "live" controversy will arise concerning this framework. Consequently, I cannot conceive of any judicial forum in which McCorvey's evidence could be aired. At the same time, because the Court's rulings have rendered basic abortion policy beyond the power of our legislative bodies, the arms of representative government may not meaningfully debate McCorvey's evidence. The perverse result of the Court's having determined through constitutional adjudication this fundamental social policy, which affects over a million women . . . each year, is that the facts no longer matter. . . . Hard and social science will of course progress even though the Supreme Court averts its eyes. It takes no expert prognosticator to know that research on women's mental and physical health following abortion will yield an eventual medical consensus. . . . That the Court's constitutional decision-making leaves our nation in a position of willful blindness to evolving knowledge should trouble any dispassionate observer not only about the abortion decisions, but about a number of other areas in which the Court unhesitatingly steps into the realm of social policy under the guise of constitutional adjudication.[30]

One answer to this might be to encourage the Court to make the standard of review, or "undue burden" standard, more deferential. As the undue burden standard becomes more lenient, evidence of the negative impact on women might become more relevant.

A critical need in the coming years is organizing medical data and experts, and bringing these to bear in abortion litigation with greater force. At the same time information on the five best medically documented risks needs to be more widely disseminated to the public.

Political prudence before and after **Roe**. The obstacles to overturning *Roe* are many and enormous. These include the current justices and the lack of a majority to overturn *Roe*, the need for at least another vacancy and confirmation if not two to three more vacancies, the Obama presidency, the makeup of the U.S. Senate (that confirms justices), fear within the Republican Party about the political impact of overturning *Roe*, the opposition to overturning *Roe* by the Democratic party leadership and many powerful interest groups, public misunderstanding about what *Roe* is and means, and public misunderstanding about what its overturning would mean.

To the extent that prudence involves successfully implementing decisions, political prudence requires successfully explaining political decisions and their impact to different audiences. To successively overturn *Roe* and to successively shape state policy in the aftermath of *Roe* will require helping the public to better understand *Roe*'s nature and breadth, and what overturning *Roe* will practically mean in people's lives.

CONSIDERATIONS FOR FUTURE ABORTION LITIGATION STRATEGY

The goals for abortion litigation in the foreseeable future need to be defined. While the ultimate goal may be to overturn the first holding of *Roe* creating an unprecedented national right to abortion, there are legitimate incremental goals that can build momentum, such as to increase legal protection for the unborn and for women, to reduce abortions, and to return authority for abortion policy to the people at the state level.

After *Gonzales* there are still at least five justices on the Court who support *Roe* and will oppose its overruling: Kennedy, Ginsburg, Souter, Stevens, Breyer. The federal Constitution makes the nomination and confirmation of justices a political issue, in the classic sense. Future U.S. presidential and Senate elections will be critical. Elections for legislatures, governors, attorney generals—those state officials who enact abortion legislation and defend it before the Supreme Court—are critical. Every abortion case in the courts is an opportunity to build the record, to educate the justices for the future. Each case is an opportunity to educate the public positively or negatively.

Sponsors of state legislation in coming years need to consider all of these factors and the following: Is a prohibition bill necessary to provoke a test case? Will the bill be passed? Will the bill be signed? Will it be upheld by five or six justices on the Supreme Court? Will the bill be vigorously and competently defended by the state attorney general? Can he or she be counted on to urge the Court to overturn *Roe?* How will prohibition bills affect future presidential and Senate elections?

The best way to approach the Roberts Court. One of the seven habits in Stephen Covey's *Seven Habits of Highly Effective People* is to "start with the end in mind." One way to apply that "habit" to *Roe* is the following thought experiment: *How do we make it easy for the Court to overturn* Roe? It will never be easy for the justices to overturn *Roe*, at least not in the foreseeable future. Some justices cannot help but consider their historical legacy in ruling on the most controversial Supreme Court decision of the past half-century. And yet, by thinking of ways to make it easier, we can identify factors that will make a case more likely to be successful.

It's important to look at an abortion law coming to the Court as the justices might view it. While an abortion regulation does not necessarily set up a direct conflict with *Roe*—an obvious test case—an abortion prohibition would unavoidably conflict with *Roe* and set up a test case. The justices can see that ahead of time, and they can avoid a test case if they choose.

The 2007 *Gonzales* decision doesn't tell us whether Chief Justice Roberts and Justice Alito will ultimately support the overruling of *Roe*. But it does tell us that they will proceed incrementally, case-by-case. We know their record before nomination, their testimony at their hearings, their opinions, and their extrajudicial writings and speeches. We can only act on what we do know; we can't act on speculation or what we don't know (e.g., some are speculating whether Roberts will persuade Kennedy to join the other four).

How would Roberts and Alito prefer to address a test case? What bill? On what time frame? What parties? There is an array of legislation options to present to the Court: enhanced informed consent, clinic regulations, bills aimed at cutting back or hollowing-out *Roe* gradually.

The next test case on abortion at the Supreme Court needs to build on the recognition in *Gonzales* of the impact of abortion on women. That could include an enhanced informed-consent bill that requires prescreening for risk factors, or an informed-consent bill that requires specific information about the five best medically documented long-term risks from abortion: placenta previa, premature delivery and prematurity in future pregnancies, suicide, alcohol and substance abuse, and the loss of protective effect from breast cancer of a first full-term pregnancy.

We cannot know how Chief Justice Roberts and Justice Alito might view *Roe* several years from now. From a justice's perspective, however, what would they want to see on the following issues: a good record; a clear understanding of the social and legal implications; minimal upheaval—social, political and legal; minimal media attack; time frame; an understanding of what will happen in the states; concern about the specter of the back alley. These will require thoughtful planning.

MEANS AND ENDS:
HOW TO THINK ABOUT STATE ABORTION PROHIBITIONS

In light of all these considerations, including the history since the *Casey* decision of 1992 and the *Gonzales* decision in 2007, what sense might be made of the effort to pass abortion prohibition bills?

What are the best *means* to *successfully* challenge *Roe* in the courts? On what time frame? These questions were, as a practical matter, put on the shelf after the Court's decision in *Planned Parenthood v. Casey* and the confirmations of Justices Ginsburg and Breyer, because a majority of the justices clearly supported *Roe*. In the wake of the *Gonzales* decision, they are back in the public debate, though the Obama presidency will largely postpone them for at least the next four years.

The justices' written opinions are the most reliable way to determine their views of the Constitution and what they might do in future cases. It was clear before and clearer after *Gonzales* that there aren't five votes on the Supreme Court to overturn *Roe*.

In response to a question as to when, if ever, he thought the high court would overturn *Roe v. Wade*, Justice Scalia told an audience of law students and professors at the University of Freiburg in March 2006, "There are still five justices on our court who voted in favor of *Roe v. Wade*." "If I had to guess, I would say, 'Not yet—maybe not [ever]—*but certainly not yet*.' "[31] The *Gonzales* decision reinforces this.

After *Gonzales*, a federal court will likely invalidate a state abortion prohibition on its face (as a whole) without hearing new facts or evidence. The lower court judgment will be affirmed on appeal, and the Supreme Court will likely refuse to even hear the case. In addition, an abortion *prohibition* will lead to a decision that will be widely reported as either approving or disapproving the prohibition and all its elements—language, penalties and so forth. This will inevitably constrain the justices in their decision and limit their options in disposing of the test case, pushing them into a corner. The obstacles to the successful defense of a state abortion prohibition are thus clear and overwhelming in 2009.

An abortion *regulation*, in contrast, does not inevitably set up a test case and does not necessarily push the justices into a corner, since they can address a regulation without inevitably considering the future of *Roe*. Regulations are thus more likely to get Supreme Court review, while prohibitions are the most likely to be rejected for review for the foreseeable future.

Does this mean that the Court will never reconsider its disastrous decision in *Roe v. Wade?* No. But it does mean that more must be done legally and politically to circumvent current obstacles, and it's likely that the Court will have to change more, in its membership and decisions, to enable it to reconsider *Roe* in the future.

Another myth is that a *prohibition* law is necessary to instigate a Supreme Court test case. This is clearly incorrect. The Court revisited *Roe* in *Webster* in 1989 and in *Casey* in 1992, neither of which contained prohibitions. The validity of *Roe* can be drawn into question whenever an abortion law is challenged. A prohibition law is not necessary to revisit *Roe*.

Indeed, prohibitions may be positively counterproductive. It would be possible that the Court might avoid a prohibition law (and refuse to hear the case) because it does not want to give the appearance that the Court positively approved the law. The justices might think that they could achieve the same result by overturning *Roe* in a case involving a regulation, with the implication that the states would be nevertheless free to enact a prohibition without the Court having to specifically approve a prohibition law. On the other hand, the dangers that the Court might take the case and reaffirm *Roe* and *Casey*, thus strengthening the precedent, are real and substantial.

CONCLUSION

In the wake of *Gonzales*, based on an evaluation of the obstacles, opportunities and risks, it is unlikely that an abortion prohibition will ever form the means for a good test case to challenge *Roe*. Regulatory bills serve that purpose well without the risks, and regulatory bills that focus on the negative impact of abortion on women can prompt the creation of a good factual record for judicial and public education.

Roe's opponents have to be able to convince a least five Supreme Court justices, and more likely six. It's clear from *Gonzales* that five justices support *Roe*, therefore abortion prohibition bills are premature, will likely result in invalidation and review denied by the Court, and could actually hurt future Supreme Court confirmation hearings.

Overturning *Roe* will take an intensely focused effort that must include at least another Supreme Court vacancy and confirmation, electing a favorable Senate and president in future elections, enacting appropriate laws in the states with governors who will sign the law and attorney generals who will both competently defend the law and ask the Court to overturn *Roe* if the case makes it to the Court.

Building public support for returning the abortion issue to the American people should be intensely and consistently pursued. The myths of public opinion that support the retention of *Roe* must be challenged through public education. Public awareness of the negative effect of abortion on women must be enhanced in the coming years.

REGULATING BIOTECHNOLOGY TO PROTECT HUMAN LIFE AND HUMAN GOODS

"The thing that has saved man from his limited visions in the past has been the difficulty of devising suitable means for reaching them."

Robert S. Morison, "Comments on Genetic Evolution"

In the spring of 2001, a few months into President George W. Bush's first term, the media and members of Congress, including prominent members of his own party, began to exert increasing pressure on the president to end a twenty-seven-year moratorium on federal funding for human embryonic research (begun by the National Research Act of 1974) and to approve federal funding for embryonic stem-cell research.

On August 9, 2001, after several months of deliberation, President Bush announced his administration's policy on embryonic stem-cell research in a prime-time television address. Bush decided that he would allow federal tax dollars to be used for an estimated "sixty genetically diverse stem-cell lines" derived from human embryos that had been destroyed prior to August 9, 2001, but would not allow federal funding for research on cell lines from embryos destroyed after that date.[1]

The president articulated some important ethical principles. He virtually quoted from the Declaration of Independence in stating that "human life is a sacred gift from our creator." He opposed human cloning and objected to "the idea of growing human beings for spare body parts or creating life for our convenience." And he emphasized that it was important to "pay attention to the moral concerns raised by the new frontier of human embryo stem-cell research. Even the most noble ends do not justify any means."

While the president's carefully nuanced limit muted criticism from both sides temporarily, the debate has intensified at the federal and state levels. If human life is truly to be respected and protected, how can human embryos be intentionally destroyed, experimented on and used when no valid consent has been given for the use of their cells?

On one hand, as the Catholic bishops pointed out, "the federal government, for the first time in history, will support research that relies on the destruction of some defenseless human beings for possible benefit to others." On the other hand, the president's policy established a legal fence that allowed very limited funding and forestalled congressional efforts to overturn it for seven years. In July 2006, both houses of Congress passed a bill to expand federal funding, which the president successfully vetoed. The president's limitation still stood at the end of his administration.

THE GROWTH OF BIOETHICAL ISSUES IN THE LAW

The president's August 2001 decision portends many complex decisions on bioethical policy that will confront state and federal officials in the coming decades.[2] One of the strong undercurrents that drives these bioethical issues is that Americans place a high value on improved health with the aid of medical advancements and technology.

This emphasis is not new. The writer of Ecclesiaticus observed that "there are no riches above the riches of health of the body" (Sir 30:16). Twenty-five hundred years ago, Aristotle recognized the relationship between health and happiness. In the thirteenth century Thomas Aquinas observed that health (the good of the body) is related to happiness, though he stressed that it is not as important as the good of the soul for happiness.[3] All of us realize that our lives have been enhanced, if not saved outright, by medical advancements that didn't exist fifty to one hundred years ago.

As technology moves ahead in the medical marketplace, what is the role of public policy, and how do we balance the desire for continued medical advancement with the need to protect human life? The law has traditionally regulated technology and medical practice. While some technologies deserve minimal regulations, other technologies clearly threaten human life and other human goods.

The Bush decision involved, in a vivid way, the practical application of the four primary factors of political prudence: good goals, wise judgment as to what's possible in the circumstances, effectively connecting means and ends, and preserving the possibility of future improvement when the ideal cannot be immediately accomplished.

Over the past four decades biotechnology issues in the law have garnered increasing public attention and debate—including the Karen Quinlan case in the 1970s, the Nancy Cruzan case in the late 1980s, fetal tissue transplantation in the 1990s, the embryonic stem cell debate since 1998, the Terri Schiavo case in 2004-2005, and throughout these years the rising cost of health care.

The history of bioethics and law over the past forty years can be broadly summarized. During the rise of biotechnology in the United States, technology has sprinted ahead of ethical understanding and social regulation.[4] Clearly, the impact of biotechnology on human life continues to grow: abortion; in vitro fertilization (IVF); commerce in sperm, eggs and embryos; surrogate motherhood; fetal tissue transplantation; pre-implantation genetic screening and selection; cyropreserved embryos; selective reduction (abortion); embryonic stem-cell research; human cloning; gene therapy; germline therapy and genetic manipulation; cybernetics; and nanotechnology.

In 2005 the President's Council on Bioethics emphasized "the growing powers over the beginnings of human life, especially as exercised ex vivo, in the clinic and laboratory. These powers emerge out of the confluence of work in reproductive biology, developmental biology, and genetics."[5]

Up to now the regulation that exists has been done largely through the states. The federal government's intervention has been limited, and the constitutional authority of Congress to legislate on these subjects may also be limited.[6] The actual procedures in the infertility industry and biotechnology are mostly unregulated. Successful human IVF has existed since 1978, for example, but neither the states nor the federal government have enacted many regulations.[7] As the prospect of genetic engineering, including human cloning, has gained momentum in the 1990s, the states and federal government have only begun to address these technologies.

The need for governmental protection of human rights. The role of legislation reflects the unique paradigm for the protection of human life in America: governmental action through legislation is needed to protect human life. In other areas of law, like free speech and religious freedom, specific clauses in the federal Constitution can be invoked, and the courts have affirmatively protected "civil liberties." By contrast, homicide law has been the locus of protection for human life traditionally, and the states, not the federal government, are charged with enforcing homicide laws. State and federal courts have rarely acted to affirmatively expand protection for the lives of human beings. This paradigm has enormous practical legal consequences: private plaintiffs may sue to protect civil liberties, but state officials are charged with enforcing homicide and new laws that might protect human life.

The Supreme Court's decision in *Roe v. Wade* in 1973, expanding the constitutional "right to privacy" to encompass abortion, has cast a long shadow over the regulation of reproductive technology and biotechnology. And while there is an express (though qualified) right to life in the Fifth and Fourteenth Amendments to the federal constitution, the Supreme Court has held that the unborn are not protected under the Fourteenth Amendment as "persons."[8] Rightly interpreted on its own terms *Roe* is limited to a so-called "right to terminate pregnancy."[9] But the broader doctrine of the "right to privacy" suggested that it might be expanded to encompass other forms of biotechnology as autonomy.[10] The Court has not yet expanded *Roe* to encompass a right to IVF, reproductive technology or human embryo research; there is no *Roe v. Wade* of cloning, no constitutional right to do reproductive technology immune from popular control.

Nevertheless such a "right" has been consistently argued for in the academic law journals, and several courts have struck down state fetal-experimentation laws for potentially inhibiting IVF. In addition, some academics argue for an unprecedented "First Amendment right to do scientific research" that would immunize researchers from any public oversight.

The threat that the Supreme Court will withdraw these technologies from popular regulation may have receded with the additions of Chief Justice Roberts and Justice Alito, but there may still be a majority of five justices on the Court—Stevens, Kennedy, Souter, Ginsburg, and Breyer—who might expand *Roe* to encompass some forms of reproductive technology, if given the opportunity. As of 2009, however, the constitutional "right to privacy" has not been extended to withdraw biotechnology from popular control. Reproductive technology and biotechnology have not been "constitutionalized." And the *Gonzales* decision in 2007 may suggest a greater humility on the part of a majority of the justices in considering whether judicial power should supplant representative government.

This means that all these forms of reproductive and biotechnology are still subject to popular control and regulation, primarily at the state level. Our elected representatives in the states and in Congress are actively debating these issues. Legislators thus face a different, more wide-open environment with reproductive technology and biotechnology than they do with abortion.

But regulation will be needed. The President's Council recounts the growth of technology that has fostered human cloning, genetic screening and the creation of human-animal hybrids, and predicts the increasing control over human life from current and new technologies.

New legal protection is needed through legislation to protect human life and human goods. Success in bioethical policymaking to protect human goods will require at least four things:

- an understanding of the human goods at stake (especially human life and dignity)

- an understanding of current policy and the need for regulation

- an understanding and accurate assessment of the possibilities of and obstacles to success and how these might be overcome

- prudential rhetoric—an ability to explain what is at stake in the common vernacular, rhetorically balancing moral principle and utilitarian concerns

It is critical for lawmakers to define the human goods at stake in promoting and regulating reproductive technology and biotechnology, to define why some legal and ethical boundaries must be drawn around reproductive technology and biotechnology to protect those human goods and values, and to articulate these principles persuasively in the public square.

In a very complex area of technology, science and medicine, specific, targeted legislation is needed that highlights distinct issues; an all-encompassing, comprehensive regulation will rarely succeed. One of the most famous examples is the Clinton Administration's health care overhaul proposed during the 1990s.

It is continually necessary to create a democratic majority in support of public policy, and that requires returning to the fundamentals of communication: knowing your audience and how to persuade them. A prudential rhetoric that defines the human goods at stake is necessary to influence public opinion and build majority support for boundaries on biotechnology that guides technology to promote human health while protecting developing human beings and human dignity. This requires combining moral principle with utilitarian concerns (especially concerns about the personal impact). As the Oxford scholar C. S. Lewis once observed: "Any fool can write learned language. The vernacular is the real test."[11]

The moral purposes of the law. How do we identify and articulate the human goods at stake?

Since at least the Declaration of Independence, moral philosophy and moral ideals have shaped American political and legal change, including policymaking in the courts and legislatures.

The protection of human life is one of those moral ideals. The protection of human life in American law is not a "special interest" but is deeply rooted in American political and constitutional documents from the earliest history of America.

The common law. It starts with the common law's solicitude for human life. The protection of vulnerable human life is reflected, for example, in the common law's clear repudiation of the absolute power of the Roman father over the life of the child and its elevation of legal protection for human life.[12]

James Wilson, a framer of the federal Constitution and one of the first Supreme Court justices, exclaimed the common law's protection of human life in hallowed terms:

> I shall certainly be excused from adducing any formal arguments to evince, that life, and whatever is necessary for the safety of life, are the natural rights of man. Some things are so difficult; others are so plain, that they cannot be proved. It will be more to our purpose to show the anxiety, with which some legal systems spare and preserve human life; the levity and cruelty which others discover in destroying or sporting with it; and the inconsistency, with which, in others, it is, at some times, wantonly sacrificed, and, at other times, religiously guarded. . . .

[I]n Sparta, if any infant, newly born, appeared, to those who were appointed
to examine him, ill formed or unhealthy, he was, without any further ceremony,
thrown into a gulph near mount Taygetus. . . . At Athens, the parent was empowered, when a child was born, to pronounce on its life or its death. . . . [A]t
Rome, the son held his life by the tenure of the father's pleasure. . . .

With consistency, beautiful and undeviating, human life, from its commencement to its close, is protected by the common law. In the contemplation
of law, life begins when the infant is first able to stir in the womb. By the law, life
is protected not only from immediate destruction, but from every degree of actual violence, and, in some cases from every degree of danger.[13]

Wilson concluded: "The formidable power of a Roman father is unknown to
the common law. But it vests in the parent such authority as is conducive to the
advantage of the child."[14]

This understanding was familiar to lawyers during the founding era of the
United States and its aftermath. It was reflected, for example, in the legal
training of John Quincy Adams, who observed that the common law "has re-
strained within proper bounds, even the sacred rights of parental authority,
and shewn the cruelty, and the absurdity of abandoning an infant to destruction for any deformity in its bodily frame."[15] That was a tradition the common
law repudiated.

Why the Declaration still matters. This moral ideal of natural human
rights came to be enunciated in the founding political document of America,
the Declaration of Independence, in 1776.

In the words of the Declaration, "governments derive their just powers from
the consent of the governed." But that principle does not stand alone. It actually follows from five preceding principles in the preamble of the Declaration:
"We hold these truths to be self-evident, that all men are created equal, that
they are endowed by their Creator with certain unalienable Rights, that among
these are Life, Liberty, and the pursuit of Happiness. That to secure these
rights, Governments are instituted . . . deriving their just powers from the
consent of the governed."

In debate on the Bill of Rights during the first Congress, James Madison
referred to the proposition that "all men are created equal" as an "absolute
truth."[16] When the founders held that all "men" are created equal, they meant
all human beings, "created as members of the same species."[17]

Decades later, Lincoln effectively employed this truth against slavery. He referred to this proposition as "an abstract truth, applicable to all men and all times." Recognizing that the principle could not be immediately enforced in America in 1776, Lincoln asserted that the founders "meant simply to declare the *right*, so that the *enforcement* of it might follow as fast as circumstances should permit."[18]

More than two hundred years after its publication, the Declaration's principles remain the moral foundation of democratic government. But they are continually under assault. Jefferson declared that the "only firm basis" for "the liberties of a nation" is the "conviction in the minds of the people that these liberties are the gift of God." Each generation of Americans must gain a renewed conviction of the truths of the Declaration.

Lincoln articulated the rationale for a long, persevering struggle to protect moral ideals in public policy. He argued that the authors of the Declaration of Independence "meant to set up a standard maxim for free society, which should be familiar to all, and revered by all; constantly looked to, constantly labored for, and even though never perfectly attained, constantly approximated, and thereby constantly spreading and deepening its influence, and augmenting the happiness and value of life to all people of all colors everywhere."[19]

The formulation of public policy in Congress and the states to protect human life and dignity must rely—morally and rhetorically—on the Declaration and its natural rights philosophy. It is important to remind our neighbors of the importance and meaning of the Declaration in protecting human rights and dignity.

How we have protected human life. The common law is subject to change and has in many ways been eclipsed by state or federal legislation. Over the past two centuries, legislation has constantly overhauled the common law, for better or worse. But these changes generally concern the means rather than the end, since respect for human life has continued to be a hallmark of American law.

Contemporary bioethical issues in the law have proliferated since the 1960s. Over those decades regulation of bioethical issues has been largely reactive, driven by technological developments or events or publicized incidents. Individual cases, like Karen Ann Quinlan's, attract publicity, and the media is a significant factor in driving the public debate.

There have been two major trends. First, legislation usually follows problems and does not anticipate them very well. Legislatures usually react when a problem is urgent. Due to limits of time and resources, legislators address what seems most urgent, which is shaped by events, the sway of public opinion and the media. Lawmakers are also dependent on medical and scientific knowledge, and they respond to medical and scientific developments as they are brought to their attention. Second, courts have often stepped in to make new law when legislatures have failed to act and a vacuum exists.

Future legislation will be shaped, in part, by bioethical developments in law over the past forty years. Here's a general survey of some major areas.[20]

Abortion. Prior to 1973, abortion policy was decided by the people through representative government at the state level. In the three-plus decades since *Roe v. Wade,* the Supreme Court has imposed in every state a rule of abortion for virtually any reason, at any time of pregnancy, punctuated by regulations around the margins enacted by the states. The Supreme Court's *Gonzales* decision in 2007 doesn't really change that, at least in the short-term, though it does suggest that the current Court is the most abortion-skeptical Court since *Roe v. Wade* and will give greater deference to the states.

Wrongful birth and wrongful life. One indication of the direction of judicial policymaking is state court decisions involving the torts of "wrongful birth" and "wrongful life." These are novel lawsuits that state judges have created based on *Roe*'s legalization of abortion, allowing suits against doctors when a child, who could have been aborted, is born with disabilities. This has been a matter left to state law, and it shows some state courts' willingness to extend the scope of the abortion license. State courts in a majority of states have *allowed* a cause of action for wrongful *birth.* But courts in a majority of states have *rejected* a cause of action for wrongful *life.* Several states, on the other hand, have eliminated wrongful birth and wrongful life suits by legislation.[21]

Protection of the developing human being (in utero). One fundamental question is the legal status of the unborn human being (in utero) and of the extra-corporeal (ex utero or IVF) human embryo. The basic law protecting human life is the criminal homicide law. (Homicide is, by definition, the killing of a human being.) Prior to *Roe v. Wade,* the states did *not* uniformly protect the unborn human under state homicide laws; that was the role of abortion laws, which focused more on criminalizing doctors' participation in the procedure than creating legal personhood for the unborn. In addition, the Supreme Court addressed only abortion in *Roe* and did not address other ways in which the unborn could be killed, *leaving the states free to protect the unborn outside the context of abortion.* Consequently, there has been a growing area of state legislation to protect the unborn child as a human being under state homicide laws *outside* the context of abortion. The developing human, in utero, is increasingly protected, outside the context of abortion, under both state homicide and wrongful death laws.[22]

In vitro fertilization and assisted reproductive technologies (ART). Abortion fostered in vitro fertilization. *Roe v. Wade* was perceived (wrongly) as stripping all legal protection from the human embryo. In 1978, five years after *Roe*, Louise Brown became the first baby born from in vitro fertilization, and IVF introduced the then-radical phenomenon of extracorporeal (out of body) human embryos. IVF is largely unregulated in the United States, except for the federal Fertility Clinic Success Rate and Certification Act of 1992.[23] The report of the President's Council on Bioethics, Reproduction and *Responsibility* outlines several reasons why IVF has gone largely unregulated for twenty-five years.[24]

IVF has fostered a whole range of alternative reproductive technologies and options. Law professor Helen Alvare has summarized the legal landscape:

> The patchwork of federal and state laws concerning ARTs may be characterized broadly as attempts to facilitate transactions in gametes and embryos by allowing the reassignment of parental rights from biological donors to intending parent(s); to prevent the transmission of some diseases; to prevent fraud on customers and promote truth in advertising; and to provide some protection for human embryos.[25]

The courts have not yet expanded *Roe v. Wade*—which technically protects "a right to terminate pregnancy"—to encompass a right of "procreation" and ARTs more generally.[26] Nevertheless, numerous activists advocate the judicial creation of a broad right of procreation by (virtually) any means.[27] One federal court has treated IVF as a fundamental right, but the Supreme Court refused to review it,[28] and the *Gonzales* decision in 2007 suggests that the current Court majority won't touch the issue. In the absence of legislation, IVF is regulated, if at all, by malpractice suits. Implicit in IVF, as it is typically done, is a right to manipulate early stage embryos, including their preservation or destruction.

Protection of the developing human being (ex utero). Since 1978 few states have acted to protect the extracorporeal (or IVF) embryo. Theoretically, the extracorporeal embryo should be protected, as all other human beings, under state homicide laws, but these have never been used by any prosecutor. When IVF became a reality five years after *Roe*, that decision (and public beliefs about that decision) inhibited any effort to use homicide laws to restrict IVF and embryo experimentation. In the absence of legislation, a number of state courts have treated cryopreserved embryos as property, under property and contract law, rather than as children under child custody law.[29]

Fetal and embryo experimentation. Some states regulate this area.[30] Some federal courts have struck down state laws regulating fetal experimentation on the grounds that the statutes using the term *experimentation* were unconstitutionally vague rather than on the grounds that there is a right to do such experimentation.[31] Several states do restrict embryo research.[32]

Human cloning. In the years since Dolly the sheep was cloned in 1997, a number of states have passed prohibitions on human cloning.[33] A federal bill to ban human cloning continues to languish in Congress, but it may be beyond Congress's constitutional authority to legislate. Some cloning of human embryos is funded by a few states as part of embryonic stem-cell research.

In each of these areas the formation of public policy has been largely reactionary—reacting to events, such as thalidomide babies in the 1960s, Karen Quinlan's ordeal in the early 1970s or the cloning of Dolly the sheep in 1997.

The formulation of public policy has also been heavily dependent on medical and scientific understanding and expertise. The scientific and medical communities have played a significant role, as have activist organizations and the media, influencing the formation of regulations. Science and medical experts are a critical part of any strategy to support (or kill) legislation. In many cases their vested interests are to prevent legal regulation, thereby preserving their own autonomy to act as they see fit.

The states, rather than the federal government, have been the primary arena for the affirmative protection of human life over the past three decades. The regulation of biotechnology should arguably be left to the states to regulate through their police power, but the courts' inclination to expand individual autonomy, and the judicial deference to the expertise of science and medicine (even if conducted in the service of commerce and not patients), are two factors that have undercut deference to the states' police power.

On the other hand, over the past three decades federal legislation on bioethical issues directly affecting the creation or destruction of human life has been limited. The President's Council on Bioethics recently acknowledged that "new powers to observe and manipulate in vitro nascent human life for purposes of scientific research are not regulated in a meaningful way by the federal government" and described the Fertility Clinic Success Rate and Certification Act as the only "federal statute that aims at the regulation of assisted reproduction as such."[34] There are many reasons for this, including the fact that such issues have traditionally been within the domain of the states in our federal system, the politics of abortion and the political makeup of the Congress, the constitutional restrictions on Congress's authority, and the vested interests of scientists and corporate entrepreneurs in this area.

THE JUDICIAL RECORD EXPANDING INDIVIDUAL AUTONOMY IN BIOETHICAL ISSUES

Since the 1960s the courts—federal and state—have intervened to control legislative regulation of sexuality, reproduction and other bioethical issues. In *Poe v. Ullman*,[35] Supreme Court justice John Harlan first questioned criminal prohibitions on the marital use of artificial contraception. The Court first struck down such laws in 1966 in *Griswold v. Connecticut*[36] creating a right to privacy not found in the text of the Constitution. It then expanded that "right" to unmarried persons in *Eisenstadt v. Baird*[37] in 1972. By 1977, in *Carey v. Population Services International*,[38] the Court summarized previous decisions as guaranteeing "an individual's right to decide to prevent conception or terminate a pregnancy" and extended the right to minors. In 2000 the Supreme Court struck down the laws of thirty states that banned partial-birth abortion in *Stenberg v. Carhart*. Most recently, in 2003, in *Lawrence v. Texas*, the Court overruled its seventeen-year-old decision in *Bowers v. Hardwick*, and struck down state criminal prohibitions on homosexual sodomy. Through these years the courts adopted a libertarian perspective, striking down legislation that regulated these issues.

Conversely, the courts have been unwilling to act independently, in the absence of legislation, *to protect developing human life.* In the abortion arena the Supreme Court has imposed a nationwide rule of abortion on demand since 1973. Virtually all protection of unborn or developing human life has come from the legislatures, almost never from the courts.[39]

Instead, the Supreme Court has adopted a very broad, existentialist definition of personal autonomy. In 1992, in *Planned Parenthood v. Casey,*[40] a plurality of justices—O'Connor, Kennedy and Souter—first adopted this definition of personal autonomy. This has come to be called, and derided, as "the mystery passage": "At the heart of liberty is the right to define one's own concept of existence, of meaning, of the universe, and of the mystery of human life. Beliefs about these matters could not define the attributes of personhood were they formed under the compulsion of the State."[41]

There are several problems with this sweeping passage. First, the issue with abortion (and most of these bioethical issues) is not "beliefs" but action—action that ends the life of a developing human being. (If that passage justifies judicial elimination of abortion law, it justifies judicial elimination of homicide laws as well.) Second, it defies the clear history that "liberty" in American history never included abortion before *Roe.*[42] Third, it has never been the proper role of judges in the American political system to play the role of Platonic guardians, and unilaterally override self-government to expand individual autonomy. When judges don't have the courage to do that overtly, they ascribe their views to the framers of the Fourteenth Amendment. But the framers clearly never intended abortion to be among the "liberties" protected by that amendment.[43]

The judiciary's promotion of individual autonomy has been strongly echoed by the legal academy. In addition, the dominant instinct in contemporary American bioethics is individual autonomy.[44] For example, prominent bioethics law expert Lori Andrews has proposed three models for evaluating the regulation of genetics: the medical, public health and fundamental rights models.[45] For the past two decades Andrews has been influential in shaping public policy in favor of the new reproductive technologies—an unlimited right to procreational freedom—based on an ethic of moral autonomy and utilitarianism. She claims that the three models she proposes are adopted from past regulations of "medical services."[46] She favors the "fundamental rights" model, essentially a moral autonomy model. For the same reason that the mystery passage in *Casey* is misguided, the rights-oriented model is flawed. Instead a patient-oriented model—encompassing all human beings—is needed.

The courts have been the biggest legal engine in American society promoting the moral autonomy model to override self-government; state legislatures, where public opinion can have a restraining effect, have been more likely to protect human life than the judiciary, based on the record since the 1960s.

WHY WE PROTECT THE EMBRYONIC HUMAN

"But I'm still an embryo with a long long way to go."
—Helen Reddy, "I Am Woman"

Debate over the status and protection of the developing human being has been a dominant issue in American public policy for the past forty years. Three cultural developments have driven this debate: a certain brand of feminism as a cultural force, the sexual revolution, and reproductive technology making possible what was not possible in the past—like developing human beings in the laboratory.

One of the most difficult challenges in regulating biotechnology's impact on human life is humanizing the embryonic human being. This is not a recent phenomenon; doctors and medical experts in the nineteenth century wrestled with a similar dilemma in midwifery and obstetrics.

Although the public debate often focuses on whether the human embryo or fetus is a person, which is more of a philosophical or ontological question, the legal question should be more precisely whether the human embryo *is* a human being, because the primary area of law that protects human life is homicide law.

A homicide is the killing of a human being. Human being is an anthropological term that is based on biology and species. A human being is simply a member of the species Homo sapiens, and it is defined biologically by species, not developmentally.[47]

That the human embryo is a human being is determined by biology (is the human embryo a whole living organism or being?) and anthropology (is it a member of the human species—is it human?).[48] Biology tells us that a human embryo (and fetus) is an organism, a whole member of the species Homo sapiens in the earliest stages of development. Like all biological organisms, human beings come into existence as a single cell (a zygote or one-celled embryo), and they progress through various stages of development—embryo, fetus, infant, adolescent, adult. The combination of chromosomes identifies the embryo as a new, distinct organism that is human.[49] The embryo is a complete human organism or being, not a part of any other organism; gametes (egg and sperm), by contrast, whose union results in an embryo, are not whole or distinct organisms. We can determine it is living by the test of living organisms at that developmental stage—it is metabolizing, its cells are growing and dividing.[50] That an entity is an organism is not undermined by the fact that it is merely one-celled. There are other one-celled organisms.[51]

The fact that the one-celled product of cloning does not result from the union of sperm and egg does not mean that it is not the same human organism that results from the union of sperm and egg. The one-celled human zygote is a member of the human species and is a human being.[52]

This leads to the scientific conclusion of the 1995 Ramsey Colloquium on Embryo Research:

> Skin and intestinal tissue, even eggs and sperm, are human life. But, unlike such instances of human life, the embryo from the earliest moment has the active capacity to articulate itself into what everyone acknowledges is a human being. The embryo is a being; that is to say, it is an integral whole with actual existence. The being is human: it will not articulate itself into some other kind of animal. Any being that is human is a human being. If it is objected that, at five or fifteen days, the embryo does not look like a human being, it must be pointed out that this is precisely what a human being looks like—and what each of us looked like—at five or fifteen days of development.[53]

Clearly, some Americans can't accept the idea that—as a May 2004 letter to *USA Today* put it—an embryo "about the size of a period at the end of a sentence" is a human being. But these are the concepts and language that human embryology has adopted in the twentieth century. And the size of the organism, and the uses to which it can be put, don't discount the scientific analysis and conclusions.

How We Have Protected the Embryonic Human

Legal protection of the developing human goes back to ancient times. At least since 1600, Anglo-American law protected the developing human being. However, the law cannot protect something that cannot be determined to be alive, so the law's protection was effectively limited by medical and scientific knowledge. As medical knowledge about human development has increased, legal protection has grown.

The primary source of legal protection for human life has been homicide law. Prior to *Roe v. Wade*, the states had two types of laws that applied to protect the human embryo—homicide law and abortion law—and the application of these two laws to human life was shaped by medical knowledge. Since the first successful IVF did not occur until 1969, there was no such thing as an extracorporeal (out of body) embryo before then, and there was no law that specifically applied to extracorporeal human embryos. The law protected embryos in a woman's body in the context of "pregnancy" and acted against the termination of pregnancy, or abortion. Roughly speaking, abortion law applied to an embryo or fetus in utero, and homicide law applied to an embryo or fetus outside the womb (born alive). Location (inside or outside) was important; gestation (the developmental stage) was not. Between 1967 and 1972, approximately fourteen states changed their abortion laws and introduced exceptions into laws which previously prohibited abortion except to save the life of the mother.

Generally, homicide law protected the *born* human being, and abortion law protected the unborn human being. The dividing line was birth, because at that point the unborn is outside the womb and can be observed, but not birth in the sense of full-term birth—just birth as outside the womb—even if premature and not viable. Another way of saying this is that the dividing line was based on location—inside or outside the womb—not gestation (the stage of development).

So, if a pregnant woman was injured and the child was born alive at three months and died thereafter, that was a homicide of the child; if the child was stillborn at term, there was no homicide. That rule—called the "born alive rule"—was rendered obsolete by medical advances, but the law virtually *never* placed any significance on the degree of development of the unborn child. That really started with the abortion debates of the 1960s and then the Supreme Court's opinion in *Roe v. Wade*.

When *Roe* was decided, the Supreme Court invalidated the laws of all fifty states and declared abortion legal for any reason, at any time of pregnancy, in every state. The Court's decision did not say that the states could not protect unborn human life under any circumstances; the Court merely said that a woman had a right to abortion and the states could not prohibit abortion. The Court said nothing about protecting the unborn *outside* the context of a woman's desire to terminate her pregnancy. That leaves open protection of the unborn in cases such as third-party assaults against a pregnant woman or the extracorporeal (out of the body) embryo.

For example, we now call the California fetal homicide law the "Lacey Peterson law," and Americans probably think that it is novel. But the so-called Lacey Peterson law was enacted in 1970, and thirty-six states have fetal homicide laws as of 2007, twenty-four of which protect the developing human being from the time of conception.

So, *Roe* blunted but did not completely eliminate legal protection of the developing human being inside the womb, and IVF threatened the developing human embryo outside the womb. Some human research protection is already afforded to human embryos as human subjects, and has been since at least 1975. That policy is shaped by federal law—against the backdrop of constitutional law, state law and international ethical codes.

The law was progressively protecting the unborn until the abortion debate of the 1960s, and then the Supreme Court's decision in *Roe v. Wade* changed almost everything. Protection of the embryonic human is now overshadowed, legally, by the Supreme Court's decision in *Roe v. Wade*. Socially, it is overshadowed by the expansion of in vitro fertilization over the past quarter century and by current social and medical debates over in vitro fertilization, embryo and fetal research, and embryonic stem-cell research. There is some legal protection for the human embryo, but it is limited, and it is counterbalanced legally by abortion on demand, and scientifically by calls for embryo research. All of this is shaped by public attitudes about whether a "fertilized egg the size of a period at the end of a sentence" is really a human being.

Why* Roe *is not determinative for legal protection of the developing human being. It is commonly assumed that *Roe* declared that government cannot protect unborn or developing human life, or human life before birth, and governs all legal treatment of the unborn. Although this broad interpretation of *Roe* was pronounced by opponents of fetal rights, the Court did not say this, which became increasingly recognized by courts and legislatures in the 1980s.

As a matter of law, *Roe* applies only in the context of abortion and, more particularly, when a pregnancy exists and the woman's interest in an abortion is at stake. Inside that context, *Roe* occupies the field. Outside that context, *Roe* does not govern.

In the case of the in vitro embryo there is no pregnancy. *Roe* does not control because it only applies to embryos in utero, in a pregnant woman. Thus it does not govern in the case of third-party assaults against an unborn child (when abortion is not at issue and the mother wants the child) or in the case of extracorporeal embryos, such as frozen embryos.

Federal policy. What is current federal policy? The January 2004 report of the President's Council on Bioethics, "Monitoring Stem Cell Research," provides a good summary of federal policy toward the human embryo since *Roe*. Federal law governing experimentation has focused on the concept of the "protection of human subjects."

The first successful IVF was performed in 1969. The Department of Health and Human Services (HHS) regulates research involving human subjects conducted or supported by the agency through regulations.[54] Regulations protecting human subjects involved in research were first published in the Federal Register in May 1974.[55] And in August 1974 a notice of proposed rule-making was published, indicating that the protections would be amended and enlarged to include the human fetus and others.

In the wake of the *Roe* decision, Congress in July 1974 enacted a moratorium on any federal funding for embryo research.[56] That moratorium continued with President Bush's veto of the embryonic stem-cell funding bill in July 2006.

Through the National Research Act (NRA), Congress also created the National Commission for the Protection of Human Subjects of Biomedical and Behavioral Research. The Commission issued a report in 1975 that called for the establishment of a national Ethics Advisory Board (EAB) to propose standards. In August or November 1975 the federal policy on protection of human subjects was amended to include the fetus.[57] The August 1974 moratorium was "lifted" but it was established that research "will be conducted or supported by the Department only in accordance with the following regulations."[58] Research would be permitted "only if it imposes minimal or no risk to the fetus." The fetus was recognized to be a human subject,[59] although *fetus* was defined as "the product of conception from the time of implantation."[60]

The Ethics Advisory Board issued a report in June 1979 that ethically supported embryo research.[61] The Department of Health, Education and Welfare did not offer funding for embryo research. The President's Council records that "the EAB's charter expired in 1980, and no renewal or replacement was put forward, creating a peculiar situation in which the regulations requiring the EAB to review proposals for funding remained in effect, but the Board no longer existed to consider such requests. Funding was therefore rendered impossible in practice. Because the EAB was never replaced, a de facto ban on funding remained in place throughout the 1980s" (i.e., throughout the Reagan and Bush Administrations).

In 1993 Congress enacted the National Institutes of Health (NIH) Revitalization Act and in 1994 NIH convened a Human Embryo Research Panel. It made recommendations to support embryo research, but Congress did not approve them.

In 1995 Congress adopted language to the 1996 budget bill that funds HHS and NIH "prohibiting the use of any federal funds for research that destroys or seriously endangers human embryos, or creates them for research purposes." This is known as the Dickey Amendment and remained the law at the end of 2008, having been attached to the HHS appropriations bill annually since 1996.[62] The Dickey Amendment applies to federal funding and *does not* prohibit *private* research using private funding. There is no federal law prohibiting *private* research on embryos.

State policy. The President's Council on Bioethics' January 2004 report, "Monitoring Stem Cell Research," points out that, in the wake of *Roe v. Wade*, twenty-four states—virtually half of all states—enacted statutes prohibiting research on human "conceptuses." Today, at least seven states ban research on in vitro embryos entirely—Florida, Louisiana, Maine, Minnesota, North Dakota, Pennsylvania and Rhode Island.

In vitro fertilization flourished after *Roe*, and it was assumed that the states could not protect the extracorporeal embryo. The first baby born from IVF, Louise Brown, was born in 1978 in Great Britain. After *Roe*, abortion laws were struck down, but abortion laws didn't accurately apply to the case of the extracorporeal embryo because there was no pregnancy to terminate. Did any other law apply?

Since the extracorporeal embryo was outside the womb and no pregnancy was at stake, did homicide laws apply? Prosecutors could have attempted to apply homicide laws, but with the potential exception of Virginia prosecutors applying state law against an IVF clinic, there is no evidence that any state or local prosecutor applied homicide law to protect an extracorporeal embryo in the United States.

It was uncertain in 1978, and doubtful today, whether state judges would establish that an out-of-body (extracorporeal) human embryo is a human being subject to the protection of the homicide code. Several state court cases support this supposition.[63] This history indicates that it would be better to continue to work through the legislatures for legislative protection than to attempt such changes through the courts.

In the face of increasing scientific pressure for embryonic research, the challenge is whether the *partial* legal protection can be made *comprehensive* and how and on what time frame. This will require a coherent strategy—led by scientists and scientific spokespeople—and not pro-life groups or activists—enlisting the support of allied organizations and a public education campaign.

PROTECTING OTHER HUMAN GOODS AND RELATIONSHIPS

Although the abortion issue has been one of the dominant bioethical issues in American public policy since the 1960s, biotechnology will have other, subtler impacts on human bodies and minds, posing more difficult ethical issues. American law and public policy has long prohibited or regulated abortion because abortion involves the *direct killing* of a human being. Some forms of reproductive technology and biotechnology may also inevitably involve the direct killing of developing human beings. But what if they don't? Are there other human goods at stake in the application of biotechnology, even if no human being is killed?

Since the 1970s, legal and medical experts have observed, for example, the important influence of reproductive technology on our view of the child and its status, on the concept of parenthood, on parent-child relationships, on children and their personal identity, and on the preservation of biological ties between parent and child. We are a quarter century into this dramatic change in the effect of reproductive technology on parent-child relationships.

Where's the harm in manipulating human life? Generally, we must encourage good medical advances that promote human health while protecting against the potential harms from the manipulation of human life. As Leon

Kass has pointed out, many have a natural, healthy "repugnance" to the notion of human cloning. But can they articulate convincing ethical or practical arguments against it?

How will human cloning "harm" the developing child that will be born? In what ways can manipulations of human beings be said to harm them?

It will not be possible, or perhaps even beneficial, to oppose genetic engineering based on vague notions of "playing God" or of "changing human nature." If the genetic engineering of the future is truly voluntary and informed, it will be very difficult to enact any legal constraints on it. Instead, it will be necessary to define and identify real harms to human beings that require social protection through public policy constraints. Americans favor autonomy, and limits on autonomy will be difficult to explain unless there are demonstrable harms. And if the harms are slight and set against advances in health, "choice" in health will triumph.

We already see this in the debate over embryonic stem-cell research (ESCR), where killing human embryos is believed by many to be justified by highly speculative claims of possible cures, despite the fact that any speculative cures won't be realized, if at all, for many years, and despite the progress already seen with adult stem cell therapies. For some people, full information and consent will be sufficient to justify any biotechnology.

Some fences around applications of biotechnology. Regulation of biotechnology will inevitably involve erecting fences and hence line-drawing. At least five constraints make comprehensive legislation virtually impossible in the foreseeable future: the absence of specific norms in the Constitution; judicial commitment to broad autonomy; the complexity of science and technology; powerful, vested interests; and ambivalent public opinion. Because of these constraints and others it is not now possible to comprehensively protect developing human life or other human goods at stake. Regulation does not in itself imply promotion or sponsorship. There can be no limitations without line-drawing.

While the ethical debate will continue, there are four hedges against certain forms of harmful genetic manipulation that have been or can be erected by the states right now:

- the prohibition of human cloning—some states have begun to do this

- the prohibition of destructive human embryo research—ten states already do this

- the prohibition of discrimination in employment or insurance against parents with children, born or unborn, with genetic disabilities—Congress and some states have already set *some* limits on *some* forms of genetic discrimination

- the protection of doctors and other health care personnel through freedom of conscience legislation from being pressured to engage in eugenic genetic manipulation. Most states already have freedom of conscience legislation protecting doctors from participating in abortion. This narrow legislation must be expanded to encompass all health care personnel and to encompass other unethical medical practices.

A quarter century of reproductive technology has produced a large, powerful, influential industry that is subject to some of the normal business and commercial regulations, but very few state or federal regulations focus on the ethical aspects of reproductive technology.

The fabric of traditional law in areas of homicide, tort, informed consent, wrongful death and malpractice will continue to shape bioethics. New legislation will inevitably rely on these traditional areas. New regulations need to rely, as much as possible, on existing legal concepts and precedents.

Particularly difficult prudential considerations will be involved in four general issues in the coming years: regulating assisted reproductive technologies after a quarter century of unregulated growth, prohibiting or regulating embryonic research, prohibiting or regulating cloning, and regulating germline gene therapy. Sweeping federal legislation may be unconstitutional. The courts will likely not contribute to the protection of human life and will be inclined to view human dignity as limited to personal autonomy.

Human goods to protect. The following is a partial list of objectives that should be pursued to protect human dignity, prevent the artificial manipulation of human nature and prevent the commodification of human beings.[64] More could be identified—and will have to be identified—as biotechnology progresses. Broad medical progress can be promoted while human dignity is preserved.

Protect the life of human beings from their beginning. Many of the new biotechnologies are problematic for the simple reason that they disregard the dignity of developing human life, inside or outside the womb. There is a long legal history of protecting developing human life to the greatest extent possible given the status of medical knowledge.[65] And outside the context of abortion, over the past thirty years many states have progressively protected human life in the law at the earliest stages. One exception is the growth of IVF and related reproductive technologies. Although it is difficult to humanize the extracorporeal embryo in the public mind, legislative protections on developing human life are necessary to make progress in other areas.

Protect the two-parent family and two-parent childbearing. By separating sexual reproduction from procreation, reproductive technologies separate biological attachment from childbearing. Intentional procreation outside of marriage is fundamentally different from adoption, which has traditionally been viewed as an exceptional option to provide a home for an existing child who has lost his or her parents. The procreative rights of the unmarried are increasingly promoted in the law schools.[66] Reproductive technologies that permit childbearing without biological parental attachments should be discouraged. Even the U.S. Supreme Court has "recognized that natural bonds of affection lead parents to act in the best interests of children."[67] Childbearing without biological parental attachments has led and will lead to cases like that of Jaycee Buzzanca in California, who was conceived from anonymous sperm and egg donors and born in 1995 to a surrogate mother.[68] "Collaborative reproductive"—"the use of the eggs, sperm, or embryos of a third party to create a child to be reared by one or more persons biologically unrelated to the child ('the intending parents')"[69]—should be discouraged. It is currently "subject to minimal regulation in the United States."[70]

Discourage surrogate parenting or surrogacy. Likewise, because surrogacy separates biological attachments and children, surrogacy should be prohibited by legislation.[71] It risks the commodification of children and the exploitation of women.[72] Such legislation has been upheld as constitutional.[73]

Preserve a child's right to a complete identity. As a general rule, children should know their biological parents; the unique exception of traditional, closed adoption does not provide a basis for *deliberately* conceiving children while cutting off their biological ties. Anonymous sperm and egg donation has allowed men and women to treat sperm and egg as merely bodily fluids for sale, a commodity, without regard for the identity of the child. Anonymous sperm and egg donation has also resulted in the negligent transmission of disease.

Discourage sex-selection and trait-selection of children. For years bioethicists have talked about the prospect of selecting the traits of children through technology. Although selection of many traits is still not technologically possible, sex is one trait that can be selected. This can be done before conception, through screening, or after conception, through abortion. Sex-selective abortion should be prohibited by legislation. Illinois has such a law in place, but its effectiveness is uncertain.[74] Other countries have enacted laws restricting abortions for sex-selection.[75] Preconception sex selection should also be prohibited by legislation.[76]

Protect ethically conscientious medical professionals in their profession. There will be no culture of life without protecting the right of ethical health care professionals to remain in American medicine without fear of retaliatory discrimination. Legislation protecting the right of conscience currently exists in nearly forty-seven states, but it is too limited—primarily protecting only physicians from "participating" in "abortion." With the growth in reproductive technologies, cloning and genetic engineering over the past three decades, broader legislation is needed to protect all medical and scientific professionals from participating in any medical or scientific procedure that violates their conscience.

Prevent discrimination in insurance or employment against parents who wish to gestate or rear a child with disabilities. Pressure is increasing against parents who wish to gestate or rear children with disabilities.[77] Since the children with disabilities, and their medical and social costs, could have been "prevented," the burden is increasing on parents to abort such unborn children or be cut off from insurance or employment for gestating and rearing such children. Legislation is needed to protect such parents.[78]

Prevent "surplus" extracorporeal embryos. A report in 2003 indicated that there might be as many as 400,000 frozen (cryopreserved) embryos in laboratories in the United States. This not only puts human beings at the embryonic stage in a terribly vulnerable situation but acts as a growing "materials supplier" for destructive embryo research in the United States. Legislation should restrict the creation of embryos, perhaps by limiting the number that can be transferred in any ART cycle.

Promote a best-interest standard for extracorporeal embryos custody disputes. In the absence of legislation the courts have treated extracorporeal embryos not as children deserving protection but as property. Statutes should create a best-interest standard to be applied by state courts in instances of domestic disputes to resolve the disposition of extracorporeal embryos.

Prevent destructive human embryo research. Destructive embryo research can and should be prohibited by state law.[79] A variation of this might be to prohibit the transference or donation of embryos from ART clinics for research.

Prohibit human cloning. Although federal legislation remains bottled up in Congress, a number of states have moved ahead with statutory prohibitions on all human cloning. Human cloning should be prohibited by state and federal law.[80]

Prevent genetic discrimination. This is clearly a public concern, and the states and federal government have addressed this issue thoroughly over the past several years.[81] In 2008 President Bush signed GINA into law—the federal Genetic Information Nondisclosure Act. Many states have also passed legislation addressing genetic discrimination in health insurance laws,[82] genetic discrimination in employment,[83] and genetic privacy.[84] If these laws do not protect parents who gestate and rear children with disabilities, they should be amended to do so.

Patenting of human beings should be expressly prohibited by federal law. Patent law is an exclusive domain of federal law under the U.S. Constitution; the states cannot issue patents. As one legal writer has recently noted: "Biotechnology companies continue to submit various patent applications for the process of human cloning and for the resulting human embryos. . . . Commentators believe, however, that it will not be long before the PTO does grant patents on human embryos. Others believe that the PTO has already granted such patents."[85] Although Congress has never addressed the subject, the Patent and Trademark Office (PTO) has, since 1987, interpreted its regulations such that "a claim directed to or including within its scope a human being will not be considered to be patentable subject matter," because "the grant of a limited but exclusive property right in a human being is prohibited by the Constitution."[86] However, biotechnology companies are lobbying to overturn such regulations, and some legal commentators claim that the PTO has no legal authority for such a policy.[87]

Regulate germline modification. While the United States may be headed toward a policy of regulating germline modification only for safety and efficacy, serious consideration of the approach of the European Union should be undertaken. "The operating principle [in Europe] is that human beings share a genetic heritage which may change naturally, but which should not be purposively changed through human intervention. In Europe, the sense is that altering the germline would compromise human dignity."[88] The Committee of Ministers of the Council of Europe adopted the Convention for the Protection of Human Rights and Dignity of the Human Being with Regard to the Application of Biology and Medicine, which "effectively rules out any uses of germline gene therapy."[89]

Prevent eugenic modification. Genetic enhancement is a term that is now commonly used to refer to anticipated technology that will allow parents to "enhance" the traits and characteristics of their children through germline or somatic procedures.[90] Like cloning, genetic manipulation will commodify children and further transform procreation into manufacture. By custom designing children, parents will create incredible, highly subjective expectations about what those children *should* become.[91] One legal commentary referred to "parents' relentless search to use reproductive technologies to create the 'best' offspring."[92] Leon Kass and others have pointed out that genetic screening and selection turns procreation into manufacture. This is manifested in a number of ways throughout ART procedures; it is exacerbated by human cloning and will be further aggravated by eugenic manipulation and the selection of genetic characteristics. Debate over "genetic enhancement" in recent years has foundered on the ambiguity of *enhancement* and the *virtual impossibility of drawing lines* using such terms as *enhancement.*[93] (Definition of *enhancement* seems to be very difficult; perhaps the only feasible definition will be negative—defining it by what it is not.)[94] If genetic manipulation cannot be completely prohibited, legislative prohibitions must limit modification to the treatment and prevention of disease.[95]

Policy on genetic modification appears to be in the earliest stages of formulation; no state has regulated it explicitly. At least one legal commentator (generally a supporter) believes that traditional regulatory mechanisms may be inadequate and that a variety of new mechanisms will be needed.[96]

Prohibit human chimeras and hybrids and their patenting. A chimera was a monster in Greek mythology with different animal or human parts. In 1997 a patent was sought for the creation of a part-human creature that was up to 50 percent human, and, because Jeremy Rifkin joined the patent application, it was likely filed, at least in part, to spark public debate.[97] Nevertheless, the creation of animal-human genetic chimeras is thought to be all but certain. Although the patenting issue is exclusively within the domain of Congress, state legislation could prohibit the creation of human-animal chimeras or chimeric embryos.

It may strike some that these public-policy proposals are negative—prohibiting and preventing. While public debate and discussion needs to emphasize positive alternatives to assisted reproduction technologies and genetic engineering, there is no getting around the fact that legal restraints are needed to inhibit the momentum of privately sponsored biotechnology toward destroying human life and violating human dignity. Positive alternatives need to be emphasized in public debate and need to be encouraged in public policy, where possible.

PROTECTING HUMAN NATURE

One of the dominant concerns in public discussion of biotechnology has been the implication that certain technological developments—current or future—will permanently change or violate human nature.[98] For example, Bill McKibben expresses concern that genetic engineering will "call into question . . . our understanding of what it means to be a human being."[99] And Francis Fukuyama, a member of the President's Council on Bioethics and author of *Our Posthuman Future*, expresses "fear that in the end, biotech will allow us to lose our humanity," that "the most significant threat posed by contemporary biotechnology is the possibility that it will alter human nature and thereby move us into a 'posthuman' stage of history."[100]

The complexity of genetics and genetic technology, the uncertainty of the future direction of genetic technology and the complexity of the notion of "human nature" make it extremely difficult to use a general notion like "human nature" to guide legal regulations of biotechnology. One's understanding of human nature is enormously important for shaping ethical understanding and practical policies. And a proper understanding of human nature is needed to identify intermediate principles for guiding public policymaking. But more specific objectives are needed to effectively shape public policy.

What is human nature? From an old and broad understanding of human nature, it is clear that acts violating human nature have been perpetrated throughout history: unjust wars, murder, slavery, rape, infanticide, abortion and forced sterilization. Genetic technology has not suddenly brought us to the brink of violating human nature for the first time.

And yet it does seem that genetic engineering—through its antecedents, reproductive technology and in vitro fertilization—have raised this question in an acute, pervasive and more permanent way because genetics is directly related to changing the human species. Previous medical and scientific advancements have not presented the challenge to human nature quite so directly because the genetic revolution may provide the technological means to change human nature pervasively, permanently and irrevocably. (Francis Fukuyama warns, however, that neuropharmacology will be able to do sooner and more easily what is feared from genetic engineering.)[101]

But these concerns assume an understanding of what is meant by *human nature*. Without such an understanding, how can we know that we are "losing our humanity," not "staying human" or "violating human nature"? A Supreme Court justice once famously said of obscenity, "I know it when I see it." Such a subjective standard won't support regulation of biotechnology.

Philosophers have considered the meaning of human nature since at least the time of Plato. It is a vast subject, sweeping within its ambit philosophical anthropology, metaphysics, sociology, biology, and the neurosciences and consciousness, at least.

Aristotle fundamentally shaped the understanding of human nature in Western civilization, such that from the time of Aristotle to the Enlightenment of the eighteenth century man was considered to be *an individual substance with a rational soul.* But with the breakdown in the Christian consensus in Western civilization since the Enlightenment, there are so many different conceptions of human nature today that it is difficult to capture the spectrum of positions. One way is to ask, as Professor Dennis Hollinger did in a lecture, "Is there a given human nature, either from Nature or God?" The Declaration of Independence, for example, decidedly came down on one side: human beings are "endowed by their Creator with certain inalienable rights."

Our understanding (or misunderstanding) of human nature has critical implications for free will and human responsibility, and thus for accurately identifying those specific human capacities that need preservation. A correct understanding of human nature is important to discern what biological or genetic modifications might truly change human nature. Those who reject any notion of human nature will obviously not be concerned about modifications that might change human nature. Those who subscribe to biological determinism and see free will as an illusion would not be concerned if modifications constrained free will (libertarian agency). Views of human nature will inevitably influence views of free will, which will influence views of consent. To the extent that consent (informed consent) is presumed to be an essential bulwark against the imposition of genetic manipulation or any medical treatment, if free will is an illusion, then consent is an illusion that can be discarded.[102] Heightened protection for informed consent has been a significant legacy of the Nuremberg Code, and yet eliminating informed consent as an illusion is one implication of a certain view of human nature.

One common approach to addressing human nature in contemporary discussions of genetic engineering is to immediately focus on specific attributes or capacities of human beings—like free will and rationality. If we start with the question "What are the things about human nature that ought not to be changed?" the focus typically moves to specific capacities. Francis Fukuyama, for example, identifies moral choice, reason, language, sociability, sentience, emotions and consciousness.[103]

Do we have a complete understanding of human nature? One limitation of the focus on specific capacities is that those with such a partial knowledge of human nature—and an ambition to overhaul human nature as an obstacle to be conquered—will strive to redesign human nature in ways that approximate their limited knowledge of human nature. But as Kevin FitzGerald, who holds the David Lauler Chair in Catholic Health Care Ethics at Georgetown University, posed the question to a group of eager genetic pioneers, "Do we know ourselves well enough to be engineering humans?"[104]

Kevin FitzGerald's question is important. The mind may be the one facet of human nature that we least understand today, despite some neuroscientists' ambitions for brain enhancement and genetic modifications.[105] What does neuroscience say about consciousness? After a review of the scientific literature, physicist Stephen Barr has concluded: "there is nothing in the laws of nature or the character of physics as they exist today which is logically incompatible with free will. After all is said and done, the fact remains that the determinism which reigned in physical science for almost three centuries, and which seemed to leave no place for freedom, has been overthrown" by quantum theory.[106] Barr says that "the crucial question is whether the human intellect is something that can be explained in purely physical and mechanistic terms, or whether it points to the existence of a reality that goes beyond the physical."[107] The nature of consciousness continues to be hotly debated.[108]

Where does the threat to human nature from new technologies lie? In *Our Posthuman Future*, Francis Fukuyama describes a number of ways that new technologies may change human nature: controlling human behavior, neuroscience and neurotransmitters, pharmacology (including Prozac and Ritalin), and the artificial prolongation of life.

The typical concern is that changes in human nature will be imposed by government, as forced sterilization or human experimentation have been. Modern legal rules—and ethical guidelines based on the Nuremburg Code—which require consent for medical treatment may provide substantial protection against this concern. The more relevant concern, however, may not be government-imposed changes but those imposed by parents on their children or freely accepted by consumers from those advertised in the marketplace.

For example, Arthur Caplan, of the Center for Bioethics at the University of Pennsylvania, in the September 2003 issue of *Scientific American*, argues for "brain enhancement" and quickly dismisses four "likely" objections to it: (1) brain enhancement doesn't threaten human equality because "the right to be treated with respect has never depended on biological sameness"; (2) possibilities of unfair access to brain enhancement should be prevented by providing fair access; (3) brain enhancement isn't any more "unnatural" than the cosmetic enhancements that we already widely employ and there is no "natural limit beyond which our nature is clearly defiled by change"; (4) brain enhancement will not "inevitably" involve coercion, and the proper response is to ensure that it is always done "by choice, not dictated by others." "It is the essence of humanness," Caplan says, "to try to improve the world and oneself."[109]

Why should we preserve or protect human nature? In the face of the ambitions of genetic enhancement proponents who suggest the whole notion of human nature needs to be rejected as a constraint on human fulfillment, it will be challenging to make the public case for the preservation of "human nature." In addition, human frustration with human limitations, including mortality, will welcome new technologies that "promise" to overcome such limitations. As we see in the embryonic stem-cell debate, people who have diseases (or children with diseases) will have little patience with those who advise caution based on vague notions of "human nature."

But there are at least three reasons to preserve human nature. First, in the words of the Declaration of Independence humans beings are endowed by their Creator with inalienable rights. That endowment is a good. Second, we do not have sufficient knowledge (e.g., as evidenced by our current lack of understanding of consciousness) to fully understand the implications of changing human nature. Third, some aspects of human nature are "hard-wired" and will be immune to change, entailing serious violations of human nature in the attempt.[110]

Francis Fukuyama suggests a "mysterious" quality about human nature that cannot be specifically named but must be preserved. "What the demand for equality of recognition implies is that when we strip away all of a person's contingent and accidental characteristics, there remains some essential human quality underneath that is worthy of a certain minimal level of respect—call it Factor X."[111] Relying on the assertion that humans are "complex wholes rather than the sum of simple parts," he argues that "Factor X cannot be reduced to the possession of moral choice, or reason, or language, or sociability, or sentience, or emotions, or consciousness, or any other quality. . . . It is all of these qualities coming together in a human whole that make up Factor X."[112] Consequently, "we want to protect the full range of our complex, evolved natures against attempts at self-modification. We do not want to disrupt either the unity or the continuity of human nature, and thereby the human rights that are based on it."[113] Such attempts will dehumanize us.

Does American law protect human nature? *Is there a legal definition of human nature?* It is one thing to talk rhetorically about "dehumanization" and "staying human." It is quite another to draft a law that will effectively and constitutionally protect against "dehumanization." Just as homicide law protects the life of a human being, laws would be needed to protect assaults against human nature. Thus a definition of *human nature* has to be legally functional (and understandable by the public).

There may be many ways at arriving at a legal definition of human nature. One is to focus on specific capacities or attributes. A second is to focus on what has come to be called "species-typicality." What capacities are typical of the species of Homo sapiens? Francis Fukuyama defines human nature as "the sum of the behavior and characteristics that are typical of the human species, arising from genetic rather than environmental factors," with *typical* referring to "a statistical artifact—it refers to something close to the median of a distribution of behavior or characteristics."[114] Fukuyama emphasizes the subset of characteristics of human nature that are not just typical of our species but unique to human beings for special protection against biotechnology. A third way of approaching this question might be purely anthropological. If Homo sapiens is "the species to which all modern human beings belong,"[115] what changes to humans might change the species or remove humans from that species? Could this be determined individually or only across the species?

How does American law currently protect human nature? The Declaration of Independence addresses both the metaphysical and epistemological questions, identifying the source of human nature and dignity: it is "self-evident" that humans are created rather than a product of chance through impersonal matter. It is this creation that confers dignity on humans. Human dignity is not the starting question but is derivative—derived from the nature of human beings.

But the Declaration was neither incorporated into the Constitution nor is it enforceable as law, and its influence has been diminished in the past two hundred years by scientific naturalism, as Edward Purcell has recorded, so its utility in twenty-first-century America is primarily educational and rhetorical.[116] Although limited, that function is still an important one and not sufficiently appreciated. Some more concrete law is needed.

Criminal law—against murder and rape, for example—has always aimed at what are, in effect, violations of human nature.[117] In addition, contemporary bioethical principles guard against some violations of human nature—in Leon Kass's summary: "to avoid bodily harm and do bodily good, to respect patient autonomy and secure informed consent, and to promote equal access to health care and provide equal protection against biohazards."[118] But is human nature per se protected in American law?

One way to identify a legal definition of human nature is to ask whether an individual could bring a claim (suit) for violating his or her human nature (a question of tort law) or whether a prosecutor could charge an individual for violating human nature (a question of criminal law). In fact, such a claim per se cannot be identified in American legal history. The President's Council on Bioethics recently noted "the absence of human dignity as an explicit concept in American law."[119] It is not possible to identify a historic claim for violation of human nature or human dignity as such, but it is possible to identify laws that protect *certain discrete aspects of human life and well-being*. And, in recent literature on reproductive technology and genetic engineering over the past decade, it is possible to identify attempts to articulate deeper human interests that are threatened by modern technology and genetic engineering.

The law's reach has generally been limited to torts and crimes, requiring specific acts and states of mind. Historically, torts and crimes are two areas of law that protect human life. Torts include invasion of privacy and intentional infliction of emotional distress. (New torts and crimes include identity theft and hate crimes.) Tort law now protects individual consent, but this is effective only for those who can consent and not for children (for whom parents substitute their consent), or incompetent persons or unborn children or extracorporeal human beings.

If legislation is to develop that will protect human nature, it will most likely come from current concepts in tort and criminal law that are refined to take account of the impact of new technologies. However, it is sobering to recognize that though IVF has been around for a quarter-century and has been challenged for offending human nature, it has been left largely unregulated in American society.

Human nature and the courts. Although there are many discrete ways in which American law protects human nature and its dignity, the rise of bioethics over the past three decades has roughly coincided with a crisis of ethics in American law that has resulted from the rise of sociological jurisprudence and legal realism since the early part of the twentieth century.[120] That crisis has been manifested in the law's treatment of the human person. Three developments stand out.

The first and most famous is the Supreme Court's 1973 decision in *Roe v. Wade*, which adopted a positivist view of human beings and held that developing, unborn human beings were not "persons" protected by the U.S. Constitution.

Second, and derived in part from the *Roe* decision, a number of state courts have treated extracorporeal human beings in IVF cases as property, applying property and contract law to their disposition, rather than principles of "best interest" inherent in child custody law.[121]

A third development is in the context of the end of life. Some courts, or individual judges, have treated patients in a persistent vegetative state (PVS) and non-PVS patients as having a diminished interest in life and have held that society has a reduced interest in their life.

For the past three decades, the U.S. Supreme Court has used the liberty clause of the Fourteenth Amendment to strike down legislation restricting personal and sexual behavior, beginning with *Griswold v. Connecticut* in 1965.[122] This has included sexual behavior, viewing pornography, contraception, abortion and, most recently, homosexual sodomy. In *Planned Parenthood v. Casey* in 1992, a plurality of justices—O'Connor, Kennedy and Souter—articulated a broad, existentialist definition of personal autonomy.[123] This has come to be derided as "the mystery passage." A majority of six justices recently reaffirmed this same passage in striking down state laws prohibiting homosexual sodomy in *Lawrence v. Texas* in June 2003.

> The *Casey* decision again confirmed that our laws and tradition afford constitutional protection to personal decisions relating to marriage, procreation, contraception, family relationships, childrearing, and education. . . . In explaining the respect the Constitution demands for the autonomy of the person in making these choices, we stated as follows:
>
> These matters, involving the most intimate and personal choices a person may make in a lifetime, choices central to personal dignity and autonomy, are central to the liberty protected by the Fourteenth Amendment. At the heart of liberty is the right to define one's own concept of existence, of meaning, of the universe, and of the mystery of human life. Beliefs about these matters could not define the attributes of personhood were they formed under the compulsion of the State.[124]

Up through *Casey*, it was possible to argue that the right created by the Supreme Court in *Roe* and reaffirmed in *Casey* was a "right to terminate pregnancy."[125] Yet there has long been an effort among interest groups and academicians to expand this into a right to "procreational freedom."[126] And *Casey* and *Lawrence* give credence to this claim. The "mystery passage" of

Casey and *Lawrence* articulates a definition of personal autonomy that may well be used to challenge any state law restricting IVF, "procreational freedom," cloning, genetic engineering, or laws seeking to protect or preserve human nature. And the Court closed its *Lawrence* decision by issuing an "existentialist" invitation, which may be used in the future to challenge any legislative "constraints" invoking "human nature" which deny personal autonomy.[127] Although there are no definite Supreme Court decisions creating a right to IVF or genetic engineering, there are lower court decisions suggesting a right to procreational freedom.[128]

The courts have by and large been hostile to unborn or developing human life. (This is especially true with the Supreme Court, with the *Casey* decision in 1992 and the *Stenberg v. Carhart* decision in 2000.) They have been enthusiastic about procreational and sexual freedom. It is doubtful that the courts will independently protect developing human life. As someone has said, the only aspect of human nature that the courts have recognized is the absolute liberty to change human nature. Given legal history and the direction of the courts, protection for human nature and legal limitations on biotechnology that threatens to permanently alter human nature will have to come from legislatures.

CONCLUSION

Although there are evident problems with starting the focus with specific human capacities, it is more difficult to communicate an understanding of the abstractions to the public (the metaphysical and epistemological questions) and much easier to identify specific human capacities that many will readily agree make us human. It is difficult to imagine crafting legislation that protects "human nature" broadly speaking, and it is probable that the focus will have to be on *protecting specific human attributes or capacities*.

Violations of human nature are committed every day. Laws are in place to prevent some violations and are enforced. Short of killing, assault and battery, future violations of human nature from reproductive and genetic technology will be more subtle and will be less apparent to Americans. It is doubtful that a complete understanding of human nature is possible today, given our admitted lack of complete understanding of the human person, particularly the human mind and consciousness. Just as the discovery of the structure of DNA fifty years ago radically changed our understanding of biology and disease—and its fullest implications are only beginning to be felt fifty years later—medical and scientific discoveries over the next fifty years may significantly change our understanding of human biology. We are only able to describe as accurate an understanding of human nature as contemporary scientific, medical and metaphysical understanding allows. Unfortunately, this has ominous parallels to the law's dependence on medicine for its protection of developing human life.

The complexity of genetics and genetic technology, the uncertainty of the future direction of genetic technology and the complexity of the notion of human nature make it extremely difficult to use the general notion of protecting human nature to guide legal regulations of biotechnology. A proper metaphysical understanding of human nature may well be needed to identify intermediate principles for guiding legal developments. Our understanding of human nature is enormously important for shaping ethical understanding and practical policies. But more specific objectives are needed to effectively shape public policy.

Some laws that exist today may be effectively used to prevent future violations of human nature, but new laws—including prohibitions on human cloning—will be needed as well. Perhaps it will be necessary to prohibit specific practices and techniques that threaten human nature where it is not possible to precisely define the aspect of human nature that will be violated. With new laws needed to take account of new technology, the necessary forum for these new laws will be legislatures. The courts will be unlikely to adopt any classical understanding of human nature or protect against its violation. The need therefore is to protect human nature, and the specific capacities, through positive legislation.

Finally, will it be possible to persuasively communicate to the public an understanding of human nature and the need to protect it? Francis Fukuyama's argument is, for this reason, very appealing in its substance and style. By relying on Aristotle's philosophical anthropology—an individual substance with a rational soul—he may retain the core of human nature. And, without making an explicit religious argument, his style and manner may be the most effective way to make the argument for human nature in twenty-first-century America.

The moral-autonomy model in biotechnology means, in practice, freeing powerful human beings to subject powerless human beings to their will. As the history of American law from the common law to 1973 shows, however, the law has progressively protected human life, as medical science has informed the law about the threats to human life. *Roe v. Wade* did not halt that progression entirely but severely disrupted it, both by legalizing abortion on demand and by opening the door for embryo research and the technological manipulation of developing human beings.

Existing law is not sufficient to protect human beings from biotechnology or genetic manipulation. Such legal protection will not come from the state or federal courts. Governmental action through new state legislation is needed to protect human beings from genetic manipulation. Francis Fukuyama puts significant emphasis on the need to design and implement effective enforcement institutions and an emphasis on establishing policies on a national basis before seeking international regulations of, for example, human cloning. Such regulatory mechanisms are needed, but federal mechanisms may lack constitutional authority. State legislation is needed to define the law, prevent eugenic modification and create enforcement mechanisms.

CONCLUSION

"Unless religious idealists have a firm grasp of the idea of prudence, religious idealism in politics has the tendency to be overzealous and even politically destabilizing. What is needed to counteract this tendency is a heavy dose of realism."

— John G. West Jr., "Nineteenth-Century America"

Prudence is necessary to make a difference in politics without moral compromise. Prudence is not mere self-interest or sheer pragmatism; it requires us to understand and aim for the good, as guided by divine, natural or positive law. Prudence is *practical* wisdom. While prudence aims to realize the good, concrete obstacles limit the good that can be achieved in this world. Prudence aims not for the perfect good but the best, the greatest good—the greatest measure of justice—possible in the concrete circumstances before us, as embodied beings in this world of complex limits and constraints.

So, how do political leaders achieve the greatest good possible in the particular circumstances?

It requires an effective integration of the complicated elements of policy-making—a belief in the pursuit of human flourishing, a real concern for public opinion and for educating our fellow Americans, and a willingness to use prudent rhetoric. It requires an accurate view of reality and of human nature, both its potential and its limits. This in turn requires an understanding of the current state of the culture, public opinion, and the limits of people, resources, and institutions. Because no political leader can be an expert in all these areas, the need for counsel is obvious.

One of the most difficult things in all of politics is accurate foresight *(prov-identia)*. As Josef Pieper emphasized, foresight is "the capacity to estimate, with a sure instinct for the future, whether a particular action will lead to the realization of the goal. At this point the element of uncertainty and risk in every moral decision comes to light."[1] Will this plan, strategy or bill achieve its goal? How do we know? What are the implications if we fail? Are there alternative strategies with a greater potential for success? Accurate foresight requires skill, experience, counsel and planning.

Understanding reality includes understanding how the world of politics and law works. The institutions through which we seek to make change—including the courts, legislatures, the electoral system and the media—must be thoroughly understood. And with complex issues like constitutional law and campaign-finance legislation subject to frequent change in the courts and legislatures, understanding that world is getting more and more difficult. The counsel and collaboration of those with experience and expertise in these institutions must be employed effectively.

There must be effective planning to be successful in public policy. The right goals must be considered and precisely identified. Needed resources must be identified, marshaled and utilized. Allies need to be identified and recruited.

A political leader or activist must have a healthy respect for constraints in the fallen world and an acute insight into their nature, impact and the potential strategies for responding to them. Even if a prudential framework is accepted for political decision making—and assuming no cooperation in an evil act is involved—difficult strategic and tactical questions remain as a challenge to the conscientious lawmaker.

Because we live in a world of constraints, prudence tells us that if we cannot prohibit a social evil entirely, we can limit it through appropriate fences. Building fences around a social evil, as part of a larger strategy to secure justice, precludes what can be prohibited now without admitting the legitimacy of what remains unprohibited. By limiting the harm done or lessening the negative consequences, we do not admit or support the rest of the evil that we do not have the power (legal or political) to touch now.

Assuming due consideration of counsel and deliberation in identifying the good, and understanding the opportunities and constraints in the concrete political conditions, lawmakers may prudently seek to establish legal fences around legal and social evils through laws that cannot, due to political and legal obstacles beyond their control, completely prohibit the evil. Court edicts or political majorities may impose limitations (exceptions) in the law due to legal, constitutional or political obstacles beyond control.

A legal fence does not admit the legitimacy of what remains unprohibited when the limitation is not caused by our will but is compelled by countervailing obstacles beyond our control. What prevents the achievement of the complete good are those obstacles—human, institutional, political, social, cultural—not the will or desire of the conscientious lawmaker. This is precisely why wise judgment *as to what is possible* is so important for prudence. And that requires a deep understanding of both the obstacles and the range of possible solutions.

It is important to realize the dynamic quality of legal fences around a social evil when prohibition is not possible. They are not simply inert; they can be provocative. This can be seen in the Southern response to the Whig-Republican line against slavery in the Western territories. The Whig-Republican fence was enough to spark secession after Lincoln's election in November 1860. And it can be seen in the abortion advocates' response to the partial-birth abortion debate in the United States between 1995 and 2007. In both cases the legal fence was a moral affront to the proponents of the established institution. Particular legal fences must always be viewed and devised in the context of the broader campaign to eliminate the injustice entirely, as circumstances make that a realistic possibility.

Opposition to legislative fences that contain but do not entirely prohibit a social evil sometimes rests on a misunderstanding of the concrete situation, the intent of the sponsors of the fences, or existing law or existing constraints. But more often it is a failure to understand the very nature of legislation. The single legislator, or a minority of legislators, is not responsible for what the majority supports or a court dictates. The minority does not "participate" in what the majority supports or a court dictates. No one cooperates in evil if they do not participate in the evil, and lawmakers can avoid participating in unjust laws or conditions by putting legal fences around unjust laws and conditions. No one compromises without making a concession, and fighting for the greatest good possible, when obstacles prevent achieving more, is not a concession.

Given the frequent possibility for misunderstanding by citizens who are outside the legislative arena, unfamiliar with the legislative process or confused by critics as to the lawmakers' intent and action, conscientious lawmakers should seek to clearly communicate to the public (including fellow legislators, constituents and supporters) their goal of complete justice, the constraints that exist and how the constraints limited that which they can achieve. Thus public education is also essential for political prudence. To secure those fences, lawmakers may have to vote for a final bill that contains their fence(s) as a part thereof. Their stated aim should be to preserve the fence, with the realization that their vote is not needed to maintain the evil that the majority retains, and that their abstention would prevent the effective establishment of the fence. This is the essence of political prudence as it has been understood and endorsed by moral philosophers and religious leaders since Aristotle.[2]

This is not a plea for taking incremental steps regardless of existing obstacles, conditions or opportunities. This is not a plea for what Dr. Martin Luther King Jr. derided as "the tranquilizing drug of gradualism." Quite the opposite. It is intended to achieve as much good as current obstacles will allow, while leaving open the chance for making progress (achieving a greater good) in the future.

Certainly, political leaders must guard against being lured into cooperation or complicity. Prudence is needed to guide judgments about cooperation in evil. This is one of the most difficult challenges. To avoid cooperation or complicity, political leaders must keep the end in mind and not get lost in the details of the means. They need to ask, What is the true end here? What are we aiding or assisting? What would happen without our involvement?

Prudent political leaders must pursue a vision of complete justice, of complete legal protection for human life. But in the democratic process they may pursue the ideal in such a way that progress is made and with the willingness to accept "something" when "all" is not achievable because of social, legal or political obstacles beyond their control.

This is particularly difficult when no effective public-policy strategy can be implemented without successfully articulating the goals of a bioethical public policy widely shared by Americans, including many who share no particular religious faith. It is necessary to Americanize the public debate by connecting the purposes of contemporary legislation to enduring themes in American history. Any effective bioethical policy must be explained effectively to secularists, utilitarians and postmoderns. And the essential elements of that must go beyond utilitarianism and engage contemporary uncertainty about the self, human nature and authority. Bridging this cultural and rhetorical divide to mobilize a democratic majority in a republic is the challenge of prudent rhetoric.

MEANS AND ENDS

Prudence in public policy inevitably involves specific policies, and specific policies are necessarily a question of means and ends.

For example, in 2008 a number of states debated a proposed state human life amendment (HLA). If the debate remains civil—in Georgia, Colorado, Montana and other states—it might prove positively useful in exploring the state of the cause for life, the progress that has been made, the opportunities and obstacles, and what more needs to be done.

A state HLA may or may not be an effective means to protect human life. It may or may not be the best goal. It may be part of the solution, or it may actually be an obstacle to the effective protection of human life. And that may depend on specific conditions in the particular state. We frankly do not know; we need to know more.

Since no state has ever *enacted*, no state official has ever *enforced*, and no state court has ever *interpreted* or *applied* a human life amendment, it raises a host of abstract and interpretative legal and strategic questions.

In 2008 I met in Atlanta with legislators of differing views who wanted to explore precisely these questions. Along the way I talked with a few of the House sponsors of the human life amendment. They seemed tired of "half measures" and truly believed that an HLA is the best bet to overturn *Roe v. Wade* and end abortion in Georgia. But, they wondered, did I have "a better idea"?

Unfortunately, there wasn't time to articulate an alternative strategy before they hurried to the House floor. But resolving the question would require us to start with the four elements of political prudence that should guide evaluation: good goals, wise judgment about what's possible, effectively connecting means and ends, and preserving the possibility of future improvement.[3] In light of these criteria, the relative merits of practical alternatives would have to be evaluated.

Abortion and the bioethical challenges to human life and dignity at the beginning and end of life raise a host of complicated challenges that may not be addressed by a silver bullet. Are state HLAs the right means to address all bioethical issues affecting the beginning of human life?

Personally, I too would like one all-encompassing solution that we could focus on like a laser, and to which I could devote the rest of my career. But the complexity of the medical, ethical and technological challenges, and of the political and social obstacles clearly prevent such a solution in the foreseeable future. Even if we can identify one common *ethical* problem, that does not mean that the host of complex bioethical problems that confront us will lend themselves to a single legal or political solution.

First, abortion is unlike virtually all of the other challenges, as a political and legal matter (if not an ethical matter), because, with *Roe v. Wade*, the U.S. Supreme Court took abortion away from the decision making of the people, out of the democratic process. The Supreme Court controls abortion from Washington, while the other bioethical challenges at the beginning and end of life are lodged in the state legislatures (or Congress, to a lesser degree). A state HLA may be useful to protect human life after *Roe* is overturned, but it cannot effectively overrule *Roe*.

One thing is certain: debate about life issues is unavoidable. It's useful that Georgia and other states are debating a human life amendment at the same time that Professors Robert George and Christopher Tollefsen have released *Embryo: A Defense of Human Life*. Their book is a philosophical argument that "human embryos are, from the very beginning, human beings, sharing an identity with, though younger than, the older human beings they will grow up to become."[4]

If public debate about the human status of the embryo is inevitable and necessary (as their book recognizes), then debate about whether a state constitutional amendment is an *effective means* to protect the embryonic human is also inevitable and necessary. The debate about the embryo's status is a philosophical and moral one, but the debate about the amendment is inevitably a *prudential* one because it is a debate about practical wisdom—the best practical means to protect human life.

Second, it is not possible for one law to solve all of these issues. One way of thinking about political problems and solutions is in terms of "projects" and "tools." Is the tool well-adapted to the problem at hand? Is this a project that needs a hammer, a saw or a screwdriver?

For example, we don't need to dislodge the federal courts from the embryonic stem-cell issue as we do with abortion (though we do need to prevent the courts from taking over other bioethical issues and further stripping the people of the right to self-government). And abortion has huge overtones involving women's health and well-being that aren't involved in quite the same way in the stem-cell issue.[5]

We cannot look to one law to perfectly solve all of these problems; human law may simply be unequal to the task. We can work for an overarching vision of a culture of life, but the practical road map may be as complex as the ethical, medical and technological nuances of the bioethical issues themselves.

Third, it's necessary to accurately understand the reality of obstacles—social, political, institutional—that impede success. Too often political activists think that zeal and good intentions are self-justifying and disregard a sustained analysis of the obstacles that block legal and political change.

Fourth, it's necessary to devise effective means to overcome the obstacles. In determining whether a constitutional amendment will be an effective law, it will be useful to recall and learn from Professor Joseph Dellapenna's 2006 encyclopedic history, *Dispelling the Myths of Abortion History*. Dellapenna's exhaustive account of historical attempts to protect developing human life sheds important light on the limits of law, the importance of culture, the interaction of technology and law, and the practical difficulties of effective law enforcement. Will an amendment help or hurt the effective protection of human life? And how might its language be framed to make that protection more effective? Since no state has ever enacted or enforced a human life amendment, we really do not know.

Fifth, if government is necessary to protect human life, as the Declaration of Independence affirms, what is the role of the judiciary? There is a curious tension between the fact of judicial hostility to protecting human life since the 1960s and the current belief of some that ultimate protection will come from the judiciary, or the belief that judges can be trusted to protect human life. Constitutional amendments shift authority from the legislatures, as representatives of the people, to judges. Is that a good shift or a bad shift? How could we forecast that? The chairman of the Georgia House subcommittee that held hearings on the Georgia HLA stated that a major reason he voted to table the HLA was because it signaled a huge shift in power over a wide range of bioethical issues from the representatives of the people (the legislature) to the state judiciary.

Does the record of the state supreme court indicate that this makes sense? Does the record of the federal and state judiciary, generally speaking, over the past three decades, as the most hostile toward protecting human life of the three branches of government, justify such a shift of power? Can a state constitutional amendment bind judges? Or will it simply be putty for them to shape any way they want? Should any supreme court have such power?

Sixth, in effectively connecting means to ends, it's important to build momentum through partial gains. Kings (or tyrants) who hold all power can change their mind and simply order change (though the implementation may involve widespread destruction). But the more broadly that political power is diffused in a democracy, the more difficult it is to bring about change. And the more that power is diffused, the more likely it will be that sudden change will come in smaller steps (dare I say "incrementally"), not by desire but in relation to the very real obstacles that exist.

Seventh, it is important to have complementary strategies. The cultural and educational strategies must be aligned with the legal and political strategies. For example, some anti-abortion activists focus completely on the humanity of the unborn, without realizing, apparently, that there always has been and will likely always be "two sides to the coin" to the problem of abortion: the impact on the child *and* the woman. Focusing solely on the child is only half of the problem.

One paradigm in American public opinion against which the supporters of an HLA are butting their heads—perhaps unwittingly—is the public belief that legalized abortion has been good for women. That myth must be dismantled through public education of the serious medical risks to women, and yet an HLA is *not* well-crafted to do that because it addresses only one side of the coin, the impact on the child. Until that paradigm is overcome, however, an HLA (or any abortion prohibition) will almost certainly fail.

While there is rarely, if ever, a silver bullet that will be the one, single answer in politics, there are initiatives, improvements and new ideas that can bring change and momentum and eventual success. But these are almost invariably based on a deep understanding of what has gone before and what will be effective in the particular circumstances, and they require effective execution based on a deep understanding of media and public education.

Thus William Wilberforce's (and his allies') strategy in England in 1805-1806 to legislate against the "neutral flag" ships that carried slaves—after decades of failing to outlaw the slave trade outright—was brilliant. As depicted in the 2007 film *Amazing Grace*, it was an astute response to the new political conditions brought about by the war with France, and it was the result of deep understanding of admiralty laws and conditions related to the war. And ultimately, this creative side-swipe at the slave trade did more good than so many attempts straight on. Based on a deep understanding of the legal, cultural and political problem, such initiatives and improvements must be identified, formulated and implemented. Wilberforce must inspire us—after almost forty years of our own struggle for justice—to think more imaginatively about possible steps.

The supporters of an HLA may suffer from the same imprudence as Wilberforce and his allies did early on: they may assume that a moral argument alone is enough. Wilberforce and his allies eventually learned that simply presenting the facts of the slave trade to parliament was not enough. As the sociologist Peter Berger observed, "Ideas don't succeed in history because of their inherent truthfulness but rather because of their connection to very powerful institutions and interests."[6] Wilberforce and his allies eventually began to rebut the notion that the slave trade was a "necessary evil" to the British economy, just as abortion has been said to be a "necessary evil" in our society, and it took them almost twenty years to successfully overcome that myth.

Eighth, evaluation of something as broad and final as a constitutional amendment must consider "the law of unintended consequences." It may apply to future technologies that are unimaginable today. If the amendment protects the developing human being from "fertilization," for example, how does the amendment apply if a human being begins with cloning, a process that doesn't involve fertilization?

Ninth, leadership is essential. But the role of leadership is *not simply* lofty rhetoric or moral purpose, or single-minded determination. Leadership also requires wise judgment of how much of the good is possible in the historical circumstances and requires effective execution in connecting means and ends. It requires humility in bringing together the people, allies and resources necessary for an effective plan. And when inexperienced and zealous troops want to take *all the hills* in sight, leaders must make the difficult decision, in the face of limited resources, regarding *which hill* should be taken.

Tenth, like it or not, the right timing is an inescapable part of human endeavor and thus of politics. Isn't it obvious that timing is essential, for example, in football and comedy and economics? Does anyone believe that the spring of 2008 was the "right time" to max out your credit card, buy a gas-guzzling car or a second home when it was difficult to make payments on the first one? But some activists suggest that "timing" is irrelevant in public policy and politics. In their view, it's just another "excuse" by "incrementalists," another example of their traitorous cowardice, another reason why they should be condemned and purged.

This response is tragic and misguided. That timing is essential in politics is shown by studying—to cite just two examples—Lincoln's strategy regarding the Emancipation Proclamation in 1862 and Reagan's strategy toward the Soviet Union from 1981 to 1989.

However, the "right timing" is not—and should not be—based on the mere whim or self-interest of political actors. Instead, it should be based on a calculation of two prudential factors: (1) wise judgment as to what's possible under the circumstances, and (2) having the plans and resources in place to effectively connect means to ends. Identifying the "right timing" is a consequence of careful attention to these factors. The "right time" is when these obstacles have been effectively addressed (even if not perfectly solved) so as to make success *reasonably possible.*

The success of Wilberforce (and his numerous allies) in prohibiting the slave trade in the British empire in 1807 after a twenty-year struggle suggests the significance of a "historical moment." After struggling for eighteen to twenty years and being rebuffed to the point of despair at many points, they took advantage of shifting historical circumstances (the war with France) and learned to connect their goals with larger national-security issues. And that connection, based on the momentum they had built through incremental successes, led to their ultimate success. Then they spent another twenty-five years enforcing the ban on the trade and working to prohibit slavery, until slavery was prohibited in 1833.

Finally, one of the likely outcomes of *ill-prepared* efforts to enact a state HLA is more frustration and discouragement among activists. Instead of questioning the failed strategy with an open mind, with the benefit of experience, some may conclude that politics itself (or the goal of protecting human life through the law) is fruitless. This points out the need for an effective plan that identifies the right goal, creates an effective coalition and marshals the necessary resources to reasonably connect mean and ends.

Good ideas withstand the test of time and are enhanced by questioning analysis. They can be defended against thoughtful critics and make sense *despite* criticism. So the supporters of any novel policy proposal should not shy away from or bristle at questions about their proposal and its implications. They should be willing to actually debate the proposal and be prepared to answer questions about their strategy. They are instigating a *public* debate. Certainly, if they cannot answer the questions of their friends, they will not able to effectively answer the challenges of their opponents.

These factors have to be part of any prudential analysis of public policy initiatives, such as the pursuit of state HLAs.

Obstacles to Success

Unfortunately, prudence is a virtue often undervalued and underutilized by Americans with strong moral positions on political issues. Numerous vices and weaknesses tempt us all. There are pitfalls to prudence at every level: identifying the good (discernment), deliberation, decision and implementation.

We can fail in *discernment* by excessive zeal that leads to oversimplifying or overgeneralizing moral principles, by overspiritualizing a problem in a way that obscures right reason and by undue reliance on a narrow perception of law or moral philosophy.

We can fail in *deliberation* by misunderstanding existing constraints and obstacles, by failing to identify solutions to those obstacles and by lack of counsel. Deliberation also needs to address the precise outline of the decision and the resources needed to effectively implement it.

We can fail in *decision* by making no decision—indecisiveness—or by making too broad or too narrow a decision. A decision needs to be precisely envisioned and stated. We may also fail to clearly communicate the decision to those who are necessary to effectively implement it.

We can fail in *implementation* by making imprudent decisions that seem good but cannot, by their very nature, be effectively implemented—a "bridge too far." We can also fail by insufficient planning for effective implementation, by insufficient follow-up or a failure in perseverance.

People of faith, it seems, are particularly susceptible to imprudence when it comes to their involvement in political and social causes. People of faith may overspiritualize the problem or situation. They sometimes replace prudent action with religious clichés based on a phrase or a verse in Scripture that is unmoored by the truths of the faith as a whole.[7] They see the moral evil so clearly, and they rightly desire its elimination so strongly, that they are apt to strike out against it with insufficient study and knowledge of the most effective ways to do so.

A frequent problem is excessive zeal that is not supported by knowledge or experience. Religious (or ideological) zeal without knowledge is counterproductive. Without having considered what has been tried and failed before, some are always looking for "the silver bullet," the undiscovered new thing that will change everything. While improvements and innovations are always to be sought, what is an improvement or innovation requires knowledge of what has gone before, and why.

A religious piety that disdains reason, planning or preparation is also counterproductive. Prudence does not cancel out prayer; instead, it should make an individual's prayer life wiser and more effective. Prayer rests on a right understanding of providence, and prudence directs us to understand providence and the constraints of the fallen world more accurately. A false doctrine of providence (and prayer, which is based on the reality of providence) can work dangerously to minimize human responsibility and capability.

Some contemporary believers may assume a "divine anointing" of people, organizations and events, or a special revelation. The grounds for this are typically never expressed. And the notion suggests that their judgments are necessarily true and immune from evaluation. This assumes a subjectivity in *discernment* that is immune from objective evaluation and cannot be communicated to others.

Making a practical difference is sometimes prevented by a religious self-pity or self-condemnation that often sees the biggest problem in the colleagues who "compromise." There is a fundamental ethical and practical difference between compromise and prudently fighting for the most good that can be gained in the face of overwhelming odds.

The complexities of the serious bioethical challenges we face should give us the humility to seek counsel in identifying solutions. And the complexities of social reform movements should help us appreciate, without criticism, the different roles that many others, with different gifts, fulfill. Many different roles filled well and many different gifts skillfully exercised will be needed to successfully address unprecedented challenges. There is great strength and flexibility in diversity.

Debilitating frustration is often linked to unrealistic expectations. Realizing the constraints and limits of this world should guard us against unrealistic expectations of what politics can or should achieve.

And yet, the examples of Wilberforce and Lincoln, among many others, demonstrate that moral purpose can be successfully pursued in politics with prudence. Such prudence will be necessary to effectively preserve human lives and human dignity in American law and culture in the years ahead.

NOTES

Preface

[1]For an excellent introduction to the complexities of American politics, see Professor Amy Black's *Beyond Left and Right* (Grand Rapids: Baker, 2008).

Introduction

[1]Richard Carwardine, *Lincoln: A Life of Purpose and Power* (New York: Alfred A. Knopf, 2006), p. 135; David Herbert Donald, *Lincoln* (New York: Simon and Schuster, 1995), pp. 255-56.

[2]Allan Nevins, *The Emergence of Lincoln: Prologue to Civil War 1859-1861* (New York: Charles Scribner's, 1950), p. 386.

[3]Ibid., pp. 387-88.

[4]Ibid., p. 388.

[5]Ibid., pp. 390-91.

[6]Ibid., pp. 392-93. See also William Lee Miller, *Lincoln's Virtues: An Ethical Biography* (New York: Vintage Books, 2002), pp. 435-36.

[7]Nevins, *Emergence of Lincoln*, p. 397.

[8]Doris Kearns Goodwin, *Team of Rivals: The Political Genius of Abraham Lincoln* (New York: Simon and Schuster, 2005), pp. 296, 300. "The first resolved that 'the Constitution should never be altered so as to authorize Congress to abolish or interfere with slavery in the states.' The second would amend the Fugitive Slave Law 'by granting a jury trial to the fugitive.' The third recommended that all state personal liberty laws in opposition to the Fugitive Slave Law be repealed" (ibid., p. 296). Republican hardliners, including Senator Charles Sumner, Representative Thaddeus Stevens and Senator Salmon Chase, were outraged by the concessions in the speech.

[9]Nevins, *Emergence of Lincoln*, p. 394. Daniel Farber, *Lincoln's Constitution* (Chicago: University of Chicago Press, 2003), pp. 13-14. Farber's thoughtful book needs to be read in conjunction with Michael Stokes Paulsen's thoughtful critique of the book (Michael Stokes Paulsen, "The Civil War as Constitutional Interpretation," *University of Chicago Law Review* 71 [2004]: 691). See also Michael Stokes Paulsen, "The Constitution of Necessity," *Notre Dame Law Review* 79 (2004): 1257.

[10]Goodwin, *Team of Rivals*, p. 294. "When asked by the editor of a Democratic paper in Missouri to make a soothing public statement that would keep Missouri in the Union, Lincoln replied: 'I could say nothing which I have not already said, and which is in print and accessible to the public. Please pardon me for suggesting that if papers, like yours, which heretofore have persistently garbled, and misrepresented what I have said, will now fully and fairly place it before their readers, there can be no further misunderstanding. . . . I am not at liberty to shift my ground—that is out of the question. . . . The secessionists, per se believing they had alarmed me, would clamor all the louder" (ibid.).

[11]Miller, *Lincoln's Virtues*, p. 202.

[12]Ibid.

[13]See, for example, the Declaration of Independence (1776): "Prudence . . . will dictate that Governments long established should not be changed for light and transient cases"; and Thomas Paine, *Common Sense* (1776): "the same prudence which in every other cases advises him out

of two evils to choose the least." The sermons of George Whitefield (1710-1770), who toured America, are replete with references to the need for prudence, referring to "young converts, that have honesty, but not much prudence" (Sermon 30, "Christ's Transfiguration"); James T. Kloppenberg says, "[Benjamin] Franklin just as surely prized the virtues of prudence, temperance, and fortitude, qualities that his contemporaries as well as later commentators such as Max Weber associated with him, and that made Poor Richard's Almanac so widely read" (Review of *Becoming America* by Jon Butler, *Common-Place* 1, no. 1 [2000] <www.history cooperative.org/journals/cp/vol-01/no-01/reviews/butler.shtml>).

[14]See, e.g., George Weigel, *Faith, Reason, and the War Against Jihadism: A Call to Action* (New York: Doubleday, 2007); George Weigel, "Just Wars and Iraq Wars," *First Things*, April 2007, p. 14; Jean Bethke Elshtain, *Just War Against Terror: The Burden of American Power in a Violent World* (New York: Basic Books, 2003).

[15]Aileen S. Kraditor, *Means and Ends in American Abolitionism: Garrison and his Critics on Strategy and Tactics 1834-1850* (New York: Pantheon, 1969).

[16]Difficult questions of political prudence are international in scope. In 2006, political leaders in Canada debated the prudence of an anti-abortion bill in the context of a 1988 abortion decision by the Supreme Court of Canada.

[17]"It is said that the abolition party 'quickly fell into two sections, one of which was ready to make any reasonable sacrifice in order to attain success, while the other firmly opposed all compromise, looking on it as a breach of principle. This latter section, dissatisfied with the moderate counsels of the original committee, established another of its own, under the name of the 'Agency committee' " (George Stephen, cited in R. Jay Sappington, *Legislative Compromise as Moral Strategy* [master's thesis, Trinity Evangelical Divinity School, 1998], p. 1).

CHAPTER 1: PRUDENCE AND THE FULFILLED LIFE

[1]Aristotle *Nicomachean Ethics* 1140a (Indianapolis: Bobbs-Merrill, 1962).

[2]Thomas Aquinas, *Summa Theologica* (Westminster, Md.: Christian Classics, 1981). Cf. Proverbs 1:3: "for acquiring a disciplined and prudent life."

[3]John Finnis, *Aquinas* (New York: Oxford University Press, 1998), p. 84.

[4]Aquinas *Summa Theologica* I-II. Q57. A4. (The *Summa Theologica*'s citations are designated by part [I or II], question [Q], article [A], and reply objections [RO]).

[5]Josef Pieper, *The Four Cardinal Virtues* (Notre Dame, Ind.: University of Notre Dame Press, 2003), p. xi.

[6]Cicero *De officiis* (Duties). See Marcus Tullius Cicero, *The Basic Works of Cicero*, Modern Library (New York: Random House, 1951). See also Anthony Everitt, *Cicero: The Life and Times of Rome's Greatest Politician* (New York: Random House, 2001), p. 258.

[7]"And if a man love righteousness, her labors are virtues: for she teacheth temperance and prudence, justice and fortitude: which are such things, as men can have nothing more profitable in their life" (Wisdom 8:7).

[8]Edward F. McClennen, the Centennial Professor of Philosophy, Logic and Scientific Method at the London School of Economics, adopts the definition of prudence as "careful management" and comments, "This latter sense is the one in which I am interested. The wide and somewhat erratic range of connotations for the term renders the history of the concept not very helpful for my purposes. Suffice it to say that what I shall call 'prudence' is clearly one of the things that was traditionally associated with this term" ("Prudence and Constitutional Rights," *University of Pennsylvania Law Review* 917 [2003]: 151).

[9]Brian Hook and R. R. Reno, Heroism and the Christian Life (Louisville, Ky.: Westminster/John Knox, 2000), pp. 217-18.

[10]Kenneth W. Starr, *First Among Equals: The Supreme Court in American Life* (New York: Warner Books, 2002), p. 279.

[11]See Richard E. Rubenstein, *Aristotle's Children* (Orlando: Harcourt, 2003).

[12]See e.g., Carson Holloway, *The Right Darwin? Evolution, Religion and the Future of Democracy*

(Dallas: Spence, 2005); Peter Augustine Lawler, *Stuck with Virtue: The American Individual and Our Biotechnological Future* (Wilmington, Del.: ISI Books, 2005), pp. 155-74.

[13]See Leon R. Kass, *Life, Liberty and the Defense of Dignity: The Challenge for Bioethics* (New York: Encounter, 2002), p. 10; Francis Fukuyama, *Our Posthuman Future: Consequences of the Biotechnology Revolution* (New York: Picador, 2002).

[14]Douglas J. Den Uyl, *The Virtue of Prudence* (New York: Peter Lang, 1991), p. 56.

[15]Pieper, *Four Cardinal Virtues*, p. xii. An excellent contemporary book on the education of children in the virtues is David Isaacs's *Character Building: A Guide for Parents and Teachers* (Dublin: Four Courts Press, 1993).

[16]Aristotle, cited in Den Uyl, *Virtue of Prudence*, p. 60.

[17]J. Budziszewski, *Written on the Heart: The Case for Natural Law* (Downers Grove, Ill.: Inter-Varsity Press, 1997), pp. 28-31

[18]Den Uyl, *Virtue of Prudence*, p. 49.

[19]Pieper, *Four Cardinal Virtues*, p. 6. Aquinas cites Gregory the Great: "The other virtues cannot be virtues at all unless they effect prudently what they desire to accomplish" (*Moralim libri* 2.46)

[20]"Since Aristotle had admitted the validity of sense knowledge as a necessary means through which man must grasp the nature and meaning of the theoretic order, which man discovers but does not make, he denied that the objects of the senses were mere reflections or images of true reality [as Plato's philosophy implied]. They were themselves realities, substances, even though they were not the complete causes of what they were" (James V. Schall, *Reason, Revelation, and the Foundations of Political Philosophy* [Baton Rouge: Louisiana State University Press, 1987], pp. 31-32).

[21]John H. Hallowell, *The Moral Foundation of Democracy* (Chicago: University of Chicago Press, 1954), pp. 24-25.

[22]Doris Kearns Goodwin, *Team of Rivals* (New York: Simon and Schuster, 2005), p. xvii.

[23]Pieper, *Four Cardinal Virtues*, p. xi-xii.

[24]"I want you to be wise about what is good, and innocent about what is evil" (Romans 16:19 NIV).

[25]Budziszewski, *Written on the Heart*, pp. 22-23.

[26]Ibid., p. 26.

[27]Ibid., p. 24.

[28]Augustine *City of God* 19 (New York: Image Books, 1958). Of prudence, Augustine wrote: "Is not this virtue [prudence] constantly on the lookout to distinguish what is good from what is evil, so that there may be no mistake made in seeking the one and avoiding the other? So it bears witness to the fact that we are surrounded by evil and have evil within us. This virtue teaches that it is evil to consent to desires leading to sin and good to resist them. And what prudence preaches temperance puts into practice. Yet, neither prudence nor temperance can rid this life of the evils that are their constant concern."

Other Christian writers on politics in the early middle ages relied on prudence. See e.g., Agapetos Diaconus (A.D. 530), deacon of Hagia Sophia in Constantinople, in his letter to Justinian: "Prolonged deliberation, energetic performance. It is risky to embark on ill-considered measures. As one appreciates the blessing of health after being sick, so anyone who has acted imprudently will know the value of prudence well enough. You, then, most prudent king, should redouble the penetrating counsel and earnest prayer which go to frame your detailed policies for the whole world's benefit" (cited in Oliver O'Donovan and Joan Lockwood O'Donovan, eds., *From Irenaeus to Grotius: A Sourcebook in Christian Political Thought 100-1625* [Grand Rapids: Eerdmans 1999], p. 184); Sedulius Scottus (A.D. 840-860), "On Christian Rulers": "In human affairs, no art . . . is more difficult than to rule well amidst the stormy tempests of this turbulent world and to govern the state wisely. And this art attains its highest degree of perfection when the state itself has prudent and superlative counselors" (ibid., p. 224).

[29]James V. Schall, *The Politics of Heaven and Hell: Christian Themes from Classical, Medieval and Modern Political Philosophy* (Lanham, Md.: University Press of America, 1984), p. 44. See

also Reinhold Niebuhr, *Moral Man and Immoral Society* (New York: Charles Scribner's, 1932); Reinhold Niebuhr, "Augustine's Political Realism," in *The City of God: A Collection of Critical Essays*, ed. Dorothy F. Donnelly (New York: Peter Lang, 1995).

[30]Rufus Black observes that "the term 'moral realism' has been subject to a range of definitions which have variously emphasized it as a form of moral theory which is concerned with: (i) the literal truth or falsity of moral claims; (ii) the objectivity of moral claims; (iii) natural realities having moral properties; (iv) moral truth consisting in the correspondence with 'some fact or state of affairs'; or, (v) it being a moral theory analogous to scientific realism." In contrast to these Black starts with the broadly foundational definition that "moral realism" is "the claim that the ultimate epistemological grounding for moral truth is a given reality external to the will" (*Christian Moral Realism: Natural Law, Narrative, Virtue, and the Gospel* [New York: Oxford University Press, 2000], p. 8).

[31]Graham Walker, "Virtue and the Constitution: Augustinian Theology and the Frame of American Common Sense," in *Vital Remnants: America's Founding and the Western Tradition*, ed. Gary L. Gregg II (Wilmington, Del.: ISI Books, 1999), pp. 135-37. See also Jean Bethke Elshtain, *Augustine and the Limits of Politics* (Notre Dame, Ind.: University of Notre Dame Press, 1996); Gilbert Meilaender, *The Way That Leads There: Augustinian Reflections on the Christian Life* (Grand Rapids: Eerdmans, 2006), pp. 77-116.

[32]Schall, *Politics of Heaven and Hell*, p. 57.

[33]Walker, "Virtue and the Constitution," p. 139.

[34]Aquinas *Summa Theologica* I-II. Q57. A4-6; Q65. A2; *Summa Theologica* II-II. A47-56. *Summa Theologica* I-II. Q90-108.

[35]Thomas Aquinas *Summa Contra Gentiles* 3.1.37, ed. Vernon J. Bourke (Notre Dame, Ind.: University of Notre Dame Press, 1975).

[36]Aquinas *Summa Theologica* I-II. Q57.

[37]Ibid., I-II. Q57. A5.

[38]Ibid., Q94. A4.

[39]Den Uyl, *Virtue of Prudence*, p. 64.

[40]Thomas Aquinas, *On the Virtues in General* A7, in *Selected Writings of Thomas Aquinas*, trans. Robert P. Goodwin (Indianapolis: Bobbs-Merrill, 1965).

[41]James V. Schall, "On the Relation Between Art and Politics," in *Jacques Maritain: The Philosopher in Society*, 20th Century Political Thinkers (Lanham, Md.: Rowman and Littlefield, 1998), p. 29.

[42]Raymond J. Devettere, *Introduction to Virtue Ethics: Insights of the Ancient Greeks* (Washington, D.C.: Georgetown University Press 2002), p. 81.

[43]Aquinas *Summa Theologica* I-II. Q57. A5. Similarly, Aquinas says in *Summa Theologica* I-II. Q58. A2, RO4, "Right reason, which flows from prudence is included in the definition of moral virtue, not as part of its essence, but as something belonging by way of participation to all the moral virtues, in so far as they are all under the direction of prudence."

[44]This general teaching remains part of Catholic teaching in the twenty-first century. The Catechism calls prudence a human virtue (as distinguished from a theological virtue (§1805), but "the human virtues are rooted in the theological virtues." "Four virtues play a pivotal role and accordingly are called 'cardinal'; all the others are grouped around them. They are: prudence, justice, fortitude, and temperance" (§1812). "Prudence is the virtue that disposes practical reason to discern our true good in every circumstance and to choose the right means of achieving it; 'the prudent man looked where he is going.' . . . Prudence is 'right reason in action,' writes St. Thomas Aquinas (citing *Summa Theologica* II-II. Q47. A2), following Aristotle. . . . It is called auriga virtutum (the charioteer of the virtues); it guides the other virtues by setting rule and measure. It is prudence that immediately guides the judgment of conscience. The prudent man determines and directs his conduct in accordance with this judgment. With the help of this virtue we apply moral principles to particular cases without error and overcome doubts about the good to achieve and the evil to avoid" (§1806).

[45]By comparison Cicero emphasized "memory of the past, understanding of the present, and foresight of the future" (Cicero *De Inventione Rhetorica* 2).

[46]Reinhold Niebuhr, "Augustine's Political Realism," in *The City of God: A Collection of Critical Essays*, ed. Dorothy F. Donnelly (New York: Peter Lang, 1995).

[47]See Pieper, *Four Cardinal Virtues*, pp. xi-40. See also Dennis P. Hollinger, *Choosing the Good* (Grand Rapids: Baker Academic, 2002).

[48]Pieper defines synderesis as "innate conscience, natural conscience, or primary conscience" (*Four Cardinal Virtues*, p. 10 n.*). J. Budziszewski says, "Conscience is really two things, not one. Synderesis, which we may call deep conscience, is the universal interior witness to the foundational principles of moral law, along with their first few rings of implications. . . . Conscientia, which we may call surface conscience, is conscious moral belief, especially about the details of morality. This is the realm in which deep conscience is applied to particulars" (*Evangelicals in the Public Square* [Grand Rapids: Baker Academic, 2006], p. 54).

Teachers of moral philosophy in the American colonies in the eighteenth century debated the nature of synderesis or conscience. The seventeenth-century Puritans differed from the Scholastic tradition. "The primary difference between the Protestant and Catholic theories of conscience . . . concerned the degree to which each group believed that external authority is binding upon conscience. Both accepted that only the word of God could bind the conscience, that is, could supply the authoritative and obligatory general rules by which individual judgments were to be made" (Norman Fiering, *Moral Philosophy at Seventeenth Century Harvard: A Discipline in Transition* [Chapel Hill, N.C.: University of North Carolina Press, 1981], pp. 52-53, n. 93).

[49]Freddoso, *Syllabus on the Cardinal Virtues* <www.nd.edu/~freddos/courses/453/prudence. htm>.

[50]Abraham Lincoln, quoted in Richard Carwardine, *Lincoln: A Life of Purpose and Power* (New York: Alfred A. Knopf, 2006), p. 268.

[51]Josef Pieper writes that " 'prudence as cognition,' as cognition of the concrete situation of concrete action, includes above all the ability to be still in order to attain objective perception of reality. There is in addition the patient effort of experience . . . which cannot be evaded or replaced by any arbitrary, short-circuiting resort to 'faith'—let alone by the 'philosophical' point of view which confines itself to seeing the general rather than the particular" (Pieper, *Four Cardinal Virtues*, pp. 13-14).

[52]Pieper calls this " 'true to being' memory" and emphasizes "the danger that the truth of real things will be falsified by the assent or negation of the will" (Pieper, *Four Cardinal Virtues*, p. 15).

[53]Goodwin, *Team of Rivals*, p. 100 ; Robert V. Bruce, "The Riddle of Death," in *The Lincoln Enigma: The Changing Faces of an American Icon*, ed. Gabor Boritt (New York: Oxford University Press 2001), p. 141.

[54]Pieper, *Four Cardinal Virtues*, p. 16.

[55]See Wayne Barrett and Dan Collins, *Grand Illusion: The Untold Story of Rudy Giuliani and 9/11* (New York: HarperCollins, 2006).

[56]Aristotle *Nichomachean Ethics* 1141.

[57]Pieper, *Four Cardinal Virtues*, p. 18 (emphasis added).

[58]Goodwin, *Team of Rivals*, p. 104.

[59]Carwardine, *Lincoln*, p. 221.

[60]"Experience is simultaneously a necessary condition for that part of moral virtue called 'habituation' and for those parts of practical wisdom dealing with choice, deliberation, and judgment" (Den Uyl, *Virtue of Prudence*, p. 67).

[61]Aristotle *Nichomachean Ethics* 1142a11-15.

[62]Pieper, *Four Cardinal Virtues*, p. 19.

[63]Aristotle, *Nichomachean Ethics* 1140a19-20; 1144a23-27; Charles O'Neil, *Imprudence in St. Thomas Aquinas* (Milwaukee: Marquette University Press, 1955), p. 9.

[64]Budziszewski, *Written on the Heart*, p. 27.

[65] Aristotle *Nichomachean Ethics* 1144a25-35.

[66] Pieper, *Four Cardinal Virtues*, pp. 19-20.

[67] Aristotle *Nichomachean Ethics* 1144a25-35, cited in ibid.

[68] David Mark Nelson, *The Priority of Prudence: Virtue and Natural Law in Thomas Aquinas and the Implications for Modern Ethics* (University Park: Pennsylvania State University Press, 1992). For those who are skeptical that natural law has any relevance to moral questions, see J. Budziszewski, *What We Can't Not Know: A Guide* (Dallas: Spence, 2003).

[69] Aquinas *Summa Theologica* I-II. Q57. A4.

[70] See generally, Douglas W. Kmiec and Stephen B. Presser, "The Philosophical and Natural Law Basis of the American Order," in *The American Constitutional Order: History, Cases, and Philosophy* (Cincinnati: Anderson Publishing, 1998), pp. 1-120. The American founders relied on a long philosophical tradition espousing natural law. In *De Re Publica (The Republic)*, Cicero gave this classic statement of natural law: "True law is right reason in agreement with nature; it is of universal application, unchanging and everlasting; it summons to duty by its commands, and averts from wrongdoing by its prohibitions. . . . It is a sin to try to alter this law, nor is it allowable to attempt to repeal any part of it, and it is impossible to abolish it entirely. We cannot be freed from its obligations by senate or people, and we need not look outside ourselves for an expounder or interpreter of it. And there will not be different laws at Rome and at Athens, or different laws now and in the future, but one eternal and unchangeable law will be valid for all nations and all times, and there will be one master and rule, that is, God, over us all, for he is the author of this law, its promulgator, and its enforcing judge. Whoever is disobedient is fleeing from himself and denying his human nature, and by reason of this very fact he will suffer the worst penalties, even if he escapes what is commonly considered punishment" (Kmiec and Presser, "Philosophical and Natural Law," pp. 15-16).

[71] See Edward S. Corwin, *The "Higher Law" Background of American Constitutional Law* (Ithaca: N.Y.: Cornell University Paperbacks, 1995). James Madison, for example, "operated within the framework of a natural law outlook that was unquestioned for the most part by men of his age" (Neal Reimer, *James Madison* [New York: Washington Square Press, 1968], p. 15). James Wilson "relied on a Christian conception of natural law" (Mark David Hall, *The Political and Legal Philosophy of James Wilson, 1742-1798* [Columbia: University Missouri Press, 1997], p. 5).

[72] See generally, David Van Drunen, *A Biblical Case for Natural Law* (Grand Rapids: Acton Institute, 2006); J. Budziszewski, *What We Can't Not Know*.

[73] Aquinas *Summa Theologica* I-II. Q90. A4.

[74] Ibid., I-II. Q90. A4. RO1.

[75] As William E. May, writing within the Thomistic tradition, summarizes natural law: "At bottom, natural law can best be understood as consisting in ordered sets of true propositions of a practical nature meant to help us choose well. Natural law directs us to the goods perfective of human persons and enables us to distinguish alternatives of choice compatible with respect for these goods and the persons in whom they are meant to flourish from alternatives that are not so compatible" (William E. May, "Bioethics and Human Life," in *Natural Law and Contemporary Public Policy*, ed. David F. Forte [Washington, D.C.: Georgetown University Press 1998], p. 41). Or as May adds, "ordered sets of true propositions about what is to be done" (ibid., p. 43). See also William E. May, *An Introduction to Moral Theology* (Huntington, Ind.: Our Sunday Visitor, 1991).

[76] Thomas calls synderesis a habit, "a habit being that by which we act" (*Summa Theologica* I-II. Q79. A12, cited in I-II. Q94. A2) and states that "synderesis is said to be the law of our mind [by Basil], because it is a habit containing the precepts of the natural law, which are the first principles of human action" (I-II. Q94. A1. RO2).

[77] Ibid., I-II. Q94. A2.

[78] Ibid. This is, of course, reflected in the Christian Scriptures, e.g., "Hate what is evil; cling to what is good" (Romans 12:9 NIV); "Hold on to the good. Avoid every kind of evil" (1 Thessalonians 5:21-22 NIV).

79This roughly parallels the distinction between primary, second and tertiary principles of the natural law.

80Nelson, *The Priority of Prudence*, p. 70.

81Ibid., p. 75.

82Terry Hall, "Legislation," in *Natural Law and Contemporary Public Policy*, ed. David F. Forte (Washington, D.C.: Georgetown University Press 1998), p. 144, emphasis added. See also Charles N. R. McCoy, *The Structure of Political Thought: A Study in the History of Political Ideas* (New York: McGraw Hill, 1963), p. 32. McCoy explains the implications of contingency in political prudence: "Reason can be engaged in action either (1) by making things (in which cases its action passes into external matter, as we see in the case of the architect or shoemaker), or (2) by doing (in which case the action remains intrinsic to the agent, as we see in one who deliberates, or chooses, or wills)" (ibid.) Prudence is part of the latter. "This distinction between art and prudence entails other most important consequences for political science . . . . Prudence, unlike art, does not proceed by fixed and clear rules" (ibid., p. 33). McCoy quotes Aristotle: "Deliberation is concerned with things which happen in a certain way for the most part, but in whose the event is obscure, and with things in which it is indeterminate" (*Nichomachean Ethics* 3.1112b, quoted in ibid.). McCoy: "But the 'art' of politics does not proceed in most certain and determinate ways; the means to its end are infinitely variable and hence require the greatest deliberation" (ibid., p. 34). "Granted . . . that there are fixed ends in the nature of man as well as in the natural associations that guarantee the ends of human life, the task of the statesman is infinitely complicated by the contingency and obscurity of the means for attaining the end—for these are found in the concrete circumstances, contingent and variable, of a community. An awareness of this fact is the first step in the 'art' of politics" (ibid., p. 34). See also Yves Simon, "Between law and action there always is a space to be filled by decisions which cannot be written into law. . . . If law is a premise rather than a conclusion, if, universally, law admits of no immediate contact with the world of action, the ideal of a social science which would in each particular case, procure a rational solution and render governmental prudence unnecessary is thoroughly deceptive. Whatever the science of man and of society has to say remains an indeterminate distance from the world of action, and this distance can be traversed only by the obscure methods of prudence. . . . [T]he requirements of prudence [are] to extend, in the obscurities of contingency, the work of reason down to immediate contact with the world of action" (*The Tradition of Natural Law* [Bronx, N.Y.: Fordham University Press, 1965], pp. 83, 85). See also A. P. D'Entreves: "Despite the stress which is laid upon the absolute and immutable character of the natural law, the notion of it seems to be curiously flexible and adaptable. Positive laws are not expected to be molded upon it as upon a rigid pattern. A considerable sphere of freedom is left to the human lawgiver in the interpretation of general precepts" (*Natural Law: An Introduction to Legal Philosophy* [London: Hutchinson, 1951], p. 46).

83Robert P. George, "Natural Law, the Constitution, and the Theory and Practice of Judicial Review," in *Vital Remnants: America's Founding and the Western Tradition*, ed. Gary L. Gregg II (Wilmington, Del.: ISI Books, 1999), p. 164. This distinction is affirmed by other Thomistic scholars. See also McCoy: "For positive law derives from the natural law not in the way of conclusions from its first principles, but by way of determination of these common notions. It derives from the natural law in such fashion simply that what it prescribes may not of itself be contrary to natural right" (*Structure of Political Thought*, p. 150).

84Schall, *Reason, Revelation*, pp. 12-13.

85Jim Collins, *Good to Great* (New York: HarperBusiness, 2001), p. 85.

86Roy Jenkins, *Churchill: A Biography* (New York: Plume, 2001), pp. 513-14.

87Ibid., pp. 475-80.

88John Lukacs, *The Duel: The Eighty Day Struggle Between Churchill and Hitler* (New Haven, Conn.: Yale University Press, 1990).

89The works of Edmund Burke and Gertrude Himmelfarb, among many others, have observed the real constraints of culture, tradition and political arrangements.

[90]See, e.g., Isaacs, *Character Building.*

[91]Arthur Bryant, *The Turn of the Tide* (Garden City, N.Y.: Doubleday, 1957); Arthur Bryant, *Triumph in the West* (Westport, Conn.: Greenwood, 1959).

[92]Bryant, *Triumph in the West*, p. 20.

[93]Ibid.

[94]Aquinas, cited in Pieper, *Four Cardinal Virtues*, p. 16.

[95]Stephen E. Ambrose, *D-Day, June 6, 1944: The Climactic Battle of World War II* (New York: Simon & Schuster, 1994), p. 61. See also Michael Korda, *Ike: An American Hero* (New York: HarperCollins, 2007).

[96]Ambrose, *D-Day*, p. 62.

[97]Ibid., p. 66.

[98]Ibid., p. 61. See also Finnis, *Aquinas*, p. 61.

[99]An article in the *New York Times* emphasized uncertainty as an element in business decision making. "Uncertainty was an inevitable part of life and only the foolish imagined they could eliminate it. To make the best possible decisions, bond traders and policymakers alike had to weigh every relevant piece of information, estimate the risks that something unexpected would happen and then make a judgment based on the odds, aware all the while that success could not be guaranteed. They had to understand that a good decision could produce a bad outcome. That is what uncertainty meant, and recognizing it maximized the chances that they would succeed next time" (David Leonhardt, "This Fed Chief May Yet Get a Honeymoon," *New York Times*, August 23, 2006, p. C1).

[100]Ethan M. Fishman, *Prudential Presidency* (Westport, Conn.: Praeger, 2000), pp. 6-7.

[101]"Prudence may be defined as the ability to judge well in practical matters; it is tantamount to right reason applied to the realm of moral and political action" (Joseph R. Fornieri, "Lincoln and the Emancipation Proclamation: A Model of Prudent Leadership," in *Tempered Strength*, ed. Ethan M. Fishman [Lanham, Md.: Lexington Books, 2002], p. 126). Aquinas said that "it belongs to prudence to govern and command, so that wherever in human acts we find a special form of governance and command, there must be a special kind of prudence. Now it is evident that there is a special and perfect kind of governance in one who has to govern not only himself but also the perfect community of a city or kingdom; because a government is the more perfect according as it is more universal, extends to more matters, and attains a higher end. Hence prudence in its special and most perfect sense, belongs to a kind who is charged with the government of a city or kingdom: for which reason a species of prudence is reckoned to be regnative" (*Summa Theologica* II-II. Q50. A1).

[102]Aristotle *Nichomachean Ethics* 1140a; Thomas Aquinas, *Commentary on the Nicomachean Ethics*, trans. C. I. Litzinger (Chicago: Regnery, 1964), p. 558.

[103]Erwin C. Hargrove, foreword to Fishman's *Prudential Presidency*, p. xii.

[104]Pieper, *Four Cardinal Virtues*, p. 25. The classical tradition of "moderate realism was built around three core convictions," including "politics is an arena of rationality and moral responsibility. . . . Power should be understood in classical terms: as the ability to achieve a corporate purpose, for the common good" (George Weigel, *Tranquilitas Ordinis: The Present Failure and Future Promise of American Catholic Thought on War and Peace* [New York: Oxford University Press, 1987], pp. 43-44).

[105]Schall, *Reason, Revelation*, p. 3.

[106]John Cardinal O'Connor expressed support for "imperfect legislation" along similar lines as Harry Jaffa's: "It certainly seems to me . . . that in cases in which perfect legislation is clearly impossible, it is morally acceptable to support a pro-life bill, however reluctantly, that contains exceptions if the following conditions prevail: There is no other feasible bill restricting existing permissive abortion laws to a greater degree than the proposed bill; The proposed bill is more restrictive than existing law, that is, the bill does not weaken the current laws' restraints on abortion; and The proposed bill does not negate the responsibility of future,

more restrictive laws. In addition, it would have to be made clear that we do not believe that a bill which contains exceptions is ideal and that we would continue to urge future legislation which would more fully protect human life. I recognize that some in the pro-life movement may consider it politically or strategically unwise to take the course outlined above, but that is a matter of prudential judgment. It is not a matter of supporting intrinsic evil as such" (John Cardinal O'Connor, "From My Viewpoint: Abortion: Questions and Answers," *Catholic New York*, June 14, 1990 <www.priestsforlife.org/magisterium/cardocqanda.html>). This is evaluated at greater length in chap. 5.

[107]Cf. Leo Strauss: "The true statesman in the Aristotelian sense . . . takes his bearings" from the view that "there is a universally valid hierarchy of ends, but there are no universally valid rules of action. . . . [W]hen deciding what ought to be done, i.e., what ought to be done by this individual (for this individual group) here and now, one has to consider not only which of the various competing objectives is higher in rank but also which is most urgent in the circumstances" (Leo Strauss, *Natural Right and History* [Chicago: University of Chicago Press, 1953], p. 162).

[108]Hargrove, foreword to Fishman's *Prudential Presidency*, p. xii. Fishman addresses "point-counterpoint comparisons of prudence with idealism, pragmatism, and cynicism. . . . illustrations of the deal-making pragmatist, the naïve idealist, and the cynical realist through a number of case studies of presidential leadership."

[109]Fornieri, "Lincoln and the Emancipation Proclamation," p. 126.

[110]See Merrill D. Peterson, *The Great Triumvirate: Webster, Clay, and Calhoun* (New York: Oxford University Press, 1987). pp. 464-83.

[111]William Wilberforce, cited in John Pollock, *Wilberforce* (Herts, U.K.: Lion, 1986), p. 213.

[112]Winston Churchill, *Thoughts and Adventures* (London: Odhams, 1932), p. 39.

[113]See Germain Grisez, *The Way of the Lord Jesus*, vol. 3, *Difficult Moral Questions* (Quincy, Ill.: Franciscan Press, 1997), p. 876; Russell Smith, "The Principles of Cooperation and Their Application to the Present State of Health Care Evolution," in *Catholic Health Ministry in Transition* (Silver Spring, Md.: National Coalition on Catholic Health Care Ministry, 1995). See also John J. Coughlin, "Lawyers and Cooperation with Evil in Divorce Cases," in *The Catholic Citizen: Debating the Issues of Justice*, ed. Kenneth D. Whitehead (Chicago: St. Augustine's Press, 2004), p. 163, n. 22.

[114]See, e.g., John Finnis, "Helping Enact Unjust Laws Without Complicity in Injustice," *American Journal of Jurisprudence* 49 (2004): 11-42; John Finnis, "Unjust Laws in a Democratic Society: Some Philosophical and Theological Reflections," *Notre Dame Law Review* 71 (1996): 595-604; William E. May, "Unjust Laws and Catholic Citizens: Opposition, Cooperation and Toleration," *Homiletic and Pastoral Review* (November 1995): 12. As we will see in chap. 5, Colin Harte, in *Changing Unjust Laws Justly* (Washington, D.C.: Catholic University of America Press, 2005), unfortunately dismisses the doctrine of cooperation and its insights. Harte does not get to the issue of material cooperation until page 122 of his book and only then to dismiss it.

[115]See Pontifical Academy for Life, *Moral Reflections on Vaccines Prepared from Cells Derived from Aborted Human Fetuses*, June 5, 2005, reprinted in *National Catholic Bioethics Quarterly* 6 (2006): 541, 545.

[116]See e.g., ibid.; Angel Rodriguez Luno, "Ethical Reflections on Vaccines Using Cells from Aborted Fetuses," *National Catholic Bioethics Quarterly* 6 (2006): 453.

[117]Ligouri, *Theologia Moralis*, 1905-1912, 1:357 (lib. 1, §63), cited in Grisez, *The Way of the Lord Jesus*, p. 876.

[118]Germain Grisez and Russell Shaw, *Fulfillment in Christ: A Summary of Christian Moral Principles* (Notre Dame, Ind.: University of Notre Dame Press, 1991), pp. 146-48.

[119]A number of religious leaders and moral philosophers and commentators have agreed with this general conclusion, if not the specific reasoning. See e.g., Cardinal O'Connor, cited in Finnis, "Helping Enact Unjust Laws," pp. 11, 16 nn. 15-16; Anthony Fisher, "Some Problems of Conscience in Bio-lawmaking," in *Culture of Life—Culture of Death: Proceedings of the International Conference on "The Great Jubilee and the Culture of Life,"* ed. Luke Gormally (South

Bend, Ind.: St. Augustine Press, 2002); Peter Bristow, *The Moral Dignity of Man*, 2nd ed. (New York: Scepter, 1997).

[120]Grisez and Shaw, *Fulfillment in Christ*, p. 147.

[121]Coughlin, "Lawyers and Cooperation with Evil," pp. 159-60.

[122]Wayne R. LaFave and Austin W. Scott Jr., *Handbook on Criminal Law* (Eagan, Minn.: West, 1972), §65.

[123]See e.g., Damian P. Fedoryka, "What Happens to the Victims of Compromise Abortion Laws?" in *Life and Learning XIV: Proceedings of the Fourteenth University Faculty for Life Conference*, ed. Joseph W. Koterski (Washington, D.C.: University Faculty for Life, 2005), p. 51.

[124]Abraham Lincoln, speech of October 16, 1854, in Lincoln, *Speeches and Writings 1832-1858* (New York: Library of America, 1989), 1:310 (I'll refer to the 1832-1858 volume as volume 1 and the 1859-1865 volume as volume 2).

[125]Hallowell, *Moral Foundation of Democracy*, p. 49.

[126]Carwardine, *Lincoln*, p. 261.

[127]See e.g., Quentin Schultze, *An Essential Guide to Public Speaking* (Grand Rapids: Baker Academic, 2006).

[128]See Budziszewski, *Evangelicals in the Public Square*, p. 46.

[129]C. S. Lewis, *A Preface to Paradise Lost* (New York: Oxford University Press, 1961), pp. 53-54.

[130]The American founders, who will be addressed more fully in chap. 2, were familiar with the examples of prudential rhetoric in Scripture. This is exemplified in the teachings of the apostle Paul. At Mars Hill in Athens, Paul talked with Greeks, referring to their own pagan poets, with whom he was obviously familiar. With the Roman governor Felix, Paul started with a common point of reference; he sought to achieve a common understanding of morality. Contemporary Christians don't know what to make of Paul's testimony in 1 Corinthians 9:22 that he strived to be "all things to all people." It reflected logical, rhetorical, even social adaptability in presenting his message and persuading people.

[131]Lincoln, *Speeches*, 1:398 (speech of June 26, 1857, on the Dred Scott decision); Lincoln, *Speeches*, 1:794 (seventh debate with Douglas at Alton, October 15, 1858).

[132]Goodwin, *Team of Rivals*, p. 100.

[133]Joseph W. Dellapenna, *Dispelling the Myths of Abortion History* (Durham, N.C.: Carolina Academic Press, 2006). See Erika Bachiochi, ed., *The Cost of Choice* (New York: Encounter Books, 2004).

[134]James Davison Hunter makes this clear in his pathbreaking analysis, *Before the Shooting Begins: Searching for Democracy in America's Culture War* (Washington, D.C.: Free Press, 1994).

[135]Gallup Poll, "Abortion and Moral Beliefs," cited in ibid., pp. 86-90.

[136]Ibid. See Hunter's extensive analysis of this poll in *Before the Shooting Begins*.

[137]Leon R. Kass, "The Wisdom of Repugnance," *The New Republic*, June 2, 1997, pp. 17-26.

[138]Those who recognize the natural law might consider the harm-to-women argument not as a utilitarian argument but as one way of highlighting the natural consequences of violating the natural law.

[139]George Weigel, *Catholicism and the Renewal of American Democracy* (Mahwah, N.J.: Paulist Press, 1989), p. 201.

[140]Abraham Lincoln, cited in Clarke D. Forsythe, "A Legal Strategy to Overturn *Roe v. Wade* After Webster: Some Lessons from Lincoln," *Brigham Young University Law Review* (1991): 519, 530 (citing Harry Jaffa, *Crisis of the House Divided: An Interpretation of the Issues in the Lincoln-Douglas Debates* [Chicago: University of Chicago Press, 1959], pp. 231, 286-87, 309-10).

[141]Carnes Lord, "Bringing Prudence Back In: Leadership, Statecraft, and Political Science," in *Tempered Strength: Studies in the Nature and Scope of Prudential Leadership*, ed. Ethan M. Fishman (Lanham, Md.: Lexington Books, 2002).p. 75.

[142]Den Uyl, *Virtue of Prudence*, p. 41.

[143]"The epistemological approach taken by Hobbes damaged the intellectual character of prudence and severed the connection between prudence and ethics and politics" (ibid., p. 114).

"The Hobbesian framework altered the course of ethics and thereby the role and value of prudence" (p. 123). "It was Kant who dealt the virtue of prudence its death blow" (p. 143).

[144]Robert Kraynak, *Christian Faith and Modern Democracy: God and Politics in the Modern World* (Notre Dame, Ind.: University of Notre Dame Press, 2001), p. 154.

[145]James Davison Hunter, *The Death of Character: Moral Education in an Age Without Good or Evil* (New York: Basic Books, 2000).

[146]Ibid., p. 51 (noting Ralph Waldo Emerson's essay, "Character and the Children's Morality Code" of 1916).

CHAPTER 2: POLITICAL PRUDENCE IN THE THOUGHT OF THE AMERICAN FOUNDING

[1]Michael Novak, *On Two Wings: Humble Faith and Common Sense at the American Founding* (New York: Encounter Books, 2002).

[2]"Prudence . . . will dictate that Governments long established should not be changed for light and transient causes; and accordingly all experience hath shown, that mankind are more disposed to suffer, while evils are sufferable, than to right themselves by abolishing the forms to which they are accustomed" (U.S. Declaration of Independence [1776], reproduced in *The American Republic: Primary Sources*, ed. Bruce Frohnen [Indianapolis: Liberty Fund, 2002], p. 189).

[3]Reflections on the best regime have a long history in the works of Plato, Aristotle, Cicero, Augustine and Aquinas. See generally, James V. Schall, *The Politics of Heaven and Hell* (Lanham, Md.: University Press of America, 1984), esp. chap. 8, "The Best Form of Government."

[4]Forrest McDonald, *Novus Ordo Seclorum: The Intellectual Origins of the Constitution* (Lawrence: University Press of Kansas, 1985), pp. 67-68.

[5]McDonald, *Novus Ordo Seclorum*, p. 68; Martin Diamond, *The Federalist*, in Leo Strauss and Joseph Cropsey, *History of Political Philosophy* (New York: Basic Books, 1964), p. 575.

[6]James Davison Hunter, *The Death of Character: Moral Education in an Age Without Good or Evil* (New York: Basic Books, 2000), p. 37.

[7]These texts included Theophilus Golius (or Gottlieb), *Epitome Doctrinae Moralis* (1592): "one of the earliest published of the moral philosophy texts commonly used at Harvard" (Norman Fiering, *Moral Philosophy at Seventeenth-Century Harvard: A Discipline in Transition* [Chapel Hill: University of North Carolina Press, 1981], p. 67); Eustache de Saint-Paul, *Summa Philosophiae (Ethica)* (1609); and Henry More's *Enchiridion Ethicum* (1667) (adopted by Harvard in 1680s: "definitely extracted Harvard from the Scholastic pattern in ethics"; in Fiering, *Moral Philosophy*, p. 64).

[8]Fiering, *Moral Philosophy*, pp. 74-75.

[9]Ibid., pp. 52, 83. David Fordyce was a "Scottish moralist . . . whose ethics text was dominant at Harvard for the last half of the eighteenth century."

[10]Walter Stahr, *John Jay: Founding Father* (London: Hambledon and London, 2005), p. 10. Prudence was part of Jay's common vocabulary. Seeking to be kept informed while at the Continental Congress in Philadelphia in May 1775, Jay asked his wife, when writing, to be "as particular as may be consistent with prudence, for in times like these we should be cautious what we commit to paper" (ibid., p. 47). In a January 1779 letter to Lafayette supporting Washington's decision to not invade Canada, Jay concluded that "prudence therefore dictates that the arms of America should be employed in expelling the enemy from her own shores, before the liberation of a neighboring province is undertaken" (ibid., p. 109). When writing to Washington about the contemporary difficulties and obstacles, Jay wrote that "all of these factors and others portend evils which much prudence, vigor and circumspection are necessary to prevent or control" (ibid., p. 111). While president of the Continental Congress, Jay judged the priority of the issues to be considered by the Congress, concluding that it would "have been improper and imprudent to have called upon them" to decide a dispute between New York and Vermont (ibid., p. 112).

[11]E.g., The prudent man "gives thought to his steps" (Proverbs 14:15).

[12]The most frequently used Hebrew words that are translated prudent are *aruwm*, meaning "cunning," and *biyn*, meaning "to understand, be able, deal wisely, consider, pay attention to, regard, notice, discern, perceive, inquire." *Biyn* is used ninety-four times in the Old Testament to mean "understand" or "understanding." The Greek word most commonly used in the New Testament is *synētos*, which means "intelligent, sagacious, understanding." This is related to to *synēsis* (quickness of comprehension, the penetrating consideration which precedes action) and *syniēmi* (to comprehend mentally). Two passages, Luke 1:17 and Ephesians 1:8, actually use Aristotle's word for practical wisdom, *phrōnesis*. A number of other passages also use Aristotle's word for the prudent man (or the man of practical wisdom), *phrōnimos*. For Hebrew and Greek terms see *Strong's Exhaustive Concordance* (Grand Rapids: Zondervan, 2001).

[13]See also Jeremiah 49:7: "Is there no longer wisdom in Teman? / Has counsel perished from the prudent?"

[14]"Every prudent man acts out of knowledge" (Proverbs 13:16; see also Proverbs 14:18). For references for the characteristics of this sentence, see Proverbs 2:5-8; 3:21; 8:20; 10:17, 21, 31; 11:3, 12, 14; 12:1, 5, 15; 13:10, 18; 14:33; 15:1, 4, 22, 31; 16:3.

[15]Thomas Aquinas, *Commentary on the Nicomachean Ethics*, vol. 2, trans C. I. Litzinger (Chicago: Regnery, 1964).

[16]"To fill you with the knowledge of his will through all spiritual wisdom and understanding" (Colossians 1:9); "We proclaim him, admonishing and teaching everyone with all wisdom" (Colossians 1:28); "Christ, in whom are hidden all the treasures of wisdom and knowledge" (Colossians 2:2-3); "have an appearance of wisdom" (Colossians 2:23); "And over all these virtues put on love, which binds them together in perfect unity" (Colossians 3:14); "as you teach and admonish one another with all wisdom" (Colossians 3:16); "Be wise in the way you act toward outsiders; make the most of every opportunity" (Colossians 4:5).

[17]"This calls for wisdom" (Revelation 13:18); "this calls for patient endurance and faithfulness on the part of the saints" (Revelation 14:12); "This calls for a mind with wisdom" (Revelation 17:9).

[18]Paul Johnson, *A History of the American People* (New York: HarperCollins, 1997), pp. 28-117.

[19]Robert Filmer's *Patriarchy* (1680) was answered by John Locke and others.

[20]David Walsh, for example, says, "Just as Christianity is in some fundamental sense the truth of the liberal conception, so the liberal order can be considered the political truth of Christianity" (*The Growth of the Liberal Soul* [Columbia: University of Missouri Press, 1997], p. 201).

[21]Rousas John Rushdoony, *The Institutes of Biblical Law* (Nutley, N.J.: Craig Press, 1973).

[22]But others were convinced that they found direct support for a republic and the principle of the consent of the governed in the Bible. See J. Budziszewski, *Evangelicals in the Public Square* (Grand Rapids: Baker Academic, 2006), pp. 21-22.

[23]See Psalm 2:6: "I have installed my King on Zion"; Proverbs 8:16: "by me princes govern, and all nobles who rule on earth"; Isaiah 45:1: "to Cyrus, whose right hand I take hold of to subdue nations before him"; Daniel 2:21: "he sets up kings and deposes them"; Daniel 4:25: "until you acknowledge that the Most High is sovereign over the kingdoms of men and gives them to anyone he wishes"; Jeremiah 27:6: "I will hand all your countries over to my servant Nebuchadnezzar"; John 19:11: "You would have no power over me if it were not given to you from above"; Romans 13:1: "There is no authority except that which God has established. The authorities that exist have been established by God"; Revelation 1:5: "Jesus Christ . . . the ruler of the kings of the earth."

[24]See Amos 1:3–2:3; Psalm 2:10-12; Ezekiel 26–32; Daniel 5:18-30; Revelation 6:15, 16; 19:17-21.

[25]Nevertheless, some of the leaders in the founding generation did specifically believe that the raising of the American republic was part of God's sovereign plans in history. See e.g., Novak, *On Two Wings*, p. 170 n. 37, 218 n. 63; Budziszewski, *Evangelicals in the Public Square*, pp. 15-37.

[26]See, e.g., Judges 2:22: "I will use them to test Israel."

[27]See, e.g., C. F. B. Cranfield, *A Critical and Exegetical Commentary on the Epistle to the Romans*

(Edinburgh: T & T Clark, 1975), 2:663; Douglas Moo, *The Epistle to the Romans* (Grand Rapids: Eerdmans, 1996), p. 798; J. W. McGarvey and Philip Pendleton, *Commentary on Romans* (Cincinnati: Standard Publishing, 1916), p. 507.

[28]Compare 1 Timothy 2:2, where Paul requests prayers "for kings and all those in authority."

[29]See Luke 12:11: "synagogues, rulers and authorities"; Ephesians 3:10; 6:12; Colossians 1:16; 2:15; 1 Peter 3:22; Titus 3:1: "rulers and authorities."

[30]Ellis Sandoz, ed., *Political Sermons of the American Founding Era 1730-1805* (Indianapolis: Liberty Fund, 1991).

[31]See, e.g., Deuteronomy 25:1: "acquitting the innocent and condemning the guilty."

[32]He specifies three basic moral principles that the leaders and the people violated: (1) seek justice, (2) encourage the oppressed, (3) defend the cause of the poor, the fatherless, and the widow (Isaiah 1; 5:20, 23; 10:1-2). Micah spoke to Judah in the same vein (see Micah 3:2-11; "despise justice" [v. 9]). Amos speaks to Israel similarly (see Amos 2:7; 4:1; 5:7-15: "trample on the poor," "oppress . . . and take bribes"). They condemn the injustice of the legal system for violating prohibitions on bribes for rendering justice (Exodus 23:1-8; Deuteronomy 16:18-20; Isaiah 1:23; 3:13-15; 5:8, 23; 10:1-2; Micah 2:2, 9; 3:9; 6:8; 7:3). Isaiah indicts the people, not just the leaders (Isaiah 5:25).

[33]See Ken Connor and John Revell, *Sinful Silence: When Christians Neglect Their Civic Duty* (Nashville: Ginosko, 2004). An influential Christian leader of the nineteenth century, Alexander Campbell, shared this view, denying any biblical basis for the divine right of kings, affirming that Scripture permitted a multitude of forms of government, yet affirming a certain moral standard for all civil government. "Civil government is itself a divine appendix to the volumes of religion and morality. Though neither Caesar nor Napoleon, Nicholas nor Victoria, were, 'by the grace of God,' king, emperor or queen; still the civil throne, the civil magistrate, and, therefore, civil government, are, by the grace of God, bestowed upon the world. Neither the church nor the world could exist without it. God himself has, therefore, benevolently ordained magistrates and judges. . . . The Bible has sanctioned republics, and commonwealths and kingdoms, without affixing any particular name to them. It prescribes no form of human government, because no one form of government would suit all the countries, climes and people of the earth. But the Bible, in the name and by the authority of its Author, demands of all persons in authority that they protect the innocent, that they punish the guilty, and that they dispense justice to all" (*Popular Lectures and Addresses* [Philadelphia: James Challen, 1861], pp. 313-14).

[34]Daniel Boorstin, quoted in Russell Kirk, *The Roots of American Order* (Chicago: Open Court, 1974), p. 46.

[35]Samuel Cooper, in Ellis Sandoz, ed., *Political Sermons of the American Founding Era 1730-1805* (Indianapolis: Liberty Fund, 1991), p. 642.

[36]In the seventeenth century, colonial America was settled "not only by Anglicans (of the Church of England who had broken from Rome and undergone a reformation in the sixteenth century) but also by dissenters from a great variety of sects and denominations spawned out of the Protestant Reformation: Anabaptists and Pietists from Germany, Huguenots from France, Presbyterians from Scotland, Baptists, Puritans, Independents, Quakers, Mennonites" (Clarence B. Carson, *Basic American Government* (Columbus, Ga.: American Textbook, 2001), p. 118.

[37]Kirk, *Roots of American Order*, p. 73.

[38]See generally, Robert P. Kraynak, *Christian Faith and Modern Democracy: God and Politics in the Fallen World* (Notre Dame, Ind.: University of Notre Dame Press, 2001), for a thorough scriptural and prudential treatment of a theory of Christian constitutionalism.

[39]Ibid., pp. 4-5, 89-90.

[40]Ibid., pp. 89-90.

[41]John H. Hallowell, *The Moral Foundation of Democracy* (Chicago: University of Chicago Press, 1954), p. 2.

[42]John Wild, *Introduction to Realistic Philosophy* (New York: Harper and Row, 1948), cited in ibid., pp. 15-16; see also John Wild, ed., *The Return to Reason* (Chicago: University Chicago Press, 1953).

[43]McDonald, *Novus Ordo Seclorum*, pp. 4-5.

[44]Ibid., pp. 66-67.

[45]Ibid., p. 67.

[46]Kenneth Deutsch, "Thomas Aquinas on Magnanimous and Prudent Statesmanship," in Ethan M. Fishman, ed., *Tempered Strength: Studies in the Nature and Scope of Prudential Leadership* (Lanham, Md.: Lexington Books, 2002).

[47]Samuel Adams to Joseph Warren, November 4, 1775, referring to "Principles of Virtue," in William J. Bennett, *Our Sacred Honor* (New York: Simon & Schuster, 1997), p. 261.

[48]Joseph Ellis, *New England Mind in Transition* (New Haven, Conn.: Yale University Press, 1973), pp. 225-26. Jay likely read Cicero's *De Officiis* and Samuel von Puffendorf's (1632-1694) *De Officio*.

[49]Wilson maintained that parents have a duty to "maintain their children decently, and according to their circumstances; to protect them according to the dictates of prudence; and to educate them" (James Wilson, cited in Mark David Hall, *The Political and Legal Philosophy of James Wilson 1742-1798* [Columbia: University of Missouri Press, 1997], p. 59).

[50]Virtue "being necessary for the preservation of their rights and liberties" (John Adams, Massachusetts Constitution, 1780, cited in Bennett, *Our Sacred Honor*, p. 263).

[51]James Madison, quoted in Jean Yarbrough, "The Constitution and Character: The Missing Critical Principle?" in *To Form a More Perfect Union: The Critical Ideas of the Constitution*, ed. Herman Belz, Ronald Hoffman and Peter J. Albert (Charlottesville: University Press of Virginia, 1992), p. 217.

[52]Benjamin Rush, quoted in Novak, *On Two Wings*, p. 34.

[53]Benjamin Rush, quoted in James Hunter, *Death of Character*, pp. 40-41. See also Novak, *On Two Wings*, p. 34.

[54]Samuel Cooper, quoted in Novak, *On Two Wings*, p. 38.

[55]McDonald, *Novus Ordo Seclorum*, p. 90.

[56]Paul Eidelberg, *The Philosophy of the American Constitution* (Washington, D.C.: Free Press, 1965), pp. 264-71.

[57]Bruce Frohnen, ed., *The American Republic: Primary Sources* (Indianapolis: Liberty Fund, 2002), p. 227.

[58]Thomas Jefferson, quoted in Bennett, *Our Sacred Honor*, pp. 254-55.

[59]Ibid.

[60]Pierce Butler, quoted in Ethan M. Fishman, *Prudential Presidency* (Westport, Conn.: Praeger, 2000), p. 113.

[61]Terry Brennan, "Natural Rights and the Constitution: The Original 'Original Intent,' " *Harvard Journal of Law and Public Policy* 15 (1992): 965, 971-77.

[62]For example, "Luther Martin cited several theorists of natural law" at the Constitutional Convention of 1787. McDonald, *Novus Ordo Seclorum*, p. 7.

[63]Novak, *On Two Wings*, p. 36.

[64]See McDonald, *Novus Ordo Seclorum*, pp. 7, 59; and Douglas W. Kmiec and Stephen B. Presser, *The American Constitutional Order: History, Cases, and Philosophy* (Cincinnati: Anderson, 1998), pp. 1-163.

[65]Novak, *On Two Wings*, p. 36. Terence Marshall writes: "The Madisonian synthesis of rights and prudence derives finally from another source than Montesquieu or Hume, Locke or Voltaire. An attentive reading of *The Federalist* reveals that the practical reason it manifests is founded not on a passion for security but on a concern for the disposition of soul requisite to a just or reasonable deliberation of public affairs" (Novak, *On Two Wings*, p. 165).

[66]McDonald, *Novus Ordo Seclorum*, p. 60.

[67]John Adams, quoted in Novak, *On Two Wings*, p. 86.

[68]Thomas Jefferson, quoted in Novak, *On Two Wings*, p. 87.

[69]James Wilson, quoted in Novak, *On Two Wings*, p. 37. A similar concept was expressed by Samuel Cooper in a sermon in October 1780 at the Commencement of the Massachusetts Constitution of 1780, written by Adams (Novak, *On Two Wings*, p. 38).

[70]Hall, *Political and Legal Philosophy of James Wilson*, p. 67.

[71]Ibid.

[72]Novak, *On Two Wings*, pp. 87-88.

[73]Clinton Rossiter, introduction to *The Federalist Papers* (New York: Mentor Books, 1961), p. vii.

[74]Prudence is explicitly invoked in *The Federalist* at least eighteen times. Ten by Hamilton: "every prudent and honest man of whatever party" (*Federalist* 8, p. 71); "the discretion and prudence of the legislature" (*Federalist* 42, p. 162); "if its powers are administered with a common share of prudence" (*Federalist* 27, p. 177); "must be left to the prudence and firmness of the people" (*Federalist* 31, p. 197); "mutually questions of prudence" (*Federalist* 32, p. 200); "as the exigency may suggest and prudence justify" (*Federalist* 33, p. 203); "the prudent mean" (*Federalist* 65, p. 400); "a single man of prudence and good sense" (*Federalist* 74, p. 448); "an ordinary degree of prudence" (*Federalist* 81, p. 491); "I can reconcile it to no rules of prudence" (*Federalist* 85, p. 527). Eight by Madison: "The prudent inquiry, in all cases, ought surely to be not so much from whom the advice comes, as whether the advice be good" (*Federalist* 40, p. 254); (*Federalist* 41, p. 258 [twice]); (*Federalist* 43, p. 280); (*Federalist* 44, p. 283); (*Federalist* 51, p. 322); (*Federalist* 57, p. 353); (*Federalist* 63, p. 376); (*Federalist* 62, pp. 378, 380 [three times]). All page citations are to the Mentor Book 1961 edition.

[75]Graham Walker, "Virtue and the Constitution: Augustinian Theology and the Frame of American Common Sense," in *Vital Remnants: America's Founding and the Western Tradition*, ed. Gary L. Gregg II (Wilmington, Del.: ISI Books, 1999), p. 138.

[76]Rossiter, introduction to *The Federalist Papers*, p. xiv.

[77]Yarbrough, "Constitution and Character," pp. 220-21. See also Barry Alan Shain, *The Myth of American Individualism: The Protestant Origins of American Political Thought* (Princeton, N.J.: Princeton University Press, 1994), esp. chap. 2: "A Sketch of 18th-Century American Communalism."

[78]James Wilson, quoted in Hall, *Political and Legal Philosophy of James Wilson*, p. 59.

[79]Ibid., p. 60 (citing John B. McMaster and Frederick D. Stone, eds., *Pennsylvania and the Federal Constitution 1787-1788* [1888; reprint, Cambridge, Mass.: Da Capo Press, 1970], p. 312).

CHAPTER 3: WILBERFORCE'S PERSEVERANCE

[1]George Macaulay Trevelyan, *British History in the Nineteenth Century and After, 1782-1919* (New York: Harper & Row, 1962), p. 51. Indeed, Trevelyan declared that "if slavery had not been abolished before the great commercial exploitation of the tropics began, Africa would have been turned by the world's capitalists into a slave-farm so enormous that it must have eventually corrupted and destroyed Europe herself, as surely as the world-conquest under the conditions of slavery destroyed the Roman Empire" (ibid.).

[2]See generally, William Hague, *William Wilberforce: The Life of the Great Anti-Slave Trade Campaigner* (Orlando: Harcourt, 2007); Eric Metaxas, *Amazing Grace* (New York: HarperCollins, 2007); Kevin Belmonte, *Hero for Humanity: A Biography of William Wilberforce* (Colorado Springs: NavPress, 2002); John Pollock, *Wilberforce* (Herts, U.K.: Lion Publishing, 1977); Robin Furneaux, *William Wilberforce* (London: Hamish Hamilton, 1974); Reginald Coupland, *Wilberforce* (London: Collins, 1945); Reginald Coupland, *Wilberforce: A Narrative* (London: Collins, 1923). The six biographies complement one another in presenting slightly different information and perspectives. Metaxas's has insight into Wilberforce's campaign on the reformation of manners and his network. Chapters 5-7 of Belmonte's present more than other biographers on Wilberforce's campaign on the reformation of manners. The biographies are complemented by Roger Anstey's insightful history of the campaign, *The Atlantic Slave Trade*

and British Abolition, 1760-1810 (Atlantic Highlands, N.J.: Humanities Press, 1975). See also Christopher Leslie Brown, *Moral Capital: Foundations of British Abolitionism* (Chapel Hill: University of North Carolina Press, 2006); Jay Sappington, "Legislative Compromise as Moral Strategy: Lessons for the Pro-Life Movement from the Abolitionism of William Wilberforce" (masters thesis, Trinity International University, April 1998); Kevin Belmonte, "William Wilberforce," in *Building a Healthy Culture: Strategies for an American Renaissance,* ed. Don Eberly (Grand Rapids: Eerdmans, 2001), p. 159.

[3]Belmonte, *Hero for Humanity,* p. 143 (in an 1802 letter to Prime Minister Henry Addington).

[4]Sappington, "Legislative Compromise as Moral Strategy," p. 8.

[5]Frank J. Klingberg, *The Anti-Slavery Movement in England: A Study in English Humanitarianism* (1926; reprint, North Haven, Conn.: Archon Books, 1968), p. 22, cited in ibid., p. 13.

[6]Sappington, "Legislative Compromise as Moral Strategy," p. 10.

[7]*Lewis v. Stapylton* (1771) (the case of Thomas Lewis) and *Somerset v. Stewart* (Somerset's Case), 98 English Reports 499, 20 Howell's State Trials 1 (1772). Granville Sharpe published *A Representation of the Injustice and Dangerous Tendency of Tolerating Slavery in England.* Furneaux, *William Wilberforce,* p. 66. See also Steven M. Wise, *Though the Heavens May Fall: The Landmark Trial That Led to the End of Human Slavery* (Cambridge, Mass.: Da Capo Press, 2005).

[8]Furneaux, *William Wilberforce,* p. 62.

[9]Ibid., p. 61.

[10]Belmonte, *Hero for Humanity,* p. 109.

[11]Ibid., p. 108.

[12]Pollock, *Wilberforce,* p. 250. Pitt's biographer William Hague comments that the French Revolution and the slave revolt in Saint Domingue "in practice . . . made the atmosphere deeply unpromising" (William Hague, *William Pitt the Younger: A Biography* [New York: Harper-Perennial, 2005], p. 255).

[13]Anstey, *Atlantic Slave Trade,* p. 276.

[14]Furneaux, *William Wilberforce,* p. 63.

[15]Ibid., p. 63.

[16]"St. Athanasius [297-373], Bishop of Alexandria, Egypt, became the champion of the faith against Arianism in the Council of Nicaea. He suffered much persecution, including seventeen years of intermittent exile," *Daily Roman Missal,* 6th ed. (Huntington, Ind.: Our Sunday Visitor, 2003).

[17]Furneaux, *William Wilberforce,* p. 14.

[18]Ibid., p. 21.

[19]Many speeches by Burke, Fox, Sheridan, Pitt and Wilberforce are published in Brian MacArthur, ed., *The Penguin Book of Historic Speeches* (New York: Penguin, 1995), including Wilberforce's May 12, 1789, speech and Pitt's April 2, 1792, speech against the slave trade.

[20]Michelle Steel, "William Wilberforce: The Persevering Parliamentarian," *Vision,* Winter 2007 <www.vision.org/visionmedia/article.aspx?id=2266>.

[21]George Canning, quoted in Belmonte, *Hero for Humanity,* p. 220.

[22]William Wilberforce, quoted in ibid., p. 112. Excerpts of the speech can be found in MacArthur, *Penguin Book of Historic Speeches,* p. 134.

[23]Pollock, *Wilberforce,* p. 147.

[24]Ibid., p. 89.

[25]Wilberforce, quoted in Belmonte, *Hero for Humanity,* p. 218.

[26]John Pollock, *William Wilberforce: A Man Who Changed His Times* (Washington, D.C.: Trinity Forum, 1996).

[27]Furneaux, *William Wilberforce,* p. 27.

[28]Ibid., p. 29.

[29]This does not mean that Boswell supported Wilberforce or his opposition to the slave trade. He later wrote a hateful doggerel against Wilberforce (Belmonte, *Hero for Humanity,* p. 115).

[30]Pollock, *Wilberforce*, p. 266.

[31]Sappington, "Legislative Compromise as Moral Strategy," p. 15.

[32]Belmonte, *Hero for Humanity*, p. 98.

[33]Sappington, "Legislative Compromise as Moral Strategy," p. 16; Belmonte, *Hero for Humanity*, p. 109.

[34]Belmonte, *Hero for Humanity*, p. 204.

[35]Pollock, *Wilberforce*, p. 267.

[36]Belmonte, *Hero for Humanity*, p. 208.

[37]Furneaux, *William Wilberforce*, p. 53.

[38]Ibid., pp. 34-35.

[39]Pollock, *Wilberforce*, p. 37.

[40]Furneaux, *William Wilberforce*, p. 37.

[41]Belmonte, *Hero for Humanity*, p. 96.

[42]See e.g., Pollock, *Wilberforce*, pp. 20, 111, 138; Furneaux, *William Wilberforce*, p. 19 (citing an early speech of February 22, 1782). It is certainly possible, since Wilberforce read classical Greek and Roman writers and could read, write and translate Greek and Latin. His letters are laced with Latin phrases. He was "an accomplished classicist" and "had read widely among the many great authors of Greek and Roman antiquity" (Belmonte, *Hero for Humanity*, p. 223). He was "well acquainted" with "Aristotle, Cicero, Juvenal, Lucan, Ovid, Sophocles, and Tacitus" (ibid., p. 227). We do know that Wilberforce read Francis Bacon's *Essays* "avidly all his life and from which he derived much guidance." He also read Pascal's *Pensées* and recommended him to others, and he read Milton and had "a natural love of classical learning" (ibid., pp. 89, 93-93, 97). See also Anstey, *Atlantic Slave Trade*, p. 367 (quoting Wilberforce's letter to Grenville of March 24, 1806).

[43]Wilberforce, quoted in Belmonte, *Hero for Humanity*, p. 91.

[44]Furneaux, *William Wilberforce*, p. 19.

[45]Pollock, *Wilberforce*, p. 71.

[46]Wilberforce, quoted in Sappington, "Legislative Compromise as Moral Strategy," p. 58.

[47]Furneaux, *William Wilberforce*, pp. 140-41.

[48]Wilberforce, quoted in Belmonte, *Hero for Humanity*, p. 133.

[49]Pollock, *Wilberforce*, p. 213.

[50]Belmonte, *Hero for Humanity*, p. 116; Sappington, "Legislative Compromise as Moral Strategy."

[51]Sappington, "Legislative Compromise as Moral Strategy," p. 59.

[52]Pollock, *Wilberforce*, p. 288.

[53]James Davison Hunter, "To Change the World" <www.workforceministries.com/articles/Hunter-To%20Change%20the%20World.doc>.

[54]Sappington, "Legislative Compromise as Moral Strategy," p. 9.

[55]Furneaux, *William Wilberforce*, p. 68; see also Metaxas's account, *Amazing Grace*, p. 103-6.

[56]Sappington, "Legislative Compromise as Moral Strategy," p. 10.

[57]Pollock, *Wilberforce*, p. 307.

[58]Wilberforce, quoted in Belmonte, *Hero for Humanity*, p. 100.

[59]Belmonte, *Hero for Humanity*, p. 100.

[60]See generally, William Hague, *William Pitt the Younger: A Biography* (New York: HarperPerennial, 2005). Hague offers this explanation of Pitt's caution in February 1788: "While he and the leading members of the opposition favored change, many of his senior colleagues in the government and a likely majority of the country gentlemen of the House of Commons were unpersuaded. They feared the economic and international consequences of renouncing the slave trade. . . . Pitt faced opposition to any serious move against the slave trade from members of the Royal Family and much of his own cabinet, including Sydney, who was responsible for the colonies, and, inevitably Thurlow. Even Pitt's closet confidant in the government, Dundas, was opposed to abolition because of the tens of millions of pounds of assets involved in the West Indies and his view that a ban would be an encroachment on the legislative rights of the colonies" (ibid., p. 252).

[61]Furneaux, *William Wilberforce*, p. 14.

[62]Sappington, "Legislative Compromise as Moral Strategy," p. 27.

[63]See Bernard Martin, *John Newton: A Biography* (London: William Heinemann, 1950), p. 303.

[64]Furneaux, *William Wilberforce*, pp. 69-71; Sappington, "Legislative Compromise as Moral Strategy," pp. 10-11.

[65]Thomas Clarkson, *The History of the Rise, Progress and Accomplishment of the Abolition of the African Slave Trade by the British Parliament* (1808; reprint, London: Frank Cass, 1968).

[66]Pollock, *Wilberforce*, p. 252.

[67]Belmonte, *Hero for Humanity*, p. 274.

[68]Anstey, *Atlantic Slave Trade*, p. 272.

[69]Sappington, "Legislative Compromise as Moral Strategy," p. 52.

[70]Anstey, *Atlantic Slave Trade*, p. 326

[71]Ibid., pp. 255-56 (quoting Clarkson, *History of the Rise, Progress and Accomplishment*).

[72]Furneaux, *William Wilberforce*, pp. 72-73. Sappington observes that the emotional overtones of "property" in eighteenth-century England paralleled the mantra of "choice" in America in the late twentieth century (Sappington, "Legislative Compromise as Moral Strategy," p. 49 n. 3).

[73]One historian of the slave trade concluded, "Wilberforce, who had dreamed in 1781 of becoming 'the instrument of breaking or, at least easing, the yoke' of West Indian slaves, concluded by 1787 that Africa and the Atlantic slave trade should be the key objectives for reform. It was to be expected, then, that the 1787 Abolition Committee would decide to limit its goal, over Sharp's objections, to an outlawing of the slave trade. The only surprise, if we may believe Clarkson's later testimony, is that the Committee considered alternatives and concluded that it did not really matter where they began, since an ending of either slavery or the slave trade would bring an end to the other evil" (David Brion Davis, *Slavery in the Age of Revolution*, cited in Sappington, "Legislative Compromise as Moral Strategy," p. 54).

[74]Pollock, *Wilberforce*, p. 71.

[75]Ibid., p. 71.

[76]Ibid., p. 213.

[77]Pollock, *William Wilberforce*, p. 15; Belmonte, *Hero for Humanity*, p. 95.

[78]Pollock, *Wilberforce*, p. 336 n. 76.

[79]Ibid., p. 213.

[80]Sappington, "Legislative Compromise as Moral Strategy," p. 15.

[81]Anstey, *Atlantic Slave Trade*, p. 266.

[82]Quoted in Charles Colson, "William Wilberforce," in *Chosen Vessels: Portraits of Ten Outstanding Christian Men*, ed. Charles Turner (Ann Arbor, Mich.: Servant, 1985), pp. 53, 51.

[83]William Pitt directly addressed the notion of the trade as a "necessary evil" in his April 2, 1792, speech (Brian MacArthur, ed., *The Penguin Book of Historic Speeches* [New York: Penguin, 1995], p. 139).

[84]Pollock, *Wilberforce*, p. 209.

[85]Earl of Abington, quoted in Coupland, *Wilberforce*, p. 174.

[86]Belmonte, *Hero for Humanity*, p. 111.

[87]Anstey, *Atlantic Slave Trade*, p. 260.

[88]Thomas Clarkson, *An Essay on the Impolicy of the African Slave Trade in Two Parts* (1788; reprint, Freeport, N.Y.: Books for Libraries Press, 1971).

[89]Anstey, *Atlantic Slave Trade*, p. 260.

[90]Ibid., pp. 348-49.

[91]Sappington, "Legislative Compromise as Moral Strategy," p. 75. See also Anstey, *Atlantic Slave Trade*, p. 331.

[92]Anstey, *Atlantic Slave Trade*, p. 279.

[93]Sappington, "Legislative Compromise as Moral Strategy," p. 81.

[94]Wilberforce, quoted in ibid.

[95]Sappington, "Legislative Compromise as Moral Strategy," pp. 88-89.

96Anstey, *Atlantic Slave Trade*, p. 395.

97Clarkson, *History*, 1:528, cited in Sappington, "Legislative Compromise as Moral Strategy." Dolben stated that the object of his bill "went only to limit the number of persons to be put on board to the tonnage of the vessel which was to carry them, in order to prevent them from being crowded too closely together; to secure to them good and sufficient provisions; and to take cognizance of other matters, which related to their health and accommodation; and this only till Parliament could enter into the general merits of the question" (Clarkson, *History*, 1:529).

98Dale Herbert Porter, *The Abolition of the Slave Trade in England, 1784-1807* (Hamden, Conn.: Archon Books, 1970), p. 49 n. 60.

99Anstey, *Atlantic Slave Trade*, p. 336.

100Anstey's book (ibid.) and Sappington's thesis, "Legislative Compromise as Moral Strategy," are excellent resources for this purpose.

101Sappington, "Legislative Compromise as Moral Strategy," p. 75. Pitt's biographer, William Hague, offers these strategic insights: Dolben's bill "duly went through, but only narrowly and with many amendments. With Pitt's help, a replacement bill was rammed through the Commons in a single day, . . . Pitt apparently refusing to let Parliament rise for the summer recess until the measure was passed. He had got his way, but it had been a Pyrrhic victory. If so much political capital was required to get such a minor measure through Parliament, what hope could there be of outright abolition? The hope lay in eloquence and inquiry. The inquiries of the Privy Council and the Commons' Committee on Trade produced evidence which Pitt thought 'irresistible' " (ibid., pp. 252-53).

102Furneaux, *William Wilberforce*, p. 85.

103Belmonte, *Hero for Humanity*, p. 116.

104Pollock, *Wilberforce*, p. 116.

105Ibid., p. 284.

106Sappington, "Legislative Compromise as Moral Strategy," p. 109.

107Anstey, *Atlantic Slave Trade*, p. 276.

108Ibid., p. 281.

109Hugh Thomas, *The Slave Trade: The Story of the Atlantic Slave Trade, 1440-1870* (New York: Simon and Schuster, 1997), p. 538.

110Sappington, "Legislative Compromise as Moral Strategy," p. 23.

111Belmonte, *Hero for Humanity*, p. 132.

112Anstey, *Atlantic Slave Trade*, p. 321.

113Hague, *William Pitt the Younger*, p. 376.

114Thomas, *Slave Trade*, p. 541.

115Anstey, *Atlantic Slave Trade*, p. 322.

116Ibid., p. 322.

117Ibid., p. 321.

118Ibid., p. 326.

119Colson, "William Wilberforce," p. 58.

120Belmonte, *Hero for Humanity*, p. 144.

121Sappington, "Legislative Compromise as Moral Strategy," p. 19.

122Klingberg, cited in ibid., pp. 19-20.

123Anstey says that by mid-1804, "the abolitionists were already flexing their muscles on strategies which wove significant measures of abolition into the received wisdom of national interest. In the next three years, aided by a change in government which enhanced the degree of ministerial support, they were helped by events and their own insights to develop a strategy which by 1806 was to end up to two-thirds of the British slave trade, basically by appeal to national interest. This made easier, but does not fully explain, the triumph of humanitarian principle in 1807" (Anstey, *Atlantic Slave Trade*, p. 342).

124Sappington, "Legislative Compromise as Moral Strategy," p. 27; Anstey, *Atlantic Slave Trade*, pp. 348-49, 358-59.

[125]Pollock, *Wilberforce*, p. 194.

[126]For example, Anstey documents instances of Pitt's delay and lack of commitment in 1804-1805 (Anstey, *Atlantic Slave Trade*, p. 348). Pitt's biographer William Hague concludes that Pitt's greatest failure was his "inability to secure final abolition of the slave trade. The sincerity of his opposition to this dreadful trade was all too plain, but so is the fact that he lost the energy, focus and will to pursue the matter to a successful conclusion in the early 1800s. The fact that abolition was so speedily secured by Grenville and Fox soon after Pitt's death suggests that he too could have secured it if he had marshaled his forces to do so. The truth is that by 1805, weighed down by the conduct of the war and deeply troubled by domestic controversies, Pitt was a spent force as a reformer. It is a lesson that the energy and focus of a political career are finite" (Hague, *William Pitt the Younger*, pp. 494-95).

[127]Belmonte, *Hero for Humanity*, p. 147.

[128]Anstey, *Atlantic Slave Trade*, pp. 357, 365.

[129]Ibid., p. 368.

[130]Ibid., p. 370.

[131]Ibid., pp. 366-68.

[132]Thomas, *Slave Trade*, p. 553.

[133]Anstey, *Atlantic Slave Trade*, p. 357.

[134]James Stephen's books are *The Crisis of the Sugar Colonies* (1802) and *War in Disguise, or the Frauds of the Neutral Flags* (1805). See Anstey, *Atlantic Slave Trade*, pp. 349-54.

[135]Sappington, "Legislative Compromise as Moral Strategy," p. 28; Anstey, *Atlantic Slave Trade*, pp. 370-73.

[136]Anstey, *Atlantic Slave Trade*, pp. 400-401.

[137]Pollock, *William Wilberforce*, p. 17.

[138]Colson, "William Wilberforce," p. 65.

[139]Pollock, *Wilberforce*, p. 214.

[140]Klingberg, *Anti-Slavery Movement*, pp. 157-58.

[141]Sappington, "Legislative Compromise as Moral Strategy," p. 31.

[142]Ibid., p. 32.

[143]Ibid., p. 92.

[144]Pollock, *Wilberforce*, p. 250.

[145]Ibid., p. 251.

[146]Ibid.

[147]Ibid., p. 241.

[148]Sappington, "Legislative Compromise as Moral Strategy," p. 34.

[149]Ibid., p. 35.

[150]Hague, *William Wilberforce*, pp. 426-27.

[151]Sappington, "Legislative Compromise as Moral Strategy," p. 33.

[152]Pollock, *Wilberforce*, p. 284.

[153]Ibid., pp. 283-84.

[154]Belmonte, *Hero for Humanity*, p. 279.

[155]Klingberg, *Anti-Slavery Movement*, p. 211.

[156]Ibid., pp. 273-74.

[157]At the Anti-Slavery Society's annual meeting in 1831, Wilberforce stressed the theme of perseverance (Pollack, *Wilberforce*, p. 304).

[158]Sappington, "Legislative Compromise as Moral Strategy," p. 43.

[159]Ibid., p. 44.

[160]Ibid.

[161]Belmonte, "William Wilberforce," p. 164.

[162]Beilby Porteus, quoted in ibid., p. 156.

[163]Pollock, *Wilberforce*, p. 218.

[164]Wilberforce, quoted in Belmonte, *Hero for Humanity*, p. 207.

[165]Belmonte, *Hero for Humanity*, p. 214.

[166]Pollock, *Wilberforce*, pp. 223-24, 242 (Wilberforce recorded in his diary that he was "so busy with charities."). Eberly puts the figure at sixty-seven (*Building A Healthy Culture*, p. 348).

[167]Furneaux, *William Wilberforce*, p. 83.

[168]Pollock, *Wilberforce*, pp. 218-19.

[169]Ibid., p. 219.

[170]Ibid., pp. 218-19.

[171]J. Douglas Holladay, foreword to John Pollock, *William Wilberforce: A Man Who Changed His Times* (Washington, D.C.: Trinity Forum, 1996), p. 9.

[172]Sappington, "Legislative Compromise as Moral Strategy," pp. 88, 115.

CHAPTER 4: LINCOLN'S JUDGMENT

[1]William Lee Miller, in his *Lincoln's Virtues: An Ethical Biography* (New York: Vintage Books, 2002), contains a discourse on the meaning of "prudence." Miller used the words *prudence* and *responsibility* "in quotation marks instead of some variant of the overworked American word 'pragmatism,' because they imply a combination of practical wisdom with moral purpose, as 'pragmatism' does not" (p. 222).

[2]In July 1858, in his "Fragment on the Struggle Against Slavery," Lincoln wrote: "I have never failed . . . to remember that in the republican cause there is a higher aim than that of mere office. I have not allowed myself to forget that the abolition of the Slave-trade by Great Britain [*sic*], was agitated a hundred years before it was a final success; that the measure had it's [*sic*] open fire-eating opponents; it's stealthy 'don't care' opponents; it's dollar and cent opponents; it's inferior race opponents; its negro equality opponents; and its religion and good order opponents; that all these opponents got offices, and their adversaries got none. But I have also remembered that though they blazed, like tallow-candles for a century, at last they flickered in the socket, died out, stank in the dark for a brief season, and were remembered no more, even by the smell. School-boys know that Wilberforce, and Granville Sharpe, helped that cause forward; but who can now name a single man who labored to retard it? Remembering these things I can not but regard it as possible that the higher object of this contest may not be completely attained within the term of my natural life" (Abraham Lincoln, *Speeches and Writings*, 2 vols. [New York: Library of America, 1989], 1:438).

[3]Harry Jaffa, *Crisis of the House Divided* (Chicago: University of Chicago Press, 1959), p. 371.

[4]Allen Guelzo, *Abraham Lincoln: Redeemer President* (Grand Rapids: Eerdmans, 1999).

[5]Joseph Fornieri, *Abraham Lincoln's Political Faith* (DeKalb, Ill.: Northern Illinois University Press, 2003), pp. 142-43 (citing Jaffa, *Crisis of the House Divided*, pp. 330-46).

[6]Richard Carwardine, *Lincoln: A Life of Purpose and Power* (New York: Alfred A. Knopf, 2006), p. 310. Carwardine's is one of the best Lincoln biographies in coherently addressing prudence and the prudential uses of political power. He confronts this more directly than David Donald, for example, whose pragmatism rarely addresses the moral purpose of political power. Carwardine gives this summary of Lincoln's ethics: "What strikes the neutral reader is the tenacity of Lincoln's ethical convictions: his faith in meritocracy; his belief that no one's opportunities for self-improvement should be limited by class, religious beliefs, or ethnicity; his repugnance for slavery as a system that denied people their chance of moral and economic self-fashioning; his unwavering commitment to a Union freighted with moral value, as a democratic model; and his refusal to be complicit in the destruction of the Union. Lincoln's moral understanding of the demands of power was not founded on a conventional Christian faith. But the evolution of his religious thought, his quest to understand divine purposes during the war, his Calvinistic frame of reference, and the ease with which he rooted his arguments in Scripture, make it essential to take his religion seriously" (ibid., p. 325).

[7]Ibid., p. 311.

[8]Ibid.

[9]Ibid., p. 312.

[10]Daniel Farber, *Lincoln's Constitution* (Chicago: University of Chicago Press, 2003), p. 176.

[11]David Herbert Donald, *"We Are Lincoln Men": Abraham Lincoln and His Friends* (New York: Simon & Schuster, 2004), p. 150.

[12]Doris Kearns Goodwin, *Team of Rivals: The Political Genius of Abraham Lincoln* (New York: Simon & Schuster, 2005), p. xviii.

[13]William Lee Miller asks, "So now we have to ask a further question—what ends do these realistic politicians serve? . . . When we responsibly ask 'can we all do better?'—what is the criterion of better? When we realistically ask, 'Which is preferable?'—what is the measure? Which of the fruits is good? Which 'consequences' are worthy?" (*Lincoln's Virtues*, p. 229).

[14]Ibid., p. 192.

[15]Lincoln, *Speeches and Writings*, 1:111.

[16]Ibid. 1:112, emphasis in original.

[17]Abraham Lincoln, quoted in Miller, *Lincoln's Virtues*, pp. 207-8.

[18]Abraham Lincoln, quoted in Carwardine, *Lincoln*, p. 234. Joseph Fornieri observes that "Lincoln's ethics were far more Aristotelian and Thomistic than Kantian. He presumed that the process of moral judgment began with an apprehension 'that' something could be intuitively recognized by human experience as good or evil before proceeding on to a discursive reasoning of 'why' it is wrong or to a systematic account of 'what' makes it wrong. For Kant, the order of moral inquiry is reversed: the formal account and rational demonstration of why something is good or evil seems to precede the commonsense acknowledgment that something can be grasped initially as evil without relying upon discursive reasoning" (*Abraham Lincoln's Political Faith*, p. 122).

[19]Richard Current, *The Political Thought of Abraham Lincoln* (Indianapolis: Bobbs-Merrill, 1967), p. xxix.

[20]Lincoln, *Speeches and Writings*, 1:18.

[21]James Nuechterlein, "Lincoln Both Great and Good," *First Things*, August-September 2006, p. 39.

[22]Carwardine, *Lincoln*, p. 22.

[23]Miller, *Lincoln's Virtues*, p. 192.

[24]Henry Mayer, *All on Fire: William Lloyd Garrison and the Abolition of Slavery* (New York: St. Martin's Press, 1998), p. 52.

[25]See William Lee Miller, *Arguing About Slavery: John Quincy Adams and the Great Battle in the United States Congress* (New York: Vintage, 1996).

[26]Lincoln, *Speeches and Writings*, 1:312 (speech on Kansas-Nebraska Act at Peoria, October 16, 1854).

[27]Ibid., 1:227.

[28]Miller, *Lincoln's Virtues*, p. 230.

[29]Ibid.

[30]Lincoln, *Speeches and Writings*, 1:306 (editorial in the *Illinois Journal*).

[31]Ibid., p. 317 (Peoria speech). See also Lewis E. Lehrman, *Lincoln at Peoria: The Turning Point* (Mechanicsburg, Penn.: Stackpole Books, 2008).

[32]Lincoln, *Speeches and Writings*, 1:807-8 (seventh debate, October 15, 1858); see also ibid., 1:477-78 (speech at Springfield, July 17, 1858); 1:581 (speech at Edwardsville, Ill., September 11, 1858). Emphasis in original.

[33]Ibid., 1:512 (first debate, August 21, 1858).

[34]Lincoln, *Speeches and Writings*, 2:15 (speech at Chicago, March 1, 1859).

[35]Abraham Lincoln, quoted in Richard H. Sewell, *A House Divided: Sectionalism and Civil War, 1848-1865* (Baltimore: Johns Hopkins University Press, 1988), p. 75.

[36]Lincoln, *Speeches and Writings*, 2:120 (Cooper Union Address, February 27, 1860).

[37]Mark Neely writes that Lincoln "reluctantly bowed to the constitutional necessity of enforcing the fugitive-slave law and disapproved of state legislation aimed at frustrating the fugitive slave clause in the Constitution. In 1859, he insisted on Republican adherence to the law and

criticized the Ohio party platform, which had called for its repeal" (Mark E. Neely Jr., *The Fate of Liberty: Abraham Lincoln and Civil Liberties* [New York: Oxford University Press, 1991], p. xvi).

[38]Mayer, *All on Fire*, p. 486.

[39]Ibid., p. 488.

[40]Ibid., p. 489. "The explosion came at the annual Mass anti-slavery society meeting in January 1859" (ibid., p. 491).

[41]Carwardine, *Lincoln*, p. 297.

[42]See generally Sewell, *House Divided*.

[43]See "Declaration of Causes of Seceding States" <http://sunsite.utk.edu/civil-war/reasons. html>.

[44]Goodwin, *Team of Rivals*, p. 403. The army grew from 16,000 in March to 670,000 in December 1861.

[45]The case for the South, or against Lincoln, is made by Thomas J. DiLorenzo, *The Real Lincoln* (New York: Three Rivers Press, 2002); Jeffrey Rogers Hummel, *Emancipating Slaves, Enslaving Free Men: A History of the American Civil War* (Chicago: Open Court, 1996); Charles Adams, *When in the Course of Human Events: Arguing the Case for Southern Secession* (Lanham, Md.: Rowman & Littlefield, 2000); Greg Loren Durand, *America's Caesar: The Decline and Fall of Republican Government in the United States of America* (Dahlonega, Ga.: Confederate Reprint Co., 2006) (also available at <www.americascaesar.com>). These challenges are effectively rebutted by Thomas L. Krannawitter, *Vindicating Lincoln: Defending the Politics of Our Greatest President* (Lanham, Md.: Rowman & Littlefield, 2008).

[46]Abraham Lincoln, quoted in Goodwin, *Team of Rivals*, p. 356.

[47]Lincoln, *Speeches and Writings*, 2:246, 250.

[48]"It was to be remembered that the Union must be preserved in the purity of its principles as well as in the integrity of its territorial parts. It must be 'Liberty and Union, now and forever, one and inseparable'" (ibid., 1:365 [speech at Bloomington, Ill., May 29, 1856]).

[49]Articles of Confederation, reprinted in *The American Republic: Primary Sources*, ed. Bruce Frohnen (Indianapolis: Liberty Fund, 2002), p. 200.

[50]U.S. Constitution, reprinted in *The American Republic*, p. 234.

[51]Carwardine, *Lincoln*, pp. 275-76.

[52]Goodwin, *Team of Rivals*, p. 300.

[53]Ibid., p. 348.

[54]Ibid.

[55]John J. Crittenden, quoted in Allen C. Guelzo, *Lincoln's Emancipation Proclamation: The End of Slavery in America* (New York: Simon & Schuster, 2004), pp. 39-40. Joseph R. Fornieri, "Lincoln and the Emancipation Proclamation," in *Tempered Strength: Studies in the Nature and Scope of Prudential Leadership*, ed. Ethan M. Fishman (Lanham, Md.: Lexington Books, 2002).

[56]In the case of actions against slavery by Fremont and Cameron during 1861, Lincoln's position was that "any decision regarding the future of slavery rested with the president, not with a subordinate official" (Goodwin, *Team of Rivals*, p. 405). "While Lincoln understood that the slaves coming into the Union hands 'must be provided for in some way,' he did not believe, he later wrote, that he possessed the constitutional authority to liberate and arm them. The only way that such actions, 'otherwise constitutional, might become lawful,' was if those measures were deemed 'indispensable' for 'the preservation of the nation,' and therefore for 'the preservation of the constitution' itself" (ibid.). In December 1861 he was not yet "convinced that arming seized slaves was 'an indispensable necessity' " but that it would "alienate the moderate majority of his coalition" (ibid.).

[57]Lincoln, *Speeches and Writings*, 2:357-58.

[58]Farber, *Lincoln's Constitution*, pp. 118-19; Vasan Kesavan and Michael Stokes Paulsen, "Is West Virginia Unconstitutional?" *California Law Review* 90 (March 2002): 291, 303-4.

[59]Harry V. Jaffa, *A New Birth of Freedom: Abraham Lincoln and the Coming of the Civil War* (New York: Rowman & Littlefield, 2000).

[60]See Ronald C. White Jr., *The Eloquent President* (New York: Random House, 2005), pp. 77ff.

[61]Michael Stokes Paulsen, "The Civil War as Constitutional Interpretation," *University of Chicago Law Review* 71 (Spring 2004): 706. See also Kesavan and Paulsen, "Is West Virginia Unconstitutional?" pp. 291, 302-13.

[62]Goodwin, *Team of Rivals*, p. 334.

[63]James F. Simon, *Lincoln and Chief Justice Taney: Slavery, Secession, and the President's War Powers* (New York: Simon & Schuster, 2006), p. 185.

[64]Lincoln, *Speeches and Writings*, 2:215, 218, emphasis in original.

[65]Madison's letter to Edward Everett, August 28, 1830, published in the *North American Review* in October, "opposing nullification and upholding the supremacy of federal law" (Jack Rakove, notes in *James Madison, Writings* [New York: Library of America, 1999], pp. 842, 913). See also David P. Currie, *The Constitution in Congress: Descent into the Maelstrom, 1829-1861* (Chicago: University of Chicago Press, 2005), pp. 225ff.; Farber, *Lincoln's Constitution*, pp. 62-69, 83-91; Paulsen, "The Civil War as Constitutional Interpretation," pp. 707-8 and n. 49; Kesavan and Paulsen, "Is West Virginia Unconstitutional?"

[66]Farber, *Lincoln's Constitution*, pp. 61-62.

[67]Paulsen, "The Civil War as Constitutional Interpretation," p. 706.

[68]Ibid.

[69]Simon, *Lincoln and Chief Justice Taney*, pp. 180-83.

[70]Ibid., p. 181; Goodwin, *Team of Rivals*, p. 334.

[71]Lincoln, *Speeches and Writings*, 2:232 ("Proclamation Calling Militia and Convening Congress").

[72]Ibid.

[73]Farber, *Lincoln's Constitution*, p. 133.

[74]Simon, *Lincoln and Chief Justice Taney*, p. 200. See also Phillip Shaw Paludan, *The Presidency of Abraham Lincoln* (Lawrence: University of Kansas Press, 1994), p. 71. See The Prize Cases, 67 U.S. (2 Black) 635 (1863) (J. Nelson, dissenting) (citing the federal laws).

[75]67 U.S. 635, 682-99 (1863).

[76]Simon, *Lincoln and Chief Justice Taney*, p. 231.

[77]See Clarke D. Forsythe, "The Historical Origins of Broad Federal Habeas Review Reconsidered," *Notre Dame Law Review* 70, no. 5 (1995): 1079. See also William Rehnquist, *All the Laws But One: Civil Liberties in Wartime* (New York: Vintage, 1998); Neely, *Fate of Liberty*.

[78]"The Maryland legislature assembles to-morrow . . . and, not improbably, will take action to arm the people of that State against the United States. The question has been submitted to . . . me, whether it would not be justifiable . . . for you . . . to arrest or disperse members of that body. I think that it would not be justifiable; nor, efficient for the desired object. First, they have a clearly legal right to assemble; and, we can not know in advance, that their action will not be lawful, and peaceful. And if we wait until they shall have acted, their arrest, or dispersion, will not lessen the effect of their action. Secondly, we can not permanently prevent their action. If we arrest them, we can not long hold them as prisoners; and when liberated, they will immediately re-assemble, and take their action. And, precisely the same if we simply disperse them. They will immediately re-assemble in some other place. I therefore conclude that it is only left to the commanding General to watch, and await their action, which, if it shall be to arm their people against the United States, he is to adopt the most prompt, and efficient means to counteract, even, if necessary, to the bombardment of their cities—and in the extremest necessity, the suspension of the writ of habeas corpus" (Abraham Lincoln, quoted in Neely, *Fate of Liberty*, p. 7).

[79]Neely, *Fate of Liberty*, p. 4.

[80]Simon, *Lincoln and Chief Justice Taney*, pp. 184-89; Ex parte Merryman, 17 F. Cas. 144 (Cir. Ct. Md. 1861), 9 Am. Law Reg. 524, 24 Law Rep. 78 (1861).

[81]Abraham Lincoln, quoted in Farber, *Lincoln's Constitution*, p. 159.

[82]Lincoln, *Speeches and Writings*, 2:253, emphasis in original.

[83]Edward Bates, quoted in Farber, *Lincoln's Constitution*, p. 159; USAG, Suspension of the Privilege of the Writ of Habeas Corpus, 10 U.S. Op. Atty. Gen. 74 (1861).

[84]Edward Bates, quoted in Goodwin, *Team of Rivals*, p. 355.

[85]Neely, *Fate of Liberty*, p. 52.

[86]Abraham Lincoln, cited in Paulsen, "The Civil War as Constitutional Interpretation," p. 721; Lincoln, *Speeches and Writings*, 2:585.

[87]Farber, *Lincoln's Constitution*, p. 163.

[88]Carwardine, *Lincoln*, p. 249.

[89]Lincoln, *Speeches and Writings*, 2:250, emphasis in original.

[90]Gideon Welles, quoted in Neely, *Fate of Liberty*, p. 31.

[91]See Michael Stokes Paulsen, "The Constitution of Necessity," *Notre Dame Law Review* 79, no. 4 (2004): 1257.

[92]Farber, *Lincoln's Constitution*, p. 118; Paludan, *Presidency of Abraham Lincoln*, p. 71.

[93]Simon, *Lincoln and Chief Justice Taney*, p. 233.

[94]Carwardine, *Lincoln*, p. 251.

[95]Lincoln, *Speeches and Writings*, 2:247 ("Special Message to Congress").

[96]Jeffrey Manber and Neil Dahlstrom, *Lincoln's Wrath: Fierce Mobs, Brilliant Scoundrels and a President's Mission to Destroy the Press* (Naperville, Ill.: Sourcebooks, 2005).

[97]Geoffrey R. Stone, review of *Lincoln's Wrath*, by Jeffrey Manber and Neil Dahlstrom, *Chicago Tribune Sunday Book Review*, 12 February 2006, 5.

[98]Simon, *Lincoln and Chief Justice Taney*, pp. 246-47; Ex parte Vallandigham, 68 U.S. 243 (1864); Goodwin, *Team of Rivals*, pp. 522ff.

[99]Ex parte Milligan, 71 U.S. 2 (1866).

[100]Neely, *Fate of Liberty*, p. xii.

[101]Paulsen, "Civil War as Constitutional Interpretation," pp. 691, 700-701 and n. 23.

[102]Simon, *Lincoln and Chief Justice Taney*, p. 250; Ex parte Vallandigham, 68 U.S. 243 (1864).

[103]Lincoln, *Speeches and Writings*, 2:454 (letter to Corning); ibid., 2:465 (letter to Ohio Democratic Convention). See Goodwin, *Team of Rivals*, p. 524; Neely, *Fate of Liberty*, p. 67.

[104]Lincoln, *Speeches and Writings*, 2:459, emphasis in original.

[105]Neely, *Fate of Liberty*, p. 68.

[106]Ibid., pp. 53, 61.

[107]Carwardine, *Lincoln*, p. 255.

[108]Neely, *Fate of Liberty*, p. 54.

[109]Ibid., pp. 60, 62.

[110]Goodwin, *Team of Rivals*, p. 567.

[111]Lincoln, *Speeches and Writings*, 2:518, emphasis in original. Quoted in Goodwin, *Team of Rivals*, p. 569.

[112]Neely, *Fate of Liberty*, p. 9.

[113]Ibid., p. 20.

[114]Ibid., p. 23.

[115]Ibid., pp. 115, 234. See Neely's thorough discussion of statistics on pp. 124-38.

[116]Ibid., p. 49.

[117]Ibid., p. 51.

[118]Ibid., p. 234.

[119]Simon, *Lincoln and Chief Justice Taney*, p. 281. Simon, however, never actually comes to grips with, never really weighs in the balance, the threats that Lincoln faced (p. 272). Except briefly, but not thoroughly (pp. 281-82), Simon's failure to thoroughly weigh the obstacles, threats and uncertainty that Lincoln actively faced is reflected in his gratuitous, offhand criticism of the current Bush administration without any attempt to weigh the threats and uncertainty that it faces in the war on terror (p. 285).

[120]Lincoln, *Speeches and Writings*, 2:467 (letter to Ohio Democratic Convention, June 29, 1863).

[121]Goodwin, *Team of Rivals*, pp. 389ff.

[122]Ibid., pp. 390-91.

[123]Lincoln, *Speeches and Writings*, 2:266 (letter to Fremont, September 2, 1861).

[124]Ibid., 2:267 (letter of September 11, 1861).

[125]Simon, *Lincoln and Chief Justice Taney*, pp. 202-3; Carwardine, *Lincoln*, pp. 177-80; Lincoln, *Speeches and Writings*, 2:268 (letter to Orville Browning); ibid., 2:279 (message to Congress, December 1861).

[126]See generally, Guelzo, *Lincoln's Emancipation Proclamation*; Fornieri, "Lincoln and the Emancipation Proclamation."

[127]Lincoln, *Speeches and Writings*, 1:315 (speech on Kansas-Nebraska Act in Peoria, October 16, 1854), emphasis in original.

[128]Simon, referring to Lincoln's June 1858 speech, commented: "Lincoln had never spoken with such urgency about slavery. He had always opposed the institution but, until the passage of the Kansas-Nebraska Act four years earlier, had assumed that it would gradually disappear" (*Lincoln and Chief Justice Taney*, p. 145).

[129]Ibid., p. 146.

[130]Ibid.

[131]Lincoln, *Speeches and Writings*, 2:585-86 (letter to Albert Hodges, April 4, 1864).

[132]Ibid., 2:585.

[133]Carwardine, *Lincoln*, pp. 204-11; Goodwin, *Team of Rivals*, pp. 459-70, 497-502.

[134]"I lay this down as the law of nations. I say the military authority takes for the time the place of all municipal institutions and of slavery among the rest, and that under that state of things, so far from its being true, that the States where slavery exists have the exclusive management of the subject, not only the President of the United States, but the command of the army, has power to order the universal emancipation of slaves" (quoted in Neely, *Fate of Liberty*, pp. 219-20; see also Miller, *Arguing About Slavery*, pp. 206-9).

[135]Carwardine, *Lincoln*, p. 211.

[136]Goodwin, *Team of Rivals*, pp. 571-72.

[137]Simon, *Lincoln and Chief Justice Taney*, p. 274.

[138]Farber, *Lincoln's Constitution*, pp. 146-52.

[139]Ibid., pp. 174-75. Some of the contemporary arguments that Lincoln violated the Constitution or was a dictator dredge up constitutional arguments over internal improvements between Whigs and Democrats from the 1830s and 1840s.

[140]Ibid., p. 164.

[141]Ibid., p. 174.

[142]Ibid., p. 172.

[143]Ibid., p. 170.

[144]Lincoln, *Speeches and Writings*, 2:459 (letter to Erastus Corning and others, June 12, 1863), emphasis in original.

[145]Ibid.; Farber, *Lincoln's Constitution*, pp. 170-71.

[146]Farber, *Lincoln's Constitution*, p. 163.

[147]Neely, *Fate of Liberty*, p. 68.

[148]Ex parte Milligan, 71 U.S. 2 (1866).

[149]Neely, *Fate of Liberty*, p. 161.

[150]Carwardine notes that "as Lincoln explained, he had to exercise that power under constraint. Constitutional duty, the obstinate realities of the battlefield, and opinion on the home front severely hemmed in his freedom of action. These, however, were evolving, not static, constraints" (*Lincoln*, pp. 192-93).

[151]Farber, *Lincoln's Constitution*, pp. 170-75; Paulsen, "The Civil War as Constitutional Interpretation," pp. 700-701 n. 23.

[152]Abraham Lincoln, quoted in Goodwin, *Team of Rivals*, p. 588.

[153]Simon, *Lincoln and Chief Justice Taney*, pp. 256-57 (December 1864 Report to Congress with preliminary ideas on reconstruction plan).

[154]Lincoln, *Speeches and Writings*, 2:552 (annual message to Congress, December 8, 1863).

[155]Michael Les Benedict, *A Compromise of Principle: Congressional Republicans and Reconstruction, 1863-1869* (New York: W. W. Norton, 1974), p. 80.

[156]Abraham Lincoln, quoted in Goodwin, *Team of Rivals*, p. 589.

[157]Carwardine, *Lincoln*, p. 236. See also William C. Harris, *With Charity for All: Lincoln and the Restoration of the Union* (Lexington: University Press of Kentucky, 1997).

[158]Carwardine, *Lincoln*, p. 242.

[159]Ibid.

[160]Benedict, *Compromise of Principle*, p. 81.

[161]Ibid., p. 83.

[162]Carwardine, *Lincoln*, p. 243.

[163]Ibid.

[164]Lincoln, *Speeches and Writings*, 2:700 (speech on reconstruction, April 11, 1865).

[165]Ibid., 2:247.

[166]David Herbert Donald, *Lincoln* (New York: Simon & Schuster, 1995), pp. 446-47.

[167]Carwardine, *Lincoln*, p. 253.

[168]Ibid., pp. 252-53.

[169]Ibid., pp. 313-14.

CHAPTER 5: THE CHALLENGE OF MORAL PERFECTIONISM

[1]See e.g., Charles E. Rice, *The Winning Side: Questions on Living the Culture of Life* (Mishawaka, Ind.: EMR, 1999); Charles E. Rice, *Fifty Questions on Abortion, Euthanasia and Related Issues* (Notre Dame, Ind.: Cashel Institute, 1986); Charles E. Rice, *Fifty Questions on the Natural Law: What It Is and Why We Need It* (Ft. Collins, Colo.: Ignatius Press, 1993); Charles E. Rice, *No Exception: A Pro-Life Imperative* (Front Royal, Va.: Human Life International, 1990), p. 85 ("The incremental approach should be rejected not as immoral but as counterproductive"); Charles E. Rice, "A Cultural Tour of the Legal Landscape: Reflections on Cardinal George's Law and Culture," *Ave Maria Law Review* 1, no. 1 (2003): 81; Charles E. Rice, "Should We Blame the Lawyers?" in *Back to the Drawing Board: The Future of the Pro-Life Movement*, ed. Teresa R. Wagner (Chicago: St. Augustine's Press, 2003).

[2]Colin Harte, *Changing Unjust Laws Justly* (Washington, D.C.: Catholic University of America Press, 2005). Harte's is a book-length treatment of a debate he had with Oxford professor John Finnis at Cambridge University in June 2003 on the morality of imperfect legislation in the context of abortion. Harte has conducted an ongoing debate for the past several years with Finnis and others in various periodicals. In 2000, the then-secretary of the Congregation for the Doctrine of the Faith, Archbishop Tarcisio Bertone, presented a paper at a meeting of the Pontifical Academy for Life ("Catholics and Pluralist Society: 'Imperfect Laws' and the Responsibility of Legislators") in which he noted that "it would be morally licit to become promoters of a new law on abortion that is more restrictive than the one in force, but that legalizes or de-penalizes some cases of abortion." In a subsequent article, "Inconsistent Papal Approaches Towards Problems of Conscience?" (*National Catholic Bioethics Quarterly* [spring 2002]), Harte, who is convinced that the aforementioned article by Professor Luño takes a similar view to that of Bertone, critiqued some of Archbishop Bertone's article, notably his support for "imperfect" legislation as a "lesser evil."

[3]Harte, *Changing Unjust Laws Justly*, p. 9. Harte argues that "any proposal obligating, permitting, or tolerating abortion is intrinsically unjust and unworthy of support" (ibid., p. 218).

[4]Ibid., pp. 108-10. Harte's position is that a just abortion law is "one that prohibits all direct abortions and does not make an exception even to save the life of the mother" (ibid., p. 106).

[5]"It must in any case be clearly understood that whatever may be laid down by civil law in this matter, man can never obey a law which is in itself immoral, and such is the case of a law

which would admit in principle the liceity of abortion. Nor can he take part in a propaganda campaign in favor of such a law, or vote for it. Moreover, he may not collaborate in its application" ("Declaration on Procured Abortion" §22, Congregation for the Doctrine of the Faith, June 1974).

[6]John Finnis points out that " 'intrinsically unjust laws' replaces the term 'intrinsically immoral' predicated of such laws in [§22 of] the Declaration on Procured Abortion made by the Congregation of the Doctrine of the Faith in November 1974. Neither term, as predicated of a kind of law, is traditional" ("Helping Enact Unjust Laws Without Complicity in Injustice," *American Journal of Jurisprudence* 49 [2004]: 11, 13 n. 6).

[7]Harte, *Changing Unjust Laws Justly*, p. 88 (emphasis added).

[8]Ibid.

[9]Ibid., p. 74.

[10]Ibid., p. 22.

[11]Ibid., p. 159.

[12]Cf. the 1987 publication by the Congregation for the Doctrine of the Faith, *Donum vitae [Instruction on Bioethics]:* "In various states certain laws have authorized the direct suppression of innocents" (*Donum vitae*, quoted in Rice, *Fifty Questions*, p. 290 [emphasis added]).

[13]Numerous Catholic Church leaders and scholars have rejected Harte's conclusions, by implication, and affirmed the morality of "imperfect legislation," at least under certain circumstances. See John Paul II, *Evangelium vitae* §73 (1995). *Catholic Church officials:* Cardinal Ratzinger, "Comments on the Hatch Amendment" (1982); Statement of Italian Conference of Bishops on Modification of Law 194/78 (February 11, 1981); Catholic Bishops of England, Wales, Scotland, Ireland Joint Committee on Bioethical Issues, "Imperfect Laws: Some Guidelines," in 19 Briefing No. 14 (July 7, 1989) ("Catholics may support and vote for a bill or other proposal which would strength [sic] the law's protection for the unborn, even when the bill fails to extend such protection to the full extent that justice truly requires"); John Cardinal O'Connor, "Abortion: Questions and Answers," *Catholic New York*, 14 June 1990; Archbishop Tarcisio Bertone, secretary of the Congregation for the Doctrine of the Faith, "Faith, Catholics and Pluralistic Society: 'Imperfect Laws' and the Responsibility of Legislators" (2001), in *Evangelium Vitae: Five Years of Confrontation*, ed. J. Vial Correa and E. Sgreccia; Congregation for the Doctrine of the Faith, "Symposium: Catholics and the Pluralistic Society: The Case of 'Imperfect Laws' " (Rome, November 9-12, 1994), proceedings published in Italian, *I Cattolici e la Societa Pluralista*, ed. Joseph Joblin and Real Tremblay (Bologna: Edizioni Studio Domenicano 1996); Louisiana Catholic Bishops, "Statement on Anti-Abortion Legislation" (1991) (agreeing with Cardinal O'Connor's statement of July 1990); Bishop John Myers, "The Obligations of Catholics and the Rights of Unborn Children," *Origins* 70, no. 20 (1990); Cardinal Edouard Gagnon, president of the Pontifical Council for the Family, letter of June 20, 1987, to Paul Weyrich, *Origins* 17, no. 9 (1987) ("If they have reason to believe that the proposed legislation will not be the final stage, Catholics could decide to work toward legislation which prohibits abortion or abortion funding, but which allows certain exceptions such as danger to the life of the mother. . . . In the political situation, where 'the art of the possible' prevails, Catholics may push for imperfect legislation. . . . However, even as they work for imperfect legislation, they must make it clear in the public forum that they remain opposed to all abortions."). *Scholars:* William E. May, "The Misinterpretation of John Paul II's Teaching in *Evangelium Vitae* n. 73," *National Catholic Bioethics Quarterly* 6, no. 4 (2006): 705 (2006); Peter Bristow, *The Moral Dignity of Man* (Dublin: Four Courts, 1997); John Finnis, "Restricting Legalised Abortion Is Not Intrinsically Unjust," in *Cooperation, Complicity and Conscience*, ed. Helen Watt (London: Linacre Centre, 2005); Finnis, "Helping Enact Unjust Laws," p. 11; John Finnis, "The Catholic Church and Public Policy Debates in Western Liberal Societies: The Basis and Limits of Intellectual Engagement," in *Issues for a Catholic Bioethic*, ed. Luke Gormally (Queensland, Australia: St. Austin Press, 1999); John Finnis, "Unjust Laws in a Democratic Society: Some Philosophical and Theological Reflections," *Notre Dame Law Review* 71, no. 4

(1996): 595; Anthony Fisher, "On the Duties of a Catholic Politician with Respect to Abortion Law Reform, with Particular Reference to *Evangelium vitae* §73" <www.priestsforlife.org/articles/imperflefisher.html>; Robert George, "Political Action and Legal Reform in *Evangelium Vitae*" <www.nccbuscc.org/prolife/programs/rlp//96rlpgeo.shtml>; Robert George and Alfonso Gómez-Lobo, personal statement in "Reproduction and Responsibility: The Regulation of New Biotechnologies, a report of the President's Council on Bioethics," March 2004, pp. 243-44; Ángel Rodriguez Luño, "*Evangelium Vitae:* The Catholic Lawmaker and the Problem of a Seriously Unjust Law," *L'Osservatore Romano*, September 18, 2002; Ángel Rodriguez Luño, "The Dilemma of Catholic Legislators Faced with Proposals Seeking to Ameliorate Unjust Laws Promoting Artificial Procreation," paper to Tenth General Assembly of the Pontifical Academy for Life, February 21, 2004; William E. May, "Unjust Laws and Catholic Citizens: Opposition, Cooperation, and Toleration," *Homiletic and Pastoral Review*, November 1995, p. 12; William E. May, "Why Hatch Is Necessary," *National Catholic Register*, January 17, 1982, pp. 1, 8.

As John Finnis points out, " 'Intrinsically unjust' replaces the term 'intrinsically immoral' predicated of such laws in [§22 of] the *Declaration on Procured Abortion* made by the Congregation for the Doctrine of the Faith in November 1974. Neither term, as predicated of a kind of law, is traditional" ("Helping Enact Unjust Laws," pp. 11, 13 n. 6).

[14]Harte's evaluation of the "realities" of legislation is much more truncated and conclusory. Harte claims that there are "three underlying realities of legislation." First, he asserts "laws to restrict abortion do not simply save some lives but always exclude from protection some unborn children" (Harte, *Changing Unjust Laws Justly*, p. 15). He fails to ask, By whose will and power? Second, he asserts that "restrictive abortion laws . . . inevitably distort the truth of the pro-life perspective." There's nothing "inevitable" about it. It depends on the language of the bill or amendment, the obstacles imposed, and the skill and rhetoric of the legislators in communicating the goals, and how and why the outcome occurred. Third, he asserts that "those unborn children excluded . . . are further marginalized" (Harte, *Changing Unjust Laws Justly*, p. 15). He fails to ask, By whom are they marginalized? The majority who preserved abortion for those conditions? Whether they are "further" marginalized depends on two prudential conditions that legislators must seriously consider: whether abortions were reduced and whether future progress (in reducing or prohibiting abortion) was somehow permanently compromised or prevented. Harte's is an incomplete and fragmented picture of legal and political action. It views legislation in isolation, outside its proper context. Who or what is doing the "excluding," "distorting" and "marginalizing"? The legislation? Or the controlling Supreme Court decision? Or the majority of legislators who want to exclude or marginalize and prevent the minority from overcoming this in any legislative vote? Or majority public opinion?

[15]*Roe v. Wade*, 410 U.S. 113 (1973).

[16]*Cruzan v. Director*, Missouri Department of Health, 497 U.S. 261 (1990).

[17]*Vacco v. Quill*, 521 U.S. 793 (1997); *Washington v. Glucksberg*, 521 U.S. 702 (1997).

[18]The Court defines "health" in abortion law as "all factors—physical, emotional, psychological, familial, and the woman's age—relevant to the well-being of the patient" (*Doe v. Bolton*, 410 U.S. 179, 192 [1973]).

[19]*Gonzales v. Carhart*, 127 S.Ct. 1610 (2007).

[20]*Planned Parenthood v. Casey*, 505 U.S. 833 (1992).

[21]The fences themselves were opposed by abortion advocates in litigation as embodying an unconstitutional motive or purpose to restrict or prohibit abortion.

[22]Bret Stephens, "Being Ehud Olmert," *Wall Street Journal*, 25 July 2006.

[23]Carl Hulse, "Senate Restricts Abortion Option for Young Girls," *New York Times*, 26 July 2006.

[24]As Princeton professor Robert George has recently written, "So long as incrementalism is not a euphemism for surrender or neglect or compromises that leave grave injustices permanently in place, it can be entirely honorable. The goal must be to accomplish in law and policy all that

can be accomplished in the prevailing circumstances, while working to move public opinion in directions more respectful of human life so as to make possible further advances in law and policy. Indeed, often it is small victories in the political domain that help get public opinion moving in the right direction, thus establishing the conditions for greater achievements" ("Families and First Principles," *National Review*, February 12, 2007, pp. 33-34).

[25]See e.g., Leslie Lenkowsky: "Measured against the high expectations that accompanied the program's launching, its accomplishments may seem modest to some of its supporters. . . . But politics rarely works miracles; more typically, it leads to an accumulation of incrementally useful steps" ("Devil's Bargain?" review of *Tempting Faith,* by David Kuo, *Commentary,* January 2007, 57, 61). Recently, for example, the *Wall Street Journal* noted "positive, incremental change" in China's financial system ("Review & Outlook: The Long China View," *Wall Street Journal,* 20 April 2006). A recent review of the presidency of George H. W. Bush examined the president's goals in the context of a political system that changes by increments (Ryan J. Barilleaux and Mark J. Rozell, "Incrementalism in Theory and Practice," in *Power and Prudence: The Presidency of George H. W. Bush* [Bryan: Texas A & M University Press, 2004]). Barilleaux and Rozell define prudence as "a realistic assessment of possibilities" (ibid., pp. 114, 131). In a recent book on the work of the Supreme Court and its impact on American society, Ken Starr also notes that the Supreme Court's development of legal doctrine can also work "incrementally" (Kenneth W. Starr, *First Among Equals: The Supreme Court in American Life* [New York: Warner Books, 2002], p. xxviiii). Starr referred to the Supreme Court in 2002 as "a Court dedicated to stability, not change; moderation and incrementalism, not liberalism or progressivism." See also Richard Carwardine: "Over sixteen months, by increments, Lincoln had moved. From firmly repudiating emancipation as a weapon of war, he had moved to declare the advancing Union forces the liberators of millions in bondage" (*Lincoln: A Life of Purpose and Power* [New York: Alfred A. Knopf, 2006], p. 220).

[26]Containment was also the moral purpose of Republican opposition to the extension of slavery in the 1850s. "Containment provided a plausible means of eventually extirpating a moral wrong" (Carwardine, *Lincoln,* p. 118).

[27]George and Gómez-Lobo, personal statement in "Reproduction and Responsibility," pp. 243-44.

[28]Harte, *Changing Unjust Laws Justly,* p. 28.

[29]Ibid., p. 228.

[30]Ibid., p. 225.

[31]Ibid.

[32]Ibid., p. 19.

[33]In the same vein an online reviewer of Harte's book, Francis Phillips, argues that "restrictive abortion legislation invariably sends the weakest to the wall" <www.theotokos.org.uk/pages/breviews/francisp/colinh.html>. This rhetoric too fails to consider context and countervailing constraints, and ignores the action of the majority and the conflicting intent of the majority versus the minority. Did a court or the majority or the minority "send the weakest to the wall"?

[34]"By trying, however, to gain support for a bill that had no chance of being enacted without an exclusion for disabled babies, their actions and statements distorted their true view, because they effectively colluded with the prejudices of those legislators who positively favor disability abortions" (Harte, *Changing Unjust Laws Justly,* p. 33). This is overblown rhetoric. A collusion is a secret agreement to gain something illegally or fraudulently. How is a bill a secret agreement, and what did the minority of pro-life legislators gain? How can a person "collude" with "prejudices"?

[35]Ibid., pp. 3-5.

[36]Ibid., p. 5.

[37]Ibid., p. 8.

[38]See the analysis in James Davison Hunter's *Before the Shooting Begins: Searching for Democ-*

racy in America's Culture War (Washington D.C.: Free Press, 1994).

[39]This scenario assumes legislative discretion in the matter. In reality, under current U.S. law—meaning the Supreme Court's decisions in *Roe* and *Casey*—abortion is legal throughout pregnancy, with some regulations in some states.

[40]Harte, *Changing Unjust Laws Justly*, pp. 226-27. "If the Act as amended remains intrinsically unjust, then the amendment bill is intrinsically unjust" (ibid., p. 230).

[41]Aquinas *Summa Theologica* I-II. Q93. A3. RO3.

[42]Harte, *Changing Unjust Laws Justly*, pp. 74-75.

[43]Ibid., p. 88.

[44]Cf. ibid., pp. 73-74 n. 40, p. 289.

[45]Ibid., p. 75.

[46]Ibid.

[47]Ibid., p. 76. Harte also recognizes that Aquinas and others "blur the distinction" between permit and tolerate (cf. ibid., p. 79) including Aquinas's recognition that law "permit[s] certain things, not as approving them, but as being unable to direct them" (Aquinas *Summa Theologica* I-II. Q93. A3. AD3), but Harte concludes that Aquinas "means not 'to approve' but rather 'to tolerate' " (Harte, *Changing Unjust Laws Justly*, p. 79). After giving examples where Aquinas uses *permit* to mean *tolerate*, Harte says that "the verbs 'to tolerate' and 'to permit' have different meanings, and each should be used with precision. . . . Aquinas' two statements are by no means inconsistent, though the use of the verb 'to permit' as a synonym for 'to tolerate' would suggest that they are" (ibid., pp. 79, 80). In arguing that *permit* and *tolerate* are different, Harte cites numerous statements where they have been used interchangeably or as synonyms. Elsewhere, Harte uses the term *tolerate* to mean "not punish" (ibid., p. 82). Finally, Harte quotes the 1974 *Declaration on Procured Abortion* but adds his terms *tolerate* and *permit* in brackets: "Human law can abstain from punishment [i.e., tolerate], but it cannot declare to be right [i.e., permit] what would be opposed to the natural law" (ibid., p. 80).

[48]Harte, *Changing Unjust Laws Justly*, p. 81.

[49]Provoking further confusion, Harte inserts his term *permit* into *Evangelium vitae* §4 and §72.1 in referring to the pope's teaching. But *Evangelium vitae* §72 does not use the term *permit*. Instead, §72 refers to "laws which legitimize the direct killing," and "laws which authorize and promote abortion," and "a civil law authorizing abortion." Likewise, *Evangelium vitae* §73.1 states that "abortion and euthanasia are thus crimes which no human law can claim to legitimize." Thus *Evangelium vitae* refers to laws which "authorize" or "legitimize" but not to laws that "permit," and doesn't define *permission*. The only clear definition of *permit* that Harte provides is in referring to the U.S. Supreme Court as creating "a right to abortion," while more than once he refers to *tolerate* as meaning "not punish." Harte observes that the pope's use of terms hasn't clearly distinguished what Harte means by *permit* and *tolerate*. While Harte uses the term *permit* to mean "authorize," John Paul does not. Again, Harte reads into John Paul's writings words and implications that are not there. This is important because, eventually, Harte will include, within the condemnation of laws that "permit" abortion, bills that the pope authorizes in *Evangelium vitae* §73.3 and bills that attempt to prohibit a class of abortions or that attempt to limit the number of abortions but can't prohibit all.

[50]Augustine, quoted by Aquinas *Summa Theologica* I-II. Q96. A2. RO3.

[51]Aquinas *Summa Theologica* I. Q79. A12. I-II. Q94, cited in *St. Thomas Aquinas on Politics and Ethics*, ed. Paul E. Sigmund (New York: W. W. Norton, 1988), p. 182.

[52]"If tyranny be not excessive it is certainly wiser to tolerate it in limited measure, at least for a time, rather than to run the risk of even greater perils by opposing it" (A. P. d'Entreves, *Natural Law: An Introduction to Legal Philosophy* [London: Hutchinson, 1951], p. 29).

[53]Aquinas *Summa Theologica* I-II. Q93. A3. RO3.

[54]Aquinas *Summa Theologica* I-II. Q96. A2, emphasis added.

[55]See, e.g., Christopher Wolfe, "Abortion and Political Compromise," *First Things*, June-July 1992, pp. 22-29.

[56]Quoted in Sigmund, ed., *St. Thomas Aquinas on Politics and Ethics*, pp. 174-76.

[57]Chaps. 1, 9; d'Entreves, *Natural Law*, p. 51.

[58]Aquinas *Summa Theologica* I-II. Q96. A2. RO3.

[59]Harte, *Changing Unjust Laws Justly*, p. 94. Harte condemns use of term *imperfect legislation* that the CDF has adopted from time to time, and asserts that laws are either categorically just or unjust. "The judgment as to whether a restrictive abortion law is just or intrinsically unjust is not a matter of perspective" (ibid., p. 94 n.16). "Descriptions like 'imperfect' law should have no place in serious discussions of this question, and restrictive abortion laws should be identified for what they are—either 'just' or 'unjust' " (ibid., p. 94).

[60]Cf. Professor Charles Rice's translation of §22: "a man may never obey an intrinsically unjust law, such as a law approving abortion in principle" (Rice, *Fifty Questions on the Natural Law*, p. 287).

[61]This is consistent with Pope Benedict's (then-Cardinal Ratzinger's) 1982 statement, in response to a request by American bishops evaluating the proposed Hatch Amendment: "According to the principles of Catholic morality, an action can be considered licit whose object and proximate effect consist in limiting an evil insofar as is possible. Thus, when one intervenes in a situation judged evil in order to correct if for the better, and when the action is not evil in itself, such an action should be considered not as a voluntary acceptance of the lesser evil but rather as the effective improvement of the existing situation, even though one remains aware that not all evil present is able to be eliminated for the moment" (quoted in May, "The Misinterpretation of John Paul II's Teaching," pp. 705, 713).

[62]May, "Misinterpretation of John Paul II's Teaching," p. 705.

[63]Harte, *Changing Unjust Laws Justly*, p. 290.

[64]Ibid., pp. 291, 16.

[65]Ibid., p. 221 n. 4.

[66]Ibid., pp. 95-96. O'Donovan and O'Donovan observe, "Construing right *(ius)* as the objectivity of justice, Thomas distinguishes natural right *(ius naturale)* from the right of nations *(ius gentium)* as the self-standing and self-evident principle from its concrete consequences or implications (*Summa Theologica* 2a2ae.57.4), and includes within the latter not only property right (and derivative rights of exchange) and slavery, but also the waging of war" (Oliver O'Donovan and Joan Lockwood O'Donovan, eds., *From Irenaeus to Grotius: A Sourcebook in Christian Political Thought 100-1625* [Grand Rapids: Eerdmans, 1999], p. 326).

[67]Aquinas *Summa Theologica* I-II. Q95. A2. RO3. RO4.

[68]See Aquinas *Summa Theologica* I-II. Q18. A2-A4: "Hence a fourfold goodness can be considered in human action. The first is the goodness an action has in terms of its genus, namely as an action. . . . Second, an action has goodness according to its species, which it has from its appropriate object. Third, it has goodness from its circumstances."

[69]Harte, *Changing Unjust Laws Justly*, pp. 112-13. "The moral goodness or badness of voting for unjust restrictive legislation depends principally on the 'object' of the chosen act, and I have referred to the determination of the object in terms of establishing the purpose(s) or proximate end(s) of the act. It is at the level of the 'object,' not 'intention,' that this question must be principally considered, the meaning I am ascribing to these terms being that given in *Veritatis splendor*, not alternative meanings. . . . If the action of a pro-life legislator doing what appears to be voting to enact unjust restrictive legislation can in fact be judged to have a different object from that of actually voting to enact unjust restrictive legislation, then it can be said to have a different purpose" (ibid., p. 181).

[70]May, "Misinterpretation of John Paul II's Teaching," p. 705. May notes that many theologians and philosophers have joined in understanding that *Evangelium vitae* §73 permits incremental, legislative fences around abortion, calling this the "consensus position." May rejects Harte's view that "the 'object' that specifies the moral act of the legislator [with restrictive legislation] is precisely to permit the killing of unborn children" (ibid., p. 708). He criticizes Harte for "his failure to consider adequately the context in which the passages he cites are situated, context

necessary for understanding properly the positions of the authors whom he criticizes" (p. 709). William May, Robert George and Bishop Myers have all focused on the restriction (the fence) that the legislator is trying to achieve. George supports the restrictive amendment when the legislator "supports the law precisely, and only, because the alternative is even less protective." In a separate statement, Bishop Myers has stated that it is appropriate if the legislator "will[s] only the law's protections, while accepting, though not willing, the injustices that he is power-less to remove. A legislator or voter is justified in supporting a law whose protections fall short of all that justice requires where the unjust aspects of the law do not figure in his deliberation and choice as reasons for his decision to vote for it." May quotes then-Cardinal Ratzinger's 1982 statement, in response to a request by American bishops evaluating the proposed Hatch Amendment: "According to the principles of Catholic morality, an action can be considered licit whose object and proximate effect consist in limiting an evil insofar as is possible. Thus, when one intervenes in a situation judged evil in order to correct it for the better, and when the action is not evil in itself, such an action should be considered not as a voluntary acceptance of the lesser evil but rather as the effective improvement of the existing situation, even though one remains aware that not all evil present is able to be eliminated for the moment" (ibid., p. 713). May points out that Harte "has allowed the ambiguity of the term *intendere* to lead him to a considerable misunderstanding of Aquinas' view of the morality of human acts" (p. 714).

[71]See also Douglas Den Uyl, *Virtue of Prudence* (New York: P. Lang, 1991), p. 68: "One must ... con-front particulars in context, that is with an eye towards their relationship to our final good."

[72]*Catechism of the Catholic Church* §1750 (Norwalk, Conn.: Easton, 1994), pp. 433-34.

[73]Ibid., §1755, p. 435.

[74]Ibid.

[75]Harte, *Changing Unjust Laws Justly*, p. 330.

[76]Ibid., p. 106. Harte argues that it is an "unsound theory of legislative voting" to "focus ... on the legislator's intention and side effects (i.e., the double effect principle) rather than on con-sideration of the justness of the norm being enacted" (p. 112).

[77]Aquinas says that "scandal is ... something less rightly done or said, that occasions another's spiritual downfall" (*Summa Theologica* II-II. Q43.

[78]Ibid., II-II. Q47.A9. R02.

[79]To support this proposition, Harte takes two biblical passages out of context: Matthew 25:45 and John 11:50 (Harte, *Changing Unjust Laws Justly*, pp. 10-11). Harte cites the concept of solidarity in the writings of Pope John Paul II and claims that the concept of solidarity means a moral obligation to protect every single human being in legislation. ("Support for restric-tive abortion legislation violates the requirements of solidarity.") Harte asserts that opposing regulatory legislation that doesn't ban all abortions is a question of solidarity with "the last and least," and argues that "support for restrictive abortion legislation violates the require-ments of solidarity" as if solidarity was a code, but nowhere identifies this code (ibid., p. 5). Harte tries to draw a connection between "solidarity" and a legal obligation to protect every single human being that John Paul never draws. Similarly, for Harte, the common good means the perfect good of every individual (ibid., pp. 4, 136). Does the "common good" require that every bill perfectly protect every human being? Like Harte's construction of "solidarity," his is an idiosyncratic reading. O'Donovan and O'Donovan observe, "The controlling idea of the art of ruling for Thomas is the 'common good' that embraces the mesh of communal ends—religious, moral, legal, political, and economic. In places he defines the civil *bonum commune* in terms of a single (albeit complex) concept such as peace (*Summa Theologica* 1a2ae.72.4; 2a2ae.96.6 ad 2; 97.1) or justice (2a2ae.58.5, 6; 59.1), sometimes to draw out its more narrowly political or legal character. In *De regno* he takes the alternative route of elaborating three components of the 'good life' of the community, which the ruler has the task of establishing, preserving, and extending: the continuation of peaceful unity, the orientation to well-doing, and a sufficiency of the material goods indispensable to virtuous action (2.4)" (*From Irenaeus to Grotius*, p. 323).

[80]Thomas Aquinas, "On Princely Government," *Aquinas: Selected Political Writings*, trans. A. P. d'Entreves (Oxford: Basil Blackwell, 1970), p. 49.

[81]Cf. Erwin Hargrove, quoted in *Tempered Strength: Studies in the Nature and Scope of Prudential Leadership*, ed. Ethan Fishman (Lanham, Md.: Lexington Books, 2002), p. 10 (prudential leadership is "the rare capacity to 'keep in mind not only the absolute best but the best in the historical context'").

[82]In the form of attorneys' fees paid to the attorneys for the abortion clinics, as "prevailing parties," as required under federal law, 42 U.S.C. §1988.

[83]Twenty-five states define the killing of an unborn child at any stage of gestation as a form of homicide: Ala., Alaska, Ariz., Ga., Idaho, Ill., Kans., Ky., La., Mich., Minn., Miss., Mo., Nebr., N.D., Ohio, Okla., Penn., S.C., S.D., Tex., Utah, Va., W.Va. and Wis. California defines the killing of an unborn child after the "embryonic stage" as a form of homicide. Arkansas defines the killing of an unborn child after twelve weeks of gestation as a form of homicide. Four states define the killing of an unborn child after "quickening" (discernible movement within the womb) as a form of homicide: Fla., Nev., R.I. and Wash. Five states define the killing of an unborn child after "viability" as a form of homicide: Ind., Md., Mass., N.Y. and Tenn. "A wave of new state fetal homicide laws recognizing a fetus 'of any gestational age' as a person and potential crime victim has abortion rights advocates worried the statutes could undermine a woman's right to end her pregnancy. . . . This year, Alabama, Alaska, Oklahoma, South Carolina and West Virginia passed new fetal homicide statutes making it a separate offense to kill a fetus when a pregnant woman is murdered or assaulted. All five new laws apply to fetuses starting at conception" (Christine Vestal and Elizabeth Wilkerson, "States Expand Fetal Homicide Laws," *Kansas City infoZine*, August 23, 2006 <www.infozine.com/news/stories/op/ storiesView/sid/17254>).

[84]In 2006, legislators in South Dakota concluded that the additions of Chief Justice Roberts and Justice Alito to the Supreme Court changed everything.

[85]Michael J. New, "Getting It Wrong: How the New York Times Misinterprets Abortion Statistics and Arrives at Incorrect Conclusions," The Heritage Foundation, July 18, 2006 <www .heritage.org/Research/Family/cda06-05.cfm>; Michael J. New, "Using Natural Experiments to Analyze the Impact of State Legislation on the Incidence of Abortion," The Heritage Foundation, January 23, 2006 <www.heritage.org/Research/Family/cda06-01.cfm>; Michael J. New, "Analyzing the Effect of State Legislation on the Incidence of Abortion During the 1990s," The Heritage Foundation, January 21, 2004 <www.heritage.org/Research/Family/cda04-01 .cfm>; Michael J. New, "Analyzing the Effect of State Legislation on the Incidence of Abortion Among Minors," The Heritage Foundation, February 5, 2007 <www.heritage.org/Research/ Family/cda07-01.cfm>.

[86]"The natural law teaching presented in the *Summa Theologica* is intended primarily to give an account of the principles that should inform the moral actions of individual human beings rather than to provide a detailed description of the fundamental legal code of every political community" (Marc D. Guerra, "Beyond Natural Law Talk: Politics and Prudence in St. Thomas Aquinas's On Kingship," *Perspectives on Political Science* 31 [Winter 2002]: 6, 9).

[87]Ibid., p. 6.

[88]As Den Uyl points out, "The perspective Kant brings to prudence is simple enough: morality is one thing; prudence is another. Prudence is another name for self-interest; morality is disinterested. Prudence is tied to experience; morality is not. Prudence is caught up in the particular; morality represents the universal. Prudence is hypothetical; morality is categorical. In short, prudence and morality are polar opposites" (*Virtue of Prudence*, p. 143). "It must not be supposed that practical wisdom, in Kantian fashion, first discovers something called a moral principle and then tries to put that principle into action. Moral rules per se are not the objects of practical wisdom. Rather moral principles are themselves fashioned out of an application of reason to passion or action in light of our natural end" (ibid., p. 65). Kant "takes universality as the sine quo non of ethical judgment" (ibid., p. 115).

[89]See Harte, *Changing Unjust Laws Justly*, pp. 268-69, on "prudential judgment." See also ibid., p. 163, where he rejects the notion of political prudence to support restrictive legislation.

CHAPTER 6: OVERTURNING *ROE V. WADE* SUCCESSFULLY

[1]Though some are calling it, at least in the short-term, the "Kennedy Court" in recognition that Justice Anthony Kennedy will be the decisive fifth vote in many important cases.

[2]*Roe v. Wade*, 410 U.S. 113 (1973).

[3]*Gonzales v. Carhart*, 127 S.Ct. 1610 (2007).

[4]See, e.g., Joseph Dellapenna, *Dispelling the Myths of Abortion History* (Durham: Carolina Academic Press, 2006); Clarke D. Forsythe, "Homicide of the Unborn Child: The Born Alive Rule and Other Legal Anachronisms," *Valparaiso University Law Review* 21 (1987): 563.

[5]Paul Benjamin Linton, "*Planned Parenthood v. Casey:* The Flight from Reason in the Supreme Court," *St. Louis University Public Law Review* 13 (1993): 15, 121-37.

[6]Robert P. George and Christopher Tollefsen, *Embryo: A Defense of Human Life* (New York: Doubleday, 2008).

[7]See Clarke D. Forsythe and Stephen Presser, "The Tragic Failure of *Roe v. Wade:* Why Abortion Should Be Returned to the States," *Texas Review of Law and Politics* 10 (2005): 85.

[8]Dellapenna, *Dispelling the Myths*.

[9]See Erika Bachiochi, ed., *The Cost of Choice* (New York: Encounter Books, 2004).

[10]See Charles Pickering, *A Price Too High: The Judiciary in Jeopardy* (Macon, Ga.: Stroud and Hall, 2007); Charles Pickering, *Supreme Chaos: The Politics of Judicial Confirmation and the Culture War* (Macon, Ga.: Stroud and Hall, 2006); Benjamin Wittes, *Confirmation Wars: Preserving Independent Courts in Angry Times* (Lanham, Md.: Rowman and Littlefield, 2006).

[11]*Ayotte v. Planned Parenthood*, 546 U.S. 320 (2006).

[12]See, e.g., "Assessing the Viability of a Substantive Due Process Right to in Vitro Fertilization," *Harvard Law Review* 118 (2005): 2792.

[13]See, e.g., Daniel Farber, "Did *Roe v. Wade* Pass the Arbitrary and Capricious Test?" *Missouri Law Review* 70 (2005): 1231. No one should assume, however, that legal academics who support *Roe* are well-informed about the decision, the wealth of scholarly criticism of the decision or its practical impact over the past thirty-three years. Legal academics seem to support *Roe* for emotional or political reasons, without feeling any necessity to give a reasoned logical or legal basis for the decision and without apparent knowledge of some of the basic facts. Farber supports *Roe* even though he gives no evidence of having read the many books and articles criticizing every aspect of the decision in the past twenty years, and hasn't had any "fresh insight about the abortion issue" since 1988. For example, he contends that Justice Blackmun "seems quite correct that the strong form of abortion opposition, which regards the fetus as a legal persona and abortion as murder, has not taken hold in our legal system or commanded any societal consensus." Farber seems completely oblivious to the legal protection of the unborn child at the time of *Roe* and the fact that thirty-six states in 2006 have fetal homicide laws. See also Daniel Farber, "Legal Pragmatism and the Constitution," *Minnesota Law Review* 72 (1988): 1331.

[14]See Kenneth Starr, *First Among Equals: The Supreme Court in American Life* (New York: Warner Books, 2003). As U.S. Solicitor General, Starr unsuccessfully argued before the justices for the overturning of *Roe* in 1992 in *Planned Parenthood v. Casey.*

[15]*Planned Parenthood v. Casey*, 505 U.S., p. 856.

[16]See, e.g., Charles I. Lugosi, "Conforming to the Rule of Law: When Person and Human Being Finally Mean the Same Thing in Fourteenth Amendment Jurisprudence," *Georgetown Journal of Law and Public Policy* 4 (2006): 361; Forsythe, "Homicide of the Unborn Child," p. 563.

[17]Clarke D. Forsythe and Stephen Presser, "Restoring Self-Government on Abortion: A Federalism Amendment," *Texas Review of Law and Politics* 10 (2006): 301; Paul Benjamin Linton, "The Legal Status of Abortion in the States If *Roe v. Wade* Is Overturned," *Issues in Law and Medicine* 23 (2007): 3.

[18]James Witherspoon, "Reexamining Roe: 19th-Century Abortion Statutes and the 14th Amendment," *St. Mary's Law Journal* 17 (1985): 29.

[19]"There is of course no way to determine [whether the human fetus is a human life]; it is in fact a value judgment. Some societies have considered newborn children not yet human, or the incompetent elderly no longer so" (Thomas Scalia, concurring in the judgment in part and dissenting in part: *Planned Parenthood v. Casey*, 505 U.S. 833, 982 [1992]). Judge Robert H. Bork criticizes this position, claiming that "by making the determination of human life a value judgment, Justice Scalia forecloses the possibility that any scientific proof or rational demonstration can establish that an unborn child is a human being. Indeed, he ultimately forecloses the possibility that there can be any rational discussion of the matter at all, insofar as values by their very nature are subjectively determined" (Nathan Schlueter and Robert H. Bork, "Constitutional Persons: An Exchange on Abortion," *First Things*, January 2003 <www.firstthings.com/article.php3?id_article=424& var_recherche=Scalia+personhood>).

[20]For a more extended evaluation see Clarke Forsythe, "Let the People Decide," in *Back to the Drawing Board: The Future of the Pro-Life Movement*, ed. Teresa R. Wagner (Chicago: St. Augustine's Press, 2003).

[21]See, e.g., Paul Benjamin Linton, *"Planned Parenthood v. Casey:* The Flight from Reason in the Supreme Court," *St. Louis University Public Law Review* 15 (1993): 490, 530.

[22]*Webster v. Reproductive Health Services*, 492 U.S. 13 (1989).

[23]Despite its exasperating subjectivity and elasticity, the "undue burden" phrase has a considerable history in the Supreme Court's abortion cases stretching back to the 1970s. Professor Victor Rosenblum raised the issue of the undue burden standard as a more deferential standard to the justices in his oral argument to the Court in *Harris v. McRae* in 1980 (available at www .oyez.org/cases/1970-1979/1979/1979_79_1268/argument) and the U.S. Solicitor General Rex Lee offered it to the Court in 1982 in the oral argument in Akron (available at www.oyez.org/ cases/1980-1989/1982/1982_81_746/argument).

[24]*Stenberg v. Carhart*, 530 U.S. 911, 921 (2000) (quoting *Casey*, 505 U.S. at 877), emphasis added. Although the Court allowed several state regulations of abortion (including informed consent, parental involvement and physician-only regulations) to go into effect between *Casey* and *Stenberg*, it reviewed no abortion case on the merits until *Stenberg* in 2000.

[25]*Gonzales v. Carhart*, 127 S. Ct., p. 1634.

[26]John Thorp Jr. et al., "Long-Term Physical and Psychological Health Consequences of Induced Abortion: Review of the Evidence," *Obstetrical and Gynecological Survey* 58 (2003): 67, 68.

[27]See, e.g., *Planned Parenthood v. Casey*, 505 U.S. (1992), pp. 945, 979 (Scalia, J., dissenting).

[28]*McCorvey v. Hill*, 385 F.3d, p. 846 (5th Cir. 2005).

[29]Ibid., p. 852.

[30]Tom Strode, "Supreme Court Not Ready to Reverse Roe, Scalia Says," *Baptist Press*, March 13, 2006 <www.bpnews.net/bpnews.asp?ID=22830>, emphasis added.

CHAPTER 7: REGULATING BIOTECHNOLOGY TO PROTECT HUMAN LIFE
AND HUMAN GOODS

[1]Nearly six years later, President Bush issued an Executive Order on June 20, 2007, to promote "alternative sources of pluripotent stem cells" (Executive Order No. 13,435, 72 Fed. Reg. 34, 591 [June 20, 2007]).

[2]For a retrospective see Jay P. Lefkowitz, "Stem Cells and the President: An Inside Account," *Commentary* (January 2008): 19-24.

[3]Thomas Aquinas *Summa Theologica* I-II. Q2. A5; Thomas Aquinas, *Treatise on Happiness*, trans. John A. Oesterle (Notre Dame, Ind.: University of Notre Dame Press, 1983), pp. 20-22.

[4]See Debora L. Spar, *The Baby Business: How Money, Science, and Politics Drive the Commerce of Conception* (Boston: Harvard Business School Press, 2006).

[5]President's Council on Bioethics, "U.S. Public Policy and the Biotechnologies That Touch

the Beginnings of Human Life: A Detailed Overview," June 2003 <bioethics.gov/background/ biotechnology.html>.

[6]Ibid.; Daniel Avila, "The Present Standing of the Human Embryo in U.S. Law," *National Catholic Bioethics Quarterly* 1 (2001): 203.

[7]See, e.g., President's Council on Bioethics, "Reproduction and Responsibility," March 2004; Lars Noah, "Assisted Reproductive Technologies and the Pitfalls of Unregulated Biomedical Innovation," *Florida Law Review* 55 (2003): 603; The New York State Task Force on Life and the Law, "Assisted Reproductive Technologies: Analysis and Recommendations for Public Policy," April 1998.

[8]*Roe v. Wade*, 410 U.S. 113 (1973).

[9]Clarke D. Forsythe, "Human Cloning and the Constitution," *Valparaiso University Law Review* 32 (1998): 469, 520 (discussing legal limits on cloning).

[10]See David M. Smolin, "The Jurisprudence of Privacy in a Splintered Supreme Court," *Marquette Law Review* 75 (1992): 975.

[11]C. S. Lewis, quoted in Michael Aeschliman, *The Restoration of Man: C. S. Lewis and the Case Against Scientism* (Grand Rapids: Eerdmans, 1998), p. 5.

[12]William Blackstone, *Commentaries on the Laws of England* (Chicago: University of Chicago Press, 1979), 1:440.

[13]James Wilson, "Lectures on Law," *The Works of James Wilson*, ed. Robert G. McCloskey (Cambridge, Mass.: Harvard University Press, 1967), pp. 596-97. See also Adam Smith, *Lectures on Jurisprudence*, ed. R. Meek, D. Raphael and P. Stein (Indianapolis: Liberty Classics, 1982), pp. 172-75.

[14]Wilson, "Lectures on Law," p. 604.

[15]John Quincy Adams, *Diary of John Quincy Adams* (entry of April 2, 1787), p. 193.

[16]James Madison, "Madison's Introduction to the Bill of Rights," U.S. Constitution Online <www.usconstitution.net/madisonbor.html>.

[17]Morton White, *The Philosophy of the American Revolution* (New York: Oxford University Press, 1978), pp. 213-27.

[18]Abraham Lincoln, speech on the Dred Scott Decision, Springfield, Illinois, June 26, 1857.

[19]Abraham Lincoln, quoted in James Nuechterlein, "Lincoln Both Great and Good," *First Things* (August-September 2006): 36-41.

[20]See generally, Americans United for Life, "Defending Life 2008" (and prior editions). Much of the data is available at www.aul.org.

[21]See Thomas A. Warnock, "Scientific Advancements: Will Technology Make the Unpopular Wrongful Birth/Life Causes of Action Extinct?" *Temple Environmental Law & Technology Journal* 19 (2001): 173.

[22]Denise M. Burke, "Unborn Victims of Violence Laws: Protecting Society's Most Vulnerable," *Defending Life 2007: Proven Strategies for a Pro-Life America* (Chicago: Americans United for Life, 2007), pp. 171-87 (twenty-four states protect unborn victims at any stage of gestation, while six states protect unborn victims before "viability" and five states have protections after "viability").

[23]Pub. Law No. 102-493, 106 Stat. 3146 (codified as amended at 42 U.S.C. sec. 263a-1 to 7 [2000]); see Noah, "Assisted Reproductive Technologies," pp. 614-15.

[24]See President's Council on Bioethics, "U.S. Public Policy and the Biotechnologies That Touch the Beginnings of Human Life: A Detailed Overview," June 2003 <http://bioethics.gov/ background/biotechnology.html>. See also Helen Alvare, "The Case for Regulating Collaborative Reproduction: A Children's Rights Perspective," *Harvard Journal on Legislation* 40, no. 1 (2003): 31-33.

[25]Alvare, "Case for Regulating Collaborative Reproduction," p. 26.

[26]See Forsythe, "Human Cloning and the Constitution," pp. 469, 514.

[27]See, e.g., John A. Robertson, "Embryos, Families, and Procreative Liberty: The Legal Structure of the New Reproduction," *Southern California Law Review* 59 (1986): 942; John A. Robertson,

"Procreative Liberty and the Control of Conception, Pregnancy, and Childbirth," *Virginia Law Review* 69 (1983): 405.

[28]*Lifchez v. Hartigan*, 735 F.Supp. 1361 (N.D. Ill. 1990), aff'd without opinion, 914 F.2d 260 (7th Cir. 1990), cert. denied sub. nom., *Scholberg v. Lifchez*, 498 U.S. 1069 (1991).

[29]*Litowitz v. Litowitz*, 48 P.3d 261 (Wash. 2002), cert. denied, 71 U.S.L.W. 3548 (U.S. Feb. 24, 2003) (No. 02-916); *J.B. v. M.B.*, 783 A.2d 707 (N.J. 2001); *A.Z v. B.Z.*, 725 N.E.2d 1051 (Mass. 2000); *Kass v. Kass*, 696 N.E.2d 174 (N.Y. 1998); *Davis v. Davis*, 842 S.W.2d 588 (Tenn. 1992), cert. denied sub. nom., *Stowe v. Davis*, 507 U.S. 911 (1993), cert. denied, 61 U.S.L.W. 3581 (U.S. Feb. 22, 1993) (No. 92-910). It is somewhat remarkable that the first case of this kind did not arise until ten years after Louise Brown's birth.

[30]See Christine Feiler, "Human Embryo Experimentation: Regulation and Relative Rights," *Fordham Law Review* 66 (1998): 2435.

[31]*Forbes v. Napolitano*, 236 F.3d 1009 (9th Cir. 2000); *Margaret S. v. Treen*, 597 F.Supp. 636 (D.La. 1984), aff'd on other grounds, *Margaret S. v. Edwards*, 794 F.2d 994 (5th Cir. 1986); *Jane L. v. Bangerter*, 794 F.Supp. 1537 (D. Utah 1992).

[32]Mailee R. Smith, "'The Brave New World' of Bioethics," *Defending Life 2007: Proven Strategies for a Pro-Life America* (Chicago: Americans United for Life, 2007), p. 325 n. 4 (noting that six states restrict funding for Destructive Embryo Research: Arizona, Indiana, Kansas, Missouri, Texas and Virginia); for more information on specific statutes, see National Conference of State Legislatures, State Embryonic and Fetal Research Laws <www.ncsl.org/programs/health/genetics/embfet.htm>.

[33]See Heidi Forster and Emily Ramsey, "Legal Responses to the Potential Cloning of Human Beings," *Valparaiso University Law Review* 32 (1998): 433.

[34]President's Council on Bioethics, "U.S. Public Policy and the Biotechnologies."

[35]*Poe v. Ullman*, 367 U.S. 497, 554-55 (1961) (Harlan, J., dissenting from dismissal on jurisdictional grounds).

[36]*Griswold v. Connecticut*, 381 U.S. 479 (1965).

[37]*Griswold v. Connecticut*, 405 U.S. 438 (1972).

[38]*Carey v. Population Services International*, 431 U.S. 678 (1977).

[39]See Forsythe, "Human Cloning and the Constitution," pp. 494-98 (surveying tort law developments). The one exception might be in the area of tort law, where some state courts have extended the scope of state wrongful death laws to include the unborn child.

[40]*Planned Parenthood v. Casey*, 505 U.S. 833 (1992).

[41]Ibid., 539 U.S. 558, 574 (2003).

[42]See Dellapenna, *Dispelling the Myths.*

[43]See ibid.

[44]See, e.g., Susan M. Wolf, "Law and Bioethics: From Values to Violence," *Journal of Law, Medicine and Ethics* 32 (2004): 293.

[45]Lori B. Andrews, "A Conceptual Framework for Genetic Policy: Comparing the Medical, Public Health, and Fundamental Rights Model," *Washington University Law Quarterly* 79 (2001): 221.

[46]Ibid., p. 223.

[47]The 1991 international edition of the *Encyclopedia Americana* defines "human being" as follows: "humankind is a species with a scientific name Homo sapiens." The 1992 edition of the *Encyclopedia Britannica* defines it as, "hominid, any creature of the family Hominidae (order Primates), of which only one species exists today—Homo sapiens, or human beings."

[48]See generally George and Tollefsen, *Embryo.*

[49]The January 2004 report *Monitoring Stem Cell Research*, of the President's Council on Bioethics, states: "the term 'embryo' refers to an organism in the early stages of its development. In humans, the term is traditionally reserved for the first two months of development. . . . At the beginning of the individual's development, the entity is a single cell. . . . So the term 'embryo' applies to an individual throughout a vast range of developmental change."

[50]Robert P. George and Alfonso Gómez-Lobo, "The Moral Status of the Human Embryo," *Perspectives in Biology and Medicine* 48, no. 2 (2005) <muse.jhu.edu/journals/perspectives_in_biology_and_medicine/v048/48.2george.html>. An article by Stephen Hall in the May 2004 issue of *Discover* notes, "Once the two packets of DNA meld into one complete set of 46 chromosomes, the one-celled embryo begins to cleave, or divide, becoming a two-celled embryo at around 22 to 28 hours after fertilization" ("The Good Egg," *Discover*, May 29, 2004 <http://discovermagazine.com/2004/may/cover/article_view?b_start:int=1&-C=>). The human is a species. Carl Zimmer in *Discover* refers to "humans and all other living species" ("What Came Before DNA?" *Discover*, June 26, 2004 <http://discovermagazine.com/2004/jun/cover>). It is an organism. The difference between one cell and a one-celled organism is that the organism is genetically complete and a self-directing entity. A human being is the name used in anthropology to refer to a member of the human species. A human being is a human being at every stage of its biological development by virtue of the fact that it is an individual, genetic member of the human species.

[51]Carl Zimmer refers to an attempt to "create life" by "transform[ing] chemicals into a single-celled organism that will grow, divide, and evolve." Zimmer mentions a "single-celled creature named Tetrahymena" ("What Came Before DNA?").

[52]Genetics and human embryology confirm that the life of a unique human being begins with fertilization. "Human pregnancy begins with the fusion of an egg and a sperm," according to Bruce M. Carlson's *Human Embryology and Developmental Biology*, 3rd ed. (Philadelphia: Mosby, 2004), p. 3. In his text *Human Embryology* (New York: Churchill Livingstone, 1993), William J. Larsen states that "the nuclei of the male and female gametes unite, resulting in the formation of a zygote containing a single diploid [having the full complement of chromosomes] nucleus. Embryonic development is considered to begin at this point." Larsen also states that "the moment of zygote formation may be taken as the beginning or zero time point of embryonic development." At a point in the process of fertilization, called syngamy, an individual member of the species Homo sapiens—or human being—begins and before which that unique being does not exist. That is the point at which the pronuclei of the sperm and ovum merge and the twenty-three chromosomes of the male and the twenty-three chromosomes of the female combine to form a new, unique, individual human entity. Carlson states that "through the mingling of maternal and paternal chromosomes, the zygote is a genetically unique product of chromosomal reassortment" (p. 36). Fertilization of the human ovum by human sperm results in the full complement of forty-six chromosomes that mark the human species. There is then one single entity (variously called fertilized ovum, zygote, or embryo). Carlson states that when "the maternal and paternal chromosomes . . . become organized around the mitotic spindle in preparation for an ordinary mitotic division . . . the process of fertilization can be said to be complete and the fertilized egg is called a zygote" (ibid.). In their text on human embryology, *Human Embryology and Teratology*, 3rd ed. (New York: John Wiley & Sons, 2001), Ronan O'Rahilly and Fabiola Müller state that "the zygote . . . is a unicellular embryo and a highly specialized cell" (p. 33). They explain that "although life is a continuous process, fertilization is a critical landmark because, under ordinary circumstances, a new, genetically distinct human organism is thereby formed" (p. 8). They add, "this remains true even though the embryonic genome is not actually activated until 4-8 cells are present, at about 2-3 days" (ibid.). O'Rahilly and Müller quote from a pioneering work in human embryology by C. H. Heuser and G. L. Streeter (Development of the Macaque Embryo [1941]): "It is to be remembered that at all stages the embryo is a living organism, that is, it is a going concern with adequate mechanisms for its maintenance as of that time" (ibid., p. v.). The human zygote or embryo has undoubted genetic individuality. The developing embryo's sex and its separate and individual genetic identity are determined at fertilization. As Carl J. Pauerstein states in his text *Clinical Obstetrics* (New York: J. Wiley, 1987), "each member of a species begins with fertilization—the successful merging of two different pools of genetic information to form a new individual" (p. 11). Joseph Levine and David Suzuki concur in their text, *The Secret of Life:*

Redesigning the Living World (Boston: WGBH Educational Foundation, 1993): "For better or for worse, every individual's genetic endowment is determined at the moment of conception. Sperm and egg each carry a random selection of parental genes. Their fusion creates a genetically unique individual" (3rd photo page after p. 122). Lennart Nilsson, in his text *A Child Is Born* (New York: Bantam, 1990), referred to "fertilization" as "the moment the sperm and egg fuse and a new individual begins to form."

[53]Ramsey Colloquium, "The Inhuman Use of Human Beings: A Statement on Embryo Research," *First Things* 49 (Jan. 1995): 17-21 <www.firstthings.com/article.php3?id_article=3985>.

[54]66 Fed. Reg. 56776 (November 13, 2001). These were codified at 45 CFR 46. Subpart B of 45 CFR 46, established in August 1975, pertains to research on fetuses, pregnant women and humans in vitro fertilization.

[55]39 Fed. Reg. 18914.

[56]National Research Act (NRA), Pub. Law No. 93-348, sec. 2123, 88 Stat. 342 (enacted by the 93rd Cong as HR 7724, July 12, 1974).

[57]40 FR 33526 (45 CFR 46 Subpart B).

[58]Ibid., 33528.

[59]Ibid., 33526 (August 8, 1975); 45 C.F.R. 46.208 and 46.209.

[60]Ibid., p. 33529.

[61]Ibid., 35,033 (June 18, 1979).

[62]The Dickey Amendment reads: "None of the funds made available in this Act may be used for—the creation of a human embryo or embryos for research purposes; or research in which a human embryo or embryos are destroyed, discarded, or knowingly subjected to risk of injury or death greater than that allowed for research on fetuses in utero under 45 CFR 46.204 and 46.207, and subsection 498(b) of the Public Health Service Act (42 USC 289g[b]) [the federal regulations and statute relating to research on living human fetuses].

(b) For purposes of this section, the term 'human embryo or embryos' includes any organism, not protected as a human subject under 45 CFR 46 as of the date of the enactment of the governing appropriations act, that is derived by fertilization, parthenogenesis, cloning, or any other means from one or more human gametes or human diploid cells." The 2003 version of the Dickey Amendment is found in Consolidated Appropriations Resolution, 2003, Pub. Law No. 108-7, 117 Stat. 11 (2003).

[63]Five or six other state supreme court decisions apply property or contract law to the question of the disposition of frozen embryos during divorce proceedings, not homicide or custody law, indicating that they consider the embryo to be a thing, not a human being. *Davis v. Davis*, 842 S.W.2d 588 (Tenn. 1992), cert. denied sub. nom., *Stowe v. Davis*, 507 U.S. 911 (1993); *Kass v. Kass*, 696 N.E.2d 174 (N.Y. 1998); *A.Z. v. B.Z.*, 725 N.E. 2d 1051 (Mass. 2000); *J.B. v. M.B.*, 751 A.2d 613 (N.J. App. 2000), cert. granted, 760 A.2d 783 (N.J. 2000); *Litowitz v. Litowitz*, 10 P.3d 1086 (Wash.App. 2000), rev'd, 146 Wn.2d 514, 48 P.3d 261 (2002) cert. denied, 537 U.S. 1191 (2003).

[64]See generally, Helen M. Alvare, "Catholic Teaching and the Law Concerning the New Reproductive Technologies," *Fordham Urban Law Journal* 30 (2002): 107, 118-30.

[65]See Forsythe, "Homicide of the Unborn Child," p. 563.

[66]See, e.g., "Reproductive Technology and the Procreation Rights of the Unmarried," *Harvard Law Review* 98 (1985): 669; Barbara Kritchevsky, "Unmarried Women's Right to Artificial Insemination: A Call for an Expanded Definition of Family," *Harvard Women's Law Journal* 4 (1981): 1.

[67]*Parham v. J.R.*, 442 U.S. 584, 603 (1979).

[68]In re Buzzanca, 61 Cal.App.4th 1410, 72 Cal.Rtpr.2d 280 (Ct. App. 1998). See, e.g., A. M. Noble-Allgire, "Switched at the Fertility Clinic: Determining Maternal Rights When a Child Is Born from Stolen or Misdelivered Genetic Material," *Missouri Law Review* 64 (1999): 517.

[69]Alvare, "Case for Regulating Collaborative Reproduction," p. 3.

[70]Ibid., p. 4 and n. 13.

[71]*Johnson v. Calvert*, 5 Cal.4th 84, 851 P.2d 776, 19 Cal.Rptr.2d 494 (1993); In re Baby M, 109 N.J. 396, 537 A.2d 1227 (1988).

[72]Marjorie Maguire Schultz, "Surrogacy Legislation in California: Legislative Regulation of Surrogacy and Reproductive Technology," *U.S.F Law Review* 28 (1994): 613.

[73]*Doe v. Attorney General*, 487 N.W.2d 484 (Mich.Ct.App. 1992).

[74]720 Ill. Comp. Stat. 510/6(8) (2002). The use of the term *solely* may make the law unenforceable.

[75]Kelly Plummer, "Ending Parents' Unlimited Power to Choose: Legislation Is Necessary to Prohibit Parents' Selection of Their Children's Sex and Characteristics," *St. Louis University Law Journal* 47 (2003): 517, 557.

[76]Ibid., p. 517; Rachel E. Remaley, " 'The Original Sexist Sin': Regulating Preconception Sex Selection Technology," *Health Matrix* 10 (2000): 249; Jodi Danis, "Sexism and 'The Superfluous Female': Arguments for Regulating Pre-implantation Sex Selection," *Harvard Women's Law Journal* 18 (1995): 219; Owen D. Jones, "Reproductive Autonomy and Evolutionary Biology: A Regulatory Framework for Trait Selection Technologies," *American Journal of Law and Medicine* 19 (1993): 187; Marian Damewood, "Ethical Implications of a New Application of Preimplantation Diagnosis," *JAMA* 285 (2001): 3143.

[77]See, e.g., Eric Rakowski, "Who Should Pay for Bad Genes?" *California Law Review* 90 (2002): 1345.

[78]Lois Shepherd, "Protecting Parents' Freedom to Have Children with Genetic Differences," *University of Illinois Law Review* 4 (1995): 761.

[79]Christine Feiler, "Human Embryo Experimentation: Regulation and Relative Rights," *Fordham Law Review* 66 (1998): 2435; June Coleman, "Playing God or Playing Scientist: A Constitutional Analysis of State Laws Banning Embryological Procedures," *Pacific Law Journal* 27 (1996): 1331.

[80]Forsythe, "Human Cloning and the Constitution," p. 469. See also Forster and Ramsey, "Legal Responses to the Potential Cloning of Human Beings," p. 433.

[81]See Sonia Suter, "The Allure and Peril of Genetics Exceptionalism: Do We Need Special Genetics Legislation?" *Washington University Law Quarterly* 79 (2001): 669, 691-97.

[82]See National Conference of State Legislatures, State Genetic Nondiscrimination in Health Insurance Laws <www.ncsl.org/programs/health/genetics/ndislife.htm>.

[83]See National Conference of State Legislatures, State Genetics Employment Laws < www.ncsl .org/programs/health/genetics/ndiscrim.htm>.

[84]See National Conference of State Legislatures (NCSL), State Genetic Privacy Laws <www.ncsl .org/programs/health/genetics/prt.htm>.

[85]Esther Slater McDonald, "Patenting Human Life and the Rebirth of the Thirteenth Amendment," *Notre Dame Law Review* 78 (2003): 1359, 1361; Damon Whitaker, "The Patentability of Embryonic Stem Cell Research Results," *University of Florida Journal of Law and Public Policy* 13 (2001): 361.

[86]McDonald, "Patenting Human Life," p. 1382 (citing U.S. Patent and Trademark Office "Policy on Patenting of Animals," April 7, 1987, reprinted in U.S. Congress, Office of Technology Assessment, New Developments in Biotechnology: Patenting Life 93 (1990).

[87]Ibid., p. 1382 n. 192.

[88]Emily Marden and Dorothy Nelkin, "Displaced Agendas: Current Regulatory Strategies for Germline Gene Therapy," *McGill Law Journal* 45 (2000): 461, 479. See also Charles F. De Jager, "The Development of Regulatory Standards for Gene Therapy in the European Union," *Fordham International Law Journal* 18 (1995): 1303.

[89]Marden and Nelkin, "Displaced Agendas," pp. 479-80.

[90]See, e.g., Allen Buchanan, *From Chance to Choice: Genetics and Justice* (Cambridge: Cambridge University Press, 2000); Michael Shapiro, "Does Technological Enhancement of Human Traits Threaten Human Equality and Democracy," *San Diego Law Review* 39 (2002): 769; Maxwell J. Mehlman, "The Law of Above Averages: Leveling the New Genetic Enhancement

Playing Field," *Iowa Law Review* 85 (2000): 517; Michael Shapiro, "The Impact of Genetic Enhancement on Equality," *Wake Forest Law Review* 34 (1999): 561; Roberta M. Berry, "Genetic Enhancement in the Twenty-First Century: Three Problems in Legal Imagining," *Wake Forest Law Review* 34 (1999): 715; Maxwell J. Mehlman, "How Will We Regulate Genetic Enhancement?" *Wake Forest Law Review* 34 (1999): 671; Roberta M. Berry, "From Involuntary Sterilization to Genetic Enhancement: The Unsettled Legacy of *Buck v. Bell*," *Notre Dame Journal of Law, Ethics and Public Policy* 12 (1998): 401; Michael Shapiro, "The Technology of Perfection: Performance Enhancement and the Control of Attributes," *Southern California Law Review* 65 (1991): 11; Michael Shapiro, "Who Merits Merit? Problems in Distributive Justice and Utility Posed by the New Biology," *Southern California Law Review* 48 (1974): 318.

[91]Berry, "From Involuntary Sterilization," pp. 401, 438-448; Nicholas Agar, "Designing Babies: Morally Permissible Ways to Modify the Human Genome," *Bioethics* 9 (1995): 1 (arguing for regulations that ensure that "enhancements" "do not limit the range of opportunities available to a child"). See also Lee Silver, "How Reprogenetics Will Transform the American Family," *Hofstra Law Review* 27 (1999): 649.

[92]Kelly Plummer, "Ending Parents' Unlimited Power to Choose," pp. 517 n. 3; Thomas Patterson, "The Outer Limits of Human Genetic Engineering: A Constitutional Examination of Parents' Procreative Liberty to Genetically Enhance Their Offspring," *Hastings Constitutional Law Quarterly* 26 (1999): 913.

[93]As Kass points out, " 'Enhancement' is, of course, a euphemism for 'improvement,' and the idea of improvement necessarily implies a good, a better and perhaps even a best" (Leon Kass, *Life, Liberty and the Defense of Dignity: The Challenge of Bioethics* [New York: Encounter, 2002], p. 132).

[94]One legal commentator offers the following: "A genetic enhancement . . . refers to an intervention that is not undertaken for purposes of treating or preventing diseases or disorders" (Mehlman, "How Will We Regulate Genetic Enhancement?" p. 671, 675).

[95]Vicki G. Norton, "Unnatural Selection: Nontherapeutic Preimplantation Genetic Screening and Proposed Regulation," *UCLA Law Review* 41 (1994): 1581.

[96]Maxwell J. Mehlman, "How Will We Regulate Genetic Enhancement?" *Wake Forest Law Review* 34 (1999): 671, 689.

[97]See Nathan Adams, "Creating Clones, Kids and Chimera: Liberal Democratic Compromise at the Crossroads," *Notre Dame Journal of Law, Ethics and Public Policy* 17 (2003): 71; Thomas A. Magnani, "The Patentability of Human-Animal Chimeras," *Berkeley Technology Law Journal* 14 (1999): 443; Patrick J. Coyne and John N. Coulby, "Man or Monster: A Recent Application for Chimeric Embryos Brings into Question What It Is to Be 'Human,' " *Patent World* 116 (1999): 14.

[98]See, e.g., Bill McKibben, *Enough: Staying Human in an Engineered Age* (New York: Times Books, 2003), p. xii; Kass, *Life, Liberty and the Defense of Dignity*, p. 9; Francis Fukuyama, *Our Posthuman Future: Consequences of the Biotechnology Revolution* (New York: Picador, 2002); Dinesh D'Souza, *The Virtue of Prosperity: Finding Values in an Age of Techno-Affluence* (New York: Free Press, 2000); Bryan Appleyard, *Brave New Worlds: Staying Human in the Genetic Future* (New York: Viking Adult, 1998).

[99]See, e.g., McKibben, *Enough*, p. xii; Kass, *Life, Liberty and the Defense of Dignity*, p. 9; Fukuyama, *Our Posthuman Future*; D'Souza, *Virtue of Prosperity*; Appleyard, *Brave New Worlds*; Robert P. Kraynak, "Defending Human Dignity: The Challenge of Our Times," in *In Defense of Human Dignity: Essays for Our Times*, ed. Robert P. Kraynak and Glenn Tinder (Notre Dame, Ind.: University of Notre Dame Press, 2003), p. 2.

[100]Fukuyama, *Our Posthuman Future*, p. 7.

[101]"The widespread and rapidly growing use of drugs like Ritalin and Prozac demonstrates just how eager we are to make use of technology to alter ourselves. If one of the key constituents of our nature, something on which we base our notions of dignity, has to do with the gamut of normal emotions shared by human beings, then we are already trying to narrow the range of

the utilitarian ends of health and convenience" (ibid., p. 173).

[102]For example, Bruce Reichenbach advanced a form of Christian physicalism but conceded its implications: "if we are to hold that man is governed by moral oughts, and that human performance or failure of performance of these yields moral responsibility, it would seem that we must reject the monistic [i.e., physicalist] view of man, for on this view both of these appear to be impossible because man is not free" (Bruce Reichenbach, quoted in J. P. Moreland and Scott B. Rae, *Body & Soul: Human Nature and the Crisis in Ethics* [Downers Grove, Ill.: InterVarsity Press, 2000], p. 155).

[103]Fukuyama, *Our Posthuman Future*, p. 171.

[104]Kevin FitzGerald, quoted in Gregory Stock and John Campbell, eds., *Engineering the Human Germline: An Exploration of the Science and Ethics of Altering the Genes we Pass to Our Children* (New York: Oxford University Press, 2000), p. 107.

[105]See, e.g., Fukuyama's discussion of the limits of modern understanding of consciousness (Fukuyama, *Our Posthuman Future*, pp. 166-71).

[106]Stephen M. Barr, *Modern Physics and Ancient Faith* (Notre Dame, Ind.: University of Notre Dame Press, 2003), p. 184.

[107]Ibid., p. 190.

[108]See e.g., Adam Zeman, *Consciousness: A User's Guide* (New Haven, Conn.: Yale University Press, 2003); Julian Paul Keenan, Gordon Gallup and Dean Falk, *The Face in the Mirror: The Search for the Origins of Consciousness* (New York: Ecco, 2003); John Horgan, *The Undiscovered Mind* (New York: Free Press, 1999); David J. Chalmers, *The Conscious Mind: In Search of a Fundamental Theory* (New York: Oxford University Press, 1996); Daniel Dennett, *Consciousness Explained* (New York: Back Bay, 1995); Roger Penrose, *Shadows of the Mind: The Search for the Missing Science of Consciousness* (New York: Oxford University Press, 1994); John R. Searle, *The Rediscovery of the Mind* (Boston: MIT Press, 1992); Avshalom Elitzur, "Consciousness and the Incompleteness of the Physical Explanation of Behavior," *The Journal of Mind and Behaviour* 10, no. 11 (1989): 1-20.

[109]Arthur L. Caplan, "Is Better Best?" *Scientific American*, September 2003, p. 104.

[110]See Peter Augustine Lawler, *Stuck with Virtue: The American Individual and our Biotechnological Future* (Wilmington, Del.: Intercollegiate Studies Institute, 2005).

[111]Fukuyama, *Our Posthuman Future*, p. 149.

[112]Ibid., p. 171.

[113]Ibid., p. 172.

[114]Ibid., p. 130.

[115]*The New Encyclopedia Britannica*, 15th ed., 6:28.

[116]Edward A. Purcell Jr., *The Crisis of Democratic Theory: Scientific Naturalism and the Problem of Value* (Lexington: University Press of Kentucky, 1973).

[117]Ironically, old statutes against homosexual sodomy often called it a "crime against nature," and that is apparently the only crime ever called by that name.

[118]Kass, *Life, Liberty and the Defense of Dignity*, p. 10.

[119]President's Council on Bioethics, "U.S. Public Policy and the Biotechnologies."

[120]See Purcell, *Crisis of Democratic Theory*; Phillip E. Johnson, *Reason in the Balance: The Case Against Naturalism in Science, Law and Education* (Downers Grove, Ill. InterVarsity Press, 1995); Arthur Leff, "Unspeakable Ethics, Unnatural Law," *Duke Law Journal* (1979): 1229.

[121]*Davis v. Davis*, 842 S.W.2d 588 (Tenn. 1992), cert. denied sub. nom.; *Stowe v. Davis*, 507 U.S. 911 (1993); *Kass v. Kass*, 696 N.E.2d 174 (N.Y. 1998); *A.Z. v. B.Z*,. 725 N.E. 2d 1051 (Mass. 2000); *J.B. v. M.B.*, 751 A.2d 613 (N.J. App. 2000), cert. granted, 760 A.2d 783 (N.J. 2000); *Litowitz v. Litowitz*, 10 P.3d 1086 (Wash.App. 2000), rev'd, 146 Wn.2d 514, 48 P.3d 261 (2002), cert. denied, 537 U.S. 1191 (2003). See Daniel Avila, "The Present Standing of the Human Embryo in U.S. Law," *National Catholic Bioethics Quarterly* 1 (2001): 203; President's Council on Bioethics, "U.S. Public Policy and the Biotechnologies."

[122]*Griswold v. Connecticut*, 381 U.S. 479 (1965).

123*Planned Parenthood v. Casey*, 505 U.S. 833 (1992).

124*Lawrence v. Texas*, 539 U.S. 558 (2003).

125Forsythe, "Human Cloning and the Constitution," p. 469.

126See, e.g., Rakowski, "Who Should Pay for Bad Genes?" p. 1345.

127"Had those who drew and ratified the Due Process Clauses of the Fifth Amendment or the Fourteenth Amendment known the components of liberty in its manifold possibilities, they might have been more specific. They did not presume to have this insight. They knew times can blind us to certain truths and later generations can see that laws once thought necessary and proper in fact serve only to oppress. As the Constitution endures, persons in every generation can invoke its principles in their own search for greater freedom" (*Lawrence v. Texas*, 123 S.Ct., p. 2484).

128For example, a federal court in *Lifchez v. Hartigan* struck down an Illinois statute restricting IVF (735 F.Supp. 1361 [N.D. Ill.1990], aff'd without opinion, 914 F.2d 260 [7th Cir. 1990], cert. denied sub. nom., *Scholberg v. Lifchez*, 498 U.S. 1069 [1991]).

CONCLUSION

1Josef Pieper, *The Four Cardinal Virtues* (Notre Dame, Ind.: University of Notre Dame Press, 2003), pp. 17-18.

2Terry Hall provides some specific advice to legislators: "[Natural law and prudence] connects the opposition, support, or toleration to a principled understanding of what is good for humans. It provides one with reasons and a certain course (a 'direction') of reasoning. It enables one to oppose the practice on grounds other than mere taste and opinion. By doing so, it invites others to reason along. . . . We constantly are in the situation of having to seek the good, to bring what is truly perfective for us as the beings we are to light. We do not know this, in all details, in advance, because we cannot hold before us all the actual contingencies in which deliberations must perforce occur. . . . The principles of the natural law present an elevated plane to which we can look up, away from the particulars of the convoluted issues of the legislature, not in order to spy premises from which to make deductions or to gain access to the sort of clarity that obviates the need for prudential judgment and resolves all disagreements, but to remind ourselves of the proper reference point for engaging in legislative determinations" (Terry Hall, "Legislation," in *Natural Law and Contemporary Public Policy*, ed. David F. Forte [Washington, D.C.: Georgetown University Press, 1998], pp. 144-45).

3John Cardinal O'Connor expressed support for "imperfect legislation" along similar lines as Jaffa's: "It certainly seems to me . . . that in cases in which perfect legislation is clearly impossible, it is morally acceptable to support a pro-life bill, however reluctantly, that contains exceptions if the following conditions prevail: There is no other feasible bill restricting existing permissive abortion laws to a greater degree than the proposed bill; the proposed bill is more restrictive than existing law, that is, the bill does not weaken the current laws' restraints on abortion; and the proposed bill does not negate the responsibility of future, more restrictive laws. In addition, it would have to be made clear that we do not believe that a bill which contains exceptions is ideal and that we would continue to urge future legislation which would more fully protect human life. I recognize that some in the pro-life movement may consider it politically or strategically unwise to take the course outlined above, but that is a matter of prudential judgment. It is not a matter of supporting intrinsic evil as such" (John Cardinal O'Connor, "From My Viewpoint: Abortion: Questions and Answers," *Catholic New York*, July 1990 <www.priestsforlife.org/magisterium/cardocqanda.html>).

4Robert P. George and Christopher Tollefsen, *Embryo: A Defense of Human Life* (New York: Doubleday, 2008), p. 3.

5See Erika Bachiochi, ed., *The Cost of "Choice": Women Evaluate the Impact of Abortion* (San Francisco: Encounter Books, 2004).

6Peter Berger, quoted in James Davison Hunter, *To Change the World* <www.workforceministries .com/articles/Hunter-To Change the World.doc>.

[7]J. P. Moreland points out that, in interpreting Scripture, believers often "go straight to the question, What does this passage mean to me? while bypassing the prior question, What does the passage say and why do I think my interpretation is correct? We allow [an application] . . . of a passage that is based on vague feelings or first impressions. . . . For many, religion is identified with subjective feelings, sincere motives, personal piety, and blind faith. . . . In other words, we test the truth of our religion not by a careful application of our God-given faculties of thought, or even by biblical mandates . . . but rather by our private experiences" (J. P. Moreland, *Love Your God with All Your Mind: The Role of Reason in the Life of the Soul* [Colorado Springs: NavPress, 1997], p. 26). See also Mark A. Noll, *The Scandal of the Evangelical Mind* (Grand Rapids: Eerdmans, 1994); Os Guinness, *Fit Bodies, Fat Minds: Why Evangelicals Don't Think and What to Do About It* (Grand Rapids: Baker, 1994).

BIBLIOGRAPHY

BOOKS

Aeschliman, Michael. *The Restoration of Man: C. S. Lewis and the Case Against Scientism*. Grand Rapids: Eerdmans, 1998

Alvarez, Leo Paul S. de, ed. *Abraham Lincoln, The Gettysburg Address and American Constitutionalism*. Dallas: University of Dallas Press, 1976.

Ambrose, Stephen E. *D-Day: June 6, 1944: The Climactic Battle of World War II*. New York: Simon & Schuster, 1995.

Anstey, Roger. *The Atlantic Slave Trade and British Abolition, 1760-1810*. Atlantic Highlands, N.J.: Humanities Press, 1975.

Aristotle *Nicomachean Ethics*. Translated by Martin Ostwald. Englewood Clilffs, N.J.: Prentice Hall, 1962.

Arkes, Hadley. *Natural Rights and the Right to Choose*. Cambridge: Cambridge University Press, 2002.

Barilleaux, Ryan J., and Mark Rozell. *Power and Prudence: The Presidency of George H. W. Bush*. Bryan: Texas A & M University Press, 2004.

Belmonte, Kevin. *Hero for Humanity: A Biography of William Wilberforce*. Colorado Springs: NavPress, 2002.

Benedict, Michael Les. *A Compromise of Principle: Congressional Republicans and Reconstruction, 1863-1869*. New York: W. W. Norton, 1974.

Bennett, William J. *Our Sacred Honor*. New York: Simon and Schuster, 1997.

Biskupic, Joan. *Sandra Day O'Connor: How the First Woman on the Supreme Court Became Its Most Influential Justice*. New York: Harper Perennial, 2005.

Black, Rufus. *Christian Moral Realism: Natural Law, Narrative, Virtue, and the Gospel*. New York: Oxford University Press, 2000.

Budziszewski, J. *Evangelicals in the Public Square*. Grand Rapids: Baker Academic, 2006.

———. *Written on the Heart: The Case for Natural Law*. Downers Grove, Ill.: InterVarsity Press, 1997.

Burns, James MacGregor. *Roosevelt: The Lion and the Fox, 1882-1940*. New York: Harcourt, Brace, 1956.

Canavan, Francis. *The Political Ideas of Edmund Burke*. Durham, N.C.: Duke University Press, 1960.

———. *The Political Reason of Edmund Burke*. Durham, N.C.: Duke University Press, 1960.

————, ed. *The Ethical Dimension of Political Life*. Durham, N.C.: Duke University Press, 1983.

Carrese, Paul. *The Cloaking of Power: Montesquieu, Blackstone and the Rise of Judicial Activism*. Chicago: University of Chicago Press, 2003.

Carwardine, Richard. *Lincoln: A Life of Purpose and Power*. New York: Alfred A. Knopf, 2006.

Childress, James. *Moral Responsibility in Conflict: Essays on Nonviolence, War and Conscience*. Baton Rouge: Louisiana State University Press, 1982.

Clarkson, Thomas. *The History of the Rise, Progress and Accomplishment of the Abolition of the African Slave Trade by the British Parliament*. 1808. Reprint, London: Frank Cass, 1968.

Cochran, Clarke E., Lawrence C. Mayer, T. R. Carr and N. Joseph Cayer. *American Public Policy: An Introduction*. 3rd ed. New York: St. Martin's Press, 1990.

Corwin, Edward S. *The "Higher Law" Background to American Constitutional Law*. Ithaca: N.Y.: Cornell University Paperbacks, 1995.

Cromartie, Michael, ed. *Caesar's Coin Revisited: Christians and the Limits of Government*. Grand Rapids: Eerdmans, 1996.

Dahl, Norman O. *Practical Reason, Aristotle and Weakness of the Will*. Minneapolis: University of Minnesota Press, 1984.

d'Entreves, A. P. *Natural Law: An Introduction to Legal Philosophy*. London: Hutchinson, 1951.

————, ed. *Aquinas: Selected Political Writings*. Translated by J. G. Dawson. Oxford: Basil Blackwell, 1970.

Den Uyl, Douglas J. *The Virtue of Prudence*. New York: Peter Lang, 1991.

Devettere, Raymond J. *Introduction to Virtue Ethics: Insights of the Ancient Greeks*. Washington, D.C.: Georgetown University Press, 2002.

Dunne, Joseph. *Back to the Rough Ground: "Phronesis" and "Techne" in Modern Philosophy and in Aristotle*. Notre Dame, Ind.: University of Notre Dame Press, 1993.

Eberly, Don, ed. *Building a Healthy Culture: Strategies for an American Renaissance*. Grand Rapids: Eerdmans, 2001.

Ellis, Joseph. *The New England Mind in Transition*. New Haven, Conn.: Yale University Press, 1973.

Elshtain, Jean Bethke. *Augustine and the Limits of Politics*. Notre Dame, Ind.: University of Notre Dame Press, 1998.

Engeman, Thomas S., and Michael P. Zuckert, eds. *Protestantism and the American Founding*. Notre Dame, Ind.: University of Notre Dame Press, 2004.

Fiering, Norman. *Moral Philosophy at Seventeenth Century Harvard: A Discipline in Transition*. Chapel Hill: University of North Carolina Press, 1981.

Finnis, John. *Aquinas*. New York: Oxford University Press, 1998.

Finnis, John, Joseph Boyle and Germain Grisez. *Nuclear Deterrence, Morality and*

Realism. New York: Oxford University Press, 1987.

Fishman, Ethan M. *The Prudential Presidency: An Aristotelian Approach to Presidential Leadership.* Westport, Conn.: Praeger, 2001.

———, ed. *Tempered Strength: Studies in the Nature and Scope of Prudential Leadership.* Lanham, Md.: Lexington Books, 2002.

Fleming, Thomas. *The Morality of Everyday Life: Rediscovering an Ancient Alternative to the Liberal Tradition.* Columbia: University of Missouri Press, 2004.

Fordyce, David. *The Elements of Moral Philosophy.* 1754. Reprint, Hildesheim, Germany: Georg Olms Verlag, 1991.

Fornieri, Joseph R. *Abraham Lincoln's Political Faith.* DeKalb: Northern Illinois University Press, 2003.

Forte, David F., ed. *Natural Law and Contemporary Public Policy.* Washington, D.C.: Georgetown University Press, 1998.

Furneaux, Robin. *William Wilberforce.* London: Hamish Hamilton, 1974.

Garver, Eugene. *Machiavelli and the History of Prudence.* Madison: University of Wisconsin Press, 1987.

George, Robert P. *Natural Law, Liberalism, and Morality: Contemporary Essays.* New York: Oxford University Press, 1996.

George, Robert P., and Christopher Tollefsen. *Embryo: A Defense of Human Life.* New York: Doubleday, 2008.

Gilson, Etienne. *The Christian Philosophy of Saint Augustine.* New York: Random House, 1960.

Goldstone, Lawrence. *Dark Bargain: Slavery, Profits and the Struggle for the Constitution.* New York: Walker, 2005.

Goodwin, Doris Kearns. *Team of Rivals: The Political Genius of Abraham Lincoln.* New York: Simon & Schuster, 2005.

Gregg, Gary L., II, ed. *Vital Remnants: America's Founding and the Western Tradition.* Wilmington, Del.: ISI Books, 1999.

Guelzo, Allen C. *Lincoln's Emancipation Proclamation: The End of Slavery in America.* New York: Simon & Schuster, 2002.

Hague, William. *William Pitt the Younger: A Biography.* New York: HarperPerennial, 2005.

———. *William Wilberforce: The Life of the Great Anti-Slave Trade Campaigner.* New York: Harcourt, 2007.

Hall, Mark David. *The Political and Legal Philosophy of James Wilson, 1742-1798.* Columbia: University Missouri Press, 1997.

Hallowell, John. *The Decline of Liberalism as an Ideology.* 1943. Reprint, New York: Howard Fertig, 1971.

———. *Main Currents in Modern Political Thought.* New York: Henry Holt, 1950.

———. *The Moral Foundation of Democracy.* Chicago: University of Chicago Press, 1954.

Hallowell, John, and Jene Porter. *Political Philosophy: The Search for Humanity and Order.* New York: Prentice Hall, 1997.

Hargrove, Erwin C. *The President as Leader: Appealing to the Better Angels of our Nature.* Lawrence: University Press of Kansas, 1998.

Harte, Colin. *Changing Unjust Laws Justly: Pro-Life Solidarity with "The Last and Least."* Washington, D.C.: Catholic University of America Press, 2005.

Hartmann, Herbert E., Jr. *St Thomas and Prudence.* Ph.D. dissertation, University of Toronto, 1979.

Hittinger, Russell. *The First Grace: Rediscovering the Natural Law in a Post-Christian World.* Wilmington, Del.: ISI Books, 2003.

Hook, Brian S., and R. R. Reno. *Heroism and the Christian Life: Reclaiming Excellence.* Louisville, Ky.: Westminster/John Knox, 2000.

Hooker, Richard. *Of the Laws of Ecclesiastical Polity.* Edited by A. S. McGrade and Brian Vickers. New York: St. Martin's Press, 1975.

Hummel, Jeffrey Rogers. *Emancipating Slaves, Enslaving Free Men: A History of the American Civil War.* Chicago: Open Court, 1996.

Hunter, James Davison. *Before the Shooting Begins: Searching for Democracy in America's Culture War.* Washington, D.C.: Free Press, 1994.

———. *The Death of Character: Moral Education in an Age Without Good or Evil.* New York: Basic Books, 2000.

Isaacs, David. *Character Building: A Guide for Parents and Teachers.* Dublin: Four Courts Press, 1993.

Jaffa, Harry. *Crisis of the House Divided.* Chicago: University of Chicago Press, 1959.

Kirk, Russell. *The Politics of Prudence.* Wilmington, Del.: ISI Books, 1993.

———. *The Roots of American Order.* Chicago: Open Court, 1974.

Klingberg, Frank J. *The Anti-Slavery Movement in England: A Study in English Humanitarianism.* 1926. Reprint, North Haven, Conn.: Archon Books, 1968.

Kraditor, Aileen S. *Means and Ends in American Abolitionism: Garrison and His Critics on Strategy and Tactics, 1834-1850.* New York: Pantheon Books, 1969.

Krannawitter, Thomas L. *Vindicating Lincoln: Defending the Politics of Our Greatest President.* Lanham, Md.: Rowman and Littlefield, 2008.

Kraynak, Robert. *Christian Faith and Modern Democracy: God and Politics in the Modern World.* Notre Dame, Ind.: University of Notre Dame Press, 2001.

Kreeft, Peter. *Back to Virtue.* Ft. Collins, Colo.: Ignatius Press, 1992.

Lawler, Peter Augustine. *Aliens in America: The Strange Truth About Our Souls.* Wilmington, Del.: ISI Books, 2002.

Lehrman, Lewis E. *Lincoln at Peoria: The Turning Point.* Mechanicsburg, Penn.: Stackpole Books, 2008.

Maritain, Jacques. *The Rights of Man and Natural Law.* London: Geoffrey Bles, 1944.

McCoy, Charles N. R. *The Structure of Political Thought: A Study in the History of*

Political Ideas. New York: McGraw Hill, 1963.

McDonald, Forrest. *Novus Ordo Seclorum: The Intellectual Origins of the Constitution*. Lawrence: University Press of Kansas, 1985.

McInerny, Ralph. *Art and Prudence: Studies in the Thought of Jacques Maritain*. Notre Dame, Ind.: University of Notre Dame Press, 1988.

Meek, Esther Lightcap. *Longing to Know*. Grand Rapids: Brazos, 2003.

Meilaender, Gilbert. *The Theory and Practice of Virtue*. Notre Dame, Ind.: University of Notre Dame Press, 1984.

Miller, William Lee. *Arguing About Slavery: John Quincy Adams and the Great Battle in the United States Congress*. New York: Vintage, 1996.

———. *Lincoln's Virtues: An Ethical Biography*. New York: Vintage, 2002.

Moreland, J. P. *Love Your God with All Your Mind: The Role of Reason in the Life of the Soul*. Colorado Springs: NavPress, 1997.

Nelson, Daniel Mark. *The Priority of Prudence: Virtue and Natural Law in Thomas Aquinas and the Implications for Modern Ethics*. University Park: Penn State University Press, 1992.

Nevins, Allan. *The Emergence of Lincoln: Prologue to Civil War, 1859-1861*. New York: Scribner, 1950.

Novak, Michael. *On Two Wings: Humble Faith and Common Sense at the American Founding*. New York: Encounter, 2002.

O'Donovan, Oliver, and Joan Lockwood O'Donovan, eds. *From Irenaeus to Grotius: A Sourcebook in Christian Political Thought, 100-1625*. Grand Rapids: Eerdmans, 1999.

O'Neil, Charles. *Imprudence in St. Thomas Aquinas*. Milwaukee: Marquette University Press, 1955.

Pieper, Josef. *The Four Cardinal Virtues*. Notre Dame, Ind.: University of Notre Dame Press, 1965.

———. *Guide to Thomas Aquinas*. New York: Pantheon Books, 1962.

Planinc, Zdravko. *Plato's Political Philosophy: Prudence in the Republic and the Laws*. Columbia: University of Missouri Press, 1991.

Rasmussen, Douglas B., and Douglas J. Den Uyl, *Norms of Liberty: A Perfectionist Basis for Non-Perfectionist Politics*. University Park: Penn State University Press, 2005.

Reid, John Phillip. *The Ancient Constitution and the Origins of Anglo-American Liberty*. DeKalb: Northern Illinois University Press, 2005.

———. *Rule of Law: The Jurisprudence of Liberty in the Seventeenth and Eighteenth Centuries*. DeKalb: Northern Illinois University Press, 2004.

Reimer, Neal. *James Madison*. New York: Washington Square Press, 1968.

Rice, Charles E. *Fifty Questions on Abortion, Euthanasia and Related Issues*. Notre Dame, Ind.: Cashel Institute, 1986.

———. *Fifty Questions on the Natural Law: What It Is and Why We Need It*. Ft. Collins, Colo.: Ignatius Press, 1993.

————. *No Exception: A Pro-Life Imperative*. Front Royal, Va.: Human Life International, 1990.

————. *The Winning Side: Questions on Living the Culture of Life*. Mishawaka, Ind.: EMR, 1999.

Rosen, Gary. *American Compact: James Madison and the Problem of Founding*. Lawrence: University Press of Kansas, 1999.

Rubenstein, Richard E. *Aristotle's Children*. Orlando: Harcourt, 2003.

Salkever, Stephen G. *Finding the Mean: Theory and Practice in Aristotelian Political Philosophy*. Princeton, N.J.: Princeton University Press, 1990.

Sandoz, Ellis. *A Government of Laws*. Baton Rouge: Louisiana State University Press, 1990.

Sandoz, Ellis, ed. *Political Sermons of the American Founding Era, 1730-1805*. Indianapolis: Liberty Fund, 1991.

Sappington, Jay. *Legislative Compromise as Moral Strategy: Lessons for the Pro-Life Movement from the Abolitionism of William Wilberforce*. Master's thesis, Trinity International University, 1998.

Simon, Yves R. *The Tradition of Natural Law*. Bronx, N.Y.: Fordham University Press, 1965.

Schall, James V. *At the Limits of Political Philosophy*. Washington, D.C.: Catholic University of America Press, 1996.

————. *Jacques Maritain: The Philosopher in Society*. Lanham, Md.: Rowman and Littlefield, 1998.

————. *The Politics of Heaven and Hell: Christian Themes from Classical, Medieval and Modern Political Philosophy*. Lanham, Md.: University Press of America, 1984.

————. *Reason, Revelation, and the Foundations of Political Philosophy*. Baton Rouge: Louisiana State University Press, 1987.

Simon, Yves. *Philosophy of Democratic Government*. Chicago: University of Chicago Press, 1951.

Stahr, Walter. *John Jay: Founding Father*. London: Hambledon and London, 2005.

Starr, Kenneth W. *First Among Equals: The Supreme Court in American Life*. New York: Warner Books, 2002.

Strauss, Leo. *Natural Right and History*. Chicago: University of Chicago Press, 1953.

Thomas Aquinas. *Commentary on the Nicomachean Ethics*. Translated by C. I. Litzinger. Chicago: Regnery, 1964.

————. "On Kingship or the Governance of Rulers." In *St. Thomas Aquinas on Politics and Ethics*. Edited by Paul E. Sigmund. New York: W. W. Norton, 1988.

————. *Summa Contra Gentiles*. Translated by Vernon J. Bourke. Grand Forks: University of North Dakota Press, 1975.

————. *Summa Theologica*. 5 vols. Westminster, Md.: Christian Classics, 1981.

———. *Treatise on Happiness.* Translated by John A. Oesterle. South Bend, Ind.: University Notre Dame Press, 1963.

———. *Treatise on the Virtues.* Translated by John A. Oesterle. South Bend, Ind.: University Notre Dame Press, 1966.

VanDrunen, David. *A Biblical Case for Natural Law.* Grand Rapids: Acton Institute, 2006.

Weaver, Richard. *Ideas Have Consequences.* Chicago: University of Chicago Press, 1948.

Weigel, George. *Catholicism and the Renewal of American Democracy.* Mahwah, N.J.: Paulist Press, 1989.

———. *Tranquillitas Ordinis.* New York: Oxford Press, 1987.

———. *Witness to Hope: The Biography of Pope John Paul II.* New York: HarperCollins, 1999.

Westberg, Daniel. *Right Practical Reason: Aristotle, Action and Prudence in Aquinas.* New York: Oxford University Press, 1994.

White, Ronald C., Jr. *The Eloquent President: A Portrait of Lincoln Through His Words.* New York: Random House, 2005.

Wilentz, Sean. *The Rise of American Democracy.* New York: W. W. Norton, 2005.

Williams, Frank J., William D. Pederson and Vincent J. Marsala, *Abraham Lincoln: Sources and Style of Leadership.* Westport, Conn.: Greenwood Press, 1994.

Zagzebski, Linda Trinkaus. *Virtues of the Mind: An Inquiry into the Nature of Virtue and The Ethical Foundations of Knowledge.* Cambridge: Cambridge University Press, 1996.

Articles and Chapters

Anastaplo, George. "American Constitutionalism and the Virtue of Prudence." In *Abraham Lincoln: The Gettysburg Address and American Constitutionalism*, edited by Leo Paul S. de Alvarez. Dallas: University of Dallas Press, 1976.

Cochran, Clarke. "Aquinas, Prudence and Health Care Policy." In *Public Policy and the Public Good*, edited by Ethan Fishman. Westport, Conn.: Greenwood Press, 1991.

———. "The Radical Gospel and Christian Prudence." In *The Ethical Dimension of Political Life*, edited by Francis Canavan. Durham, N.C.: Duke University Press, 1983.

Deutsch, Kenneth. "Thomas Aquinas on Magnanimous and Prudent Statesmanship." In *Tempered Strength*, edited by Ethan Fishman. Lanham, Md.: Lexington Books, 2002.

Finnis, John. "Is Natural Law Theory Compatible with Limited Government?" In *Natural Law, Liberalism, and Morality: Contemporary Essays*, edited by Robert P. George. New York: Oxford University Press, 1996.

Fisher, Anthony. "Some Problems of Conscience in Bio-Lawmaking." In *Culture of Life,*

Culture of Death, edited by Luke Gormally. South Bend, Ind.: St. Augustine Press, 2002.

Fishman, Ethan. "Under the Circumstances: Abraham Lincoln and Classical Prudence." In *Abraham Lincoln: Sources and Styles of Leadership*, edited by Frank J. Williams, William D Pederson and Vincent J. Marsala. Westport, Conn.: Greenwood Press, 1994.

Glendon, Mary Ann. "The Philosophical Foundations of the Federalist Papers: Nature of Man and Nature of Law." *Harvard Journal of Law and Public Policy* 16 (1992).

Guelzo, Allen C. "Abraham Lincoln and the Doctrine of Necessity." *Journal of the Abraham Lincoln Association* 18 (1997).

———. "Lincoln's Prudence." Review of *Lincoln's Virtues: An Ethical Biography*, by William Lee Miller. *First Things*. October 2002.

———. "The Prudence of Abraham Lincoln." *First Things*. January 2006.

Guerra, Marc D. "Beyond Natural Law Talk: Politics and Prudence in St. Thomas Aquinas's *On Kingship*." *Perspectives on Political Science* 31 (2002).

McKenna, George. "On Abortion: A Lincolnian Position." *Atlantic Monthly* 276 (1996).

McClennen, Edward F. "Prudence and Constitutional Rights." *University of Pennsylvania Law Review* 151 (2003).

Mawhinney, Brian. "Christian Leadership and Public Policy: Making a Difference." In *Bio-Engagement: Making A Christian Difference Through Bioethics Today*, edited by Nigel M. de S. Cameron, Scott E. Daniels and Barbara J. White. Grand Rapids: Eerdmans, 2000.

Nelson, Eric. "Moral and Political Prudence in Kant." *International Philosophical Quarterly* 44 (September 2004).

Niebuhr, Reinhold. "Augustine's Political Realism." In *The City of God: A Collection of Critical Essays*, edited by Dorothy F. Donnelly. New York: Peter Lang, 1995.

O'Neil, Charles J. "Prudence, the Incommunicable Wisdom." In *Essays in Thomism*, edited by Robert E. Brennan. London: Sheed and Ward, 1942.

Rice, Charles E. "A Cultural Tour of the Legal Landscape: Reflections on Cardinal George's Law and Culture." *Ave Maria Law Review* 1 (2003).

Ruderman, Richard. "Aristotle and the Recovery of Political Judgment." *American Political Science Review* 91 (1997).

Shapiro, Martin. "Prudence and Rationality Under the Constitution." In *The Constitution and the Regulation of Society*, edited by Gary Bryner and Dennis L. Thomson. Provo, Utah: Brigham Young University Press, 1988.

Walker, Graham. "Virtue and the Constitution: Augustinian Theology and the Frame of American Common Sense." In *Vital Remnants: America's Founding and the Western Tradition*, edited by Gary L. Gregg II. Wilmington, Del.: ISI Books, 1999.

Williams, Harry T. "Abraham Lincoln—Principle and Pragmatism in Politics: A Review Article." *Mississippi Valley Historical Review* 40 (1953).

Yarbrough, Jean. "The Constitution and Character: The Missing Critical Principle?" In *To Form a More Perfect Union: The Critical Ideas of the Constitution*, edited by Herman Belz, Ronald Hoffman and Peter J. Albert. Charlottesville: University Press of Virginia, 1992.

Index